The Liturgical Dictionary of Eastern Christianity

Peter D. Day

A Michael Glazier Book
THE LITURGICAL PRESS
Collegeville, Minnesota

Peter D. Day has also written *Eastern Christian Liturgies: The Armenian, Coptic, Ethiopian and Syrian Rite* (Eucharistic Rites with Introductory Notes and Rubrical Instructions) published by Irish University Press in 1972.

Cover design by David Manahan, O.S.B.

A Michael Glazier Book published by The Liturgical Press

Published in North America by The Liturgical Press, Collegeville, Minnesota.

1	2	3	4	5	6	7	8	9

Library of Congress Cataloging-in-Publication Data

Day, Peter D., 1936–
    The liturgical dictionary of Eastern Christianity / Peter D. Day.
        p.   cm.
    ISBN 0-8146-5848-2
    1. Eastern churches—Liturgy—Dictionaries. 2. Liturgics—Dictionaries. 3. Catholic Church—Oriental rites—Liturgy—Dictionaries. I. Title.
BX106.2.D38 1993
264′.015′003—dc20   93-20377
                                              CIP

To Anne,
who launched the idea

Contents

Introduction

It is my intention that this book should be an easy-to-read guide to the multitude of Eastern Christian liturgical terms. The readership of this book is likely to be drawn from those who are looking for a simple explanation of a term rather than a definitive, lengthy, and scholarly explanation, which is beyond the intended scope of this book.

For those readers who wish to find an Eastern Christian equivalent term for a familiar Western term, the Quick Reference Guide at the end of the book will be of help in directing such readers to the Dictionary proper.

The Eastern terms have been anglicized and doubtless many purists may take exception to the final presentation, for which I make my apologies in advance.

The following authors are cited throughout the text, and should any readers want further information they should consult their works: R. Aigrain, J. Assemani, D. Attwater, G. Badger, Bar Hebraeus, A. Baumstark, Dom B. Botte, O.S.B., F. E. Brightman, H. Brockhaus, Bute, John (Marquis of), A. J. Butler, G. Codinus, F. C. Conybeare, J. D. Crichton, H. Denziger, Dom G. Dix, O.S.B., L. Duchesne, A. Fortescue, C. E. Hammond, Isabel Hapgood, A. A. King, E. Martene, Mother Mary (of the Monastery of the Veil), Dom P. de Meester, O.S.B., J. M. Neale, J. Pargoire, E. Renaudot, S. Salaville, J. H. Srawley, Vansleb of Erfurt, Bishop Kallistos Ware.

I wish to acknowledge the generous assistance and patience of my wife, Anne, who so ably edited my original typescript. I would also like to thank some of the people who helped me in many ways with advice and essential material: particularly Dom Robert Gibbons, O.S.B., and the monks of St. Michael's Abbey, Farnborough, Hampshire, for the generous use of their library; the community of the Religious of Christian Education and Miss R. A. Yarnold, librarian of Farnborough Hill Convent College, Hampshire; Richard Hardy of London and Toronto; Philip and Rosalind Lund of Chesterton Books, Cambridge, and Mary Gilborson of Redill, Surrey, for supplying me with books; and my cousins Nerrida and Stephan Kogitz of Toronto and Zell and Eric Cunningham of Sydney for their warm encouragement.

P.D.D.
Farnborough Hill, Hampshire
Feast of St. Bartholomew, 1989

Use of Dictionary

Most entries list that entry's liturgical family, for example,

ANABATHMOI (Byzantine/Greek)

An entry may show alternative but unlisted names. Alternative names that are listed are marked with an *asterisk, for example,

ANAGNOSTES (Byzantine/Greek/Coptic)
(also called Anagnust; Anagu'stis; *Karianjili; *Tchetz)

Cross references are either given at the end of the entry or are marked with an *asterisk within the entry.

The Quick Reference Guide at the end of the Dictionary lists familiar English terms against which are listed the less familiar Eastern Christian terms, which the reader may then locate in the Dictionary.

A

ABA (Syro-Jacobite)

A black cassock worn as part of the outside dress of a cleric over which a wide-sleeved, open gown called a *jubba is sometimes worn.

See SULTANA.

ABA SALAMA (Ethiopian)

Literally, "father of peace." An alternative title for the head of the *Ethiopian Church; it derives from a name given to St. Frumentius, a fourth-century *metropolitan of Aksum and primate of Ethiopia who was consecrated for the Ethiopian Church by St. Athanasius. St. Frumentius was for a long time credited with having translated the New Testament into his native tongue, but modern research suggests that this was not done until the 5th or 6th century.

See ABUNA.

ABBA

Literally, "father." A word derived from Aramaic or late Hebrew. The name suggests attachment and confidence and was in common use when referring to the superior of a male community. Originally, this office could be held by a layman, but in time it became the practice that candidates must have received at least the diaconate to be eligible.

ABBAS (Coptic/Arabic)

The title of a *Coptic *bishop or *metropolitan, both of whom are consecrated by the *patriarch. The Liturgy of consecration is identical in either case except that in the case of the consecration of a metropolitan a special invocation is made on his behalf at the end of the *Liturgy. A Coptic bishop, who must never have been married, is elected by a council composed of both clergy and laity. Should the chosen candidate be a *deacon, the intervening orders of *priest and *archpriest (*kummus) are given on successive days.

The bishop-elect must receive the *monastic habit prior to consecration, and he is expected to spend the evening before his consecration in a vigil, during which he must read the Psalter and the Gospel of St. John in their entirety. During the consecration Liturgy and after the giving of the *peace, the senior deacon cries, "Lift up your hands, O bishops," whereupon they all lay hands on the shoulders of the new bishop, while the patriarch places his on the new bishop's head. At a later stage in the Liturgy the patriarch places the Book of Gospels on the consecrand's head, and says the Peace, following which the deacon reads the Gospel from the *ambo. During the reading of two passages from John 20 the Gospels book is held over the consecrand's head, but at verse 22, "Receive ye the Holy Spirit," the patriarch breathes on his face in the form of a cross and proclaims, "Axios" (He is worthy), which is repeated by all the faithful while the bells are rung.

See ORDERS, HOLY.

ABBATEIA (Byzantine/Greek)

An abbey or monastery.

See MONASTICISM (Byzantine Tradition).

ABEGHA (Armenian)

A *monk-*priest.

ABSOLUTION OR PENITENCE, PRAYER OF (Coptic/Ethiopian)

In practice there seem to be two such prayers, one to the Son, the other to the Father. The former occurs in the *Coptic *Liturgy as part of the *enarxis and in the *Ethiopian Liturgy in a similar position, just before the Liturgy of the *Catechumens when the *priest says, "Lord Jesus Christ . . . who breathed on the face of your disciples . . . said receive the Holy Spirit . . . whatsoever mens' sins you remit, they are remitted."

The prayer to the Father is found in both Liturgies just before the distribution of *Communion, when the priest prays silently, "Lord God Almighty . . . who said to Peter . . . you are Peter, upon this rock I will build my Church . . . I will give you the keys . . . what you shall loose on earth shall be loosed in heaven."

ABUDIYAKUN (Coptic)

Literally, "subdeacon." During the ordination of a *subdeacon the ordinand stands at the door of the sanctuary, and when the *bishop has concluded the Prayer of the Morning Incense, he places one hand on each of the candidate's temples with the thumbs meeting on the forehead, and the ordination prayer is recited. The *sign of the cross is made on the subdeacon's head once and then three times, and the *orarion is placed over his left shoulder. Throughout this Liturgy the subdeacon holds a lighted candle in one hand.

See YPODIAKON.

ABU-HALIM (East Syrian/Nestorian) (also called Abukhalima)

A book of collects used at the conclusion of Night Prayers on Sundays. This book owes its name to its alleged editor, Elias III Abu-Halim, *metropolitan of Nisibis and *patriarch from 1176 to 1190, who included many of his own compositions with the *Divine Office.

See LITURGICAL BOOKS.

ABUNA (Ethiopian)

Literally, "our father." A title of the *patriarch of the *Ethiopian Church.

See ABA SALAMA.

ACATHISTOS (Byzantine)
(also called Acathistus; Akathistos)

Literally, "without sitting." The liturgical hymn or *canticle that is sung solemnly in *Byzantine-rite *Slavonic churches on the Saturday of the fifth week of Lent, called The Saturday of the Acathistos. In *Greek churches it is sung on the first five Fridays of the *fast during *Small Compline. Its recitation in Small Compline differs on the first four Fridays from the last, or fifth, Friday of the fast.

Alternatively, the word may be used to indicate a day on which that hymn is said or sung by clergy and laity alike while all stand, hence the name "without sitting." The text of twenty-four stanzas is based on the Gospel narratives of the Nativity, each stanza's initial letter being in strict alphabetical sequence, with the whole representing a complete Office in honor of the Virgin Mary commemorating the Annunciation. The hymn is therefore suitable for use on various *feasts of the Mother of God. The authorship of the hymn is uncertain, but some assign it to St. Romanos the Melodist (d. 560), while others have suggested that the author was George Pisides, *chartophylax at St. Sophia in Constantinople in the early 7th century, and yet others claim that it was composed by the *Monothelite *patriarch of Constantinople, Sergius, as a thanksgiving for

that city's deliverance from the Avars and Slavs in 626.

It is known that its recitation was recommended by the patriarch St. Germanus (715–732) as a thanksgiving to the Mother of God for protecting Constantinople in the sieges of 626, 677, and 718, and, as a further sign of special gratitude to the Mother of God, the Church decreed that the hymn should be sung standing, hence the name "acathistos." Other acathistoi include that to "our All-Sweetest Jesus" and that of "the Resurrection of Christ" composed by Patriarch Sergei of Moscow, while some are devoted to saints, for example, the acathistos to "the Orthodox Prince St. Alexander Nevsky" and to "St. Panteleimon."

ACMAM (Ethiopian)

Liturgical *cuffs, not to be confused with the *alb (*kamis). These cuffs are worn only by Catholic *Ethiopian clergy.

See EDJGE; VESTMENTS, TABLE OF.

ACOEMETAE (Byzantine/Greek)
(also called Acoemeti)

Literally, "watchers" or "sleepless ones." A general term that is applied at times to all *Eastern Christian ascetics but more specifically to some Basilian *monks (see RULE OF ST. BASIL) who devoted themselves to ceaseless prayer day and night. This was organized by dividing the community into three choirs, each of which performed its duties in relays throughout the twenty-four hours. The "order" was probably established by Alexander, a 5th-century nobleman who together with a congregation of some three hundred monks built a monastery on the banks of the Euphrates. They moved later to Constantinople where they occupied the Monastery of St. John the Baptist, built by John Studius, from whom the Acoemetae came also to be called Studites.

ACOLOUTHIA (Byzantine)
(also called Akalouthia; Akolouthia)

Specifically the fixed arrangement of the *Divine Office, but the term may also be applied to the fixed sequence of events in any religious ceremony.

ACOLYTE

Literally, "attendant." The office is a very ancient one, since it is mentioned in the 3rd and 4th centuries, and a form of ordination is preserved in the *Sacramentary* of St. Gregory (590–640). Prior to this time it was less an order (with the laying on of hands) and more an appointment by a *bishop. The terms "acolyth" and "acolythist" were also used in the Western Church, where the order of acolyte was regarded as the highest of the *minor orders. The function of the acolyte was to serve the *deacon and *subdeacon at a Western-rite Mass, to light tapers, prepare cruets, and attend to the *incense. In the East, the order of acolyte is incorporated in the ordination to the lowest order conferred within a specific rite.

ADAM AIYUB (Arabic)
See ECHOS ADAM.

ADIANI JAMARKIK (Armenian)
See JAMARKIK.

AER (Byzantine)
(also called Kalymma; *Kalymmata; *Nephele; Vosdukh)

Literally, "cloud." The outermost *veil used to cover the Eucharistic veils that conceal the unconsecrated *bread and wine during the *Liturgy. Following its removal from the sacred vessels, it is placed on the *altar, folded according to a set pattern: first the upper third and then the lower third and the left side are folded in. A four-part veil, or pokrovets (Slavonic), is placed on top folded so that its pattern lies inward. Finally, the right side of the aer is turned in so as to cover the folded parts. When the *Creed is being sung by the people, the *priest takes the aer and gently lifts it up and down over the sacred vessels as a symbol of the grace-giving action of the Holy Spirit, which is likened to a breeze. If there are concelebrating clergy, they jointly fan the oblation with the aer while silently reciting the Creed, after which the second senior priest presents the aer to be kissed by the principal celebrant alone, and it is then handed to the youngest priest to be placed by him on the *prothesis. According to pious tradition, the aer represents the stone in front of the Holy Sepulcher.

AETOS (Byzantine/Greek)

This may be either (1) a marble inset placed into the choir floor to mark the place where formerly the emperor's throne was positioned or (2) a round mat embroidered with the figure of an eagle soaring above the battlements of a city. During the Middle Ages aetoi were sometimes no more than rough sketches on the floor, and it is known that during their history they have been made from various other materials including wood and paper. The aetos is used by *bishops as part of the rite of consecration of bishops. The consecrand reads the *Creed and profession of faith while standing on it. The mat is sometimes known as a *psathion, or little mat, and can be stood upon by a bishop when celebrating the *Liturgy.

See ORLETZ; PSATHION.

AGAPE

A meal that was taken in common after the *Eucharist had been celebrated, despite the impression one might gain from St. Paul's comments in 1 Corinthians 11. The Agape and Eucharist were undoubtedly separated by the middle of the 2nd century, for when Ignatius was writing around 115, he told the Smyrnaeans that neither the Agape nor the Eucharist was to be celebrated apart from the *bishop, and it is obvious that he was referring to two separate rites. In Egypt, the Agape survived as a single ceremony well into the 5th century, but the Trullan canons (can. 74) forbade the Agape's celebration in churches from 692.

AGBIAH (Coptic/Arabic)
(also called Egbiyah)

A breviary in Arabic containing the *Divine Office, which is read by the Catholic clergy.

See COPTIC CHURCH, DIVINE OFFICE OF; LITURGICAL BOOKS (Coptic Tradition).

AGGOI (Byzantine)

Tiny cups that separately hold wheat, wine, and oil. These are blessed on some major feasts when *Vespers is followed by a night *vigil, or *agrypnia. The three cups sometimes have a common base.

See ARTOKLASIA.

AGHIA TRAPEZA
(Byzantine/Greek)

See ALTAR.

AGIASMATARION
(Byzantine/Greek)

See BOOK OF NEEDS; LITURGICAL BOOKS (Byzantine Tradition).

AGIASMOS (Coptic)

A general term describing the three Anaphoras in common use among the *Copts.

See ANAFORA; ANAPHORA; KUDDAS.

AGIOS ATHANATOS
(Byzantine/Greek)

Literally, "holy immortal." The third part of the *Trisagion, sung during the *Byzantine Liturgy.

AGIOS ISCHYROS
(Byzantine/Greek)

Literally, "holy strong." The second part of the *Trisagion, sung during the *Byzantine Liturgy.

AGIOS O THEOS (Byzantine/Greek)

Literally, "holy God." The opening words of the *Trisagion, sung during the *Byzantine Liturgy.

AGNETZ (Byzantine/Slavonic)

A square portion of *bread called the "lamb," which is removed from the first loaf as part of the *prothesis, or rite of preparation, in the *Byzantine Liturgy. In performing this ceremony the *priest takes the *lance (kopyo) in his right hand and the bread in his left, and having blessed the *seal, which is a square set into the top of the bread and marked in a cross between the letters IC, XC, NI, KA, he inserts the lance into the right side of the loaf, saying, "As a sheep, he was led to the slaughter." He then puts the lance into the left side, then the upper, and then the lower sides of the loaf.

Once the seal has been removed, it is placed upside down on the *diskos, or *paten, as the priest says, "The Lamb of God is sacrificed . . . ." The bread is then placed with its stamped side uppermost and is pierced on its right side just below the letters IC, as the priest says, "One of the soldiers pierced his side with a lance . . . ." This piercing and cutting of the bread was certainly customary in the 9th and 10th centuries, and it seems that the practice was known to St. Germanus of Constantinople early in the 8th century.

See AMNOS.

AGRYPNIA (Byzantine)

The night *vigil, which follows the ceremony of *Artoklasia, which may occur at the end of *Vespers.

AHL-ALMANTAL-KAH
(Coptic/Arabic)

Literally, "people of the girdle." A term applied to the *Copts and *Syrian Jacobites dating from the mid-9th century. Its use stems from the Muslim insistence that Christians in Egypt be identified by wearing a girdle as a symbol of humiliation.

AINED (Ethiopian)

The *Ethiopian paten, which measures about 7″ in diameter.

See PATEN.

AINOI (Byzantine/Greek)

The name derives from the frequent repetitions of the "Aineite," or "Praise Ye," which are found throughout Psalms 148 and 150 and which form part of the Office that follows the *Exapostilarion on great feasts at Matins. It is possible to find *stichera inserted between the last few verses of the Office, but just how many such insertions are made depends on the rules governing the feast.

See KHVALITNYI; LAUDS.

AISAHHAR (Armenian)

See ENERGUMEN; METHTA'BRONO.

AITESIS (Byzantine/Greek)

Either a long series of invocations interspersed with congregational responses or any series of invocations. In the *Byzantine Liturgy, one aitesis occurs at either side of the *Canon.

AJUS (Coptic/Arabic)

See ALTHALATHAN; TRISAGION.

AKAZ (Coptic/Arabic)
(also called Schvot [Coptic])

The *crozier carried by all *Coptic *bishops and by the *patriarch. It probably derives from the crutch, or leaning stick, which acts as a support for Eastern *monks during the long monastic services.

While a patriarch may carry the akaz anywhere and at any time, a bishop may only carry it if the patriarch is not at that moment within the bishop's diocese. Among the Copts it seems to be a staff of authority rather than a symbol of pastoral care. The akaz is about 5'6" long, its upper end terminating in a cross with two short symmetrical branches usually in the shape of serpents' necks with their heads facing in. A small green silk veil is secured to the staff at the point where it is usually held. There is little information from the Coptic Pontificales to indicate exactly when the akaz is presented to the new bishop during his consecration. At the conclusion of the ceremony the new bishop or patriarch sits on the throne holding the Gospel book and not a crozier.

See DIKANIKION; RABDOS.

AKOIMETONA (Byzantine/Greek)

The light that burns before the *reserved Sacrament.

AKOIMETOS LYCHNIA
(Byzantine/Greek)

Literally, "watchful light." The perpetually lit lamp that faces the *royal doors of the *iconostasis.

AKROSTICHIS (Byzantine/Greek)
(also called Akrosteech [Slavonic])

The initial letters of the *troparion of a *Canon that make up an alphabet, a name, or even a phrase. The word or phrase may sometimes run backward.

AKUATEA QUERBAN (Ethiopian)

Literally, "thanksgiving of the Eucharist." Since the word *"anaphora" does not usually appear in Ethiopian *Ge'ez, this expression substitutes for it and describes that section of the *Liturgy that lies between the preface and the *epiclesis.

ALABASTRON (Byzantine/Greek)
(also called *Alavastr)

The great glass or metal vessel used to contain the holy *chrism. When the *priest administers *chrismation he uses his thumb for the anointing, but with the administration of *unction to the sick, or *euchelaion, he applies the oil with a small cotton wand or even a fine brush.

ALAVASTR (Byzantine/Slavonic)

See ALABASTRON.

ALB

See STIKHARION; VESTMENTS, TABLE OF.

ALBANIAN ORTHODOX CHURCH
(also called the Orthodox Church of Albania)

Christianity probably came to what is present-day Albania through commerce from Epirus and Macedonia; however, there is archaeological evidence that suggests an early Christian community existed in Albania from A.D. 58. This evidence is in the form of the remains of a Christian chapel found beneath a recently excavated Roman amphitheatre at Durres, a large seaport town. Albania was certainly evangelized in the 3rd century by Constantinople and toward the end of the

4th century by Rome, but with the fall of the Western empire in the 5th and 6th centuries, Christianity went into a decline. During the later Turkish occupation of the Balkans many Christians converted to Islam. It has been suggested that their conversion in the 16th and 17th centuries was inspired less by conviction and more by the Albanians' desire to be accepted as equals of the Turks, since imperial favor depended on the profession of Muhammedanism.

After the Balkan wars (1912-1913) and Albanian independence, *Orthodox Albanians argued for autocephaly (*autocephalous) at the end of World War I. Despite the *ecumenical patriarch's fair-mindedness in this matter, which culminated in the *phanar's offer of autocephaly, it was met with refusal by King Ahmad Zoghu (Zog), possibly at Italy's behest.

In 1929, with the consecration of two Albanian *bishops by a Serbian bishop and the Yugoslav *patriarch Dmitry, the foundations of a synod were laid so that the Albanians could declare their autocephaly at Tirana. Initially the *ecumenical patriarch refused to recognize this action but finally capitulated in April 1937. After World War II, in which the Orthodox clergy had played an important role in the Resistance, events took a downturn, and by 1947, with the detention of some *priests by the communist government under General Enver Hoxha, pressure was applied to the Church; by 1951 the bishops of the dioceses of Tirana, Berat, Gjirokastes, and Kora were arrested and replaced by clergy more amenable to socialist ideologies.

The years from 1946 to 1963 saw a further decline in a liberal attitude toward religion on the part of the government, which was highlighted at the Sixth Communist Party Conference (1966) when it was declared that a set goal was the elimination of religion in Albania. Subsequently, in October 1967 Albania was declared to be the "first atheistic state of the world," the clergy was abolished, and all decrees concerning religion and all signs of religion in Albania were eliminated. The few Orthodox who practice religion are concentrated in the south among the Tosk, using *Greek or Albanian as their liturgical language and receiving the holy *chrism from the ecumenical patriarch. The more numerous Catholic communities are in the north among the Ghegs.

ALEIPTRON (Byzantine/Greek)

The small brush or cotton wand with which to anoint the faithful with oil that has been burning in a lamp before a holy *icon; this anointing of the sick is known as the *euchelaion.

See UNCTION OF THE SICK.

ALEXANDRIA, ORTHODOX PATRIARCHATE OF

The *patriarch's title is "His Holiness, the Pope and Patriarch of the Great City of Alexandria and of All Egypt." He resides at Alexandria. The orthodox patriarch has jurisdiction over the Orthodox Church of Alexandria, an apostolic Church founded by St. Mark that included among its *bishops Sts. Athanasius and Cyril. The patriarchate was displaced by Constantinople following Chalcedon in 451, and since 567 there have been two unbroken lines of patriarchs, one for the *Orthodox and the other for the *Monophysites, who refused to accept the Chalcedon decrees.

ALEXANDRIA, PATRIARCHS OF

There are three: (1) for Catholic Copts, who use a modified *Coptic rite; (2) for *non-Chalcedonian Copts; and (3) for *Orthodox Copts.

ALEXANDRIAN LITURGY

See ANAPHORA; LITURGY (Coptic Tradition).

ALLELUIA (Hebrew)

Literally, "Praise the Lord." The use of this Latinized Hebrew word in Christian worship is attributed to Pope St. Damasus I (ca. 304–384), a great biblical scholar who did much to encourage St. Jerome. The word is often found in the *Orthodox Lenten *Liturgies, contrary to Western usage.

ALPHABETOS (Byzantine/Greek)

A *troparion whose initial letters are arranged alphabetically.

ALTAR

Armenian Tradition

The altar is of Western design, with about a half-dozen gradines, above which stands an alcove to accommodate a cross. The table of the altar is narrow and covered with bright cloths and many objects including books, relics, *fans, and a chalice *veil. Made from stone, the altar recesses into a screen, which extends across the apse

against the east wall of the *sanctuary. A space is left at the rear of the altar that permits the passage of the clergy behind it. There may be a tabernacle on the altar in which to reserve the intincted consecrated *bread and before which a lamp may be burning. It is usual to have curtains hanging in front of the altar, which may be drawn as occasion demands.

Byzantine Tradition

Here the word "altar" may be used to refer to the whole sanctuary (*bema) or more correctly to the *hagia or *hiera trapeza (holy table), whose design has not changed much since the 6th century. The table of the altar should be made from solid stone, a requirement said to have been laid down by Pope St. Silvester (314–335), and it should be square in shape and supported either on four or more columns or else on a single pillar, the *calamos, or *bomos.

When the altar is consecrated a special type of cement called *keromastikos, which is made from wax, powdered marble chips, putty, and ground *relics, is used to secure the altar top to its support. At each corner of the altar it is usual for the *bishop to attach a small piece of material with the keromastikos. These small pieces of linen are called hyphasmata (*hyphasma) and contain a picture of one of the Four Evangelists. Over this an all-embracing cloth, the *katasarkion, is placed and secured by cords that cross over the altar top. All is then covered with a silk or velvet cloth (*altar cloths). A small hand cross used to bless the faithful and an *artophorion, which serves as a tabernacle for the *reserved Sacrament but which may be replaced by a hanging Eucharistic dove (*peristera), are placed on the altar top. Above the artophorion may be set a painting of the Crucifixion, while either two candlesticks or a single, branched candlestick are placed on the altar itself, as there are no gradines. It is customary to place the metal *fans, or hexapteriga (*hexapterygon), or *flabella, in front of these candlesticks. The Gospel book is also placed on the altar top. This arrangement recalls something of the practices in Edessa to which Narsai alludes in his *Homily* 17 (ca. 450), when he describes the altar furniture as being a cross upon the altar along with the Gospel book.

Behind the altar a seven-branched candlestick is sometimes found, which is said to symbolize the gifts of the Holy Spirit. In *Byzantine-rite churches only one altar is usual, and only one *Liturgy may be celebrated upon it in any one day, which explains the importance of concelebration in the East.

Ethiopian Tradition

The altar, or *meshwa'e, is usually square and made from stone or wood, enclosed within the innermost circle of the church building, the sanctuary, or *kedest, kedesta, kedusan. The mensa of *Monophysite *Ethiopian altars is made from hardwood upon which is placed the *tabot, or ark, an object of great reverence. The entire altar is sometimes referred to as a tabot, but this is inaccurate. Among *Ethiopian Catholics altars are usually made from stone and are covered with a silk cloth.

East Syrian/Nestorian Tradition

There may be three altars, or tables, two of which are called "the altar of prayer" and "the altar of the Gospel." The third is a small stone altar set into the east end of the *kedush, or sanctuary. This is the Eucharistic altar, on which may be found a plain cross, two candles, and a Gospel book.

West Syrian Tradition

It is usual to have only one altar, but in large churches there may be side chapels with their own altars. There are no sanctuary screens as a rule, but, as with the Armenians, there may be a curtain hanging before the altar. In front of the sanctuary, or madhbh'ha (literally, "altar"), there may be one or two lecterns.

ALTAR CLOTHS

From very ancient times altars were covered by rich cloths of tapestry and linen; for example, Constantine made a gift of a tapestry altar cloth to the church at Jerusalem, while St. John Chrysostom, in one of his homilies, mentions altar cloths of silk that were often ornamented with gold; thus they must have been commonplace in the 4th century. Sadly, many such cloths were destroyed by the *Iconoclasts in the 7th century because they were decorated with figures of the saints and angels. Sts. Isidore and Gregory both mention fine linen cloths that were used in the celebration of the *Liturgy, so it seems likely that the covering of the altar was fine linen, with ornamented cloths of silk or wool used to cover and protect the linen cloths when they were not in use.

The first cloth upon the altar is the katasarkion (Greek) or stratchitza (Slavonic), which is secured to the supports of the altar by means of knots; it is said to represent the burial shroud of Christ.

The second cloth, said to represent the glory of God, is variously known as the endytia, endyton, ependytes, ephaploma (Greek), and inditia (Slavonic). It is richly decorated and of a color appropriate to the liturgical season, and it is on this cloth that the eileton rests. The eileton (Greek), or iliton (Slavonic), is a silken cloth found lying folded on the altar and containing the *antimension (Greek), or *antimins (Slavonic). This cloth is only unfolded during the Liturgy and is said to represent the linen cloth that was wrapped around Christ's head during his entombment. According to St. Simeon of Thessalonica, the cloth is to remind us of the Resurrection, for it was this cloth that the apostles found in a place by itself when they found the tomb empty. Other pious commentators have written that the eileton symbolizes Christ's swaddling clothes.

In the *Coptic rite there is no general term used to cover the altar cloths. The altar is covered by a tight-fitting case of silk or dyed cotton embroidered with fine needlework of silver thread patterns, and this usually extends to the ground. During a Coptic Liturgy, a second cloth covers the first, while a frontal about 18'' square embroidered with a central cross and with figures at its corners hangs on the western side of the altar.

See EILETON; ENDYTIA; ILITON; INDITIA; KATASARKION; STRATCHITZA.

ALTHALATHAH

See TRISAGION.

AMBA (Coptic)

The *Coptic patriarchal title; in full, "The Most Holy Pope and Patriarch of the Great City of Alexandria and of All the Land of Egypt, of Jerusalem the Holy City, of Nubia, Abyssinia, Pentapolis and All the Preaching of St. Mark." The seat of the *patriarch was at Alexandria, but when the Muhammadans moved their capital to Cairo, the patriarchal seat moved there also.

When the patriarch dies, an assembly of twelve *bishops is convened, and if a nominee is agreed upon he is received with the assembly's acclamation. Interestingly, if there is a disagreement, a variation of an 11th-century *Nestorian method is said to be used to rationalize the problem. A final short list of three names is written on slips of paper and placed with a fourth slip of paper bearing the inscription "Jesus Christ, the Good Shepherd" under an altar for a period of three days, during which time the *Liturgy is celebrated above them. A child then selects one of the pieces of paper, and if the one with Christ's name is chosen, then all three candidates are considered unworthy and the process is repeated with other names.

Ideally, the patriarch should be a first son of a first husband of a woman, he should be sound in body and mind, unmarried and not less than fifty years of age, a desert dweller and not a bishop. The tradition of requiring that he not be a bishop seems to have been the custom from the time of St. Mark until 1235. The elected cleric is brought in chains to the cathedral to be consecrated, this custom being thought to reflect the nominee's unwillingness to be so ordained. For example, in the 9th century Joseph LII refused to leave his monastery and, like Sanutius LV, a successor, was dragged in chains to the cathedral. Any missing orders are supplied on successive days, it being possible for the nominee to be ordained *deacon on Thursday, *priest on Friday, and *kummus (archpriest) on Saturday.

In times past the patriarch, after his ordination, would sit on his throne holding the head of St. Mark, but this has recently been superseded by the holding of the Gospel book.

AMBO (Byzantine/Greek)

Literally, "ascend." The word suggests an elevation from which the Bible is read to the congregation during the *Liturgy. It once stood in the middle of the church and was the place reserved for the *readers and *singers and from which a sermon was preached. Today it is a medium-sized projection opposite the holy doors of the *iconostasis, from which the Gospel is announced and the homily is preached. Occasionally, in some churches, an eagle with outstretched wings forming a lectern may be found, on which the Gospel book may be placed.

The prayer behind the ambo (eukhe opisthambonos) is the concluding prayer of the Liturgy, which the *priest recites while standing in front of the holy doors of the iconostasis and facing the *icon of Christ. In times past when the ambo stood in the middle of the choir, the priest was indeed standing "behind the ambo" when he recited the final prayer.

AMCHA (Ethiopian)

In the *Ethiopian rite the Peace is transmitted by the congregation bowing to each other.

See PEACE, KISS OF.

AMFORION (Coptic)

See FELONION; VESTMENTS, TABLE OF.

AMICE

See MASNAPHTHO; TAILASAN; VA(R)KAS; VESTMENTS, TABLE OF.

AMNOS (Byzantine/Greek)

See AGNETZ.

AMURA (East Syrian/Nestorian)

A *reader.

See ORDERS, HOLY.

AMVON (Byzantine/Slavonic)

That part of the *soleas immediately in front of the holy doors of the *iconostasis.

See AMBO.

ANABATHMOI (Byzantine/Greek)
(also called Anavathmoi)

Literally, "steps." Either of two meanings: (1) the Song of Degrees, which describes each of the fifteen gradual psalms (Pss. 119–133), which the ancient pilgrims sang on their way to the Temple at Jerusalem and which are now sung before the *prokimenon; or (2) each section of a series of eight troparia (*troparion; *troparia eothina) or hymns that are sung at *Orthros, or Matins. For each *tone there is one hymn or psalm, and each is divided into three *antiphons; each antiphon is further divided into three troparia except for Tone 8, which has four antiphons.

See STEPENNYI ANTIFONI.

ANADOCHOI (Byzantine/Greek)

A *sponsor.

See BAPTISM; KRESTNAYA ATIETS.

ANAFORA (Coptic)

See AGIASMOS; ANAPHORA.

ANAGNOSTES
(Byzantine/Coptic/Greek)
(also called Anagnust; Anagu'nstis; *Karianjili; *Tchetz)

A reader, a cleric who has received the first *minor orders. He should read the lessons, carry the tapers, and attend to the *incense.

See ORDERS, HOLY (Byzantine and Coptic Traditions); READER.

ANAKOMIDE

A ceremony that involves the transferring of *relics from one place to another.

ANALABOS (Byzantine/Greek)
(also called Analav [Slavonic])

Part of the habit worn by *monks who have been clothed with the *angelic habit, which is the habit of the highest degree (*megaloschemos). The analabos is quite distinct, consisting of two oblong pieces of material joined at the shoulder and falling in front and be-hind rather like a Western scapular. It is highly ornamented with many crosses, which has led to its being known as the *"polystavrion," and with embroidered depictions of the instruments of the Passion and the skull of Adam. Ideally, the analabos is made of wool and is either black or brown. In the past it was made of leather, which, being the hide of a dead animal, served to remind its wearer of his own death to the world.

See DEGREES OF MONASTICISM, HABITS OF.

ANALEPSIS (Byzantine/Greek)

The feast of the Ascension, which is commemorated on the Thursday of the sixth week after Easter.

See VOZNESENIA.

ANALOGION (Byzantine/Greek)

Either (1) a lectern used by singers during the *Liturgy, or (2) a table placed before the *iconostasis bearing a cross, candles, and *icons. *Marriage ceremonies take place at this table, and it is also used to distribute the *breads at the *artoklasia to give nourishment to those participating in the night *vigil (*agrypnia).

ANAMNESIS (Greek)

Literally, "to remember." The part of the *Liturgy that recalls the narrative of the Institution and records those events in the life of Christ.

ANAMPHIASIS (Byzantine/Greek)

The preparation of the *altar on Holy Thursday prior to its being washed.

ANAPHORA (Byzantine)

Literally, "offering" or "offer up." From earliest times this was the normal name for the Eucharistic Prayer, which is equivalent to the Western Canon. Many scholars think there was a common basic structure of the Eucharistic Prayer and that apparent differences are simply additions. This common structure, believed to be reflected in the *Apostolic Tradition* of Hippolytus (ca. 215), is as follows: introductory dialogue, *thanksgiving, Institution, *Anamnesis, *Epiclesis, and doxology.

There are many variations of this skeletal structure. For example, in Serapion of Egypt's Anaphora (ca. 340–360) the Institution and Anamnesis are conflated, while in the *East Syrian Anaphora of Sts. Addai and Mari the words of Institution are apparently omitted. Dom Botte asserts that the words used to be there; however, their insertion in the middle of the *Fraction in the 16th- and 17th-century *Malabarese Missals, which were based on the East Syrian mode, suggests they were not included in the *Liturgies up to that time. One can then conclude that the East Syrians believed the Consecration was effected by the Epiclesis alone. Another view, put forward by Bevenot (1946), suggests that the words were omitted in an attempt at abbreviation as part of the overall plan of Patriarch Jesu-Yab (Ishu'Yab) III of Adiabene (650–661), whose liturgical work was acknowledged by many later commentators.

Shape of Anaphoras

1. Apostolic Tradition: Dialogue, Preface, Institution, Anamnesis, Epiclesis, Doxology.

2. Testament of our Lord (4th-century Syrian document): Dialogue, Preface, Institution, Anamnesis, Epiclesis, Diptychs, Doxology.

3. *Antiochene form: Dialogue, Preface, Sanctus, Post-Sanctus, Institution, Anamnesis, Epiclesis, *Diptychs, Doxology.

4. Alexandrian form: Dialogue, Thanksgiving (part 1), Diptychs, Thanksgiving (part 2), Sanctus, Preliminary Epiclesis, Institution, Anamnesis, Epiclesis, Doxology.

5. East Syrian form: Dialogue, Preface, Sanctus, Post-Sanctus, Institution (once absent), Anamnesis, Diptychs, Epiclesis, Doxology.

See AGIASMOS; ANAFORA; ANNAPHURA; ENFORA; KEDDASE; KUDDASHA; KUROBHO; LITURGY; ZAMESHTIR.

ANASTASIMON (Byzantine)

A *troparion that commemorates the Resurrection.

ANATHEMATISMA (Byzantine)

A curse that is solemnly pronounced by the Church.

ANATOLIKON (Byzantine)

A *troparion allegedly composed in the 5th century by Anatolius, *patriarch of Constantinople, whose feast day is observed July 3.

ANBA (Coptic)

Literally, "father."

See AMBA.

ANBAL (Coptic)
(also called Anban [Coptic/Arabic])

See AMBO.

ANBERO ED (Ethiopian)

Literally, "blessing" or "prayer of blessing." This long Prayer of the Imposition of the Hands, which is recited at the end of the *Ethiopian Liturgy, was taken verbatim from the *Liturgical Instructions* of Zara-Jacob, who ruled Ethiopia with a fanatical zeal from 1434 to 1468.

ANCIENT CHURCH OF THE EAST

See CHALDEAN; EAST SYRIAN.

ANDIFNARI (Coptic/Arabic)

See DIFNARI; LITURGICAL BOOKS (Coptic Tradition).

ANDIMISI (Arabic)

See ANTIMENSION; KETHONS; MANDIL.

ANGELIC HABIT

See DEGREES OF MONASTICISM, HABITS OF.

ANIDA (East Syrian/Nestorian)

The book used for conducting the funerals of the laity.

See LITURGICAL BOOKS (East Syrian Tradition).

ANJIL (Coptic/Arabic)

At *Coptic *Liturgies this is the Gospel normally sung by the senior cleric available; if a *deacon sings the Gospel, he should face east while the *priest, censer in hand, stands at the altar or near the sanctuary veil. If a *bishop sings the Gospel, he may face west. If the cleric is wearing the *tarbush, it is removed before the Gospel is sung. At the conclusion of the Gospel, the Gospel book is kissed, except on Holy Thursday and Holy Saturday.

See EVANGELIE; EVANGELION.

ANNAPHURA (West Syrian)

Among the West *Syrians the reputation is that there are more than one hundred Anaphoras, some of which allegedly go back to apostolic times in Jerusalem—for example, the Anaphora of St. James, "which he heard and learnt from the mouth of the Lord." While it is unlikely that the attributed authorship is correct, this Anaphora was certainly in use in the 4th century, for St. Cyril of Jerusalem (ca. 315–386) knew of its existence. The *Anaphora of St. James the Brother of Our Lord,* originally in *Greek, was later translated into *Syriac. Doubtless it is the source of the *Byzantine and *Armenian *Liturgies, and the present-day *Maronite Liturgy is a simple modification of it.

Other Anaphoras date from the 2nd century, for example, that attributed to St. Ignatius (d. 107). Liturgies were being composed until the 14th century; however, most were produced from the 4th to the 7th centuries and all showed increasingly marked Byzantine influence. The many Anaphoras claimed may not have originated with those to whom they are ascribed but may originally have been used on their feast days or commemorations.

See ANAPHORA; KUROGHO; LITURGY, QUDSHO; QUROBHO.

ANNAPHURO (West Syrian)

A large *veil used to cover both the *paten and *chalice. The word may, in the past, have referred to the *altar cover itself.

See SHUSHEPO.

ANOINTING OF THE SICK

See UNCTION OF THE SICK.

ANOIXIS

The anoixis marks (1) the opening of a church after its consecration or (2) its reopening following its rededication after it has been profaned.

ANONYMOI (Byzantine/Greek)

The saints who lack a proper *kontakion for their Office, in which case it is usual to supply a hymn from the Common of saints.

ANTASDAN (Armenian)

A series of *Gospels read by *Armenian Catholics on the feast of Christ the King during the service of Matins. The Gospel *lessons are Luke 1:26-33; Matthew 2:1-12; Luke 19:11-28; Mark 11:1-10; John 1Ϛ:1-16. One Gospel is read at each of the four cardinal points of the church and the fifth from the *ambo.

ANTERION (Byzantine/Greek)

Part of the outdoor dress of the clergy. It is a long buttonless cassock, open in front, crossed over the chest, and secured at the neck with a hook. *Monastic clergy wear a black anterion, while secular clergy use blue, gray, or dark green cloth.

See ESORASON; KALASIRIS; PODRIZNIK; RASON.

ANTHOLOGION (Byzantine/Greek)

Literally, "The Festival Mineya." This general term described the many attempts that have been made over the years to amalgamate some of the *liturgical books under a single title, the Anthologion, or the Tsietoslov (Slavonic). It represents a compression into a single book of the Offices of the saints and those of the seasons. The Festal Menaion contains the services of the *twelve great feasts; an excellent English translation has been produced by Mother Mary and Bishop Kallistos (Ware).

See PRAZDITCHNAYA MINEYA.

ANTIDORON (Byzantine/Greek)

Literally, "instead of the gift." The bread that is blessed but not consecrated and is distributed to the congregation at the end of the *Liturgy. (An ancient authority for the antidoron's distribution seems to be St. Germanus, *patriarch of Constantinople [732].) Its distribution recalls the ancient custom of the *Agape and the practice of bringing the Eucharist to those who were absent from the celebration of the Liturgy.

In *Byzantine/Greek churches the portions of the single large *prosphora (loaf of bread), not used in the Liturgy are cut into small cubes, blessed, and offered to the people at the end of the Liturgy. In *Russian churches, the antidoron is prepared from those prosphora that are in excess of the five loaves used in the service of oblation (*proskomide). Russian prosphora are small, about 2" in diameter and 1½" high. Members of the congregation often take the antidoron home and keep it in a special container, consuming a small portion at the start of each weekday after their morning prayers.

See BREAD; EULOGIA.

ANTIFON (Byzantine/Slavonic)

See ANTIPHON.

ANTIMENSION (Byzantine/Greek)

The antimension serves as a portable *altar and resembles a large corporal in which are sewn and sealed *relics of saints. If there should be an accident to an altar, the *Liturgy can be served on the antimension alone. This simple form of altar probably came into use at the time of the *Iconoclastic persecution of the 8th century and provided for the needs of non-heretical *priests wishing to celebrate the Liturgy without having to use churches that had been profaned by heretical priests and their congregations. St. Theodore the Studite (759–826) refers to fabric as well as wooden altars, but the term "antimension" did not appear until the end of the 12th century.

The size of the antimension (10" x 13'14") dates at least from the 7th or 8th century. On it is depicted the entombment of Christ. The antimension is consecrated before the celebration of a pontifical Liturgy, when *chrism consecrated the previous day is used to anoint it and wine is poured over it. The whole antimension is then sprinkled with holy water. Following these ceremonies the relics of saints are fixed into a pocket in the cloth with a seal of wax and signed by the ruling *bishop of the diocese.

While it is customary to consecrate an antimension during the service of the dedication of a church, it is permitted to consecrate one outside this rite, a practice authorized by St. Simeon of Thessalonica (d. 1429), and with a bishop's permission, it is possible for a priest to perform the ceremony. The antimension is left folded in the center of the altar in such a way that the right third of the cloth is folded over the left third.

See ANTIMINS; KATHIEROSIS; THRONOS.

ANTIMINS (Slavonic)

See ANTIMENSION.

ANTIOCH, PATRIARCH OF

The principal *bishop of one of the ancient principal Sees of Christendom; in the 4th century the others were Rome and Alexandria. Today Antioch is the See of five *patriarchs: *Greek Orthodox, *Syrian Orthodox, *Melkite, *Maronite, and *Syrian Catholic.

Catholic Patriarchs

Melchite. See MELCHITES, PATRIARCH OF (IN ANTIOCH).

Syrian. "The Patriarch of Antioch, the City of God and of All the East" has jurisdiction over Catholic Syrians throughout the world. Like the Melchite patriarch, he is elected by a synod and the appointment is confirmed by the *pope. The patriarchate was established in 1783 with his residence at Sharfeh, but the See is in Beirut.

Maronite. "The Patriarch of Antioch and All the East." His election and confirmation is similar to that of the other Catholic patriarchs. He has the right to consecrate all *bishops of his rite and to nominate chorepiscopoi (*chorepiscopus), to consecrate the *chrism, and to reserve absolution for various classes of sins. His title dates from the mid-13th century, and he distinctively takes the name of Peter, which is inserted between his first and second names as a commemoration of Antioch's first bishop, St. Peter.

Non-Catholic Patriarchs

Orthodox. "The Patriarch of Antioch the Great and All the East." This is an *autocephalous part of the Eastern Orthodox Church in Syria and throughout the Near East, but now its jurisdiction is exercised universally over Syrians.

Syrian/Jacobite. "The Patriarch of Antioch and All the East" lives in Damascus and has jurisdiction over two million faithful, most of whom live in southeast Turkey, Iraq, Syria and Lebanon, southwest India, and in small scattered congregations throughout the English-speaking world.

ANTIOCHENE

The West Syrian rite, made up of *Syro-Malankarese, *Maronite, *Syrian Catholic, and Syro-*Jacobite rites.

See ANTIOCHENE LITURGY.

ANTIOCHENE LITURGY

The most apostolic of Liturgies, the *Liturgy of Apostolic Constitutions, was the original Liturgy of Antioch, which was superseded by a Liturgy from Jerusalem known as the *Liturgy of St. James. However, following the *Monophysite schism and Council of Chalcedon (451), the *Orthodox used the *Byzantine Liturgy instead of that of St. James, while the *Jacobites used a *Syriac version of St. James, which is the principal *Anaphora of the West *Syrian rite.

See LITURGY (West Syrian Tradition).

ANTIPASCHAL WEEK

The week beginning with the first Sunday after Easter.

ANTIPASHKA (Byzantine/Slavonic)

The second Sunday of the Paschal Feast, commonly called "St. Thomas' Sunday," because of the *Gospel *lesson for that day (John 20:19-31). The week that follows is sometimes called St. Thomas' Week.

ANTIPHANON (Byzantine)

See ANTIPHON.

ANTIPHON

Literally, "alternate utterance." It is alleged that St. Ignatius of Antioch introduced the system of alternate singing by two choirs, while it was introduced among the Greeks by two *monks, Flavian and Diodorus. Originally, the antiphon was a single verse taken from a psalm, repeated after (and sometimes sung before) the psalm was recited, the purpose being to place emphasis on some concept associated with that psalm.

According to St. Basil, in the latter part of the 4th century the antiphon ceased to be simply a responsory in which the two parts were taken by the two choirs and became more a dialogue between the *reader and the congregation. A good example of the antiphon is found in the *Armenian rite as part of the preparatory ceremonies of the *Liturgy, when the *priest says the *ktzord, "I will go to the altar of God . . . ," to which the deacon replies with the Phokh, "Give sentence to me, O God . . . ."

In the *Nestorian tradition, the unaya, or unitha, is simply a verse recited by the clergy and repeated by the congregation between the verses of a psalm.

See ANTIFON; ANTIPHANON; PHOKH; UNAYA; UNITHA.

ANTIPHONARIUM (Coptic)

See ANDIFNARI; DIFNARI; LITURGICAL BOOKS (Coptic Tradition).

APIR (Armenian)

See SAGHMOSERGOV; SINGER.

APOCRISARUS (Byzantine/Greek)

An ecclesiastical deputy. From the 5th century on, these clerics were sent on special missions, but by the 9th century their status had become more that of permanent legate.

APODEIPNON (Byzantine/Greek)

The equivalent of the Western Compline, this was originally a private prayer said by Eastern *monks on retiring for the night, in addition to the official and public Offices.

In structure the Apodeipnon consists of the opening prayer, "O Heavenly King, the Comforter of, Spirit of Truth . . . come and take up your abode in us and cleanse us from every stain and save our souls, O Good One," followed by the *Trisagion and "*Our Father," Psalms 50, 69, and 143 (LXX), the Nicene *Creed, a *troparion and *kontakion (whose texts vary according to the feast), prayers addressed to the *Theotokos, and a final prayer.

In Lent the Apodeipnon is called the Grand Compline, and as part of the *vigil service of Christmas and Epiphany it is joined with the *Mesonyktikon. The Office of Grand Compline is much longer than the ordinary Apodeipnon, with a complicated structure and the inclusion of more hymns and psalms.

See GREAT (OR GRAND) COMPLINE; POVECHERIE.

APODOSIS (Byzantine/Greek)

This marks the conclusion of a *feast of our Lord and of our Lady, whose commemoration is celebrated over several days and is marked by the daily recitation of the prayers of the festival being commemorated.

APOKARSIS (Byzantine/Greek)

See TONSURE.

APOKOUKOULISMOS (Byzantine/Greek)

When a *monk of the highest degree (*megaloschemos) receives the monastic cowl, he must wear it for eight days, after which it is laid aside in a little ceremony, the apokoukoulismos; the monk then resumes his normal headwear.

APOKREOS (Byzantine/Greek)

The week preceding a period of abstinence; this term can be used to describe a particular Sunday, for example, Sexagesima, the last Sunday before the period of abstinence commences.

See MASTYANEETSA.

APOLOUSIS (Byzantine/Greek)

The custom of not washing those parts of a baby that were anointed with *chrism at *baptism for eight days. At the end of this period the child is taken to the church, and the *priest washes the *chrismated parts with a sponge; the water that was used is then reverently disposed of by the clergy. The ceremony is accompanied by various prayers and concludes with the priest *tonsuring the child, cutting the hair in the form of a cross while saying: "N. the servant of God, is shorn. In the name of the Father and of the Son and of the Holy Spirit."

APOLYSIS (Byzantine/Greek)

Literally, "dismissal." The prayer recited at the end of the *Liturgy or Office; for example at the conclusion of the Liturgy the prayer which is recited by the *priest while facing the congregation and which precedes the distribution of the *antidoron.

St. Athanasius (ca. 296–373) uses the word "apolysis" in the sense of a dismissal, and as such it is found in the 4th- and 5th-century texts. The dismissal had probably fallen into disuse by the 7th century, although according to the *Epistle* of James of Edessa to Thomas the Presbyter all may not have been lost, for he writes, "All these things have now vanished from the Church, albeit sometimes the *deacon makes mention of them exclaiming after the ancient custom."

In his outline of the 7th-century *Byzantine Liturgy, St. Maximus comments that the dismissal was by this time rather theoretical, quite contrary to a 4th-century injunction that ordered that the faithful remain in the church until the apolysis had been recited.

See OTPUST.

APOLYTIKION (Byzantine/Greek)

A *troparion, or hymn of the feast or saint being commemorated, which is sung before the *apolysis at Vespers (*Hesperinos) and which precedes the hexapsalmos at *Orthros.

See OTPUST.

APOSTICHA (Byzantine/Greek) (also called *Stikheres)

Brief liturgical hymns that are added to verses from the psalms at the end of *Vespers (*Hesperinos) and Matins.

APOSTLE

The lesson selected from the Epistles of St. Paul for use in the *Liturgy and Offices.

See APOSTOL; APOSTOLOS; ARRACHEALCH; BULUS; LECTIONS; SH'LIHO; SHLIKHA.

APOSTOL (Byzantine/Slavonic)

See APOSTOLOS; LECTIONS.

APOSTOLOS (Byzantine/Greek)

The word refers to (1) one of the twelve apostles, (2) a feast kept on October 31 to honor some of the apostles, or

(3) a *liturgical book containing the liturgical Epistles for use during the year; more specifically, it can refer to the Epistle read during the *Liturgy (see LECTIONS).

As a liturgical book it is divided into two parts, (1) the Proper of the season and (2) the Proper of the saints. The Epistles for the seasons are rather rigidly arranged: from Easter until Whitmonday the readings come from the Acts of the Apostles, while from Whitmonday until Holy Saturday they are taken from St. Paul's Epistles. These readings are set out in five periods of eight seasons and correspond with the eight *tones of the *Byzantine music tradition.

See APOSTOL; BIBLION APOSTOLIKON; PRAXAPOSTOLOS.

APOTOME (Byzantine)

Literally, "cutting off." The commemoration of the beheading of St. John the Baptist, which is observed on August 29 (September 11, New Style).

APSIS (Byzantine)

The rounded end, or apse, at the eastern end of the church. In pagan basilicas, on which Constantinian basilicas were modeled, it was in the apsis, or concha, that the legal experts and judges sat.

ARABIC

See LITURGICAL LANGUAGES, TABLE OF.

ARADCHENORD (Armenian)
(also called Aradjnord, Aratshnord)

A mitered vartabed, a prelate who exercises episcopal jurisdiction but who is not in episcopal orders.

See VARTABED.

ARARAI (Ethiopian)

One of the three *tones used in the *Ethiopian rite, which is used from November 7 until the first Sunday of Advent. This tone is also used during Lent and from June 17 until September 27.

ARATSHAVORATZ (Armenian)

The week following the tenth Sunday before Easter.

See NINEVEH, FAST OF.

ARCHDEACON
(also called Archdiaconos [Greek]; Archidiakion [Slavonic])

The archdeacon was originally the same as the *protodeacon, but in time his role came to be more than simply that of the *deacon of a large church, and today an archdeacon has authority over a large district within a diocese. In the *Eastern Church the functions of a deacon are exercised specifically by a man who is in deacon's *orders, and an archdeacon is not actually a *priest.

See ARKIDYAKNA; ORDERS, HOLY (Coptic Tradition); RA'IS A-SHAMAMISH.

ARCHIERATICOS THRONOS
(Byzantine/Greek)

See THRONOS.

ARCHIERATIKON
(Byzantine/Greek)

The Archieratikon is roughly equivalent to a Western Pontificale; but unlike the Western liturgical book it contains the text of the three *Liturgies of the *Byzantine rite together with the details for the correct celebrations of the peculiarly pontifical ceremonies, such as ordinations, church consecrations, and other pontifical blessings.

See LITURGICAL BOOKS (Byzantine Tradition); TCHINOVNIK.

ARCHIEREUS (Byzantine/Greek)

The episcopacy, in the sense of representing that the episcopacy is the fullness of the priesthood. While this term is often encountered in *Orthodox *liturgical books, it must not be confused with ''*protoiereus,'' which denotes an *archpriest, a title that may be conferred on a married *priest.

See ORDERS, HOLY (Byzantine Tradition).

ARCHIGRAMMATEUS

The principal secretary of a patriarchal court.

ARCHIMANDRITE (Byzantine)
(also called Archimandret [Slavonic])

A very ancient title that has been in use in the East since the 4th century. While it refers either to the head (*hegumenos) of a single monastery or to the superior of a group of monasteries, the title suggests a higher rank than that of hegumenos. The rank is conferred by a *patriarch, *metropolitan, *bishop, or holy synod on any religious clergy as a title of honor, and the recipient need not be the superior of a community.

The *Copts regard the rank as being second only to that of patriarch,

who as grand prior of all the monasteries in the country is an archimandrite's immediate superior. A *monastic archimandrite in the *Byzantine rite has the right to a pastoral staff and an episcopal *mandyas.

ARCHISTRATEGOS
(Byzantine/Greek)

Literally, ''commander-in-chief.'' A term often applied to the archangels Michael and Gabriel.

ARCHON (Byzantine)

A cleric who is responsible for a special part of a service or for directing some special function in a cathedral.

ARCHPRIEST

A title often conferred as an honor for married clergy within the *Byzantine rite. According to St. Jerome (ca. 342–420), who may have been the first to record this title, a church could have only one archpriest. Liberatus recorded that the archpriest was not always the senior *priest of a church but was one chosen by the *bishop from the college of presbyters. Such a priest was to preside over the church next in line to the bishop and to substitute for the bishop in his absence.

In early times it is possible that archpriests were subject to *archdeacons, who had the power of censure; for example, in a passage from the acts of the Council of Chalcedon, Ibas, bishop of Edessa, says that the *deacon Maras was to be excommunicated by his archdeacon and not by the bishop himself.

In Byzantine *Liturgies a bishop may be referred to as an ''archpriest,'' but in the sense of being an *archiereus as against a *protoiereus, or proto-priest.

See KUMMUS.

ARF (Syro-Jacobite)

See KAWOK.

ARKIDYAKNA (East Syrian)
(also called Arkidyakuna)

An *archdeacon in the *East Syrian rite, but one who exercises liturgical rather than administrative functions. In the *Nestorian tradition the arkid-yakna attends to the *bishop's finan-ces, and his role approximates that of a vicar-general in the Western Church.

ARMENIAN

See LITURGICAL LANGUAGES, TABLE OF.

ARMENIAN CATHOLICS

Armenians who have been in commun-ion with Rome following a temporary union in 1198 and who were reor-ganized in 1742. These Catholics use the Armenian rite, have their own Code of Canon Law, and are governed by the *patriarch *catholicos of Cilicia, who resides in Beirut, Lebanon.

ARMENIAN CHURCH

This Church is also known as the Church of Armenia or of the Arme-nians. In 527 when the Synod of Dovin adopted *Monophysitism, the Arme-nian Church became a most national and isolated Church, not being in com-munion with the other two Monophy-site Churches—of the *Copts and the Syro-*Jacobites. It acknowledges only the first three *ecumenical councils (Nicea and Constantinople in the 4th century and Ephesus in the 5th cen-tury) and denies the remaining four, which are recognized by both the *Greek and *Latin-rite Churches.

There is a tradition that the Gospel was taken to Armenia by the apostles Bartholomew and Jude. The Church claims to be the oldest Christian state Church still extant, having been estab-lished by St. Gregory and King Tiri-dates in 301, eleven years before Constantine established Christianity in the Roman Empire.

ARMENIAN CHURCH CALENDAR

The Armenians now use the *Grego-rian Calendar, which was adopted by the *Armenian Catholics in 1892 and subsequently by the non-Catholics in 1912 and 1925. The calendar is based on two principal liturgical cycles, the first being variable and dependent on Easter with its ten weeks of prepara-tion followed by the seven weeks preceding Whitsunday as well as the subsequent seven weeks. The second liturgical cycle starts on the Sunday nearest August 15, which com-memorates the Falling Asleep, or Dor-mition, of the Virgin Mary; this cycle lasts twenty-two weeks, of which the last six are used as a preparation for Epiphany (Hainuthiun) on January 6.

The time between Epiphany and Easter is called the Time of the The-ophany, while the Time of the Trans-figuration refers to the weeks between Easter and the feast of the Dormition. Christmas is not observed as in the West but is commemorated with Epiphany (January 6–19). The origin of this practice seems to date from before the 4th century, when the Western feast of Christmas was introduced into the *Eastern Church.

Of the feasts, there are 160 *fast days and 117 days of abstinence in the Church year. During Lent (*Karasnorth) and the Fast of *Nineveh (*Aratshavoratz) a strict fast is observed during which no food is taken from sunrise until 3 P.M. Such a fast (*dzuom) is distinct from abstinence (bahkh), which forbids the partaking of flesh meat, fish, wine, and oil, while a mild abstinence (*navagadikh) forbids the eating of flesh meat only.

ARMENIAN CHURCH, DIVINE OFFICE IN

The books used for the Day Hours include the Jamarkik, which resembles both the *Byzantine *Horologion and a Western Book of *Hours, while the hymns may be supplied by the Sharagan (*Sharakan), a hymnary.

The Office in the Armenian Church displays a combination of *Syrian and Byzantine elements, especially the latter, doubtless due to the influence of the efforts of the *monks of Mar Saba. The Armenians observe nine traditional Hours, each of which is dedicated to a specific concept. For example, the *Midnight Office is in honor of God the Father, *Matins honors the risen Christ, the Dawn Office honors the Holy Spirit, and the Little Hours honor the descent of the Holy Spirit, the Passion, and the death of Christ respectively. *Vespers traditionally commemorates the burial of Christ and the Sunset Office calls for the peace of Christ, while the equiva-lent of *Compline prays for a peaceful repose. On Saturdays the Dawn and Sunset Offices are omitted.

Like all comparable Offices, the Hours consist of psalms, which are divided into seven main groups, one for each day of the week, together with various hymns attributed to St. Neres Glaietsi (d. 1173), who is not to be confused with St. Narses (d. 373). Several other prayers found in the Offices were allegedly composed by St. John Mantaguni (d. 490). Of the weekday Offices, certain days of the week are set apart for special commemorations; for example, Wednesdays are days when the Annunciation is specially honored, while Fridays commemorate the passion of Christ.

See JAMARKIK.

ARRACHEALCH (Armenian)

The Epistles, which are read on the north side of the *bema while facing west. The reading of these Epistles in the *Liturgy is always preceded by a psalm (*mesedi).

See APOSTLE; LECTIONS.

ARRHABON (Byzantine)

See MNESTRA.

ARTOKLASIA (Byzantine/Greek)

Literally, "the breaking of bread." On the eve of a major feast this ceremony is performed before the night *vigil (*agrypnia), during which five loaves of ordinary *bread and sometimes three vessels of wine, oil, and wheat are placed on the flat surface of the *analogion (lectern), in the center of the church. Among the Greeks only oil and wine are used. As the *apolytikion is sung the table is censed by the *priest and the bread is blessed, during which the feeding of the five thousand is recalled (Matt 14:15-21). The bread is then taken behind the *iconostasis, cut into pieces and dipped in wine, and then distributed to all those participating in the vigil service.

ARTOPHORION (Byzantine/Greek)

The Eastern equivalent of the Western tabernacle, used for the safekeeping of the *reserved Sacrament.

See KOUCHEG; RESERVED SACRAMENT.

ARTZEBURION (Armenian)

The Fast of Nineveh, which precedes the Lenten *fast. During Artzeburion a strict fast (*dzuom) is observed, which forbids the consumption of any food from sunrise until 3 P.M.

See ARATSHAVORATZ; NINEVEH, FAST OF.

ASBADIKON (Coptic/Ethiopian)
(also called Isbadikon; Isbadyakun; Isbodikon; *Spoudikon)

The central and largest square of the consecrated *bread, which is taken to represent our Lord and is intended for the *Communion of the clergy. It is detached at the *Fraction, and before it is placed in the *chalice at the *commixture, the celebrant says in Greek, "Holy things for the holy." This term is used mistakenly at times to refer to an unconsecrated portion of bread.

ASKEMA (Ethiopian)
(also called Askim)
See SHAMLAH.

ASOTOS (Byzantine/Greek)

The Sunday of the Prodigal Son. This Sunday occurs nine weeks before Easter and is so called because the Gospel read at the *Liturgy recalls the story of the Prodigal Son (Luke 15:11-32).

ASPASMOS (Byzantine/Greek)

Literally, "salutation." The act of kissing, specifically the kiss of *peace but also the kissing of an *icon, a *priest's hand, or a Gospel book, performed by the clergy if a *bishop is celebrating or if there is *concelebration. Having kissed the *aer, the front of the *altar, and covered vessels, the bishop stands slightly aside and the concelebrating clergy repeat the following prayer three times: "I will love you, O Lord, my strength; the Lord is my firm foundation and my deliverer." The ceremony continues with the clergy kissing the hand and then the shoulder of the bishop and finally receiving the kiss of peace. As they embrace, the clergy exchange the greeting "Christ with us, is and will be."

See TSELOVANIE.

ASSYRIANS

Members of the Ancient Church of the East, who for centuries have described themselves as *Nestorians (followers of the *patriarch Nestorius' theology, which, like *Monophysitism, was concerned with the nature of the union of divinity had humanity in Christ). Nestorius assumed that in Jesus Christ there were two persons as well as two natures and that there was a conformity of will between Christ the man and God the Word. In 1970 there were 52 congregations of the Church with 144,050 members, and by 1980 the number of faithful had risen to 167,684.

See EAST SYRIAN.

ASTERISK (Byzantine/Greek)
(also called Asteriskos)

Literally, "star." A liturgical instrument made from two curved bands of precious metal, either gold or silver, which intersect at right angles. It is used to cover the Eucharistic *bread when spread out on a *paten during the *Liturgy and is designed to prevent the *veils from brushing against the consecrated bread, but during the recitation of the *Creed it is laid aside. The asterisk may have a cross at the top, and sometimes a tiny star is suspended from the intersection of the two bands. According to some sources the use of the asterisk was introduced by St. John Chrysostom. It is known to have been in use from the 11th century; however, no mention of it appears in the *Euchologion before the 14th century.

ASTERISKOS (Byzantine/Greek)

See ASTERISK.

ATABA (Ethiopian)

The rite of *consignation, in which the central square of consecrated bread (*Asbadikon) is taken by the *priest, who uses his finger tips to intinct the bread from the *chalice, and, having signed the sides of the bread, he places it in the chalice.

ATHONITE

A *monk of Mount Athos.

See ATHOS, MOUNT.

ATHOR (Coptic)

The third month of the Coptic calendar, which corresponds to the period from October 28 to November 26. During Athor when the intercessions are recited as part of the *Coptic *Anaphora, a special prayer is recited: "Lord to bless the fruits of the earth." When Athor is ended another prayer is used: "O Lord send rains of blessing and good weather on the fruits of the earth."

See COPTIC CALENDAR.

ATHOS, MOUNT

A small projection of land stretching into the Aegean Sea from the mainland of Greece and famous for its many monasteries and hermitages. In 962 St. Athanasius (920–1003) retired to Mount Athos and with the help of several followers built the first monastery, or Great *Lavra. Other hermits joined him there and more monasteries were built, but not without opposition from the settlers, who resented the newcomers' intrusion. The spiritual and temporal government is in the hands of the representatives of the monasteries of Mount Athos, who meet regularly at Karyes. The *ecumenical patriarch seems to exercise a purely nominal authority over the foundation. Both *cenobitic and *idiorrhythmic forms of the religious life are practiced there as well as some extreme forms of the eremetical life.

ATRIUM (Byzantine)

In times past, the atrium was a round or square area containing a fountain, which could be used for washing the hands and feet before entering the church building. Certain classes of penitents were required to stand in the atrium in order to attend the *Liturgy, until they were reconciled with the Church and allowed to enter the building proper.

ATSH (Armenian)

Literally, "right arm." Allegedly the right arm of St. Gregory the Illuminator, this *relic is used at the ordination ceremony of the *Armenian *catholicos when it is laid on the head of the catholicos designate. The rest of the ceremony includes an anointing by twelve *bishops and the imposition of hands.

AULOGYA (Ethiopian)

See BARACAH.

AUTOCEPHALOUS

Any *Orthodox Church not subject to any authority outside itself. It can appoint its own chief *bishop or primate. Some *priests used to be called "autocephali," meaning that they were the clergy of a *patriarchal diocese.

AUTOMELON (Byzantine)

See IDIOMELON.

AUTONOMOUS

A self-governing Church, but one that acknowledges the jurisdiction of a *patriarch or hierarch outside itself.

AVAGUERETZ (Armenian)

An *archpriest, whose principal function is the spiritual administration of the Church.

AVANDATOUN (Armenian)

The *sacristy, where ordinarily the *priest vests prior to celebrating the *Liturgy. It may be approached from a *door on either side of the apse screen, into which it may be recessed. A *bishop usually has the privilege of vesting at the *throne in the church.

AVAT(H)RAN (Armenian)

The Gospel book. Following the reading of the *Apostle in the *Liturgy, the *deacon and *incense are blessed, then the congregation is blessed by the celebrant using a hand cross. After the announcement of the lesson, "The Holy Gospel according to N.," the choir sings "Glory be to you, O Lord our God," which is followed by the diaconal warning "Let us be attentive" (proschume) and the choir's response, "It is God who speaks." At the celebration of a non-Catholic Liturgy the celebrant removes his cap, or crown, during the reading of the Gospel, and the Gospel book is held in a veil.

See GOSPEL; LECTIONS.

AWAKENER (East Syrian/Nestorian)

See SHAHARA.

AWED (Ethiopian)

Literally, "tray."

See CACHEL.

AZF (Ethiopian)

An obsolete *alb-like vestment that was worn by *subdeacons, *deacons, and *priests.

AZYME

Unleavened *altar *bread.

AZYMITES (Greek)

Literally, "no yeast." An unflattering term of reproach applied to Catholics and used by Greeks from the 11th century because of the Catholic custom, in common with *Maronites and *Armenians, of using unleavened altar bread. The use of such bread has been thought by many in the East to invalidate the *Liturgy.

B

BABYLON, PATRIARCH OF

Known as the "*Patriarch *Catholicos of Babylon of the Chaldees," he governs the Catholics of the *Chaldean rite. He is selected by a synod of *bishops under the presidency of the apostolic delegate. His election must, however, be confirmed by the *pope, who presents him with a *pallium.

BADARAKAMADUITZ (Armenian)
(also called *Pataragamaduitz)

Literally, "Book of the Sacrament." While this book contains the text of the *Liturgy, it does not contain the Epistles or *Gospels. In 1789, however, an *Armenian Catholic edition of the Badarakamaduitz was published that contains the texts of the relevant Epistles and Gospels.

See KORHRTADEDR; LITURGICAL BOOKS (Armenian Tradition).

BAHKH (Armenian)

See ARMENIAN CHURCH CALENDAR.

BAION (Byzantine)

The palm branches and leaves that are blessed and distributed on Palm Sunday.

BAKTERIA

See PATERISSA.

BALDACHINO (Coptic)
(also called Baldakyn)

In *Coptic-rite churches this is the domed wooden canopy supported on four columns and placed over the main and side *altars. In the center of the dome there is usually a painting of Christ surrounded by angels. Between the four columns, which symbolize either the four quarters of the globe or the Four Evangelists, there may be narrow wooden rods from which altar curtains are suspended and which are sometimes decorated with painted Coptic texts. The use of such curtains is a very early custom, but in modern churches a curtain is hung before the door of the *haikal (sanctuary) and is usually decorated with an embroidered red cross and other figures. During the recitation of the *Anaphora, which commences with the Prayer of the *Iconostasis of St. James or the Prayer of the Veil, this curtain is usually kept drawn across the door.

BALLIN (Coptic/Arabic)

See AMICE; OMOFORION; TAILASAN.

BAPTISM

Besides the frequent biblical references to baptism, the Apostolic canons affirm the necessity for baptism (can. 49), and in "The Doctrine of the Twelve Apostles" there is the command that the pastors of the Church "baptize in the name of the Father and of the Son and of the Holy Spirit." With regard to infant baptism, Canon 54 of the local Council of Carthage (252) witnesses eloquently to the ideal that baptism should take place two or three days after birth. The practices observed by the different *Eastern Christian traditions in administering this *sacrament are highlighted below:

Armenian Tradition

On the eighth day after birth the family and friends bring the child to the church. Psalms are recited while the child's clothing is loosened, and it is blessed upon the forehead and chest but not anointed. This is unusual, especially since the practice of unction before baptism was common by the third century. During the preparatory singing of the psalms a small cross attached to interwoven red and white threads is laid on the child's chest. The renunciation of Satan, but with no ceremony of exorcism, occurs while the child is faced toward the west; then, while facing east, the godparents and *priest affirm their belief in the Trinity, Incarnation, and Redemption. As the party goes to the baptistery Psalm 117 is recited, and the font and water are blessed during a prayer that resembles an *Epiclesis. A reading follows, which is taken from Matthew 28:16-20.

Holding the child so that it faces east, the priest pours water over the infant at each mention of a person of the Holy Trinity, saying, "N., the servant of God, is now baptized by me, in the name of the Father and of the Son and of the Holy Spirit." The child is immersed completely three times in the water as the priest says, "Being ransomed from the slavery of sin by Christ's blood, and set free by the heavenly Father's power, he [or she] becomes a co-heir with Christ and a temple of the Holy Spirit." The newly baptized child is then anointed on the forehead, eyes, nostrils, mouth, palms of hands, heart, spine, and feet as the priest says, "Sweet oil is poured out on you in Christ's name, as the seal of gifts from heaven." Strictly speaking, this is the rite of *chrismation. The cross with the interwoven red and white threads is then placed around the neck of the child, who is given a small candle and is brought to the altar steps, where it is made to bow its head to the cross. *Communion may be received, either by the child swallowing a little of the consecrated wine or by having a particle of the consecrated *bread touch its lips. This is called "Communion of the lips."

Byzantine Tradition

Baptism is normally conferred in the *Byzantine rite by the triple immersion, and extensive anointings and prayers are said over the mother, ideally on the first day after she has given birth and then on the fortieth day following. According to St. Simeon of Thessalonica (d. 1429), the prayers on the first day after birth are said to bestow the grace of sanctification and purification on the woman and her family, while the second set of prayers are really a rite of *churching, which often directly precedes the child's baptism.

Following several exorcisms and the renunciation of Satan by the child's godparents, the contents of the font are blessed. It was St. Simeon who pointed out that the exorcisms appointed for baptism should be read many times. This multiple recital probably reflects the custom of the early Church, when the catechizing priest read the exorcisms on each of seven days and finally they were read over the *catechumens on the eighth day by the baptizing priest. This multiple recitation of the exorcisms is referred to in a 16th-century *Euchologion and emphasizes their importance in the rite of baptism.

Prior to the actual immersion, the child is anointed on the forehead, chest, back, ears, hands, and feet, and the rite of immersion is accompanied by the priest's words, "The servant of God, N., is baptized in the name of the Father, Amen. And of the Son, Amen. And of the Holy Spirit, Amen." Tertullian (ca. 160–230) asserted that "after this, having come from the bath, we are anointed thoroughly with a blessed unction," and St. Cyril of Jerusalem, writing in the 4th century, also describes this ritual in one of his catechetical lectures, stating that a special robe, "the garment of righteousness" (*sabanon), a girdle (*zonarion), and veil (*koukoulla) may be worn by the newly baptized. The putting on of these garments is accompanied by the singing of Psalm 31. When the child is dressed, the rite of chrismation is performed when the priest anoints the newly baptized with holy *chrism on the forehead, eyes, nostrils, lips, ears, chest, hands, and feet, each time saying, "The seal of the gift of the Holy Spirit. Amen." The priest and the godparents, who are carrying the child, walk around the baptistery, and an Epistle (Rom 6:3-11) and a *Gospel (Matt 28:16-20) are read. A *litany then brings the ceremony to a close. It is important to note that if an adult or child is in danger of death without having been baptized, any *Orthodox Christian may baptize that person using the same formula, but such a person must intend to baptize with suitable matter and with the right intention, using triple immersion if this is possible.

Two or more infants may be baptized in the same water, but if they are of different sexes, the male is immersed first. The sacramental words must be intoned over each separately as they are immersed, clothed in their baptismal robes, and as the crosses are placed around their necks. The placing of a blessed cross on the breast of the newly baptized is an ancient practice. First, the priest makes a sign of the cross with it over the person, say-

ing, "In the name of the Father
. . . ." Then the priest places the
cross to the person's lips and announces Jesus' commandment, "If
any man come after me, let him deny
himself" (Matt 16:14).

Coptic Tradition

The time at which baptism takes
place in the *Coptic rite depends on the
sex of the child. Males are normally
baptized forty days after birth, females
eighty days. In cases of emergency
where there is a danger of death, the
sacrament may be administered at
once. The practice of ensuring that circumcision take place about eight days
after birth and before baptism is attributed to *Patriarch Cyril (1235–1243).
It was Patriarch Christodulus (1047–
1077) who forbade the two sexes to be
baptized in the same water, and while
Epiphany was thought to be the most
appropriate time, Abu Dakn in the
17th century claimed that Easter Day
and Pentecost were the most suitable
times.

The ceremony is very long and involves the fresh consecration of the
water, which must be removed from
the font following its use. Immersion
is the usual practice, but if the child is
weak, aspersion administered three
times is thought to suffice. From the
Teaching of the Apostles, which dates
from the 2nd century, it would seem
that aspersion was then the custom.

After the renunciation of Satan the
infant is anointed, and following this
the ceremony of immersion is performed. There are three immersions
and breathings in the face of the child.
Each immersion is accompanied by a
distinct phrase: "N., I baptize you in
the name of the Father, in the name
of the Son, and in the name of the
Holy Spirit." The neophyte is then
anointed with chrism in thirty-six
places, each anointing being accompanied by various short prayers. There is
the imposition of hands and breathing
into the face accompanied by the
prayer "Be blessed with the blessing of
heaven's angels. May our Lord Jesus
Christ bless you. Receive the Holy
Spirit . . . through our Lord Jesus
Christ, to whom be glory with his Father and the Holy Spirit, now and
always."

Following the ceremony, Holy Communion may be received. If the infant
is too young to receive under both
kinds, the priest may dip his finger into
the consecrated wine and moisten the
child's lips. The newly baptized then
receives a portion of blessed milk and
honey. An account of this ceremony
provided by the patriarch Severus of
Alexandria (646) suggests that it has
changed little with the passage of time.
At the conclusion of the ceremony, the
child is carried around the church three
times accompanied by the clergy carrying candles, *cymbals, and bells.
Non-Catholic Copts do not recognize
the validity of lay baptism.

Ethiopian Tradition

Among *Ethiopian Catholics the
practice is similar to that of the Coptic rite, but non-Catholic Ethiopians
appear to administer this sacrament
rather haphazardly.

East Syrian Tradition

For both *Chaldeans and *Nestorians the ceremony is modeled along the

lines of the *Liturgy. According to tradition the Nestorians claim that the rite was established by Ishu'yab (Jesu-Yab) III (650–658). After the birth the infant is washed in blessed water and given its name in a ceremony known as the signing, when it is also anointed between the eyes. It is generally thought that this pre-baptismal ceremony is very ancient and was in general use in the 3rd century. On the first feast day following the birth and after the recitation of several psalms, prayers, and a hymn the font is filled with water. The Epistle and Gospel are read, and then oil in a flagon is blessed and added to some holy oil, which is safeguarded in the sanctuary and reserved (like the *Malca). The holy oil is thought to have been handed down from St. John the Evangelist. The mixture of oils is added to the water in the font, and into this the infant is dipped three times as the priest says, "N. is baptized in the name of the Father, Amen. In the name of the Son, Amen. In the name of the Holy Spirit, Amen." The infant is then dried by the *deacon and handed back to the godparent. A prayer of chrismation is recited as the clergy reach the sanctuary door.

After baptism the water is de-sacralized, or de-consecrated, and respectfully disposed of. The rite's parallel with the Liturgy is marked by the recitation of the *Creed, a Gospel, litany, Sursum Corda, and an Epiclesis. Chaldeans recognize lay baptism, but not so the Nestorians.

West Syrian Tradition

The rite of baptism in the West *Syrian tradition is performed prefer-ably at Epiphany or on the *vigil of St. John the Baptist.

The first anointing on the forehead, which recalls the Ritual of Theodore of Mopsuestia (5th century), is accompanied by the prayer "N. is signed with the oil of gladness, that he [or she] may be armed against the enemy and grafted into the whole olive tree in God's Holy, Catholic, and Apostolic Church." The consecration of the water follows using a (possibly) 4th-century form, which is not restricted to baptism but is also used at the blessing of the waters at Epiphany. At the baptism proper, the child sits naked at the font and water is poured over it three times by the priest, using his left hand, while his right hand rests on the child's head. As he pours, he says, "N. is baptized in the name of the Father and of the Son and of the Holy Spirit into everlasting life."

The rite of chrismation follows immediately. The priest anoints the forehead saying, "N. is signed with holy *myron, the sweet perfume of the Anointed of God, with the seal of true faith, and with the gift of the Holy Spirit, in the name of the Father. Amen." The neophyte is sometimes crowned with a small filet, or garland, at the close of the ceremony while various prayers are recited.

BAPTISMA (Byzantine/Greek)
See BAPTISM.

BAPTISTERION (Byzantine/Greek)
Literally, "place of enlightenment." The baptismal font, which is used for conferring *baptism by immersion. At its brim should be three lit candles,

while on a small table nearby are placed a cross, the *Gospel, and other requisites for the ceremony. If there is a baptistery in the church it should be in the *narthex, but often a movable trough is used. This is placed in the narthex for the ceremony, after which its contents are emptied down the *khoneuterion.

See KOLYMBETHRA; PHOTISTERION.

BARACAH (Coptic/Arabic)
(also called Baracat)

Literally, "blessing." The blessed *bread that is brought for the offertory but not used. It is distributed by the *priest or his assistant at the close of the *Liturgy.

See AULOGYA; EULOGIA.

BARDUTS (Maronite)

See PERIODEUTES.

BARSANIANS

See MONOPHYSITE.

BASHAK (Armenian)

An *Armenian *chalice, which is of Western design.

See SKI.

BASIL, ST.

Otherwise known as St. Basil the Great (330–379), one of the *four Great Doctors of the Western Church and the first of the *three Holy Hierarchs of the *Eastern Church. He was a *bishop of Caesarea, well known not only for his *monastic legislations but his long fight against Arian heterodoxy. The monastic life of the *Orthodox Church is based largely on the principles that he laid down.

See RULE OF ST. BASIL.

BASILIKOS (Byzantine/Greek)

Literally, "royal." The central *door in the *iconostasis, so called because the emperor claimed the right to enter the sanctuary by means of it. In the ancient coronation ceremony the emperor was led into the sanctuary through this door.

BASTAGARIOS (Byzantine/Greek)

A cleric whose duty it is to carry in procession the *icon of the saint whose feast is being celebrated.

BATOUSHKA (Byzantine/Slavonic)

A *priest.

See IEREUS; ORDERS, HOLY (Byzantine Tradition); PAPAS.

BATRASHIL (Coptic/Arabic)

See SHORDION.

BAUTHA DNIWAGE
(East Syrian/Nestorian)
(also called Ba'utha d'Ninwayi)

The Supplication of *Nineveh, a period of fasting thought to date from the time of Mar Saurishu, a 6th-century *bishop who was instructed by an angel to introduce the *fast in order to halt an outbreak of bubonic plague. The fast is observed on the Monday, Tuesday, and Wednesday of the third week before Lent.

See LITURGICAL BOOKS (East Syrian/ Nestorian Tradition).

BAZPAN (Armenian)

Liturgical cuffs, or strips of brocade attached to the wrists, which may originally have been small napkins that were used as towels. When they are being put on the *priest says, "Give strength, O Lord, to my hands and wash away all my filth, that I may serve you in cleanness of mind and body."

See VESTMENTS, TABLE OF.

BEARDS

The wearing of beards by clerics has been standard practice in the *Eastern Church from the 5th century, largely through *monastic influence. Western clergy gradually adopted the practice of being clean shaven, and at the time of Photius, *patriarch of Constantinople (810–895), the beardlessness of the Western Clergy became a matter of major controversy between East and West.

BEATITUDES (Byzantine)

The text for these is taken from Matthew 5:3-12. In the *Byzantine rite while the last portion of the Beatitudes is being sung, the *priest recites the Prayer of the Little Entrance prior to the entry of the *Gospels and clergy as part of the *Mikra Eisodos, or Little Entrance.

BEAUTIFUL DOORS (Byzantine)

See BASILIKOS; ROYAL DOORS.

BEIT QURBAN (Syro-Jacobite)

See PARADISCUS.

BEITH ROZE (Syrian/Catholic)

See SACRISTY.

BEKANEL (Armenian)

See FRACTION (Armenian Tradition).

BELA (Byzantine)

See KLEPALA; SEMANTRON.

BELOTHYRON (Byzantine/Greek)
(also called *Velothyron; *Vemothyron)

The curtain that is drawn across the *Holy Doors (*basilikos) to conceal the Sacred *Mysteries from view during the *Liturgy.

See ZAVIESA.

BEMA (Byzantine/Greek)

The sanctuary, in the middle of which is located the square stone *altar, an arrangement that has been in general use at Constantinople since the 6th century. To the right of the altar is the *diakonikon, the Eastern equivalent of the Western sacristy, in which there are cupboards for the vessels and *liturgical books. To the left of the altar is the *prothesis (*proskomide) where the preparation of the *bread and wine takes place. The bema is separated from the rest of the church by the *iconostasis.

BEMOTHYRON (Byzantine/Greek)

The word is sometimes used to refer to the *door leading into the sanctuary (*bema).

BET LECHEM (Ethiopian)

Literally, "house of bread." The place where the Eucharistic bread for the *Ethiopian Liturgy is prepared by the clergy.

See BETHLEHEM; BREAD (Ethiopian Tradition).

BETA MAKDAS (Ethiopian)

See KEDEST.

BETH DENHO (Syrian)

The feast of the Epiphany.

BETH DIYAKUN
(East Syrian/Chaldean)

See SACRISTY; DIAKONIKON.

BETH DIYAQON
(West Syrian/Jacobite)
(also called *Beth Diyakun)

See BEITH ROZE; DIYAQONIQON.

BETH GAZZA (East Syrian)

Literally, "house of the Holy Thing." A treasury built into the north wall of the sanctuary of *Nestorian churches in which the *paten is placed. According to *Chaldean Missals it also refers to the table that is set up by the north wall of the sanctuary.

See BETH KUDSHA; TREASURY.

BETH KADDISHE (East Syrian)
(also called Beth Sadhe)

Literally, "place of saints." A memorial, sometimes in the form of a reliquary, that is established to a particular church's patron saint; it is usually located on the south side of the sanc-

tuary, quite commonly in association with the beth'mada (baptistery).

BETH KUDSHA (East Syrian)

See BETH GAZZA.

BETH QUDSHO (Syro-Jacobite)

See QUDSHO.

BETH QURBANA
(East Syrian/Chaldean)

Literally, "house of oblation." A tabernacle in which the reserved Sacrament is kept after the *Liturgy.

See RESERVED SACRAMENT.

BETH ROZE (Syro-Jacobite)

See DIYAQONIQON.

BETH SADHE (East Syrian)

See BETH KADDISHE.

BETH SHAMASA (East Syrian)

An architectural term describing the *oven in which the Eucharistic bread (*korban) is baked in an *Ethiopian church.

See BREAD (Ethiopian Tradition).

BETH SHAMASHA
(East Syrian/Nestorian)

See SACRISTY.

BETH SLOTHA
(East Syrian/Nestorian)

Literally, "house of prayer." The covered part of the courtyard outside a *Nestorian church in which the Office may be recited from the feast of the Ascension until the feast of the Hallowing of the Church. At other times the Office is recited in the church proper at the *bema.

BETH YALDO (Syrian)

The feast of Christmas, which in times past was combined with the feast of Epiphany.

BETHLEHEM (Ethiopian)

See BREAD (Ethiopian Tradition).

BETH'MADA
(East Syrian/Chaldean)

Literally, "house of baptism." The *Chaldean baptistery, which is on the right of the east end of the sanctuary. *Syrian Jacobites often place the baptistery on the *catastroma.

See CATASTROMA.

BIBLION APOSTOLIKON
(Byzantine)

See APOSTOLOS; LECTIONS.

BIKION (Byzantine)

An inaccurate term referring to the metal flask used as an aspergill, or sprinkler. The term is sometimes used (wrongly) to refer to the container holding the *chrism, which is contained in the *alabastron.

See KANION.

BIRUN (East Syrian/Nestorian)
(also called Biruna)

A small embroidered hood worn by *bishops of this rite, roughly equivalent to a *Maronite *masnaphtho.

BISHOP

The highest *order received by a cleric. A bishop in the *Orthodox Church is always chosen from the ranks of the *monastic clergy, or "black clergy." Thus he is always celibate, but if a *priest becomes a widower he may enter the monastic state and is then eligible to be chosen as a bishop. A candidate for this order should ideally be at least thirty years of age.

See ARCHIEREUS; EPISCOPOS; EPISKOPOS; ORDERS, HOLY.

BIT QANKI (East Syrian/Nestorian)

The baptistery, which is on the south side of the sanctuary and in which are housed the font (gurna) and the oven (*tanurta) used for the preparation of the Eucharistic *bread.

BITRASHIL (Syrian)

A *stole.

See HAMNIKHO; URORO; VESTMENTS, TABLE OF.

BODIKI (Maronite)

The prayer recited in a low voice by the *deacon on behalf of the living and the dead.

See PRODIKI.

BOGORODITCHNI
(Byzantine/Slavonic)
(also called Bogorodichen)

The hymns in honor of the Holy Birth-Giver of God.

See DOGMATIKI; THEOTOKARION; THEOTOKION.

BOGOYAVLENIE
(Byzantine/Slavonic)

Literally, "manifestation of God." The commemoration on January 6/19 of the baptism of Christ by St. John the Baptist in the River Jordan.

See THEOPHANY.

BOHOD (Byzantine/Slavonic)

See EISODOS.

BOMOS (Byzantine/Greek)

See ALTAR; TRAPEZA.

BOOK OF EIGHT TONES
(Byzantine)

See OCTOECHOS; PARAKLETIKE.

BOOK OF NEEDS (Byzantine)

The book containing the prayers and rites of the *sacraments together with the funeral ceremonies and other commonly used services. The text of this book omits the *Liturgy and some specifically episcopal ceremonies such as ordination rites.

See AGIASMATARION; SMALL EUCHOLOGION; TREBNIK.

BOOK OF THREE ODES (Byzantine)

See TRIODION.

BOURWARR (Armenian)

See CENSER.

BOUTISTES

Literally, "plunger." An official whose function it was to immerse the child in the font as part of the baptismal rites while the *priest was saying the formula of *baptism.

BO'WOTHO (Syro-Jacobite)

A hymn divided into four strophes, the last of which has the doxology added.

BRAK (Byzantine/Slavonic)

See GAMOS; MARRIAGE.

BRAKA (East Syrian/Nestorian)

See LITURGICAL BOOKS (East Syrian Tradition).

BREAD

Armenian Tradition

The *Armenians use unleavened bread, which is supposed to be prepared on the morning of the day upon which the *Liturgy is to be celebrated. In its preparation only the best quality wheaten flour is to be used, and the water is expected to be taken from a pure, running source. To knead the dough, the *priest who is preparing the bread uses his right hand only and is expected to recite the Penitential Psalms. When the *neshkhar (wafer), which is usually circular and measures about 3″ in diameter and 1″ in depth, has been imprinted with the sacred monogram, it is pricked all over to prevent its baking unevenly. This baking is done on a flat pan over a charcoal heater. Three wafers are normally made from which only one is selected for use in the Liturgy. Larger, thinner, and unmarked wafers are prepared and cooked at the same time for distribution at the end of the Liturgy.

Byzantine Tradition

The *Byzantine leavened cake measures 5″ in diameter and 2″ in depth with a 2″ square inset, which is divided by a cross into four squares inscribed in turn with the characters IC, XC, NI, KA (Jesus Christ conquers). The *Russian prosfora is shaped into two spheres, one placed above the other with the top one slightly smaller, flattened and imprinted as above. This square depression is known as the holy lamb (*amnos [Greek]; agnetz [Slavonic]).

Among the Greeks there is another square with a triangle to the left of the imprinted amnos, which is set apart for the commemoration of the Mother of God, while to the right there are three rows of smaller triangles for the commemoration of the angels and the saints. This use of a single prosphora is peculiar to the *Greeks, while the Russians make use of five separate prosfora during the Liturgy.

See PROSFORA; PROSPHORA.

Coptic Tradition

The *Coptic leavened bread is made by a priest or *monk, and no woman may be present during its making. The baking should take place either after sunset of the evening before the Liturgy or on the morning the Liturgy is to be celebrated. Some sourdough, which was set aside at the last preparation, is added to the flour and leaven, and psalms are recited while the dough is kneaded. A ball of dough is then taken from the whole, and following the recitation of Psalm 1, it is flattened and imprinted with a wooden stamp. Around the outer rim are the Greek words for "Holy God, Holy Almighty, Holy Immortal," and the bread is marked into twelve small

squares surrounding a large central square, all marked with a small cross. By tradition the smaller squares are said to represent the apostles, while the center square, the *asbadikon or *spoudikon, represents our Lord. The smaller squares are detached at the *commixture ceremonies.

Up to seven korbans are made, each about 3″ in diameter and 1″ in depth, and it is from these that a selection is made at the *altar the next morning. The baking is done in an *oven attached to the church, which is called the *bethlehem, the heating provided by burning wood beneath it.

See KORBAN; QURBAN.

Ethiopian Tradition

The *Ethiopians ordinarily use leavened bread, but on Holy Thursday unleavened bread is used at the Liturgy. The preparation of the bread takes place after sunset and is the responsibility of a monk, who first washes his hands and removes his shoes. Facing south, he takes a lump of sourdough kept back from the last baking and mixes it with the fresh dough that he has made. The dough is kneaded with the right hand only, and when complete it is placed into a white basin and a deep cross is made in the dough so that the bottom of the basin can be seen. It is then covered and left to rise. After sunrise, the baking takes place in the *bethlehem (bet lechem, literally, "house of bread"). The dough is rolled into a ball and pressed on its face with a stamp, and again the right hand only is used. Six loaves are baked, and the three best ones are taken to the celebrant, who selects one for use. The rejected korbans are then broken into particles for distribution as the antidoron, after the Liturgy.

See H'BST; KORBAN.

Syro-Jacobite Tradition

The term "p'resto" (p'risto) refers to the flat cake mentioned by James of Edessa in the *Epistle* to Thomas the Presbyter, when James describes the signing of the oblation (p'resto) with a cross as part of the Liturgy. The bread used in this rite is leavened and is made in a round shape, about 3″ in diameter. The dough is prepared at sunset with leaven reserved from the last baking incorporated into the new dough. The kneading is by tradition performed by a virgin, by an unmarried priest or *deacon, or by a monk. The flour, which must be of the best quality, is sifted and mixed with pure water, leaven, salt, and a small drop of oil as the psalms are recited.

The breads are baked early on the morning of the Liturgy after being shaped and imprinted by means of a wooden stamp. In the past some use has been made of stone molds. This imprinting leaves a deep cruciform impression that extends to the edge of the bread and an elaborate system of markings upon its surface. It is divided into four equal parts by the arms of the deep cross with a circle at the center. The four small segments inside the circle are marked with a cross, and the four larger segments between the circle and the edge of the bread are further divided in half, making a total of twelve segments. The baking is carried out most carefully, always in the church, while psalms and *canticles are

recited. Women are forbidden to perform this task.

The tradition of baking the bread before each Liturgy is said to derive from apostolic times. A further tradition seems to have arisen of consecrating an unequal number of breads even at times when there are no communicants and two would seem to suffice. This was certainly the custom in the 6th century according to John Bar Cursos, *bishop of Telles (538), but Bar Hebraeus, a *Jacobite canonist of the 13th century, admitted that there was no binding authority for this.

See BUCHRO; PURSHONO; TABH'O.

East Syrian Tradition

The bread used in this rite is leavened, and the flour is, by tradition, presented by the parishioners. The preparation is carried out either in the church or in the priest's house. *Chaldeans prepare enough bread at one time to last for at least fifteen days, and no special time of day is specified for its preparation. The dough is made from flour, salt, filtered water, and leaven. The tradition of using leavened bread has been the custom among the *East Syrians since at least the 13th century. According to the comments of both St. Aphraates (4th century) and St. Rabula (5th century), it was the custom then to use unleavened bread (*azyme). An open fire and tongs with large oval engraved plates at their extremities are used in preparing the bread for both priest and laity.

In the Chaldean rite the priest's bread has a crucified Christ above the letters IHS, all enclosed within a border of a crown of thorns. This bread measures about 3" in diameter, while the laity's bread measures about 1" in diameter.

For the preparation of the *Nestorian bread (bukhra), the wheat selected for use is washed under the running water, dried and ground by a virgin, and then brought to the church. The priest prepares the dough by mixing the flour with water from a running source, and during the kneading he adds salt and a few drops of oil and a small piece of dried and powdered leaven (*h'mira), which has been left over from the last preparation. The addition of the oil and salt is said to be due to the influence of the *patriarch John V Bar Abgar (10th century), which is confirmed in the writings of Timothy II (1318–1353).

Finally the *Malca is added. This mixing of the dough takes place in the baptistery (*bit qanki), which is on the south side of the sanctuary. The priest kneads the dough in the palm of his hand while reciting twenty-seven psalms, or three *hulali. A depression is then made in the dough, oil is poured into the depression, and the dough is stamped at the four corners and then in the center. The four corner pieces are pinched off and left aside as leaven for the next mixing. Then another four pieces are pinched off and rolled into a stick about 3" long, which is called the *kaprana. From the center of this a piece of dough is taken and molded into a round flat cake, or *melkaita, which is placed inside a cruciform cup together with oil. The Malca is scattered into the melkaita and the whole is flattened with a stamp. The result is a cross-shaped loaf upon which the im-

pression called the "seal" (*rushma) can be seen. *Incense is added to the fire that will bake the bread. The loaves, which are not allowed to brown, are removed when they are crisp. Four breads are chosen and placed in a tray touching each other crosswise, and the melkaitas are placed above them in the center. According to custom at least three breads must be consecrated in the Liturgy, but if the priest and deacon are the only communicants, it was recommended by Patriarch John V Bar Abgar that two would be sufficient.

See BUKHRA.

BRODIKI (Syro-Jacobite)
(also called B'rudiki)
See CATHOLIC.

BRYIGYASMANA (Syrian/Arabic)
See R'SHOM KOSO.

BSCH

An abbreviation of the Slavic word "Boschiei," meaning "God." These letters are often found on *icons.

BUCHRO (Syro-Jacobite)
See BREAD (Syro-Jacobite Tradition).

BUKHRA (East Syrian)
See BREAD (East Syrian Tradition).

BULGARIA, ORTHODOX CHURCH OF

By the close of the 2nd century churches had been set up near Burgas on the Black Sea, and by the time of King Simeon's death in 927 the Bulgarian *bishops had declared the Church to be *autocephalous with its own *patriarch, all of this in the face of Constantinople's opposition. With the fall of Bulgaria to Byzantium the Bulgarian patriarchate was suppressed, but independence was regained in 1186. The patriarchate was re-established in 1235, but once again Bulgaria was invaded by the Ottoman Turks and fell in 1396. The Turks remained in control of Bulgaria until the 19th century, while the *Greek Orthodox Church controlled the Church. In 1870 the Turkish government approved the establishment of a national Bulgarian Church, which was promptly excommunicated by the Greeks in 1872. A reconciliation with the *Ecumenical Patriarch in Constantinople was finally effected in 1945. The present Bulgarian patriarch lives in Sofia, Bulgaria.

BULUS (Coptic/Arabic)

See APOSTLE.

BURC'THO (Syro-Jacobite)

Literally, "blessing." The blessed *bread, which is distributed by the *deacon at the *Liturgy on the days of the Holy (or *Great) *Fast of Forty Days. There are many prayers used for the blessing of the bread, but the one commonly used is, "May the grace of the Holy Trinity come from heaven and rest on this burc'tho and upon those who donated, received, and distributed it, and may the mercies of God in both worlds be upon those who have received and are receiving it, for ever and ever. Amen."

See BARACAH; EULOGIA; KHUBZ MOUBARAK.

BURNUS (Coptic)

See FELONION.

BURSHANAH (Maronite and Syrian)

Literally, "oblation" or "first fruits." Either the leavened bread formerly used in the *Maronite rite or the leavened bread of the Syro-*Jacobites. The *azyme (unleavened bread), which is now used, should be thin and is decorated with figures. Its preparation should be undertaken by a cleric, who sings psalms during the baking. The Maronites probably used leavened bread until the 12th century, for it was *Pope Innocent III at the time of the Fourth Lateran Council (regarded by the West as the twelfth *ecumenical council) who recommended the use of unleavened bread to the *patriarch Jeremias Al-Amchiti.

See QURBORO.

BYELORUSSIAN

White Russian, a sub-rite of the *Byzantine rite.

BYZANTINE

A term referring to the Church and patriarchate of Constantinople but commonly used to refer to the whole *Eastern Orthodox Church.

BYZANTINE CALENDAR

The *feasts appearing in this calendar are divided into those of our Lord, our Lady, and the saints. All Sundays are named after the theme of the *Gospel of the day; for example, the Sunday of the Prodigal Son is celebrated nine weeks before Easter. September 1 marks the start of the Church Year.

BYZANTINE CHURCH, DIVINE OFFICE OF

See ACOLOUTHIA; APODEIPNON; HESPERINOS; MESONU(Y)KTIKON; ORTHROS.

BYZANTINE CHURCH, LITURGY OF

See LITURGY (Byzantine Tradition).

BYZANTINE CHURCH, SACRAMENTS OF

See under individual headings: BAPTISM, PENANCE, etc.

BYZANTINE RITE

The system of worship originally peculiar to the Constantinopolitan Church but now used largely by the *Russian and *Greek Churches as well as by some *Eastern-rite Catholics.

C

CACHEL (Ethiopian)

The *Ethiopian *paten, a tray about 7″ wide.

See AWED.

CALAMOS (Byzantine/Greek)

See ALTAR.

CALOGERS (Byzantine)

Literally, "good old men." A designation for *Greek *monks, who follow the *Rule of St. Basil. There are three degrees of *monasticism: (1) novices (archari), (2) ordinary professed monks (microschemoi), and (3) the more perfect (*megaloschemoi).

See DEGREES OF MONASTICISM, HABITS OF.

CALPAS (Armenian)

An article of *Armenian ecclesiastical headwear bordered with fur.

CAMPANA (Byzantine)

A sanctuary bell.

See KODON.

CAMPANARION (Byzantine)
(also called *Kodonastasion)

A tower or similar building for housing the bells; it is customarily located to one side of the church.

CANCELLI (Coptic)

A standing screen that has evolved from a lattice to a solid structure and may be fitted with folding *doors.

CANON (Byzantine)
(also spelled *Kanon)

Part of the Church's *Divine Office. The Canon, probably of Syrian origin, is composed of nine odes that correspond to the nine *canticles. The second of these is sung only during Lent.

1st Canticle, of Moses
　　Exod 15:1-19
2nd Canticle, of Moses
　　Deut 32:1-43
3rd Canticle, of Anna
　　1 Kgs 2:1-10
4th Canticle, the Prayer of Habakkuk
　　Hab 3:2-19
5th Canticle, the Prayer of Isaiah
　　Isa 26:9-20

6th Canticle, the Prayer of Jonah
Jonah 2:3-10

7th Canticle, the Prayer of the Three Children
Dan 3:26-56

8th Canticle, the Song of the Three Children
Dan 3:57-88

9th Canticle, the Magnificat and Benedictus
Luke 1:46-55, 68-79

The Canon takes its theme from the feast on which it is sung. These odes are divided into heirmoi (*hirmos) and troparia (*troparion); these troparia, of which the odes of the Canon are composed, are often arranged to form an acrostic from the initial letters; it has been suggested that the appearance of these troparia dates from the 8th century. While there are fairly strict and complex rules governing the reading of the Canons, in general they should be so arranged that the total number of troparia in each of the canticles does not exceed fourteen.

CANTHAROS (Byzantine)
(also called Labron; Nymphaion; Phialla)

A fountain, now almost obsolete, in the center of the *atrium located outside an eastern basilica. It was used for washing the hands and face before entering the building.

CANTICLE (Byzantine)

The canticle in the *Byzantine rite refers not only to the nine subdivisions of the *Canon but also to the prayers used, which are biblically based.

See PESNE.

CAPPA (Ethiopian)

A *vestment used in the *Ethiopian rite, it resembles a small cloak that reaches from the neck to the knees and is secured at the top. It may be decorated with small bells of either gold or silver. More recently the cappa has been lengthened, and short sleeves have been added. The *Ethiopian Catholic *deacons and *subdeacons wear a cappa shorter than that worn by a *priest and fastened at the chest.

See KABA; LANKA.

CATABASIA (Byzantine)

A *hirmos, which is placed at the end of a hymn. The term also refers to a short hymn sung by a choir, which moves from its place into the church proper for part of the singing of the Office.

CATABASION (Byzantine)

The place beneath the *altar where the *relics may be stored.

CATASTROMA (Syro-Jacobite)
(also called *Qestroma)

The section of the church between the sanctuary and the *nave reserved for the choir. It is separated from the nave by a railing and one step; on the catastroma there may be a lectern on either side to hold the Office books, while another in the center is where the *hussoya and the *lessons of the day are read.

CATECHUMENS (Byzantine)

Those who are receiving instruction in the faith with a view to being baptized, referred to as "*hearers" in the *Liturgy of Nestorius. In the *Epistle* of James of Edessa to Thomas the Presbyter the writer refers to the "hearers" receiving the blessing of the *bishop or *priest prior to leaving the church at the beginning of the offertory.

In apostolic times it was customary for those wishing to receive *baptism to prepare for it by catechization, and the *Apostolic Constitutions* of the early Church instructs bishops and priests to test the knowledge and sincerity of their candidates. Catechization involved others as well, for as St. Justin Martyr wrote in his *First Apology,* the catechumens are "taught to pray and entreat God . . . while we join in their prayer and fasting." This joint effort is reflected in the Liturgy of the Catechumens, in the *Liturgy of St. Basil, and the *Liturgy of St. John Chrysostom.

An old liturgical Office, the *Tritekti, was directly concerned with the catechumenate. St. Simeon of Thessalonica confirmed that this Office was still taking place in the 15th century and was certainly found to exist in a Sinaitic *Euchologion of the 10th century. The Tritekti took place during Lent, a time when catechumens traditionally prepared for baptism, and was an occasion for communal prayer and fasting, as a reference in the *Didache* suggests, stating that "before baptism, the baptizer and the baptized should *fast and any others who can," thus emphasizing the community's involvement. The fast concluded with the baptism of the catechumens at Epiphany, Easter, and Pentecost.

See ERAKHAH; KATECHOUMENOS; NE'US CRESTIYAN; OGLASHENNIY.

CATHANARS (Syro-Malabarese)

Literally, "the Lord's men." A clear reference to *priests.

CATHEDRA (Byzantine)

See THRONOS.

CATHISMA (Byzantine/Greek)

A division of the Psalter.

See KATHISMA.

CATHOLIC (Syro-Jacobite)

A general intercession recited during the rite of *Fraction, or *Tukkoso dh'-q'soyo w'rushmo. This prayer, which is recited by the *deacon, is thought to be ancient.

See BRODIKI; KATHULIKI.

CATHOLICON (Coptic)
(also spelled *Katholikon)

The second Epistle from the Catholic Epistles, which follows the *lessons from St. Paul in the *Coptic *Liturgy. This Epistle is read first in Coptic and then in Arabic, and during the reading in Arabic, the *priest usually recites the Prayer of the Catholic Epistle.

CATHOLICOS

A title of honor as detailed below:

1. Catholicos of the East, or kathulika d'madhn'ha (Syrian), *patriarch of the *Nestorians and successor of the archbishop of Seleucia-Ctesiphon. "The Reverend and Honored Father of Fathers and Great Shepherd, the Catholicos and Patriarch of the East," as the Nestorians call him, always takes the name of Simon (Shim'un) and is known as Mar Shim'un. He is selected from the "patriarchal fam-

ily,'' or ''holders of the throne.'' The office has customarily passed from an uncle to his nephew, who must be celibate and who must never have eaten flesh meat, nor may his mother have eaten flesh meat during her pregnancy with him. The Catholicos consecrates all *bishops, and he may ordain a *priest for any diocese. Every seven years he consecrates the holy *chrism for use throughout the Church.

2. Catholicos-patriarch for non-Catholic *Ethiopians; he resides at Addis Ababa. Among the *Monophysite Ethiopians the head of the Church is called the catholicos-patriarch. As usual, he ordains his bishops and consecrates the holy chrism. Since the diocesan system has not been fully implemented, the bishops are delegated by the catholicos. The Ethiopians accord the *Coptic patriarch a primacy of honor, but in earlier times the Ethiopian Church was governed by a Coptic *monk chosen and ordained by the Coptic patriarch.

3. Catholicos of Etchmiadzin, patriarch of all *Armenians, and the catholicos of Cilicia, patriarch of Catholic Armenians. As the catholicos of Etchmiadzin, the principal Armenian prelate receives certain honors following his consecration. His outward symbol is the *epigonation, or konker, which is worn from the waist on the left side. As part of the consecration ceremony, at the hands of the twelve bishops the head of the catholicos is covered with a large, thick embroidered silk veil (*kogh), and in subsequent ceremonies this veil is carried in front of him when he is in procession. The title ''catholicos'' was first used of the Armenian primate, who was initially dependent

on the patriarch, but later this was reversed, and the title of patriarch came to suggest an inferior rank. The catholicos' particular functions are to consecrate bishops as the need arises and to bless the holy chrism every three to five years. The chrism is made from oil and balsam, together with forty essences from different plants and gums. Some holy chrism is left over from the last preparation and is added to the new chrism, so that a small portion of the original holy chrism is retained in it. This original holy chrism was allegedly blessed by Jesus and brought to Armenia by the apostles.

The ''Patriarch of the Catholic Armenians and Catholicos (Katholikos) of Cilicia'' resides in Beirut, Lebanon. He is elected by a synod of bishops, and this election is ratified by the *pope when he bestows the *pallium on the catholicos. By tradition, the catholicos includes the name of Peter in his official name.

4. Catholicos-patriarch of *Georgia. Probably a survival of the catholicate of Iberia, which was dependent on *Antioch. The dependency of the Iberian (Georgian) catholicate on the patriarch of Antioch probably lasted until the 11th century. Over the years it became part of the *Russian Church, but on May 18, 1918, following the fall of the Tsarist empire, the national Church with the catholicos at its head was established. When the Bolshevik administration took authority, Georgia was brought under the control of Moscow, and the catholicos and several of his bishops were imprisoned. The catholicos has the title ''Archbishop of Mtshetis and Tbilisi, Catholicos of All Iberia'' and lives at Tbilisi;

he and four other bishops form the holy synod, which governs the Georgian Orthodox Church.

CEDANA'AWED (Ethiopian)

The veil used to cover the *paten in the *Ethiopian *Liturgy.

See VEILS.

CENAE (Ethiopian)

The *chalice used in the *Ethiopian rite, which is usually covered with a *veil.

See CEWA'E.

CENOBITIC (Byzantine)
(also spelled Coenobitic)

A form of *Byzantine *Orthodox *monasticism that is traditionally contemplative and designed along the lines suggested by the teachings of St. Basil. Unlike *idiorrhythmic foundations, *cenobitic monasteries practice the communal life and are not permitted to convert to idiorrhythmic status. However, idiorrhythmic monasteries may become cenobitic, although apparently this is quite rare. The Serbian monastery of Chilander at Mount *Athos wished to do so in 1933, but for political reasons the conversion was disallowed.

At the start of his monastic life, an aspirant is admitted to the lowest grade of *monk (*rasophore [Greek]; ryasonosets [Slavonic], and after three years he may choose to become a *stavrophore (Greek) or krestonosets (Slavonic). This grade is also sometimes known as the microschemos. Few proceed beyond this grade to assume the rank of *megaloschemos (Greek) or Skhimnik (Slavonic), which is characterized by extreme penitence and discipline.

See DEGREES OF MONASTICISM, HABITS OF.

CENOBITIC SKETE (Byzantine)

A *monastic settlement, the superior of which is elected by all the *monks subject to the principal monastery's approval. The superior may be elected for life. Members of such a skete attend the *Liturgy and Offices together in the skete church (*kyriakon), eat communally, and in general practice the community life. They may not change to *idiorrhythmic status, whereas idiorrhythmic monasteries may become cenobitic but rarely do so.

See DIKAIOS; RASTOYATEL.

CENSER

The Eastern censer is always shorter than its Western counterpart and is sometimes ornamented with little bells. The chains of the censer are swung from the ends with one hand only, using a short, jerking action.

See BOURWARR; KADILNITZA; MA'ETANT; PIRMO; SHOURE; THYMATERION.

CEWA'E (Ethiopian)
(also spelled Ceuae)

The *chalice used in the *Ethiopian rite is usually Latin, or Western shaped. The wine used by the non-Catholic Ethiopians is reputedly made by soaking dried grapes in water and using the extracted juice, while the *Ethiopian Catholics use a pure fermented wine.

See CENAE.

CHALDEAN

Known variously as the Chaldean, Syro-*Oriental, or *East Syrian rite of the Roman Catholic Church. There is also a sub-rite, the *Syro-Malabarese. The name "Chaldean" was first used to describe East Syrian Catholics by *Pope Eugenius IV (1431–1447).

See BABYLON, PATRIARCH OF.

CHALDEAN CHURCH

See EAST SYRIAN.

CHALICE

The sacred vessel used to contain the wine in the *Liturgy. For most rites the Western shape is usual, but among the *Nestorians the chalice is a footless cup made of inferior metal, often copper, measuring about 6″ across.

See under individual headings: BASHAK; CENAE; COSO; POTERION; POTIR; SKI.

CHARTION (Byzantine/Greek)

Literally, "piece of paper." When an *altar is to be consecrated by a *bishop, this is the authorization; it is written on pieces of parchment and placed inside each of the supporting pillars of that altar.

CHARTOPHYLAX (Byzantine)

A diocesan chancellor, whose functions are next in importance to those of the diocesan *bishop. He is in charge of the archives and discipline among the clergy, and he usually deals with matrimonial cases.

CHASOSLOV (Byzantine/Slavonic)
(also called *Tchasolov)

See HOROLOGION.

CHASY (Byzantine/Slavonic)

One of the *Hours of the Office.

See ORAI.

CHATA (Syro-Malankarese)
(also called sradha [Sanskrit])

Funeral feasts.

CHATSVERATZ (Armenian)

The feast of the Exaltation of the Holy Cross, which is celebrated on the Sunday between September 11 and September 17. Other feasts of the Holy Cross are celebrated during the year; for example, the Invention of the Holy Cross on the seventh Sunday after Easter, as well as feasts commemorating the apparition of the Cross in 351 and 653.

CHAZRANION (Byzantine/Greek)
(also spelled *Khazranion)

Literally, "walking stick." A straight, highly decorated ebony stick, a little shorter than a *rabdos, with a knob of silver or ivory at its tip; it may serve as a substitute for a staff. A *bishop may use it when not pontificating, or it may be carried before a bishop as emblematic of his office.

CHEESE SUNDAY (Byzantine)

The last day upon which cheese and eggs may be eaten before Lent, thus making it the equivalent of the Western Quinquagesima Sunday. It is also known as "Forgiveness Sunday," and this note of reconciliation is sometimes emphasized after *Vespers by the faithful lining up and in turn bowing down to the ground before each other, saying, "Forgive me, a sinner" and replying, "God forgives us."

CHEIROTONIA (Byzantine/Greek)

Literally, "stretching of hands."

See ORDERS, HOLY.

CHEROUBIM (Coptic)

Liturgical fans, which are mentioned in the Liturgy of St. Clement (translated from the *Apostolic Constitutions* [ca. 375]); the *Catecheses* of Theodore of Mopsuestia (350–428); and St. Gregory the Great's *Liber Sacramentorum* (624). These fans are made of gold or silver and are so constructed that a disc of silver on which is embossed the figure of the seraphim has a silver socket that is secured into a short wooden handle. The fans are used at the ordination of a *priest, at the laying on of hands, and in the procession of the *chrism during its consecration, in which the holy chrism is accompanied by twelve *subdeacons carrying lamps and twelve *deacons carrying the fans.

See EXAPTERYGA; MIRWAHAH; RIPIDIA; RIPISTERION.

CHERUBIC HYMN (Byzantine)

See CHERUBIKON; EISODOS.

CHERUBIKON (Byzantine)
(also called *Cherubic Hymn; Cherubimic Hymn)

In the *Byzantine *Liturgy, this is intoned just before the *Great Entrance (Byzantine Tradition). It is sung very slowly by the choir, but the singing is suspended during the entrance procession and resumed only when the clergy reach the sanctuary. The text is as follows: "We who mystically represent the Cherubim who sing to the life-giving Trinity, the thrice-holy hymn, let us now lay aside all earthly cares" (the Cherubikon is suspended here, and then continues) "that we may receive the King of the universe born aloft by armies of unseen angels. Alleluia. Alleluia. Alleluia."

CHESCI GHEBEZ (Ethiopian)

Literally, "priest-treasurer." The cleric in whose house the *vestments and books are stored until they are needed for the celebration of the *Liturgy.

CHINOVNIK (Byzantine/Slavonic)
(also spelled *Tchinovnik)

See ARCHIERATIKON.

CHOREPISCOPUS

In "The Blessing of Chorepiscopus" the candidate receives the imposition of hands by the *bishop and is presented with the *masnaphtho (Syrian), a hood-like *vestment rather like a Western amice. The chorepiscopus may be given the right to wear a pectoral cross and a ring and may carry a hand cross.

The earliest mention of chorepiscopoi was at the Synod of Ancyra (314), and they were undoubtedly in episcopal *orders; their origin seems to have arisen from a need to supply country churches with episcopal oversight in the absence or unavailability of a diocesan bishop. Even in the early days they were restricted in the exercise of their orders; they could only ordain to the lower ranks of clergy and were subject to diocesan authorities.

They were subject to further restrictions by the Council of Laodicea (363), which ordered that they be replaced by traveling *priests (*periodeutai). The Council of Meaux (845) further forbade the chorepiscopoi to administer *confirmation, consecrate churches, or ordain priests. The office certainly seems to have disappeared in the *Byzantine Church by the 11th century. A synod held by the Armenians in 1911 resolved to call these clergy "regional inspectors" of the clergy and of the Church, and they were prohibited from conferring holy orders.

CHOSIAC (Coptic)

The season of Advent. The *fast observed permits the use of oil and fish and varies in length according to whether the individual is a cleric or layperson. This lengthy fast (allegedly) was introduced by the 11th-century *patriarch Christodulus to imitate the one-and-a-half-month fast that the *Copts believe the Blessed Virgin Mary observed prior to Christ's birth.

CHOTKI (Byzantine/Slavonic)

See KOMBOLOGION; KOMBOSCHOINION.

CHRISM

A mixture of olive oil, balsam, and either thirty or fifty-five other substances including red wine, gums, nuts, and flowers. Only *bishops have the right to consecrate the holy chrism according to the Second Council of Carthage, and in the *Eastern Church it is a privilege belonging to the *patriarch alone. In the case of the *Ecumenical Patriarch, the oil, which is used for *chrismation and other consecrations, is consecrated on Holy Thursday and then distributed to those bishops under his jurisdiction. This consecration ceremony is very long and occurs about once every ten years.

The *Byzantine order of preparation starts on Holy Monday with a *moleben and a preliminary blessing of water and an aspersion of the ingredients and blessing of the cauldron in which the chrism is to be made. The cauldron filled with the ingredients is then heated by an oven ignited by the flame of a *trikerion. The *Gospel of St. Matthew is read, followed by other scriptural readings, during which vested *deacons stir the cauldron with wooden ladles. The cauldron is kept boiling until Holy Wednesday, when it is blessed again and a compound of oil and wine is poured crosswise three times into it, the action accompanied by a blessing from a senior cleric. This chrism is then taken to the patriarchal cathedral, and during the singing of the Pentecost *troparion, "Blessed art Thou, O Christ our God . . . ," special vessels filled with chrism are set up to the north and south of the altar.

On Holy Thursday, during the patriarchal celebration of the *Liturgy and at the *Great Entrance, a vessel containing the old chrism is brought from the *prothesis through the north door to the *holy doors where it is received by the patriarch, who places the vessel on the altar. At the same time the two vessels with the new chrism are brought to the patriarch. This new chrism is consecrated at the end of the Eucharistic *Canon, with a triple blessing of the chrism in each vessel and the prayer of consecration, in which the sending of the Holy Spirit on the

...sm is supplicated. After this prayer each vessel with the new chrism is blessed three times, and then portions of the new chrism are ladled into the old chrism and vice versa. At the conclusion of the Liturgy, the vessels with the newly consecrated chrism are sealed, and during the singing of Psalm 45 these vessels are placed in the *synthronon of the patriarchal cathedral.

See MERON; MYRON.

CHRISMATION
(also called *Chrism [Greek]; *Meropomazanie)

Known in the apostolic age as the "unction" or "anointing" (2 Cor 1:21; 1 John 2:20, 27). This *sacrament is normally conferred by a *priest immediately after *baptism.

Armenian Tradition

Chrismation is administered by a priest as part of the rite of baptism. The *meron (chrism) used for the anointing is consecrated by the *catholicos, who performs the ceremony every few years on Holy Thursday. To administer the sacrament the priest dips his thumb into the oil and anoints the newly baptized child or *catechumen in nine places, but it can also be administered by anointing the forehead alone and saying, "N., may this sweet oil which is poured upon you, in the name of Christ, be a seal of the celestial gifts."

Byzantine Tradition

Commonly called "the seal of the Holy Spirit," chrismation follows immediately upon immersion and baptism. Reconciliation is also effected through this sacrament, and the holy chrism (*myron) is consecrated and distributed by the *ecumenical patriarch except in the *Russian Orthodox Church where it is consecrated by the *patriarch of Moscow. The priest administers the sacrament by anointing the forehead, eyes, nostrils, mouth, ears, chest, hands, and feet of the child or catechumen while reciting the words "The seal of the gift of the Holy Spirit" at each anointing.

Coptic Tradition

Chrismation is administered immediately after baptism; each of the thirty-six anointings, on many parts of the body, is given with a different formula followed by the imposition of hands and a breathing on the one being chrismated. This is accompanied by the words "Be blessed with the blessing of heaven's angels. May our Lord Jesus Christ bless you. Receive the Holy Spirit. Be clean vessels through our Lord Jesus Christ to whom be glory with his Father and the Holy Spirit, now and always." The ceremony ends with a *dismissal followed by a short hymn.

Ethiopian Tradition

*Ethiopian Catholics used to administer this sacrament after baptism, but now it is usually administered by the *bishop in accord with standard Catholic practice; non-Catholic Ethiopians seem to have included the rite of chrismation as an integral part of the rite of baptism.

East Syrian Tradition

Until recently the Catholic *Chaldeans administered this sacrament immediately after baptism, with the priest anointing the space between the eyes with *chrism and using the Catholic formula for its administration in *Syriac. The *Nestorians have combined chrismation with the baptismal rite: the priest lays his right hand on the head of the person being chrismated and then the forehead is signed with the right thumb, moving from below upwards and then from right to left, saying "N. is baptized and confirmed in the name of the Father and of the Son and of the Holy Spirit, for ever."

West Syrian Tradition

The sacrament is administered by a priest who anoints the forehead, eyelids, nostrils, lips, ears, hands, chest, back, and feet with the oil consecrated by the patriarch on Holy Thursday; the words of administration are "N. is sealed unto everlasting life in the name of the Father and of the Son and of the Holy Spirit with holy chrism . . . the sign and seal of true faith and of the accomplishment of the gifts of the Holy Spirit."

CHSCHOTHS (Armenian)

See FANS.

CHURCH MUSIC (Byzantine)

In the *Byzantine rite the singing is always unaccompanied and no musical instrument is ever used. There is a plainchant of eight modes that correspond to Western usage except that they are numbered differently. The four authentic modes (Doric, Phrygian, Lydian, and Mixolydian) come first and then the Plagal modes, but their scales are different from those used in the West. The plainsong is enharmonic with variable intervals.

CHURCH SLAVONIC

The form of Russian used in the *Russian Orthodox Church and some other *Byzantine-rite Churches.

See LITURGICAL LANGUAGES, TABLE OF.

CHURCHING (Byzantine)

In the *Russian and *Greek traditions, on the fortieth day after giving birth a new mother brings the child to the church in imitation of Luke 2:22. The *priest blesses the child, and after making several signs of the cross with the infant, he takes a male child into the sanctuary through the south *door of the *iconostasis and goes around the *altar, bowing at the southern, eastern, and northern sides of the altar. The infant is then touched with holy *icons. A female child is not taken into the sanctuary, but in either case the priest brings the child to the godparent, who bows three times after the Prayer of Simeon has been recited.

CIDARIS (Coptic)

A cap decorated with small crosses, mentioned in the 12th century by the *Coptic *bishop of Akhmin, who included it in a catalog of priestly *vestments. In times past it was worn only by a *priest, but now it is also worn occasionally by non-Catholic Coptic *deacons. Denzinger mistakenly confused it with the *amice. It is made from crimson velvet material, bound on upper and lower hems by a circlet of silver lace and divided into four parts by vertical bands of lace. In each of these sections is a solid silver cross with small crosses set into the branches of the large cross.

CILICIA
(also called Sis)

The See of two rival *patriarchs, the Armenian apostolic *catholicos and the Armenian Catholic patriarch.

See ARMENIAN CATHOLICS.

CINCTURE

See VESTMENTS, TABLE OF; ZONE.

CIRCUIT OF THE LAMB (Coptic)
(also called *Durat Alhamal [Coptic/ Arabic])

At the start of a solemn *Coptic *Liturgy, the *bread, or *lamb, is wrapped in a veil, held high, and carried around the *altar in procession. During this procession the choir sings "Alleluia. The thought of man shall praise you and the rest of his thought shall keep festival before you. Alleluia." According to the time of the year, other verses may be substituted. Some clergy precede the lamb, while another bears the wine and yet another a lighted taper. In the *Ethiopian tradition, as part of the ceremony of the *prothesis the bread is carried around the altar after it has been rubbed all over to remove any crumbs and then placed in a veil (*machfad; macdan). A procession forms in which the lamb is preceded by a *taperer and followed

by a *deacon with the *chalice. After the procession, wine and a little water are poured into the chalice.

CITUNAH (Syrian/Maronite)

See KUTHINO.

CLERIC

A term widely used to refer to any ecclesiastic but more correctly used in reference to anyone who has received the *tonsure.

CLOUD (Byzantine)

See AER.

COAL (Coptic, Ethiopian, East Syrian)

A widely used term referring to the Blessed Sacrament. "Coal" is a clear reference to Isaiah 6:6, 7, when a live coal was taken from the altar and laid on the lips of the prophet—an obvious reference to the Holy Sacrament. It is so called, specifically, in the *Coptic *Liturgy during the prayer at the *Fraction, "As you cleaned the lips of your servant Isaiah the prophet . . . one of the seraphim took a live coal . . . to purge our souls and bodies and our lips . . . this true coal . . . which is the Holy Body and Precious Blood of Christ . . . ."

In the *Ethiopian Liturgy it is found as part of the preparatory rites; as the *priest places the *bread on the *paten, he says, ". . . and clean this paten which is filled with live coal even your own Holy Body . . . ."

In both the *Syrian and *Nestorian (*East Syrian) rites it refers to the consecrated particles; for example, in the Syro-*Jacobite (West Syrian) Liturgy as the priest is about to receive the bread he says, ''The propitiatory Coal of the Body and Blood of Christ our God is given to . . . .''

See G'MURTHO.

COE'NATA (Ethiopian)

See KOBORO.

COLOBION (Coptic)

A very early form of *stoicharion, or dalmatic-type *vestment, with short, close-fitting sleeves. Its use was abolished by *Pope St. Sylvester (314–355) at the time of Constantine the Great.

COMMIXTURE

See ENOSIS; ISOPOLNENIE; KHARRNOUMN; SMIESHEVANIE.

COMMUNION

The reception of the Body and Blood of Christ present in the Blessed Sacrament varies according to the rite. The four methods of reception are (1) separately, when the particles of *bread and the *chalice are presented separately to the communicant; (2) singly, when the communicant receives only under one species; (3) by Intinction, when the bread particle has been intincted by dipping it into the contents of the chalice; (4) by means of a *spoon, when the particle of bread is removed from the chalice in a spoon and this spoon is then presented to the communicant; the communicant's lips are then wiped with a large corporal, or veil.

See ANAPHORA; IKADDISHE; KHAGHORDOUTHIUN; KOINONIA; KUDSHE; LITURGY; PRICHASTIYE; PRECHASTCHENIE; SUTAFE; TANAWUL; TSCHI.

Armenian Tradition

*Armenian Catholics receive a particle that may sometimes be intincted. *Communion may be received by a kneeling communicant, who is expected to be fasting from the night before and in a state of grace.

Byzantine Tradition

For Catholic (*Melchite) and non-Catholic members alike, the procedure is identical: The communicant approaches the sanctuary steps leading to the *royal doors of the *iconostasis with arms crossed over the chest. The person receives under both kinds from the chalice with the aid of a Communion spoon (*labis). Fasting and confession are required of the communicant.

Coptic Tradition

Catholic *Copts receive Communion usually under one species, and it should be received while kneeling. Non-Catholic Copts may receive both species separately with the wine administered by a Communion spoon (*kokliarion), or they may receive by means of intinction.

Ethiopian Tradition

Catholics receive under both species at a solemn Liturgy, the wine being received separately by means of a spoon while the communicant stands. At ''low'' celebrations they receive under one species only. Non-Catholic Ethiopians may receive under both kinds, but separately; like non-Catholic Copts, they receive the particle of consecrated bread in the right hand, which is crossed over the left hand. This custom may have prompted St. Anastasius Sianaita (d. 598?) or his successor, who was *patriarch of Antioch (599–610), to write that the people who were to communicate should wash their hands (probably in the *atrium) before entering the church. A Trullan canon (can. 101) forbade the use of vessels in which to receive the Sacrament (Council of Trullo, 692). In this rite it is usual for a *deacon to administer the chalice to the communicants.

East Syrian Tradition

While the *Chaldean Catholic communicant may receive under both species, it is usual to receive only under one species and then while standing at the door of the sanctuary. *Nestorians receive under both species and separately; the *priest administers the bread and the deacon administers the chalice.

West Syrian Tradition

Catholic communicants may receive while standing, either by intinction or by means of a Communion spoon. It is by means of such a spoon that deacons and *subdeacons receive the contents of the chalice. Non-Catholics, or *Jacobites, normally receive a particle of bread that has been dipped into the chalice. It is generally assumed that Communion is to be received during the Liturgy, but it is known that in the 4th century it was quite common for the faithful to carry away particles with which to communicate themselves. This was attested by St. Basil, and it was common in Alexandria. The cus-

tom was specifically condemned by Canon 58 of the Council of Trullo. Intinction in the *Eastern Church was allegedly unknown until the 10th and 11th centuries when it became quite widespread.

COMPETENTES (Byzantine)

Literally, "illuminated ones." A *catechumen who is receiving instruction during the forty days that precede Easter with a view to receiving baptism on Easter eve. In Holy Week they confirm their belief by reciting the *Creed to the *bishop or *priest and then receive last-minute instructions about the details of the baptismal ceremony. After their baptism the competentes receive their First *Communion.

COMPLETES, THE DEACON WHO (East Syrian/Nestorian) (also called Damshamli)

An archaic expression, the exact meaning of which has been lost, that refers to the *deacon who participates in the *Nestorian *Liturgy. There is a rubrical mention of this expression when the *priest washes his hands following the recitation of the *Creed: "The priest says to the deacon who has concluded [completed] . . . ."

COMPLINE

In the *Byzantine rite this is the Church's Evening Prayer, which may be either Great or Small Compline. Great Compline is said together with Matins, forming the all-night *vigil service celebrated on the eves of Christmas, Theophany, and the Annunciation.

See APODEIPNON; GREAT COMPLINE; POVECHERIE; SMALL COMPLINE.

CONCELEBRATION

Concelebration occurs when more than one *priest consecrates the bread and wine in the *Liturgy; it is usual when a *bishop celebrates. It is surprising that it is not more widespread, since only one Liturgy may be celebrated on an *altar in any one day. This custom was quite normal in the early Church.

See SOBORNIE; SYLLEITOURGON.

CONFIRMATION

See CHRISMATION.

CONSECRATION CROSSES

Crosses marking where the *altar was anointed with *chrism; they are also found on the walls of a church's sanctuary as part of the church's consecration. In the *Nestorian *Liturgy these crosses are acknowledged when as part of the *Anaphora the *priest, having washed his hands joins them and makes the *sign of the cross in the air toward the consecration crosses of the church building.

CONSECRATION OF THE ALTAR

In the *Greek tradition the *altar has three incised crosses on it (unlike the Western usage of five crosses), which are set into the altar mensa. These crosses, which are quite large, are arranged so that one is in the center and one is set on either side of the central cross. The *Copts do not have any incised crosses other than those marked on the altar board (*lax) which has a cross in the middle with the letter Alpha (*A*) set above it and Omega (*Ω*) below, and the letters IC, XC, YC, and OC at the four corners of the board.

CONSECRATION OF SACRED VESSELS

In the *Byzantine tradition the vessels are blessed and anointed with *chrism by a *bishop during a ceremony that consists of several *ectenes and an anointing accompanied by several prayers: "Lord Christ our God, send your Holy Spirit on this new *chalice and bless, hallow, and consecrate it," then making the *sign of the cross over both chalice and *paten, he says, "Behold the chalice of salvation and the *diskos of life of the New Testament are hallowed, consecrated in the name of the Father . . . ."

In the *Coptic rite the bishop takes chrism and anoints the inside of the chalice as well as the outside, saying, "Holiness, purity, blessing, and protection to all of those who shall drink of your True and Precious Blood. Amen."

CONSIGNATION

The signing of either sacred element with the other during the *Liturgy.

See ATABA; RUSHMO.

COPTIC

The name derives from the Arabic for the Greek name for Egypt. The term is applied to both Catholics and non-Catholics, the latter being the more numerous, having a world membership in 1980 of 6,027,900. The Catholic Copts are much fewer, having in 1980 only 133,544 members.

COPTIC BREAD

See BREAD (Coptic Tradition); KORBAN; PROSPHORA; QURBAN.

COPTIC CALENDAR

The *Coptic calendar year is taken from 284, which marked the start of the reign of the Roman emperor Diocletian, who in the early part of the 4th century was responsible for a huge purge of the Christian community. It was in memory of the large number of martyrs who were sacrificed and tortured for their faith that the Copts adopted the first year of Diocletian's reign to mark the starting points of the calendar. This period is known as the era of the martyrs. The Copts observe the following great *feasts of our Lord: Annunciation, his baptism, Palm Sunday, Easter, Ascension, and Pentecost, together with some lesser feasts that include the miracle of Cana and Jesus' appearing to St. Thomas.

*Coptic Catholics make use of the *Gregorian calendar, but the year is divided into three parts relating to the Nile and the crops, namely the Inundation, Sowing, and the Harvest. The Church Year, which begins in the month of Tout (approximately September 10), has twelve months of thirty days and a little month of five or six days in a leap year.

COPTIC CATHOLICS

Native Egyptian congregations that have been united with Rome since the early 17th century when Capuchin missions were established, with one in Cairo in 1630. *Pope Leo XII unsuccessfully attempted to set up a patriarchate, and it was not until 1899 that Cyril Makarios was approved as *patriarch by Pope Leo XIII. Their principal centers are the Faggalah Quarter of Cairo, the suburbs of Heliopolis, and the cities of Tahta and Luxor. The title of the Coptic Catholic patriarch is "Patriarch of Alexandria of the Copts."

COPTIC CHURCH

According to tradition the Church of Alexandria was founded by St. Mark the Evangelist (Eusebius, *Historia Ecclesia* 2, 16), and along with Rome and Antioch, it ranked as one of the chief Sees of the Early Church. During the patriarchate of St. Cyril (ca. 380–444) the renown and power of Alexandria reached its peak, but during the time of Dioscorus (444–451), St. Cyril's successor, the Church became involved in the *Monophysite heresy. After six years of controversy Dioscorus was deposed and his teaching condemned by the Council of Chalcedon (451); with the election of his successor, Proterius, schism followed. The schism divided the Catholics, or *Orthodox, and the Monophysites. The Catholics maintained faith in the two natures of Christ as determined by the Council of Chalcedon, while the Monophysites followed the teaching of Dioscorus, which alleged that there was a single divine nature in the one person of the incarnate Christ.

The Orthodox Catholics became known as *Melchites, or Royalists, while the dissidents were known as *Jacobites. The See of Alexandria became alternately occupied by these rival parties, and each communion maintained a separate and independent succession. In Upper Egypt *monasticism was flourishing, as attested by the many Lives of the Saints and Sayings of the Fathers, and this monastic influence is most readily seen in the *Coptic *Liturgy, which is very lengthy and slow in movement.

The Coptic *patriarch (non-Catholic) is elected by his fellow *bishops and clergy, who also consult the laity, and it is he who ordains all bishops himself and he alone who consecrates the *chrism, which is sent to all the dioceses of the Church. In government, the patriarch, or *pope, is assisted by a religious council.

See ANAPHORA; LITURGY.

COPTIC CHURCH, DIVINE OFFICE OF

Collectively called the al-Agbieh, the *Divine Office is made up of the traditional seven *Hours: the Prayer of Sunset (al-Ghurub); the Prayer of Repose (an-Naum); the Prayer of Midnight (Nusf-al-Lail); the Prayer of Dawn (al-Bakar); and the equivalents of Terce, Sext, and None. With the exception of the Night Office, which has three nocturns, each with twelve psalms, all the other Hours have twelve psalms each as well as a *Gospel, troparia (*troparion), prayers, *Trisagion, and *Our Father. The Dawn Office, however, has nineteen psalms in addition to prayers, the Trisagion, and the Our Father.

COPTIC FASTS

The Coptic fasts are conscientiously observed. The four principal fasts, which involve abstinence from food between sunrise and sunset as well as abstinence from many things besides flesh meat, are listed below:

1. The Great Fast of Lent, which commences fifty-five days before Easter and includes a preliminary week of modified fasting. No meat, fish, or milk are supposed to be eaten during Lent; however, many people only fast until midday at the beginning of Lent, and this fast is extended as Lent goes on, so that by Holy Week a strict fast is observed in which mainly vegetables and beans are eaten.

2. The Fast of the Apostles, which lasts about forty days before July 5 (the feast of Sts. Peter and Paul).

3. The Fast of the Mother of God, which lasts fifteen days before August 9 (16 Mesore).

4. The Little Fast of Advent, from December 1 until Christmas.

Other small fasts include the Fast of *Nineveh, which lasts three days and takes place around two weeks before Lent, and the Fast of *Heraclius, which coincides with the first week of Lent.

See FASTS.

COPTIC RITE, LANGUAGE OF

See LITURGICAL LANGUAGES, TABLE OF.

COPTIC SACRAMENTS

See under individual headings: CHRISMATION, COMMUNION, etc.

COSO (Syrian)

In the *Syrian rite the *chalice is the familiar Latin-shaped vessel, which according to the synod of Sharreh (1888) must be consecrated with *chrism, although prior to this date the chalice and *paten were consecrated in a very casual manner.

See CHALICE.

CREED
(also called Symvol [Slavonic])

The confession of faith; the text used liturgically is that of the Nicea-Constantinopolitan Creed (325). This credal statement extended the use of the Creed beyond being a simple test of belief for neophytes, and it became a solemn affirmation of belief of those already in the Church. The Nicene Creed has as its basis the old baptismal creed of Jerusalem, to which clauses were added that must exclude the Arians. It was Peter "the Fuller," the *Monophysite *patriarch of Antioch (473), who insisted that the Creed be recited at every *Liturgy in order to show disrespect for the Council of Chalcedon, or the "emperor's council," which he claimed had rejected the Council of Nicea. The Creed's insertion into the Constantinopolitan Liturgy by Timothy in the 6th century was allegedly insisted upon to secure the political support of the Monophysite emperor. But with the return of *orthodoxy to Constantinople, it was considered prudent to continue the use of the Creed as a regular feature of the *Byzantine Liturgy. It should be noted that the Creed was not introduced into the Roman Liturgy until 1014.

In the *Syrian, *Coptic, and *Nestorian rites the Creed was probably placed initially just before the *Peace, but in the present Nestorian Liturgy it is separated from the Peace by the *diptychs and by some pre-*anaphoral prayers. The position of the Creed in the Coptic rite is just before the Peace. The Creed is similarly positioned in the Syrian rite, since its recitation is immediately followed by the lavabo (washing of the hands), and then by the prayer of the Peace, which introduces the Anaphora (of St. James).

In the Coptic, *Armenian, Nestorian, *Ethiopian, and *Syrian Catholic and *Maronite Liturgies the Creed begins with the words "We believe." In the Syrian rite each of the congregation says, "I believe," while the *priest says, "We believe." Catholics add the *Filioque phrase, which St. Photius, patriarch of Constantinople (878–891), declared to be a "corruption of the faith."

See HAIYIMONUTHO; KHAVATAMCH; SYMBOLON.

CROSS, SIGN OF

The *Armenians (Catholics and non-Catholics), *Copts and *Ethiopians, and *East and West *Syrian Catholics all make the sign of the cross from left to right. West Syrian *Jacobites make the sign from left to right, using either three fingers or the middle one alone. *Byzantine-rite Christians make the sign of the cross from right to left, using the first two fingers and thumb of the right hand joined together.

See STAVROS.

CROWN

The miter worn by the senior clergy; the term may refer also to the crowns placed on the heads of the bride and bridegroom at their wedding, which they are supposed to wear for eight days, after which they return to the church for the ceremony of the deposition of the crowns.

See MITER; STEPHANOS; VIENETZ.

CROZIER

See RABDOS.

CRUCIFIX

See ESTAVROMENOS.

C'THOBKO TESHMESHTO (Maronite)

Literally, "Book of the Ministry." A collection of rubrics that are to be observed by the *deacon, servers, choir, and people during the principal ceremonies of the *Maronite rite.

CUFFS

See CUMM; CUMMAN; CUMMIN; EPIMANIKIA; KAMISION; PEDHITHO; VESTMENTS, TABLE OF; ZANDE; ZENDE.

CUMM (Coptic)

*Coptic cuffs that cover the whole forearm, being broadest at the elbow and narrowing down to the hand; in that way they differ from *Byzantine cuffs (*epimanikia). The cuffs of a *patriarch, *bishop, and *priest are seldom used except at ordinations. These *vestments are usually highly ornamented, often with gold and silver embroidery worked into a design of flowers and seraphim.

See CUMMAN; KAMAN; KAMISION.

CUMMAN (Arabic)

See CUMM; KAMAN; KAMISION.

CUMMIN (Maronite)

The cuffs worn by a traditionally vested cleric.

See ZENDE.

CURSI ALCAS (Coptic/Arabic)

The ark, or tabernacle, a cubical box 8"–9" high on the top of which is a circular opening just large enough for the top of the *chalice to be accommodated. At the Consecration during the *Liturgy the chalice is placed in the ark so that the rim is flush with the top of this box. The four walls of the cursi alcas are covered with paintings of our Lord and St. John.

Renaudot considered that the ark was a sort of *antimension and was not, as Neale thought, simply used for the reservation of the Blessed Sacrament. To judge from the prayer used at the ark's dedication, it is unquestionably set apart, "that in it, may be consecrated the Body and Blood of your Only Begotten Son, our Lord . . . ."

See PITOTE; THRONOS NTE PIPOTERION; TOTE.

CUSHAPA (East Syrian/Nestorian) (also spelled Kushapa)

The private prayers in a *Liturgy said by a *Nestorian *priest while kneeling; such prayers are always recited in a low whisper.

CUTHINO (Syro-Jacobite and East Syrian/Chaldean) (also spelled Cuthina)

An *alb worn by the clergy participating in the *Liturgy; it may be made of linen, cotton, or silk, and while there is no regulation as to the color of this vestment, it is usually embroidered with many crosses. Catholic *East Syrian clergy have adopted the custom of wearing very lacey albs. When the *priest puts on the cuthino he says, "Clothe me, O Lord, with the robe of incorruption, and girt me with the strength of your Holy Spirit, O our Lord."

See VESTMENTS, TABLE OF.

CYMBALS (Coptic)

Cymbals are used, along with hand bells and tongueless bells, to mark certain parts of the ceremonies. They are stored in a lectern until required. Renaudot cites their use in 850 to mark the *elevation of the consecrated *bread.

CYPRUS, CHURCH OF

The apostles Paul and Barnabas visited Salamis, which was Barnabas' birth place, in A.D. 46, and subsequently Barnabas became the first *bishop of Cyprus. In 431 the third *ecumenical council, at Ephesus, discussed the separation of the Church of Cyprus from the Church of Antioch, and during Emperor Zeno's reign (474–491) it received its *autocephaly, which was confirmed in 488 by Acacius, *patriarch of Constantinople, and decreed by Zeno. In the years that followed Cyprus was attacked many times by the Arabs, Franks, Genoese, and Turks, and by 1571 the local Church

had become subordinate to the Latin Church. The Turkish invasion of that year restored the *Orthodox Church to its former position, and the Latins were banished.

In 1878, when Cyprus came under British influence, a movement agitating for union with Greece (Enosis) was started in which the Church leaders took a leading role. In 1959, the ethnarch Makarios, who had been banished and allowed later to return to the island, was elected president. Cyprus was declared independent in 1960. Three-quarters of the population and 96 percent of all Christians on Cyprus are members of the Orthodox Church of Cyprus. The Orthodox Constitution of 1909 states that the Church is to be governed by a holy synod consisting of three diocesan bishops with the archbishop as the synod's president.

CZECHOSLOVAKIA, ORTHODOX CHURCH OF

An early *Orthodox community was set up by disaffected Catholics in Prague during the mid-19th century, but it was suppressed and then reactivated following World War I. During the 20th century dioceses were set up at Mikhailov, Olomouc-Brno, and Presov. Once again these Orthodox suffered persecution during World War II, but the *metropolitan See was re-established in Prague under the patriarchate of Moscow. This Church has been *autocephalous since 1951.

D

DABTARA (Ethiopian)
(also spelled *Defteras; *Depteras)

A learned layman, usually one who teaches the clergy and administers local Church affairs.

DAGHARAN (Armenian)

A hymnbook used to provide the texts of the hymns sung during the *Liturgy by the choir.

DAILY VESPERS
(also called *Hesperinos; *Vechernya)

The Evening Prayers of the Church, which may also form part of the all-night *vigil service. The *Byzantine Church, in agreement with the Jewish tradition that the day commences at sunset, begins its daily worship with *Vespers. The all-night vigil service in the early Church was intended to last all night and was composed of both Vespers and *Matins. In monasteries, where the service was read and chanted very slowly, the service did indeed last all night.

Outline of the Service

The service is composed of the following:

A blessing by the *priest and the singing of Psalm 103 (LXX), during which the priest recites the Prayers of Light.

The Great *Litany, or *Velikaya Ekteniya (Slavonic).

A Psalter reading.

The Small Litany (or *Malaya Ekteniya (Slavonic).

The *stichera.

The hymn to the *Theotokos.

The evening hymn, "O Joyful Light," attributed to Sophronius, *patriarch of Jerusalem.

The Litany of Fervent Intercession.

The *aposticha.

The Nunc Dimittis.

The *Trisagion.

The *Our Father, *apolytikion, *Theotokion, and litany.

The final blessing by the priest and the *dismissal.

See GREAT VESPERS.

DAIR (Coptic/Arabic)

A ringed wall that may be found enclosing *Coptic churches and monasteries.

DAKTYLIOS (Byzantine/Greek)

A ring worn by a *bishop, although among most *Orthodox this is almost unknown. It also refers to the rings blessed by a *priest during the espousal ceremonies (*marriage), which were traditionally made from gold for a man and from silver for a woman. Today, both rings are made from gold.

DAR (Byzantine/Slavonic)

Literally, "the gift." Specifically refers to the oblation of the *bread.
See DORON.

DARETHA (East Syrian/Nestorian)

An architectural feature found in many traditional *Nestorian churches. It is a partly covered area in the eastern part of the courtyard forming an entrance to the church building.

DA'WAH (Syrian/Catholic)

The *Epiclesis, found in the *Syrian *Anaphoras after the words of institution and the *Anamnesis. During this ceremony the *deacon censes the oblation as the prayer is recited, and the *priest flutters his hands three times over the *bread and over the *chalice. Then, standing upright with his hands stretched out over the bread and wine, he completes the Epiclesis, the text of which follows: " . . . that coming down He may make this bread the body ✛ of Christ, Amen, the life-giving body, the redeeming body ✛ of our souls . . . the very body ✛ of our great Lord God and Savior . . ." (to which the congregation responds, "Amen"). The priest then continues: "and the mixture that is in this cup, the blood of Christ, Amen ✛ the blood ✛ purifying our souls and bodies, the very blood ✛ of our Lord God and Savior . . ." (to which the congregation again responds, "Amen").
See KERYTHO.

DAWIDHA (East Syrian/Nestorian)

Literally, "the David." The Psalter, which is divided into twenty *hulali, rather like the *Byzantine *kathisma, each consisting of two or more *marmitha (marm'yatha), or "sittings." The numbering of these psalms is taken from the Hebrew, not from the Septuagint. The psalmody, which is pre-eminent among the *East Syrians, is accompanied by *antiphons (onitha), which are inserted between the psalm verses.

DAY OF THE MYSTERY
(East Syrian/Nestorian)

The meaning of this curious rubrical term seems to be lost, for "if it is a Day of the Mystery," as the rubric reads, the *deacon says, "Be still and silent." This instruction is found before the reading of the *Turgama, which precedes the *Gospel.

DEACON

Literally, "a minister." The lowest of the three major orders: *bishop, *priest, and deacon. Strictly speaking, the function of the deacon is to assist the priest at the *altar and to read the *Gospel, but in the East his role is more important than that of his Western counterpart. His selection often demands a good voice, as it is the deacon who leads much of the chant during the *Liturgy. The details of the ordination ceremony vary according to the rite, as described below:

Armenian Tradition

The order is conferred most solemnly shortly after the start of the Liturgy. The bishop sits on the *throne, and after each candidate is presented to him there follows a short liturgical examination when the candidates approach the altar and kneel there. During the singing of Psalm 119 the bishop places his right hand on the head of each in turn and prays. He then places his right hand again on the head of the candidate, who faces the congregation, which signifies its approval with shouts of "He is worthy." An assistant priest then places his hands on the ordinand's shoulders while the bishop replaces his hand on the head and says, "The Divine and Heavenly Gift, that ever fulfills the holy needs of the Apostolic Church, now calls N. from the subdiaconate to the diaconate for the service of the Holy Church according to his own and this congregation's testimony." The Liturgy recommences, and after the *Creed and presentation of the gifts the bishop once more sits on the throne and places his hands on the ordinand's head. After a prayer, he vests the deacon in his distinctive stole and presents him with the Gospel book. The new deacon then censes the altar three times and takes his place among the assistant deacons.

Byzantine Tradition

The ordination to the diaconate takes place during the Liturgy after the Consecration of the *bread and wine and before the *Fraction. The candidate is brought before the altar and, following the bishop's blessing, kneels on his right knee and places the palms of his right hand on the altar in the form of a cross. He then bows so that his forehead rests on his hands. The bishop lays his stole on the head of the ordinand, then places his right hand on the ordinand's head, saying, "The grace of God, which always strengthens the weak and fills the empty, appoints the most religious *subdeacon N. to be deacon. Let us pray for him, that the grace of the Holy Spirit may come upon him." Secret prayers are recited by the bishop while keeping his hand on the ordinand's head, and the deacon is then vested with the *orarion (stole). A *ripidion (fan) is handed to him, and the bishop says three times "axios" (he is worthy). At the conclusion of the ceremony the new deacon kisses the bishop on the shoulder, and standing at the altar, he fans the consecrated bread and wine.

Coptic Tradition

When a deacon is ordained in this rite, he is vested, but without a stole (orarion). This is given to him by the bishop, who places it over the new deacon's left shoulder. Then, according to Vansleb, the Eucharistic spoon (*kokliarion) is presented to the deacon, who holds it throughout the Liturgy, at the end of which the bishop breathes on the face of the candidate, and "axios" (he is worthy) is called three times by the clergy.

East Syrian Tradition

The prayers used by *Chaldeans and *Nestorians are similar. As part of the ceremony the candidate is led to the position on the *bema that places him below the altar or sanctuary lamp, where he kneels on his right knee with his left knee up and his head between his hands, the forefingers pointing up and the head bowed. The bishop lays his right hand on the ordinand's head, and, while stretching out his left hand he recites some lengthy prayers. The ordinand is then blessed and vested with the stole, which is placed over the left shoulder. The Book of Epistles is handed to him, and he is then signed between the eyes from below upward and then from right to left, as the bishop recites the following prayer in a loud voice: "N. has been set apart, consecrated and perfected to the work of the Ministry of the Church and to the Levitical and Stephanite Office, in the name of the Father. . . ."

West Syrian Tradition

The order is conferred within the Liturgy and involves the imposition of hands and prorection of instruments. The prayer used in the conferral of this order is the same as for other orders: "N. is ordained Deacon in the Holy Church of Jesus Christ, in the name of the Father. . . ." Prior to ordination the ordinand must sign a solemn profession of faith.

See ORDERS; DIAKON; DIAKONOS; DYAKNA; MCHAMCHONO; SARKAVAK.

DEACONESS
(Syro-Jacobite and Maronite)

The term may have one of two meanings:

1. The *chalice into which the celebrant washes his hands when water is poured over them. The contents of the deaconess are drunk as part of the ablutions at the end of the *Syrian *Liturgy.

2. Certain women who, according to the evidence of Epiphanius, were set aside to assist with the *baptism of other women, because immersion was the tradition. From Justinian and the *Apostolic Constitutions* it is clear that deaconesses anointed female *catechumens with oil as part of the rite of baptism. It also appears that these deaconesses catechized female catechumens in private. The Fourth Council of Carthage insisted that these women have sufficient understanding of the Faith that they could display the ability to instruct and prepare other women for baptism. Epiphanius records that another of their functions was to visit and attend women who were in poor health and those who were in prison, since it was thought, in the latter case, that women could more easily gain access to them and arouse less suspicion on the part of the authorities. There is a further tradition that deaconesses were employed as *doorkeepers at that time, when access to the women's part of the *nave was through a separate *door.

See M'SHAM-SHONOITHO.

DEESIS (Byzantine)

See ICONOSTASIS.

DEFTERAS (Ethiopian)
(also spelled *Depteras)

See DABTARA.

DEGGWA (Ethiopian)
(also spelled Degwa)

One of the four books needed for the *Ethiopian Divine Office. This book contains the *antiphons used throughout the entire Church Year except during Lent.

DEGREE OF THE ANTIPHON
(Byzantine)

The *antiphons that are sung at Matins (*orthros) according to the *tone of the week. These antiphons are based on the gradual psalms (Psalms 119–133).

See ANABATHMOI; STEPENNYI ANTIFORI.

DEGREES OF MONASTICISM, HABITS OF (Byzantine)

1. *Rasophore or archarios (also ryasonosets [Slavonic]). The habit for a beginner in the *monastic life is known as the proschema (fore-habit) and consists of an inner and outer *rason, a leather *girdle, *skouphos (round cap), and sandals.
2. *Stavrophore or mikroschemos (also krestonosets [Slavonic]). The little habit worn by *monks and nuns of this degree consists of the inner and outer rason, the sleeves and body of which are fuller than that for the degree of rasophore, a skouphos with a veil, and a mandyas (mantiya [Sla-

vonic]), which is a long black cloak that may be substituted for the rason. The habit is completed with a girdle and sandals and a small wooden cross.
3. *Megaloschemos, literally "great habiter" (also skhimnik [Slavonic]). Religious admitted to this degree of monasticism may wear the great habit, which consists of the inner and outer rason, mandyas, girdle, sandals, and analavos (analabos), which is like a Western scapular, made from wool or leather and covered with embroidered pictures of the instruments of the Passion. Additionally the monk or nun may wear the cowl (koukoulos) and a skouphos with a veil. Occasionally a garment called the klobuk may be substituted for the cowl. Both stavrophore and megaloschemos religious may wear the *paramandyas, or paraman, and cross.

See HABITS, COMPARATIVE TABLE OF.

DEISIS (Byzantine)

The name given to the *icon of Jesus in royal robes, which stands above the icon of the Last Supper over the *royal *doors of the *iconostasis. To its right is the icon of the *Theotokos, and to its left that of St. John the Baptist.

DEKANIKION (Byzantine/Greek)

The popular name for the *rabdos (staff), which may have a crosspiece on the top and with which the clergy and others can support themselves during long services.

See RABDOS.

DEPTERAS (Ethiopian)

See DABTARA.

DEPUTATUS (Byzantine)

A name occasionally used to describe an *acolyte in this rite.

DERDERS (Armenian)

Married *priests, who are expected to live apart from their wives for eight days preceding the celebration of the *Liturgy. If they are *Armenian Catholics they are obliged to recite the *Divine Office.

DESPOINA (Byzantine)

A title of the Virgin Mary.

DESPOTES (Byzantine)

A descriptive title of God or of Jesus Christ.

DESPOTIKON (Byzantine)

See THRONOS.

DESPOTIKOS (Byzantine)

Literally, "of the Lord." Examples of the use of this word are "Despotike Heorts" (a *feast of our Lord), and "Despotikon Troparion" (a hymn in honor of our Lord).

DEUTERON KALYMMA (Byzantine)
(also spelled Devteron Kalymma)

See KALYMMATA; VEILS.

DEVTEREVON (Byzantine)

An occasionally used title for a *deacon, implying that he is second in rank.

DIACON
(Byzantine/Slavonic and Coptic)
(also spelled *Diakonos)

See DEACON.

DIACONAL DOOR (Byzantine)

The *door to the right of the *royal *doors as one faces the *iconostasis. The door on the left of the screen is for the use of the lower clergy.

See ICONOSTASIS.

DIACONICUM (Byzantine/Greek)

The word has several meanings. It is used to refer to the *liturgical book that specifies the functions of a *deacon; it also refers to the prayers said by a deacon before the congregation. Originally the name referred to an annex of a basilica, where the necessary supplies for the *altar were maintained, as distinct from the *prothesis. In larger churches the diaconicum may have comprised several rooms, one for the reception and audience of the *bishop, another where the sacred vessels and books were kept. The prothesis and diaconicum were ordinarily on either side of the apse of the church.

See DIAKONIKON.

DIAKAINESIMOS (Byzantine)

The new week, specifically Easter Week, or the Week of Renewing.

DIAKON (Byzantine/Slavonic)

See DEACON.

DIAKONIKA (Byzantine and Coptic)

Generally refers to those parts of the *Liturgy recited by the *deacon such as the ectenes (see *ektene) or *litanies. In the *Coptic rite the term refers to the book used by the deacon containing his responses together with texts of the variable and fixed hymns.

DIAKONIKON
(East Syrian/Chaldean and Byzantine)

A place where the sacred books and vessels are kept. In *Chaldean churches the diakonikon is on the left of the east end of the sanctuary, or to the left of the apse (*qanke). To the extreme left of this diakonikon is the martyrium (*beth kaddishe), where the *relics are safeguarded. In the *Byzantine rite it is also known as the secretarium, and as the name implies, it was in the care of the *deacons.

See BEITH ROZE; BETH DIYAKUN; BETH SHAMASHA; DIAKONNIK; SACRISTY.

DIAKONNIK (Byzantine/Slavonic)
See DIAKONIKON.

DIAKONOS (Byzantine)
See DEACON.

DIASTULA
(also spelled Diastyla)
See ICONOSTASIS.

DIBAMPOULOS (Byzantine)

A two-branched candlestick that may be carried in front of a *patriarch as a mark of respect when he performs patriarchal functions in a *Liturgy. It has been suggested that it was once used by the *Byzantine emperor, and thus it symbolized both civil and ecclesiastical powers.

DIBDIKON (Ethiopian)
See DIPTYCH.

DIFNARI (Coptic/Arabic)

An antiphonary allegedly owing its origin to the *patriarch Gabriel in Taril (1131–1145). It contains two alternative hymns, written in Coptic, for each day of the year.

See ANDIFNARI; ANTIPHONARIUM; LITURGICAL BOOKS (Coptic Tradition).

DIGAMOS (Byzantine)

A person who has married a second time.

DIKAIOS (Byzantine/Greek)

Literally, "just" or "righteous." A title applied to the names of lay saints, or to the superior of a *skete. The superior of a *cenobitic skete, or monastic settlement, is elected by all the *monks of that skete subject to the principal monastery's approval and may be elected for life. Members attend the *Liturgy and Office together in the skete church (kyriakon) and have meals in common.

See RASTOYATEL.

DIKANIKION (Byzantine/Greek)

The crozier, so called because it resembles the imperial dikanikion, which was originally a staff of office, with two curved branches ornamented with serpents' heads. The imperial dikanikion had a cross standing between the two serpents.

See AKAZ; CROZIER; SHVOT.

DIKERETRIKERA (Byzantine)

A collective term that describes the two candlesticks held by a *bishop as he blesses the people.

See DIKERION; TRIKERION.

DIKERION (Byzantine/Greek)
(also called *Dikiri)

A two-branched candlestick that, together with the *trikerion, a three-branched candlestick, is used in pontifical blessings in the *Liturgy. The dikerion, which represents the two natures of Christ, is carried in the left hand, while the trikerion, representing the Holy Trinity, is carried in the right. It seems unlikely that these candlesticks were in use before the 7th century, since St. Maximus Homologetes (d. 662) makes no mention of them.

See TRIKERION.

DIKIRI (Byzantine/Slavonic)

See DIKERION.

DIPHROS (Byzantine/Greek)

The abbot's chair in a monastery.

DIPHTUCHO (Syro-Jacobite)

Literally, "book of the living."

See DIPTYCH; KANUNO; QANUNO.

DIPLOUS

A day on which there is a concurrence of two feasts.

DIPTICH (Byzantine/Slavonic)

See DIPTYCH.

DIPTICHON (Coptic)

The *diptychs of the dead in a *Coptic *Liturgy, which are recited after the institution and the *Epiclesis. Before the *priest blesses the congregation at the end of the diptichon he puts *incense into the *censer, and, according to Bute, he prays for the dead.

See TARHIM; TOUPTIKON.

DIPTYCH

Originally a notebook composed of two tablets and made from wood, ivory, bone, or metal, joined by rings or a hinge. The inner surface of these tablets had a wax coating upon which characters could be scratched using a stylus. In early Christian times the diptychs were used for listing the names of those both living and dead who were considered to be members of the Church, and in this manner the diptychs of the living and the dead came into use. In the 3rd century St. Cyprian (ca. 200–258) alluded to the naming of the dead in his *First Epistle*, but he failed to mention the naming of the living. In the early years of the Church, it is likely that these diptychs served several purposes, as a *baptismal register and also as an ecclesiastical calendar, since the diptychs included the names of *bishops, *priests, and laity who had died with a saintly reputation. The diptychs were the subject of controversy; for example, in 420 in Constantinople following the deposing of St. John Chrysostom, there was disagreement as to whether his name should be included in the list, and for the next hundred years or so its contents reflected the political temperature of the times.

In the *Liturgy of St. James the diptychs were positioned according to St. Cyril's reference to the naming of the dead, after the Consecration as part of the intercessory prayers. This "naming" occupied a similar position in the

*Antiochene and Constantinopolitan rites in the late 4th century. At Jerusalem, the naming was restricted to the dead but as time passed came to include both the living and dead, and this became the accepted practice at Constantinople in the early 5th century. The contents of the diptychs of the dead are read first, then of the living. They are read after the Consecration prayer by a priest or *deacon either from the *ambo or from the foot of the *altar.

In the *Coptic Liturgy of St. Mark after the Consecration, *Epiclesis, and intercession for the living, the deacon says, "Let those who read, publish the names of our fathers, the Patriarchs, who have fallen asleep . . . also . . . all of them . . . who are gone to rest in the priesthood and in any order of the laity." As Brightman (*Liturgies—Eastern and Western*, 1896, p. 126) notes, the names entered are those of the "parochial" dead.

The diptychs of the *East Syrian rite (diupatcin) are read at the offertory, but the list is not specific except for the mention of the current *Nestorian *patriarch, while the list of the dead is more extensive and includes many Old and New Testament saints as well as a list of past Nestorian patriarchs together with many parochial or local "saints."

DISCOS (Byzantine)
(also spelled Discus)

The *paten, or sacred vessel of the *Eastern Church on which the *bread that is to be consecrated rests during the *Liturgy. A representation of the Last Supper is sometimes found on its inner surface. In the *Byzantine and other rites it is quite usual to find this concave dish fitted with a foot, which raises it above the level of the altar table.

See DISKARION; DISKOS.

DISKARION (Byzantine/Greek)
See DISCOS.

DISKELION (Byzantine)

A lectern made up of two long shafts and presenting as an X shaped desk.

See TRISKELION.

DISKOKALYM(M)A (Byzantine)
See KALYMMATA; VEILS.

DISKOS (Coptic)
(also called Seni'a [Arabic])

A *Coptic *paten, it has a slightly raised vertical brim around its circumference. This paten lacks any engravings, and there is no depression in the middle. Coptic patens, unlike *Byzantine-rite vessels, do not have a foot. As in most rites it is necessary for a *bishop to consecrate the paten with holy *chrism before it may be used.

Catholic synods for the *Armenians, Copts, and *Syrians all confirm that the sacred vessels must receive episcopal consecration and may not be touched by those who are not *subdeacons. If the vessels contain the consecrated *bread and wine they may be touched only by a *priest or by a *deacon if he is wearing a *stole. In the Coptic rite an *asterisk (*kubbah), which is a linked pair of loops made of metal, sits over the paten and serves to protect the bread from the *veil used to cover the paten during the *Liturgy.

See DISCOS; DISKARION.

DISMISSAL (Byzantine)

The final blessing by a *priest at the conclusion of the *Liturgy, *Matins, or *Vespers. If it is a long ceremony of dismissal it is known as the Great Dismissal, and as a Small Dismissal if it is short.

See APOLYSIS; OTPUST.

DISSIDENT

A term used by the Roman Catholic Church to describe an *Eastern Christian who is not in communion with Rome.

DIUPATCIN (East Syrian/Nestorian)

See DIPTYCH.

DIVINE OFFICE

See under separate headings: EAST SYRIAN CHURCH, DIVINE OFFICE OF, etc.

DIYAQONIQON (Syro-Jacobite)

The southern apse in a Syro-*Jacobite church, where the sacred vessels are stored.

See BETH ROZE; BETH DIYAKUN.

DJACHOTZ (Armenian)
(also spelled *Giaschotz; Tschaschotz)

Literally, "Book of Noon." A lectionary that contains the Epistles, *Gospels, and other portions of the *Liturgy that are sung by the ministers and clergy.

See LITURGICAL BOOKS (Armenian Tradition).

DJEZL (Byzantine/Slavonic)

See CROZIER, RABDOS.

DOGMATIKI (Byzantine/Slavonic)

See BOGORODITCHNI.

DOGMATIKON (Byzantine)

A *troparion whose subject is some particular doctrine.

DOME (Coptic)
(also called *Kubbah)

The *Coptic asterisk, made of two loops of silver, which are crossed and riveted together and placed over the *paten and *diskos.

See ASTERISK.

DONATZVITZ (Armenian)
(also spelled Donatsoitz)

A directory, or calendar, roughly equivalent to the *Byzantine *Typikon in that under each listed festival one finds a full explanation about which Epistles, *Gospels, and hymns are to be read and sung during the *Liturgy and at the Office for the day.

DOORKEEPER

A minor cleric whose function was to guard the church *doors. According to the *Apostolic Constitutions* (ca. 375), this function may have been performed by *deacons and *subdeacons, and the role of *deaconess should be noted in this regard. The canons of Laodicea, however, suggest that the responsibility was shared among the subdeacons (n. 22, 43), who were expected not to leave the doors unguarded.

See DRRNAPAN; DVERNIK; ORDERS, HOLY; THYROROS.

DOORS

There are several doors in a *Byzantine-rite church. Those at the west end of the church leading from the *atrium to the *narthex are known as the prothyra or megale pyle, the posts of which, according to the *Antiochene writings of St. John Chrysostom (ca. 347–407), were kissed on entering through them. The doors were expected to be closed at the start of the Liturgy of the Faithful. The basilikai thyrai, or svyatya vrata (Slavonic), were the doors that separated the narthex from the *nave and were used by the *catechumens, who had to leave at the start of the Liturgy of the Faithful. There are a further three doors in the *iconostasis, the central being known as the *royal door, (bemothyra [Greek] or tsarskiys vrata [Slavonic]), behind which hangs a veil. This door is opened and closed at various points in the *Liturgy. The north and south doors are used for the inferior clergy and *deacons respectively.

In the *Coptic and Syro-*Jacobite rites there are three doors that give access to the sanctuary, and behind each door there is an *altar. Each opening is closed by a curtain (katapetasma) marked by a cross, which a pious Copt is expected to kiss when passing through the door.

See PYLE; THYRA; VRATA.

DORON (Byzantine)
(also spelled Dora)

Literally, "gift" or "gifts." While the word generally refers to the offerings of both *bread and wine in the *Liturgy, it specifically refers to the bread.

See DAR; ENTSAR; KURBAN; KURBANO.

DOXASTIKON (Byzantine)
(also called Doxa; *Slava)

Literally, "glory." The *troparion or *sticheron, which may be found after the first verse of the Gloria. If there is no prescription for a doxastikon, then the usual conclusion of the second verse of the Gloria follows.

DOXOLOGIA (Byzantine)
(also called Doxology; *Slavoslovie)

Literally, "words of glory." The hymn with which *Matins concludes and which is derived from the opening words of Luke 2:14. There are two types, the Lesser or Small Doxology, and the Great or Greater Doxology.

The lesser doxology is said and never sung and is composed of two verses, usually added at the end of the psalms and *canticles, and is the familiar "Glory be to the Father and to the Son . . . . ," and "As it was in the beginning, is now. . . . " Variants in the use of this doxology are found, when, for example, a *Coptic *priest puts the *bread on the *paten in the *Liturgy at the conclusion of the *prothesis and says, "Glory and honor unto honor and glory be to the All Holy Trinity, the Father and the Son and the Holy Spirit, now and ever and world without end. Amen." Then the *enarxis follows.

The Syro-*Jacobites intersperse special remembrances within the lesser doxology, for example, just before the *lessons in the Liturgy of the *Catechumens, when the Gloria is recited: "Glory be to the Father and to the Son and to the Holy Spirit, with this smoke . . . let the doctors and priests and the just and righteous be remembered.

From everlasting, world without end, with this smoke of spices, may the Holy Church and all her children be remembered.'' Furthermore, the *Nestorians insert a Gloria, or Lesser Doxology, immediately after the Our Father, when it is recited at the start of the enarxis.

St. Basil (ca. 330–379) suggested that it was an old custom among the Christians to use the Lesser Doxology when lighting the candles as an acknowledgment of thankfulness for the benefit of light after sunset.

The Greater Doxology is the hymn "Glory be to God on high . . .," which is sung on great feasts, Sundays, and other festivals, and the versions that exist reputedly date from the late 4th century. In the 5th-century *Codex Alexandrinus* it is called the "Morning Hymn" and appears in the Office of *Orthros (Morning Office) of the *Byzantine rite.

DPIR (Armenian)

A cleric who has received the *minor orders of verger, *reader, exorcist, and *acolyte. Today it refers to one who has received the order of acolyte alone. In church the dpir wears a buttoned-up *vestment (*shapik) made of linen or velvet over which is placed a small, heavily embroidered cloak that covers the shoulders, back, and chest. The cloak has three crosses, on the back and on each side of the front.

DRNAPAN (Armenian)

See DOORKEEPER.

DRYPHAKTA (Byzantine)

Literally, "trellis." This obsolete word specifically refers to a wooden struc-ture, trellis-like in appearance, that was the antecedent of the later, more solid *iconostasis. In the modern iconostasis, the middle or *royal doors may retain a trellis-like grille at the top.

See KATAPETASMA.

D'SH-HEEME
(East Syrian/Nestorian)

A ceremony rather like a Western "dry Mass" or "Missa sicca," in which the *priest reads the prayers of the *Liturgy without a prayer of consecration.

DUHOVNEK (East Syrian/Chaldean)

A commemoration of saints or *memorial.

DUKHRANI (East Syrian)

A class of feast or memorial of saints that is normally observed on Fridays except during Lent.

See EAST SYRIAN CHURCH, DIVINE OFFICE OF.

DURAT ALHAMAL (Coptic/Arabic)

See CIRCUIT OF THE LAMB.

DVERNIK (Byzantine/Slavonic)

See DOORKEEPER.

DYAKNA (East Syrian/Nestorian)
(also called *Shamasha)

A deacon.

See DEACON; ORDERS, HOLY.

DYOPHYSITES

A term used by *Monophysites to describe those *Eastern Orthodox and

Catholics who adopted the Council of Chalcedon's definition in 451 of the two natures in the person of Christ and so were opposed to the Monophysite view that there was only one nature in Christ. On June 23, 1984, *Pope John Paul II and the *Syrian Orthodox *patriarch Moran Mar Ignatius Zakka II of Antioch signed a historic joint statement affirming a common faith in the nature of Christ. The two "sister Churches" now state that the historic disagreement arose only because of differences in terminology and culture, and in the various formulae adopted by the different theological schools of the time, to express the same matter.

DZAIRAAKOUYN (Armenian)

A major grade of vartabed, but who lacks jurisdictional powers and whose function is to instruct the faithful in church. The status of this cleric was recognized by the Catholic Council of 1911.

See VARTABED.

DZOUM (Armenian)

A period of fasting in which no food is taken from sunrise until 3 p.m. This *fast is observed during Aratshavoratz (Fast of *Ninevah) and Lent (*Karasnorth; Karasnortk).

See ARMENIAN CHURCH CALENDAR.

E

EAST SYRIAN

Members of the East Syrian Church, that is, *Nestorian (*Assyrian) and *Syro-Chaldean Churches, the latter being Catholic. It was from Edessa (modern Urfa) in Turkey that Christianity spread through East Syria into Persia, but how Christianity came to Edessa is shrouded in legend. The most notable of these legends concerns the exploits of St. Addai, identified with Thaddeus, a Palestinian Jew, and St. Mari, a convert from Mazdaism, who according to Eusebius' account first preached at Edessa and allegedly laid the foundations of Christianity there.

EAST SYRIAN CHURCH, CALENDAR OF

While the Catholic *East Syrians, or *Chaldeans, observe the *Gregorian Calendar, the *Nestorians use the *Julian Calendar to mark the months, and the era of the Greeks in Seleucid (311 B.C.) as the basis for determining the years. However, this has now been updated. The year was divided into nine periods by the *catholicos Ishu'yab III (Jesu-Yab III) of Adiabene (650–661). Each of these periods, or *Shabho'a (literally, "seven"), is a seven-week period, but one or another Shabho'a is omitted according to the year. The first is of the Annunciation; this starts on December 1 and is made up of four Sundays corresponding to Advent, each marked by the reading of Annunciation *Gospels. The second is of Epiphany, the third that of the *Great Fast, which begins on the seventh Monday before Easter, and the fourth is the Shabho'a of the Resurrection. The fifth Shabho'a, that of the Apostles, is initiated by the feast of Pentecost and is a season of six Sundays, the last one of which is the Sunday of the Twelve Apostles and also the first Sunday of the next Shabho'a. This sixth Shabho'a lasts until the seventh Sunday after the Twelve Apostles; the next is the three Sundays of Elias followed by the four Sundays of the Dedication (Qudash'idta), which corresponds to the eighth and ninth Shabho'a.

Easter (Ad'ida Kabira) is known as the Great Feast, while the Little Feast (Ad'ida Katina) commemorates Christmas (Yalda; Beith Yalda).

EAST SYRIAN CHURCH, DIVINE OFFICE OF

The only compulsory Offices in the *Chaldean rite are Vespers (*Ramcha; Ramsha), and the Morning Office (*Sapra); all the other *Hours including *Compline are recited occasionally and either celebrated or not according to the Rule of a particular monastery.

The book of the *Divine Office is called the "Book of Before and After" (Kthawa Dagdham Wadhwathar) because of the division of the choir, which commences the Office, being either the "before" or "after" choir, that is, qdham or wathar.

When *Nestorian monasteries existed seven *Hours were the norm. Three *hulali of the Psalter were recited at each Hour, with the result that the entire Psalter was recited daily. At present in the East Syrian tradition there is a provision for seven *hulali at each ferial night service, ten on Sundays, and three on memorials (*dukhrani). The entire Psalter is recited on *feasts of our Lord.

The Office at present consists only of the Morning, Evening, and Midnight Offices. A compounding of the ancient Shara (Lauds) and the first day prayer (*Slutha Dsafra) with the nocturns of the Night Office (*Slutha Dlilya) make up the text of the Morning Office. At this service the psalms are always 109; 90; 103:1-6; 112; 92; 148; 150; and 116; these are sung with variable psalms for the *memorials. The rest of the service consists of prayers, antiphons (*onitha), *litanies, and verses (giyura), which are inserted like *stichera between the verses of the psalms.

In the evening service four to seven psalms are sung. These vary with the day of the week, and a short psalm (shuraya) with a portion of Psalm 118 is usually included. During Ramcha (Vespers) and Sapra (Morning Office) the martyrs who died during the persecution of Shapur II (4th century) are commemorated, and an important hymn peculiar to this rite, the Lakhu Mara, is sung. The text of this hymn is also found at the start of the *Liturgy: "Lord of all, we confess you; Jesus Christ, we glorify you. For you give life to our bodies. You are the Savior of our souls." Both the morning and evening services conclude with prayers, a blessing (*khuthama: literally, "sealing"), the kiss of *peace, and the *Creed.

EAST SYRIAN LITURGICAL BOOKS

Among the *Nestorians the great number of books and manuscripts used to regulate the service of the Church is both bewildering and chaotic. The *Chaldeans have carefully pruned the growth of choir books and other liturgical publications.

See LITURGICAL BOOKS (East Syrian Tradition).

EAST SYRIAN LITURGICAL LANGUAGE

This is East Syriac, or the Edessene dialect of Syriac. In practice it is more usually the vernacular and therefore Arabic, Turkish, Persian, or Kurdish.

EAST SYRIAN RITE

The rite evolved in Edessa before the 4th century; it is known that St. Ephrem (306–373) used and quoted from it. In origin it is definitely *Antiochene because of such typical features as the *litanies; however, these intercessions come just before the Consecration, whereas the usual Antiochene position is just after the Consecration. While the calendar is Antiochene, there are so many non-Antiochene features that many liturgists have argued successfully against this rite's classification.

See ANAPHORA.

EASTERN CHURCH

This collective term embraces *Eastern Orthodox, *Oriental Christians, *Assyrians (*Nestorians), and *Eastern-rite Catholics.

EASTERN ORTHODOX

The Chalcedonian Christians, that is, those Christians who belong to the Churches that accepted the Council of Chalcedon's definition of 451 concerning the nature of Christ (*Dyophysites), as opposed to the *Monophysites. This group of Churches is often referred to mistakenly as *Greek Orthodox to distinguish them from the *Oriental Christians. In 1980 the total world membership was 132,835,000, which represents 82.5 percent of the total membership of the *Eastern Christian community.

EASTERN RITE CATHOLICS

Also known as *Oriental-rite Catholics, who are in union with Rome but follow rites other than those of the *Latin rite. In 1980 their total membership was 8,799,000, which represents about 1 percent of the total Catholic population.

ECHOS (Byzantine/Greek)

The *Byzantine chant is made up of eight modes, which are numbered differently from Western modes. It is not unknown for a choir to change the mode in the middle of a chant while another singer maintains a dominant (ison) of a mode and the rest of the choir continues their tunes. The singing in this rite is traditionally unaccompanied.

See TCHLAS.

ECHOS ADAM (Coptic)

A *Coptic tone taken from the name of a typical hymn.

See ADAM AIYUB.

ECPHONESIS (Byzantine/Greek)
(also spelled *Ekphonesis)

A doxology at the conclusion of a prayer.

ECTENE

See EKTENE.

ECUMENICAL COUNCILS

Gatherings of *bishops and representatives of the world's Churches, whose decisions on doctrine are regarded as binding on all Christians in those Churches participating in the council. *Eastern Orthodox accept only the first seven *ecumenical councils, up to Nicea II (787), while Roman Catholics accept twenty-one councils including Vatican I and II. The seven ecumenical councils are the following:

1. Nicaea (325), at which Arius' heresy was condemned and Christ was declared to be Houmousian (of the same nature with the Father). The text of the *Creed was agreed upon down to the clause relating to the Holy Spirit.

2. Constantinople I (381) decreed against the Macedonians, who had denied the deity of the Holy Spirit. This council dealt with the nature of the Holy Spirit and added the relevant clauses to the Creed.

3. Ephesus (431) decreed against Nestorius and consequently declared the Virgin Mary to be the *Theotokos, or Mother of God.

4. Chalcedon (451) dealt with *Monophysitism and the heresy of Eutyches; it defined the two natures of Christ.

5. Constantinople II (553) condemned the errors of Origen as well as the writings of Theodoret, Theodore of Mopsuestia, and Ibas.

6. Constantinople III (680–681), at which 174 bishops condemned *Monothelitism; it defined the two wills of Christ as being distinct.

7. Nicaea II (787) dealt with the veneration of the holy images.

ECUMENICAL PATRIARCH

The *patriarch of Constantinople, the highest ecclesiastical office in the *Eastern Orthodox Church; he is accorded a primacy of honor.

EDJGE (Ethiopian)

See ACMAM.

EEPODIACON (Byzantine/Slavonic)

See HYPODIAKONOS; SUBDEACON.

EFISKUFA (East Syrian/Nestorian)

A *bishop; having been elected by clergy and laity alike, he is consecrated by the *patriarch. In common with the practice in the other *Eastern Orthodox Churches, he may not be married. Like all *Nestorian clergy, he is bearded and wears as his outdoor dress a cassock-like robe and turban, but in church he wears the *sudra (*kuthino; *kotina), a garment similar to an *alb, with a *zunara (a belt and a stole) resembling a *Byzantine *epitrachelion. The chasuble, known as the *kafila (*ma'apra; paina; *pakila), resembles a hoodless cope. He wears also a *birun (biruna), or amice, over the head and usually carries a small cross with which to bless the faithful, although he sometimes carries a pastoral staff as well.

See ORDERS, HOLY (East Syrian Tradition).

EGYPTIAN CHURCH

See ALEXANDRIA, PATRIARCHS OF.

EIKON (Byzantine/Greek)

See ICON; IKON.

EILETON (Byzantine/Greek)

See ALTAR CLOTHS.

EIRENIKA (Greek)

An alternative name for the Great Synapte, or prayers for peace, which are recited at *Hesperinos (Vespers) and at *Orthros (Matins and Lauds). It is also recited at the start of the *Liturgy.

See SYNAPTE.

EISODIKON (Byzantine/Greek)

Literally, "entry." The anthem, or hymn, that is sung during the Little *Entrance (*Eisodos) as the *priest and *deacon enter the sanctuary through the *royal doors.

See VKHODNOE.

EISODOS (Byzantine/Greek)

An *entrance made processionally from the sanctuary through the north *door of the *iconostasis to the center of the church; it then returns to the sanctuary through the *royal doors. These entrances may be made at *Vespers and during the *Liturgy, at which there are two such entries—the Little and *Great Entrances.

The Little Entrance occurs after the third *antiphon, or *Beatitudes, in the early part of the Liturgy, during which the *Gospel book is carried solemnly by the *deacon or by the *priest alone if he is unassisted by a deacon.

The Great Entrance is concerned with bringing the offering from the *prothesis to the *altar and occurs after the singing of the Cherubic Hymn (*Cherubikon). The veiled *paten (*diskos) is carried on the head of the deacon, who also carries a *censer in his hand. If there is no deacon available the priest carries both the *chalice and paten and a server brings the censer.

See BOHOD; VKHOD.

EKPHONESIS (Greek)

Literally, "lifting of the voice." The last words of a prayer, which are said or sung aloud when the preceding part has been said silently. This is particularly common in *Byzantine and *Armenian Liturgies.

EKPLUSIS (Byzantine/Greek)

The washing of the *altar on Holy Saturday.

EKTENE (Byzantine/Greek)

A series of short prayers constructed along litanic lines; for example, The Ektene of Supplication, The Great Ektene, and The Ektene of Peace, all of which are to be found in the *Liturgy and Office. Each of the short petitions concludes with the singing of a brief response such as "Lord have mercy upon us" or "Grant us, O Lord."

See ECTENE; EKTENI.

EKTENI (Byzantine/Slavonic)

See EKTENE.

ELEOSVASTCHENIE
(Byzantine/Slavonic)

See EUCHELAION; UNCTION OF THE SICK.

ELEVATION

Armenian Tradition

During the elevation of the consecrated *bread the *deacon censes the *altar while the *priest says the accla-

mation "To the Holiness of the Holies"; he then elevates the *chalice, and
after he has replaced it, he kisses both
the altar and the chalice, removing the
*veil from the chalice.

Byzantine Tradition

The words "Holy Things to the
Holy" signal the time when the deacon girds his *orarion crosswise. According to St. Simeon of Thessalonica,
this signifies the "angelic service" of
the diaconate, since the orarion resembles the wings of the angels. While
the *Lord's Prayer is sung, the priest
draws the curtain, and holding the consecrated bread with the tips of the
fingers of both hands, he raises it
above the *diskos (*paten), and says
the prayer above, which means that the
Things of God are for the people of
God. These words are recorded by St.
Cyril of Jerusalem (ca. 315–386), who
notes that the people responded "One
Holy, our Lord Jesus Christ." The
*sign of the cross should not be made
with the consecrated bread over the
diskos.

Coptic Tradition

The acclamation, "This is the Holy
Thing for the Holy; Blessed is the Lord
Jesus Christ, the Son of God; he has
hallowed it by his Holy Spirit," takes
place before the celebrant's *communion when the priest holds the
paten, turns to the faithful, and blesses
them with it.

Ethiopian Tradition

After the commemoration of the
dead the priest bows deeply, and
elevating the consecrated bread he

says, "Holy Things to the Holy," to
which the people respond, "One is the
Holy Father, one is the Holy Son, and
one is the Holy Spirit."

East Syrian Tradition

After the *Lord's Prayer, the priest
opens his hands and rejoins them and
says, "The Holy Thing benefits the
Holy in perfection." This use of the
singular "Thing" as opposed to
"Things" is used in the Testament of
Our Lord and by St. Ephrem (ca.
306–373), while St. Cyprian (ca. 200–
258) specifically refers to the Sanctum
Domini.

Syro-Jacobite Tradition

At the words "Holy Things to the
Holy," both the paten and chalice are
raised. This elevation was known both
to St. Cyril of Jerusalem (4th century)
and James of Edessa (8th century), and
it was James who commented that it
was a variant of the normal practice.
There was a local tradition in Ancyra
(Ankara) in 600 that involved the elevation of the bread on the paten, but
this was by no means common. In this
rite the priest takes the paten in both
hands and raises it to the level of the
eyes, moves it crosswise from east to
west and then from north to south as
he says the words of the prayer above.
The priest then touches his eyes with
the paten, kisses it, and replaces it
upon the altar and bows low. The same
is repeated with the chalice. During the
elevation, the Sacrament is censed and
lights are carried, *fans are shaken,
and the bell is rung. The kissing of the
consecrated bread, according to Mar-
tens, was common in both Syrian and

Roman usage. According to James of Sarugh (451–521) the priest chanted the acclamation in the singular only.

See VOZDNOSHT SHENIE; WERATHSOUMN; ZUYOHO.

EMBADES (Byzantine/Greek)
(also spelled Emvades)

Heelless slippers worn by some *monks in church.

See PAPOUTSIA.

EMBOLISMOS (Byzantine/Greek)
(also spelled Embolism)

Literally, "insertion." An expansion of the two last clauses of the *Lord's Prayer said by the celebrant in all *Liturgies.

In *Armenian Liturgies, while the Lord's Prayer (Hair-Mer) is being sung by the congregation, the *altar is censed and the *priest recites the following prayer silently: "Lord of Lords, God of Gods, King Eternal, Creator of all things created, Father of Our Lord, Jesus Christ, lead us not into temptation but deliver us from evil and save us from temptation."

EMIPHORON (Armenian)

An Eastern-style *pallium. In the *Armenian rite, when a *bishop has put on the emiphoron, he kneels and silently prays the Prayer to the Holy Ghost, composed by St. Gregory of Nareg (10th century). At the start of the *Great Entrance, the emiphoron is removed.

See OMOPHORION.

EMPHOTION (Byzantine/Greek)
(also called Sabanon)

The robe worn by one who is newly baptized. According to tradition, it was supposed to be worn for a period of eight days.

See BAPTISM.

ENARXIS (Byzantine/Greek)

Literally, "beginning." In general usage it refers to the start of an Office or ceremony, but more specifically it is the section of the *Liturgy between the *prothesis and the Little *Entrance. In structure it resembles a lesser Office and is found at the start of all *Eastern Liturgies. The enarxis, probably introduced into the Liturgy in the 9th century, consists of three diaconal *litanies, or *ektenes (ectene; ekteni), each of which is followed by a variable *antiphon sung by the choir, during which the *priest silently prays the prayers of the antiphon. The first litany, that "of Peace," is followed by a lesser litany, while the third litany is that "of Fervent Supplication."

ENCOLPION (Byzantine/Greek)
(also spelled Enkolpion)

A pectoral ornament worn by a *bishop and sometimes by a *priest. The term was applied to a type of early reliquary that was worn around the neck in early Christian times and to which St. John Chrysostom refers in his homily on the statutes. Inside this ornament were *relics or fragments of cloth stained with the blood of a martyr or pieces of texts from Holy Scriptures, all of which gave rise to many superstitions about which St. Jerome complained. Originally the encolpion was oval, round, or four-cornered and was made of various materials ranging from glass to gold. In the Middle Ages both oval and cruciform varieties persisted, many of which reputedly contained relics of the True Cross. Gradually the cruciform encolpion gained in popularity, so much so that St. Simeon of Thessalonica refers to the encolpion as a stavrion. Today both oval and cruciform types are worn on a chain around the neck.

When putting it on, the prelate says, "Create a clean heart in me, O God, and renew a right spirit within me" (Ps 50:12). A medallion of our Lady is also commonly worn, which is more properly called *panagia or panagion.

See PANAGIA.

ENDYTE (Byzantine)

See ALTAR CLOTHS.

ENERGUMEN (Byzantine)

A class of people who were thought to be possessed by the devil and who, according to the *Epistle* of James of Edessa to Thomas the Presbyter, were dismissed next after the *catechumens, during the *Liturgy. "Let none of the catechumens, no man imperfect in the faith, none of the *penitents, nor the unclean, draw near to the Divine *Mystery."

See AISAHHAR; METHTA'BRONO.

ENFORA (Ethiopian)

See ANAPHORA; KEDDASE; ZAMESHTIR.

ENKOMION (Byzantine)

A mournful composition of several troparia (*troparion), which is sung on Great or Holy Saturday at *Lauds and which develops the theme of the passion and death of Jesus Christ. The composition is divided into three parts, called stations, or staseis, because the people stand during its singing.

ENNEA ODAI

See ODES.

ENORIA

See PREHOD.

ENOSIS (Byzantine/Greek)

The commixture of the consecrated *bread and wine in the *chalice after the ceremony of the *Fraction. It was not known in the 6th century, but it seems to have become firmly established as a custom by the 9th century. The consecrated bread was simply divided into three parts, but now it is broken into four parts, and the part imprinted with the initials IC (Jesus) is used to make the *sign of the cross over the chalice and placed within the chalice as the *priest says, "The fullness of the faith of the Holy Spirit." The portion imprinted XC is removed for the clergy participating in the *Liturgy, while the portions NI and KA are used for the *communion of the laity.

See COMMIXTURE; ISPOLNENIE; KHARRNOUMN; SMIESHEVANIE.

ENSTAR (Armenian)
(also called *Doron, *Kurbono)

A term used generally to refer to the oblation, but more specifically it means the *bread used in the *Liturgy.

See BREAD (Armenian Tradition).

ENTHERTHSOGH (Armenian)

See READER; ORDERS, HOLY.

ENTHRONISMOS
(Byzantine/Greek)

Refers either to the enthronement of a *bishop or to the rite of consecration of an *altar.

ENTRANCE

There are two main entrances, the Little Entrance and the *Great Entrance. The former is the procession that precedes the reading of the *Gospel, while the latter is the procession of the *bread and wine to be consecrated during the *Liturgy. The ceremonies vary from rite to rite, as the following will illustrate:

Armenian Tradition

1. Little Entrance. During the singing of the *Trisagion (*Erechsrbeann) three times, a Little Entrance ceremony is made by a procession around the *altar, with the *deacon carrying the Gospels and accompanied by a *censer bearer and lighted tapers, during which the Gospel book is censed. The congregation is then blessed with the Gospels.

2. Great Entrance (Weraperum; Weraberouthiun). Proceeds around the altar, during which there is an extended censing of the altar. The *chalice and *paten are carried above the heads of the clergy, who bear *incense and lighted tapers while the *hagiology is sung.

Byzantine Tradition

1. Little Entrance (Mikra Eisodes [Greek]; Maliy Vchod [Slavonic]). Takes place during the singing of the *Beatitudes, or the third *antiphon, when the clergy bring the Gospel book accompanied by lighted tapers and the censer and emerge through the north *door of the *iconostasis, reentering the sanctuary through the *royal doors. If a *bishop is celebrating, he is brought from the *nave of the church accompanied by *priests and deacons, with a deacon carrying the Gospel book. During the procession an *eisodikon and *troparion are sung.

2. Great Entrance (Megale Eisodos [Greek]; Bolshoy Vchod [Slavonic]). In early times there was opposition to the introduction of this ceremony by St. Euthychius, *patriarch of Constantinople, but it is mentioned by John the Faster in a late 6th century *Typikon. This entrance involves the procession of the bread and wine from the *prothesis to the altar. The congregation regard this ceremony with great piety and respect, and this profound reverence for the offerings has been variously explained; for example, it could be from an ancient custom of carrying the *reserved Sacrament in this procession, which in the East seems unlikely. Alternatively, it could derive from the old tradition of the deacons having brought a portion of the local bishop's consecrated bread to each of those churches that were in communion with him. This portion of bread was known as the fermentum, and until the 4th century it was carried in procession as part of the offertory ceremonies. St. Theodore of Mopsuestia suggests that the whole ceremony of the prosthesis was a representation of the Passion, while the offertory represented the entombment of Christ. Thus the bearers of the oblation came to represent the angels, the *fan bearers synbolized the

angels gathered around the cross, and the altar represented the tomb of Christ. However, the *Epiclesis, which follows and which dates from the 6th or 7th century, is clearly consecratory in intention, and so the liturgical puzzle remains.

The oblation is censed and the veiled *diskos (paten) is either placed on the head or held above the head of the deacon, who may also be carrying a censer with one hand, while the priest carries the veiled chalice (*potir) and any concelebrants carry the cross, *lance, *spoon, and *sponge. The procession leaves the sanctuary during the singing of the Cherubic Hymn (*Cherubikon) after the altar and church have been censed. They pass from the north door accompanied by lighted tapers and fans and enter the sanctuary through the *royal doors after having made the commemorations in the apse of the church. When the priest enters the sanctuary he kisses the chalice and places it on the unfolded *antimension, then takes the diskos and puts it on the left side of the antimension, reciting a troparion as he does so. He then removes the chalice and paten *veils, kisses them, and places them on the front covers of the altar. The deacon then censes the *taperer, who is on the *ambo, closes the royal doors, and draws the curtains. The *aer, having been removed from the deacon's shoulder, is censed by wrapping it around the censer, briefly. It is then used to cover both the chalice and paten. The deacon then returns to the *soleas by means of the north door and says the *Ektene of Supplication.

Regarding the 7th century *Byzantine Liturgy, it is a matter of doubt as to whether the oblation was prepared before the Liturgy as is current practice, or whether the preparation took place just before the Great Entrance. The use of the term "protithenae" suggests the latter.

Coptic Tradition

1. The Little Entrance. Takes place after the *lessons and the Trisagion when the priest goes to the altar accompanied by the deacon, who is holding the Gospel book. They process around the altar three times, during which the book is censed. During the procession the priest secretly recites the Song of Simeon (Luke 2:29-32).

2. There is no distinctive Great Entrance along the elaborate Byzantine lines.

Ethiopian Tradition

1. The Little Entrance. Occurs during the singing of the Trisagion by the priest; the non-Catholic Little Entrance is lengthier than that observed among the Catholics.

The Gospel book is brought out of the sanctuary by a deacon accompanied by an *acolyte bearing a lighted taper. Standing before the veil of the sanctuary, the principal celebrant blesses the assembled clergy and congregation. He then processes once around the altar preceded by a lighted taper with the Gospel book behind him. He then censes the book three times and reads from it.

2. There is no distinctive Great Entrance ceremony in this rite.

East Syrian Tradition

1. The Little Entrance. After the reading from the Epistle the priest takes

up the Gospel book, and preceded by a censer and lighted tapers, he comes to the door of the sanctuary. After blessing the people with the book, he reads the Gospel of the day.

2. The Great Entrance. In the *Chaldean rite this is now much truncated. In the past the priest took the chalice and paten in his right and left hand respectively and, accompanied by assistants, processed to the altar. Today the chalice and paten are brought to the altar without an elaborate procession and then covered with a veil (*shoshepa).

West Syrian Tradition

1. The Little Entrance. There is no distinctive ceremony involved at this point in the Liturgy.

2. The Great Entrance. While there is a mention of a prayer of entrance at the start of the Liturgy of the Faithful, this "Sedro d'Ma'altho" is nothing like a Byzantine entrance, since the bread and wine have been at the altar since the start of the Liturgy. It is possible that there was a more elaborate entrance ceremony at one time.

ENTSAIARAN (Armenian)
(also called Matouthsaran)

The credence table, located on the north side of the sanctuary, which is used as a table for the *prothesis.

See PROTHESIS.

EPANOKALEMAVCHION
(Byzantine/Greek)
(also spelled Exokamelavchion; *Klobuk)

A veil placed on top of and enveloping the *kamilafka, or *skouphos in the case of the little habit (*see* DEGREES OF MONASTICISM), or it may envelop the cowl (*koukoulion [Greek]; koukoul [Slavonic]). In the case of the angelic or great habit, the veil is decorated with five crosses, or a representation of the cross on Calvary together with a spear and sponge on a reed. One cross is above the forehead, one on the back between the shoulders, and one lower, while the two other crosses are at the tips of the two lappets, or wings, of the veil. The veil is normally black, but the *metropolitan of the *Russian Church may wear a white veil. The use of the lappets (voskriliya [Slavonic]) dates allegedly from the time of St. Methodius (9th century), who suffered injuries to his face during the *Iconoclast persecutions of the emperor Theophilus. To conceal his wounds St. Methodius covered the lower part of his face with the lappets, which he secured to his veil. The use of these lappets has continued until now.

EPARCHY

Literally, "province." Originally the name of a division of the Roman Empire, but in the *Eastern Church it is a province governed by a *metropolitan having several *bishops under him. This word is frequently found in the canons of the Eastern Church, for example those of Nicea (325) and Chalcedon (451), and it was commonly used in the early days. The ecclesiastical head, or eparch, had a veto on the election of bishops in his eparchy. Among Roman Catholics the word specifically refers to an *Eastern-rite diocese.

EPENDYTES (Byzantine/Greek)
(also spelled Ephaploma)

See ALTAR CLOTHS; ENDYTE.

EPEPI (Coptic)

The eleventh month of the *Coptic calendar, which corresponds to the period from June 25 to July 24.

EPHEMERIA (Byzantine/Greek)

See PREHOD.

EPHEMERIOS (Byzantine/Greek)

The *priest who may be on duty for that particular day in a church. This is only possible in those churches served by several priests. Occasionally, the term refers specifically to a parish priest.

EPHOR

From the 10th century this term was used to describe a lay guardian, or protector, in whose charge the *monastic property was often vested.

EPHOUT (Coptic)

See BALLIN; TAILASAN.

EPICLESIS (Byzantine/Greek)

Literally, "invocation." The name of the prayer found in all *Eastern *Liturgies, although its position and text varies according to the liturgical family. While the term originally meant an *invocation, it has long been held to mean a petition for the Consecration of the *bread and wine asking the Father to send down the Holy Spirit upon the bread and wine and to make them into the Body and Blood of Christ. Such a notion is obvious from reading St. Cyril of Jerusalem, and as the use of the Epiclesis spread in the 4th century, the invocation was so understood by St. John Chrysostom.

In the 8th century St. John Damascene (676–749) had to contend with the view that the Eucharist was only a representation of Christ, an opinion he vigorously denied, declaring that the Consecration was effected not only by the words of institution but by the invocation. This view was reinforced by Cabasilas and St. Simeon of Thessalonica in the 14th century. At the Council of Florence, a short-lived agreement between East and West was reached to the effect that the institution had a consecratory force, which the invocation brought to fruition, an agreement later rejected by the Greeks. Since the 18th century the *Byzantine view has been that the institution is purely historical and that Consecration is effected by the invocation. The *Russian Church has not held unwaveringly to this opinion, as the writings of Peter Moghila, patriarch of Kiev, in his *Orthodox Confessions* suggest. Nowadays the unity of opinion is undeniable.

In the *East Syrian rite, the *g'hantha of the Epiclesis is called the Nithi Mar ("May He come, O Lord . . ."), derived from the opening words. Interestingly, older *Chaldean and *Malabar (Catholic) books have placed the institution and *elevation after the Epiclesis, but the 1901 edition puts the institution first.

See ANAPHORA; INVOCATION.

EPIGONATION (Byzantine/Greek)
(also called Konker [Armenian])

An oblong piece of stiffened material worn on the right side suspended by two tapes; this *vestment should not be confused with the *palitza, which is a lozenge-shaped piece of brocade also worn on the right. If the *priest has the right to wear both vestments, the epigonation is worn on the left while the Palitza is suspended by one corner with a tape and always hangs on the right.

The epigonation, on which may be embroidered either a cross or the head of the *Theotokos, is awarded as a privilege to *bishops and some minor prelates of the *Eastern Church. Until the end of the 12th century the privilege of wearing an epigonation was reserved to bishops alone, but today it can be extended to other clergy and is a mark of authority, symbolizing the two-edged sword of Christ or the sword of the Spirit (Eph 6:17), although some will suggest that it represents the napkin with which our Lord girded himself at the Last Supper.

See HYPOGONATION; NABEDRENNIK; PALITZA.

EPIMANIKA (Byzantine/Greek)

See EPIMANIKIA.

EPIMANIKIA (Byzantine/Greek) (also called Narukavniki)

Armlets or cuffs ornamented with a cross that form part of the Eucharistic vestments worn by *bishops, *priests, and *deacons. The cuffs worn by *Russian clergy are open, so they are secured with buttons or strings, and they are somewhat shorter than the *Coptic equivalent. There is no difference between the cuffs worn by a bishop and those worn by a priest. They represent the gloves worn by the *Byzantine emperors when they entered the sanctuary in order to receive Holy *Communion in the hand. The privilege of wearing them was extended to the *patriarchs and bishops, and in the 12th century to the priests, while the deacons waited until the 17th century to be accorded the same honor. St. Simeon of Thessalonica (d. 1429) suggested that they represent the cords that bound Christ during his passion.

See CUFFS; EPIMANIKA; HYPOMANIKA; PORUTCHI; VESTMENTS, TABLE OF; ZENDE.

EPIRIPTARION (Byzantine/Greek) (also called Exokamelavchion)

See EPANOKALEMAVCHION; KLOBUK.

EPISCOPOS (Armenian)

An *Armenian *bishop. As a member of the Armenian hierarchy an Armenian bishop works in a highly decentralized system, and as head and administrator of his diocese in the conduct of all business, he has absolute authority in the granting of licenses and in matters of censure. While he can judge matrimonial matters and may grant dispensations, his powers stop short of granting divorces.

The usual dress of a bishop is like that of a *vartabed, with the additional privilege of wearing a ring on the little finger of the right hand, while the privilege of wearing a ring on the ring finger of the right hand is the prerogative of the *catholicos. The *miter and *crozier used are of the Latin type, but the Armenian *omophorion (pallium) is wider and longer than that used elsewhere, being up to 12' in length and from 10" to 12" wide, with a great deal of decoration. When worn it extends to the feet. Armenian bishops wear the *panague, an oval-shaped pectoral cross ornamented with precious stones and bearing a picture of the Virgin Mary or Christ. Bishops have the additional privilege of preaching a sermon while seated.

See ORDERS, HOLY (Armenian Tradition); VESTMENTS, TABLE OF.

EPISKOPOS (Byzantine/Greek)
(also called Episkop [Slavonic])

A *bishop. The dress of *Eastern-rite bishops is distinctive, with certain differences according to the rite. In addition to the normal sacerdotal *vestments of *stikharion, *epitrachelion (stole), *zone (girdle), and *cuffs, a bishop may wear a *sakkos, a dalmatic-style vestment with little bells suspended from it, the use of which was once the prerogative of the *patriarch. He may also wear the *omophorion (pallium), of which there are two kinds:

1. The great omophorion, which is made of wool, is heavily decorated with crosses, and so designed that it hangs down in front and behind like a very wide stole. It is removed just before the *gospel is read, its place being taken by the little omophorion, with the great omophorion replaced at the end of the *Liturgy.

2. The little omophorion, which is a much truncated version of the great omophorion and is worn from the prayer of the *Cherubikon until the end of the Liturgy.

The *Byzantine *miter is like an imperial crown, made of metal, usually heavily ornamented, and lined with red silk. In choir, the bishop wears a *mandyas (mantiya [Slavonic]), a long brown-black cloak with four squares of pale blue material, one at each of its four corners. Around the lower edge there are two bands, one red, the other white. The cloak is secured at the neck and base in the front.

Catholic bishops of the Byzantine rite wear a pectoral cross and ring, while non-Catholic bishops wear the *encolpion and *panagia but no rings. The Byzantine crozier (*rabdos) is shorter than its Western counterpart, with the head consisting of two serpents facing each other and a cross at the top.

See ORDERS, HOLY (Byzantine Tradition).

EPISQUPO (Maronite)
(also called *Khasvo; Rzkohno)

A *bishop of the *Maronite Church, who must be celibate but not necessarily *monastic. Bishops of this rite use a Latin *miter and crozier—although a triple cross has been used on occasions—as well as a ring, pectoral cross, and *masnaphtho (hood), which features in the consecration ceremonies.

See VESTMENTS, TABLE OF.

EPITAPHION (Byzantine/Greek)

A veil, richly embroidered with a scene of Christ's burial. In the *Eastern Church on Good Friday it is carried processionally at the end of *Vespers to stand in the center of the church, where it is further adorned with flowers. During the *Orthros (Matins) on Great Saturday eve the epitaphion is carried around the church and returned to the center of the church. At the end of the Office it is taken to the sanctuary and placed upon the *altar, where it remains until the close of the Easter season on the eve of Ascension Day.

EPITIMION (Byzantine/Greek)

An imposed penance; absolution is not given until the penance is discharged.

See PENANCE, SACRAMENT OF; PNEUMATIKOS.

EPITRACHELION (Byzantine/Greek) (also spelled Epitrakhelion)

A *Byzantine vestment equivalent to a Western stole but broader than a *deacon's stole (*orarion). *Russian stoles are narrow at the neck, while the *Greek stole is broader and ornamented with a cross. The two strips hanging down in front may be joined by small hooks, buttons, cords, or even stitching. The ornamentation of these stoles varies. Among the Russians this is usually of angels, while the Greeks decorate their stoles with crosses or figures of saints.

According to St. Germanus the stole is a symbol of the rope around Jesus' neck, with the right side symbolizing the reed set in his right hand and the left side representing Jesus carrying the cross. Since the epitrachelion further symbolizes the consecrating grace of the priesthood, a *priest must always wear it in public, as confirmed by the Council of Laodicea. According to St. Simeon of Thessalonica, if a priest cannot find a stole and the occasion demands that he wear one, he should take a piece of rope or something similar, bless it, and place it around his neck. A stole is not needed at *monastic functions, since these are not public ceremonies.

The color of the stole is a matter of comparative indifference, but regular liturgical colors are used, generally white for feasts, red for *fastdays and Lent, and black for the *Liturgy of the Presanctified. *Armenian, *Syrian, *Coptic, and *Ethiopian priests wear a similar vestment, but the *Nestorians and some *Chaldeans wear a Western-style stole.

See EPITRAKHIL; ORARION; PERITRACHELION; PETRAKHELION; STOLE; VESTMENTS, TABLE OF.

EPITRAKHIL (Byzantine/Slavonic)

See EPITRACHELION.

EPITROPOI (Byzantine/Greek)

A body of the leading *monks of a monastery, who elect the abbot of a *cenobitic community in line with the *Typikon of Manuel II Paleologus (1406), which ordered that elections be in the hands of the fifteen most distinguished monks of a monastery. Once elected, the abbot's decisions are final despite any advice given by the epitropoi. *Idiorrhythmic monasteries have done away with abbots and substituted a committee of three epitropoi elected by the senior monks; this committee administers for one year only.

EQBO (West Syrian)

A short anthem, or verse, appearing in the *Liturgy, for example, "O Christ, who received the offerings of Melchisedeck, receive, O my Lord, the prayer of your servant and pardon the offenses of your people.''

ERAKHAH (Armenian)

A *catechumen. In the *Armenian *Liturgy, following the recitation of the *Creed, Nicene anathemas, and *deacon's *litany the catechumens are blessed: "May the Lord God bless you all." Then they are dismissed. The *dismissal after the Creed is quite unusual, but it included a specific dismissal of unbelievers and *penitents, and to that extent it is unique. *Chaldeans use an odd type of dismissal as well: "Let none of the catechumens, no man imperfect in the faith, none of the penitents, nor the unclean, draw near to this Divine *Mystery."

The blessing of the catechumens is found in the *Greek *Liturgy of St. James, but it disappeared in the later *Antiochene rites.

ERECHSRBEANN (Armenian)

The Trisagion, which is sung by the choir three times: "Holy God, Holy and Strong, Holy and Immortal, have mercy on us." While this is being sung, a Little *Entrance is made around the altar, during which procession the *deacon carries the *Gospel book accompanied by lighted tapers and *incense. The non-Catholic version of the Trisagion, which inserts the words "who rose from the dead" after the expression "Holy and Immortal," is thought to be unacceptable to the *Armenian Catholics (Patriarchal Synod of Constantinople, 1890, and the National Council in Rome, 1911).

See ERGSRBEANN; TRISAGION.

ERETZ (Armenian)

A *priest.

See KAHANA; ORDERS, HOLY (Armenian Tradition); YERETZ.

ERETZKIN (Armenian)

The wife of an *Armenian *priest.

ERFA MASKAL (Ethiopian)

The cross *spoon, which is used to communicate the faithful and assistant clergy from the *chalice while the communicant holds a *purificator. It is usual for a *deacon to administer the chalice.

See KASIS ZAYETRADA'E.

ERGSRBEANN (Armenian)

See ERECHSRBEANN; TRISAGION.

ERPHEI (Coptic)

The sanctuary in the east end of the church, where it is common to find three *altars in a row, each altar being dedicated to a saint whose feast day is celebrated at that altar. The *bishop's *throne is placed in the central apse, and during ordinations a specific *order is conferred on each step leading to the throne. There is usually a screen, the equivalent of an *iconostasis although lacking *icons, with three *doors that swing inward to the sanctuary. In front of these doors are curtains, the hems of which are kissed by the devout *Copt upon entering the church. Within the sanctuary there is a central altar over which may stand a low cupola with benches behind it for the convenience of the clergy.

See HAIKAL.

ESKHIM (Syro-Jacobite)
(also spelled Eskhimo)

The holy schema, or *monastic hood worn by *bishops and *monks, which is never removed. It consists of a long strip of black material shaped at one end into a hood with the other end hanging down the back. The edge of the hood forms a diagonal line from the forehead to the back of the neck. *Syrian Catholics use a gold schema for bishops and a white one for monks, each with a simple cross on the forehead section. Syro-*Jacobites have the same headgear but with two white stripes, the intervening space covered with white crosses.

See QUBH'UNO; SCHEMA.

ESONARTHEX (Byzantine/Greek)
See NARTHEX.

ESORASON (Byzantine/Greek)
(also called Inner Rason)

See ANTERION; DEGREES OF MONASTICISM, HABITS OF; PODRIZNIK; RASON.

ESPOUSALS (Byzantine)
See MNESTRA.

ESPOVIEEDNIE
(Byzantine/Slavonic)

See HOMOLOGETES.

ESPUGO (Syro-Jacobite)

The *sponge used to clean the *chalice and *paten at the end of the *Liturgy after the ablutions. The celebrant prays, "Wipe away, O Lord, with the sponge of your mercy, all my offenses and the sins which I have committed. . . ." The *Jacobites frequently substitute a piece of silk for the sponge, but every time a Jacobite *priest touches the *bread, his fingers have to be purified, so there are frequent washings of the fingers.

ESTAVROMENOS
(Byzantine/Greek)

The crucifix, which is quite unlike the Western style, is a cross with the corpus of Jesus Christ either painted directly on the cross or painted on a tablet that is attached to the cross.

See CRUCIFIX; RASPIATIE.

ESYCHIA (Coptic)

A rubrical instruction that signals that a prayer is to be recited silently at this point in the *Liturgy or Office.

ETCHEGHIE (Ethiopian)
(also spelled Echtigeh; Etchague)

The principal or senior *bishop, who is responsible for the administrative jurisdiction within the *Ethiopian rite.

ETHIOPIA

From the Greek for "burnt face."

ETHIOPIAN CATHOLICS

Members of the Ethiopian Catholic rite. Ethiopian-rite and *Latin-rite Catholics coexist in unity. A vicar apostolic in Asmara has responsibility for the Latin-rite Catholics, while an eparch (*eparchy) in Addis Ababa has responsibility for the Ethiopian-rite Catholics. More than half of the Ethiopian Catholic congregation is in Eritrea province because of the province's long-standing Italian influence. Their numbers in 1980 were estimated at 113,322.

ETHIOPIAN CHURCH

It is thought that Christianity was originally introduced into Ethiopia in the apostolic age, for both Irenaeus and Eusebius record that it was introduced through the teaching of Queen Candace's treasurer (Acts 8:26-40), but it did not take a permanent hold in the country. The existing Ethiopian Church owes its origin to the missionary work originating from Alexandria in the first half of the 4th century, and it continued to be dependent on *Coptic Egypt for many centuries. In the 20th century it became *autonomous, with the Egyptian *patriarch exercising a primacy of honor only. The number of non-Catholic Ethiopians in 1980 was 11,931,400.

ETHIOPIAN CHURCH, DIVINE OFFICE OF

The Ordinary of the Office is found in one of the books needed for its celebration, the Me'eraf. The other books include the *Deggwa, an antiphonary for the whole liturgical year except Lent, when the Tsomedeggwa is used, and the *Mawase'et, which provides an alternative form of the Daily Office. Each Office consists of several parts, the most important being the psalms and fifteen biblical hymns taken from the Old and New Testaments, special prayers for the feast and season, shorter poems or hymns known as kene (qene), scriptural readings, and, finally, prayers and assorted invocations.

ETHIOPIAN CHURCH, LITURGICAL BOOKS OF

See LITURGICAL BOOKS (Ethiopian Tradition).

ETHIOPIAN CHURCH, LITURGICAL CALENDAR OF

Based on the *Coptic calendar, the year begins on September 11 or 12 (Imaskaam) and has twelve months of thirty days each, adjusted for leap year with a thirteenth month of five or six days. Within every four-year period, each year is placed under the title of one of the Four Evangelists. Major feasts are the following:

1. The nine feasts of our Lord, namely Incarnation, Passion, Resurrection, Appearance to St. Thomas, Ascension, Pentecost, Transfiguration, Epiphany, Miracle of Cana.

2. The six Sunday feasts, namely Exaltation of the Cross, Circumcision of our Lord, Feeding of the Five Thousand, Presentation in the Temple, Invention of the Cross, Sojourn in Egypt.

3. The thirty-two Marian feasts, established in the 15th century by King Zara Jacob, who governed Ethiopia from 1434 to 1468, during which time he introduced many Judaizing elements, one of which was that Saturday was to be observed as the Sabbath. People also had to have the name of the Trinity tattooed on their foreheads.

Matters of Church discipline were settled at this time, and an abortive union with Rome was attempted.

4. The fifty main saints days.

ETHIOPIAN CHURCH, MONASTIC LIFE IN

The *monastic clergy in this rite are quite numerous, and all recognize St. Takla Haimanot (literally, "plant of life"), who is said to have introduced the "angelic life" into Ethiopia in 620. His feast is commemorated on December 24.

Most *monks live in monasteries under a komos (superior), while others are hermits. Some may be married and still wear a religious *habit, but they practice special devotions. The habit consists of a tunic, which may be of almost any color, with a belt and hooded cloak.

ETHNAHTI (Coptic)

See FAITHFUL.

ETRO (Syrian)

The Prayer of Incense, which may be recited by the *bishop during pontifical *Liturgies. The prayer may be said even if no incense is being offered.

ETSCHMIADZIN (Armenian)
(also spelled Echmiadzin)

The Armenian monastery that, since 1441, has been the ecclesiastical capital of the schismatic *Armenians and the seat of the *catholicos. It is situated about twelve miles from the city of Yerivan. According to tradition the primatial See of Armenia was founded here by St. Gregory the Illuminator in the 4th century.

EUCHARIST

See ANAPHORA; COMMUNION; KOINONIA; LITURGY; PRECHASTCHENIE; PRICHASTIYE.

EUCHARISTIC BREAD

See BREAD.

EUCHELAION

Literally, "oil of prayer."

See UNCTION OF THE SICK.

EUCHOLOGION
(Byzantine and Coptic)

The principal service book, whose composition dates from at least the 8th century. It is so called because it was first written on a long parchment wound around a stick and was designed for the use of the *priest and *deacon, since it contained the fixed parts of the *Liturgy. It also contains details of the other *sacraments, together with various prayers and blessings used on occasion. Details of the Offices of Vespers (*Hesperinos) and Matins/Lauds (*Orthros) are to be found elsewhere.

See HULAKI; KULAGI; LITURGICAL BOOKS (Byzantine Tradition); TREBNIK.

EULOGIA (Byzantine/Greek)
(also called Antidor [Slavonic])

Literally, "a blessing." In early times the word was used both actively for "a blessing" and passively for "something blessed." It was also applied to signify the Eucharist; this use is found in the writings of St. Cyril of Alexandria. Quite generally it was used to describe the *bread and wine that was customarily distributed after the *Liturgy, but more specifically it refers to the bread contributed by the faithful, which is blessed during the Liturgy and distributed at its conclusion.

In the Syro-*Jacobite rite, the burc'-tho (eulogia) is blessed twice, and then, if a *bishop is present, he takes a piece and gives a portion to all the clergy present. Otherwise, each *priest takes a piece, and the last one to receive a portion distributes to the rest of the clergy, while a *deacon distributes to the congregation.

See ANTIDORON; BARACAH; BURC'THO; M'CAPRANA.

EULOGITARIA (Byzantine/Greek)
(also called *Neporochnyi)

Literally, "blessed." *Troparia sung at *Matins after the psalms are read and accompanied by the refrain "Blessed are you, O Lord teach me your statutes."

EVANGELIE (Byzantine/Slavonic)

See EVANGELION.

EVANGELION
(Byzantine/Greek and Coptic)
(also called *Anjil; *Evangelie)

In the *Byzantine tradition this term can refer to the liturgical *Gospel announced during a *Liturgy, or it can mean the Gospel book, which contains the liturgical Gospels for use during the Church Year (*Tetraevangelion). The cover of the Evangelion is distinctive in that it must never be made from the skin of dead animals, for which reason leather and vellum may never be used; a metal covering is usual. It is placed in the center of the *altar, and during the Liturgy it is processed at the Little *Entrance and venerated with the same respect as that shown to the holy *icons.

The arrangement of the Gospel book in the Byzantine rite is by sections (pericopes). These follow the order of reading at the Liturgy and Office throughout the year; for example, St. John's readings last the seven weeks from Easter to Pentecost; St. Matthew lasts eleven weeks from Whitmonday and six other weeks the Matthean readings share with readings from St. Mark. The entire Matthean series ends on the Sunday after the Exaltation of the Holy Cross. St. Luke's readings last the nineteen weeks from the Monday after the Exaltation of the Cross until the first Sunday in Lent, but from the thirteenth week on St. Luke is read only on Saturdays and Sundays and the rest of the week is given over to readings from St. Mark. This may explain why certain Sundays in the year are called, for example, the eighth Sunday of St. Matthew or the fourth Sunday of St. Luke. An appendix, the *evangelistarion, is found at the book's conclusion.

Among the *Copts the Gospel book is usually left on the altar except when it is to be read. It consists of a manuscript enclosed in a wooden case, covered all over with metal plates affixed with nails. The plates, which are often of silver, are covered with Coptic lettering and designs of angels, flowers, and crosses. Before the reading of the Gospel during the Liturgy an *acolyte brings the Gospel book from the altar and gives it to the *deacon, who reverently places it on the Gospel stand.

Following the reading it is returned to the altar. The Gospel stand in the *Coptic rite is a four-legged table fitted with a socket that receives the book and little prickets that can accommodate lighted tapers.

EVANGELISMOS (Byzantine/Greek)

The feast of the Annunciation.

EVANGELISTARION
(Byzantine/Greek)

An appendix to the *Evangelion, which details the set of rules governing the occurrence of *Gospel readings throughout the year.

See EVANGELION.

EWANGELIYUN
(East Syrian/Nestorian)

The *Gospel book. When the Epistle is concluded during the *Liturgy, the *priest carrying the Gospel book, preceded by an assistant bearing a *censer and accompanied by *taperers and minor clergy, comes to the sanctuary *door, where the people are blessed with the Gospels. At the conclusion of the appropriate reading, the book is solemnly returned to the *altar. If a Liturgy is being solemnly celebrated, an anthem of the Gospel (*unitha d'iwangaliyun) is sung. This anthem reviews the predominant theme of the Gospel reading.

See LITURGICAL BOOKS (East Syrian/ Nestorian Tradition).

EXAGOREUTES (Byzantine/Greek)

See PNEUMATIKOS.

EXAPOSTILARION
(Byzantine/Greek)
(also called Photagogikon; Svetilen [Slavonic])

Literally, "one who is sent forth." The Hymn of Light, so named because of an old tradition of sending the singer into the center of the church to sing this hymn at daybreak. It is a *troparion that occurs at the end of the *Canon at *Matins, and while it is usually read rather than sung, it is always sung on August 15, the feast of The Falling Asleep of the Theotokos. It develops the theme of Christ as the Light of the World, and the text used on Sundays specifically refers to the Resurrection. It is from this Light of the World theme during Lent that it derives its alternative name of Photogogion.

EXAPSALMOS (Byzantine/Greek)
(also called *Shestopsalmie)

The six psalms recited at the start of *Orthros, namely Psalms 3; 37; 62; 87; 102; and 142 (LXX). During the recitation the congregation is expected to stand quietly.

EXAPTERYGA (Byzantine/Greek)
(also called Ripidi [Slavonic])

Liturgical *fans, which have a large image of a seraphim inscribed on them and which are set on poles and used during processions. During the reading of the *Gospel, either at the *Liturgy or at *Matins, it is usual for the fans to be held over the Gospel book. During the Great *Entrance they may be held over the *bread and wine that are to be consecrated.

See RIPIDIA.

EXARCH

In early days, the exarch was a viceroy of any large province. Today in the *Eastern Church he is a *bishop who holds a place of honor, appointed by the *patriarch in order that he may review the clergy, ensure that the canons of the Church are observed, and act as a type of inspector. He takes precedence over a *metropolitan.

EXARCHATE

The well-defined area of jurisdiction of an *exarch.

EXOKKLESIAI (Byzantine/Greek)

A wayside shrine that may contain an *altar, although the *Liturgy is rarely celebrated there.

EXOMOLOGESIS
(Byzantine/Greek)

See PENANCE, SACRAMENT OF.

EXONARTHEX

The outer *narthex, or porch, in *Eastern churches.

EXORASON (Byzantine/Greek)
(also called Mandorrason)

See DEGREES OF MONASTICISM, HABITS OF; RASON.

EXOSTES (Byzantine/Greek)

See NARTHEX.

EZLI (Ethiopian)

One of the three modes of chant used in the *Ethiopian rite during the Church Year. This mode is used from September 26 until November 6, from the first Sunday of Advent until the *vigil of the season of Lent (Chebela), and from Easter until June 16.

F

FAINO (Syro-Jacobite)
(also spelled *Phaino)

The *Syrian equivalent of a Western chasuble, the principal Eucharistic *vestment; it is split up the center in front and secured by a loop or button at the neck. On the upper part of the back is an embroidered cross.

FAITHFUL

One who is baptized, a believer.

See ETHNAHNTI; HHAVATATHSEAL; M'HAIMNO; PISTOS; TA'AMANI; VEROYUSCHIE.

FALUNYUN (Coptic/Arabic)

See FELONION; VESTMENTS, TABLE OF.

FANS

These fans were originally made from feathers or linen veils, and according to the Sahidic Ecclesiastical Canons, they were held by *deacons standing at either side of the *altar, who would use them "to drive away little flying crea-tures that they light not on the *chalice." Only later did they become staves with metal discs attached, which were decorated in repoussé with a seraph's face and wings (*exapteryga). In the *Armenian and Syro-*Jacobite traditions, the chschoths and marwah'tho respectively are fans with little bells attached to their rims, so that when they are shaken they form an accompaniment to the solemn part of the *Liturgy. Neither the *Nestorians nor the *Ethiopians use fans.

See CHEROUBIM; CHSCHOTHS; EXAPTERYGA; MARWAH'THO; RIPIDIA; RIPIDION; RIPISTERION.

FASTS

Armenian Tradition

Fasting is rigorously observed and, strictly speaking, implies one meal a day that excludes fish, meat, butter, and milk. Typical fast days are the days in Lent (with the exception of Sunday, which according to Tornefort is a day on which fish may be eaten with impunity) and the Fast of *Nineveh, also known as the Fast of the Forerunner. Armenian writers are divided in their opinion as to the origins of this fast; some consider it to be a commemoration of the fast of the Ninevites, while others consider it to be a remembrance of the expulsion of Adam and Eve from Paradise. Every day in Pentecost Week is also observed as a fast day. Although the fasts are strictly observed, the penitential nature of some ordinary fast days is not reflected in the services of the Church. Allied to this, sexual abstinence is meticulously observed, and it is considered virtuous for married clergy to abstain from intercourse before celebration of the *Liturgy.

Byzantine Tradition

Christmas and Easter are preceded by long fasts. The fast before Christmas lasts forty days, from November 15 to December 24, while the fast before Easter, the *Great Fast, is preceded by a week of abstinence known as "Cheese Week," or Tes Turikes (see *Cheese Sunday). The Fast of the Apostles begins on the Monday after the Sunday of All Saints and lasts until the eve of the feast of Sts. Peter and Paul (June 29). The Fast of the Mother of God takes place from August 1 to 14. All these fasts are called "forty days," or tesserakostai.

During a fast, meat, cheese, butter, and eggs are forbidden, and during the Great Fast of Lent the ban extends to include fish and all animal products as well as wine and oil. This ban is rigorously observed, especially during Holy Week. *Monastic communities also observe a fast before the Exaltation of the Holy Cross on September 14.

See NESTEIA; POST.

Coptic Tradition

During any ecclesiastical year there are five principal fasts, the pre-Lenten Fast of Nineveh, which lasts three days; the Great Fast of Lent, lasting fifty-five days; the Fast Before the Nativity, which lasts twenty-eight days; the Fast of the Apostles, which follows the Ascension; and the Fast of the Virgin, which is commemorated before the feast of the Falling Asleep of the Mother of God.

Ethiopian Tradition

The fasts observed by the *Ethiopians are similar to those of the *Copts with several minor differences; for example, the Ethiopian Lenten fast lasts forty days. Both rites observe the Fast of Nineveh and the Fast of the Virgin, the latter observed on August 22. The Ethiopian pre-Christmas fast is less protracted than that of the *Copts, being only a *vigil fast.

East Syrian Tradition

The *Nestorians observe a long Advent fast starting on December 1, whereas the *Chaldeans shorten this fast to the nine days before Christmas. The three-day Fast of Nineveh, known also as the Rogation of the Ninevites or the Supplication of Nineveh, begins seventy days before Easter and is kept by both Chaldeans and Nestorians as a fitting introduction to Lent. It is alleged that this fast was instituted in the

6th century because of a devastating plague, the progress of which was halted by a fast. During the Lenten fast (Soma raba) the restrictions are rigorously observed by both Chaldeans and Nestorians. Though some measure of relief is available to the Chaldeans, the Nestorians may be required to fast for as long as forty-nine or fifty days.

A fourth fast period, that of the Death of St. Mary, or Mart Mariam (Nestorian), is kept from August 1 to 15, and it should be noted that the feast (August 15) is characteristically not described as being of the Mother of God. The Nestorians may also observe an additional fast of several days' duration, preceding the feast of Sts. Peter and Paul in June. Obsolete fasts include that of Mar Zaya (three days after the second Sunday of the Nativity) and that of the Virgin, which is kept after the first Sunday of the Epiphany.

West Syrian Tradition

The Assumption fast lasts from August 8 to 15. In connection with the feast, the Falling Asleep of the Virgin Mary, it is the custom for *Syrians to gather in the cemeteries, sit upon the graves of their dead, and eat blessed grapes. Whatever remains of their repast is given to the poor of the locality.

Other fasts include that of Nineveh, which originated, reputedly, in the 6th century and is kept on the first three days in the third week before Lent commences, and the Fast of Great Lent, which lasts forty days and is rigorously observed. The Fast of the Apostles is kept by the *Jacobites from June 16 to 28, while the *Syrian Catholics observe as fast days the three days

preceding the feast. The Christmas fast extends from December 16 to 24, although in times past it lasted much longer.

FEASTS OF OUR LORD (Byzantine)

1. The Exaltation of the Cross (September 14-27).
2. The Nativity of Our Lord (December 25-January 7).
3. Epiphany (January 6-19).
4. The Purification of the Virgin (February 2-15).
5. Palm Sunday (movable).
6. Easter, or the Feast of Feasts (movable).
7. The Ascension (movable).
8. Pentecost (movable), commemorated fifty days after Easter).
9. The Transfiguration (August 6-19).

See GREAT FEASTS.

FEASTS OF THE THEOTOKOS (Byzantine)

1. The Birth of the *Theotokos (Mother of God) (September 8-21).
2. The Presentation in the Temple (November 21-December 4).
3. The Annunciation (March 25-April 7).
4. Dormition of the Theotokos (August 15-28).

See GREAT FEASTS.

FELON (Byzantine/Slavonic)

A short tunic, or chasuble, worn by a *reader over his shoulders when he is ordained by the *bishop after being *tonsured. This *vestment is rarely worn except on the day of ordination, and it is said to symbolize the ordinand's coming under the yoke of the priesthood and his dedication to the service of God, as the prayer that accompanies this part of the ceremony suggests: "O Lord God Almighty, elect this your servant and sanctify him and enable him with all wisdom and understanding to exercise the study and reading of your divine words, preserving him in a blameless life. . . ." The reader's usual vestment is the *stikharion.

FELONION (Coptic)

This *Coptic chasuble resembles a Western cope, but without a hood. Originally it may have been a complete coverall, but as it became cut away over the arms for lightness and ease of movement in the West, it was also reduced in size behind and in front. There has been less alteration in the *Eastern vestment, with only a little cutting in the front and over the arms. The sides of the vestment are secured by a hooked clasp. The *Coptic *Liturgy is sometimes celebrated by a *priest who is not wearing a felonion. A patriarchal felonion reaches to the ground both front and back with openings at the sides for the arms. When laid out, its overall shape is cruciform.

See AMFORION; BURNUS; FELON; KABA; KOUKLION; MA'APRA; PHAINA; PHAINOLION; PHELONION; SCHOORCHAR; VESTMENTS, TABLE OF.

FELSATA (Ethiopian)

The Assumption of the Blessed Virgin Mary, commemorated on August 22 (17 Nahase), while the Death of the Virgin Mary is observed on January 16 (21 Ter).

FENQITH (West Syrian)

A festal Office said in *Syriac.

See PENQITHO.

FESTIVAL OF THE TANK (Coptic)

Another name for Epiphany, or Theophany, which is celebrated January 6 (11 Tubeh). This celebration occurs at night, when *Matins are recited in the *narthex of the church beside a large tank filled with water. The *bishops, if present, are vested in full pontificals, and together with other clergy they form a procession preceded by an iron cross, which is held high by a *deacon. Psalms and hymns are sung around the tank and a candlestick with three branches is lit beside it. The water is blessed and prayers and *lessons are recited over the tank. The water is censed and stirred with the pastoral staff, following which those present are sprinkled. In the past there was a race to get into the tank so as to have the honor of being dipped in it three times by the *patriarch, should he be present; this custom has been discontinued. After the aspersion the *Liturgy commences. The custom is ancient, since St. John Chrysostom remarked about the practice of consecrating water at night on the Feast of the Epiphany. Early Christians are known to have followed the habit of bathing in the River Jordan in order to commemorate this festival.

FETATE (Ethiopian)

The Fraction of the consecrated *bread, during which the *priest divides the bread into thirteen parts and arranges the portions in the form of a cross while the prayer of Fraction is recited.

See FRACTION.

FETHE NEGHEST (Ethiopian)

The *Ethiopian Church calendar, which is basically *Coptic. Provision is made in the course of the Church Year for the same feast to be celebrated many times. The calendar was largely revised by King Zara Jacob (1434–1468), and it should be noted that each year is under the patronage of an evangelist. There are thirteen months in the Church Year, which commences according to *Julian reckoning on August 29 and in the *Gregorian system on September 11.

FILIOQUE PHRASE

Literally, "and from the Son." This describes the procession of the Holy Spirit from both the Father and the Son. The phrase was inserted into the *Creed and aroused great controversy. St. Photius the Great of Constantinople disclaimed it in 863 in the course of his disagreement with *Pope St. Nicholas I (858–867). It is the belief in the *Eastern Church that the Western Church arbitrarily introduced the phrase into the text. In fact, however, Pope Leo III synodically denounced the phrase in 809 and was so moved as to engrave in both Latin and Greek on two silver plates the Holy Creed of the first and second *ecumenical councils entirely, and without the addition; for while he considered it theologically sound, he felt that it would be a mistake to tamper with the wording of the Creed.

In addition, "and from the Son" probably originated in Spain as a safeguard against Arianism. It was introduced at the Third Council of Toledo in 589, and from there it came to Germany, where Charlemagne made it an issue with the Greeks. It did not make its appearance in the Western Creed until the 11th century. The *Orthodox objected to the Filioque phrase because no one section of the Church had any authority, outside an ecumenical council, to make any alteration of the Creed, and they felt that the notion was theologically unsound. It transpired, therefore, that the Western Church maintained the Filioque phrase in its Creed, while the Orthodox retained the original wording and rejected the phrase outright.

FINLAND, ORTHODOX CHURCH OF

Originally part of the *Russian Orthodox Church, but after the country gained independence from Russia in 1919 the *patriarch of Constantinople granted *autonomy to the Finnish Orthodox Church (1923). The primate of the Church bears the title "Archbishop of Karelia and All Finland," but his selection and source of holy *chrism is dependent on the *ecumenical patriarch. The Church employs both *Church Slavonic and Finnish in its services.

FLABELLA

See FANS.

FORE-HABIT

See DEGREES OF MONASTICISM, HABITS OF.

FOSH (Coptic)

The prayer of the Fraction, one of the six prayers recited aloud in a *Coptic *Liturgy, when the consecrated *bread is broken and a small particle removed. The whole bread is then replaced on the *paten.

See FRACTION (Coptic Tradition); KISM.

FOSSOR(E)S

A gravedigger; a chronicle in the 6th century includes these individuals among the "clerici." They were also called "lecticarii," from the custom of carrying the corpse on a lectica (bier). Their distinctive dress appears to have been a long white robe, rather like a dalmatic.

FOUR DOCTORS OF THE EASTERN CHURCH

Saints Athanasius, Basil the Great, Gregory of Naziansus, and John Chrysostom.

FOUR DOCTORS OF THE WESTERN CHURCH

Saints Ambrose, Jerome, Augustine, and Gregory.

FRACTION

The word is used in two ways:

1. Among the *Jacobites, during the institution and just before the words are recited over the *bread, the *priest partially divides the bread into two unequal parts but does not separate the portions. Similarly, in the *Ethiopian rite during the words of institution, at the words "and he broke and gave it to his disciples," the priest fractures the bread by partially dividing it into five parts.

2. The actual division of the consecrated bread into smaller particles.

Armenian Tradition

The consecrated bread is divided over the *chalice into three parts, although some liturgists claim the division is into four pieces. The priest puts one particle (*Masn) into the chalice as part of the rite of *commixture (kharrnoumn), and while holding the other particles, he continues to pray.

Byzantine Tradition

During the singing of the *Communion hymn the *deacon stands to the right of the priest in the sanctuary and says, "Pray Father, break the Holy Bread." This the priest does, breaking it into four parts along the crosswise incision made at the *prothesis. (Until the 9th century the bread was broken into three parts.) These four parts are placed crosswise on the *paten, the portion marked IC placed to the east, XC to the west, NI to the north, and KA to the south. The particle marked IC is taken by the priest, who makes the *sign of the cross with it over the chalice, and then lowers it into the chalice, saying, "The fullness of the Holy Spirit." The warm water, or *zeon, is added by the deacon after it has been blessed by the priest.

Nicholas Cabasilas (d. 1371), *metropolitan of Thessalonica, saw the warmth as symbolizing the descent of the Holy Spirit on the Church. St. Simeon of Thessalonica wrote that the warmth testifies that the Lord's body, although dead after the separation of the soul, remained life-giving and unseparated from the Godhead and from any action of the Holy Spirit.

Coptic Tradition

During the prayer of the Fraction the priest takes the bread in his left hand, and dipping his right finger in the chalice, he signs the bread above and below with the consecrated wine from the chalice. The bread is then broken into five portions and arranged on the paten in the form of a cross, leaving the Isbodikon portion unbroken in the center. The smaller portions are then broken into very small particles.

See FOSH; KISM.

Ethiopian Tradition

The bread is divided into thirteen parts and arranged in a definite sequence so as to form the sign of the cross, while the prayer of Fraction is recited.

See FETATE.

East Syrian/Nestorian Tradition

The rite of Fraction and *consignation as performed by the *Nestorians is different from the rite of the *Chaldeans. Having kissed the *altar three times and prayed, the priest kisses the paten crosswise without touching the bread; then he takes up the center loaf (Malkaita), which has been placed above the other four breads on the paten, and breaks it in half. He traces the sign of the cross in the chalice with the first half, partially dipping the bread as he does so by moving the particle from east to west and then from north to south; then with the intincted end he signs the other half, which he places above the four loaves (*Gmuriati). Having intincted the bread, he lifts up the two halves, bringing them together so they appear as if they were whole. Then, as in the Chaldean rite, the priest makes a cleft in the top of the right half of the bread and places one half on top of the other in the shape of a cross.

East Syrian/Chaldean Tradition

At the altar, the priest takes the bread (bukhra) between the thumb and index finger of both hands, raises it above his head, and while still holding the bread, he kisses it in the form of a cross without actually touching it with his lips. Then, taking the bread, he breaks it in half, first nicking the bread with his thumbnail in order to assist the Fraction. He puts the half that is in his left hand on the paten in such a way that its broken edge is toward the chalice. Taking the right half, he dips it into the chalice, moving it from east to west and then from north to south, saying prayers in the meantime. With the intincted right half he signs the left half, touching it from east to west and from north to south. The right half is placed over the left half so that its broken edge faces west, toward the celebrant, and the two portions form a cross. Having genuflected, the priest joins his forefingers around the portions of bread, rather like a wheel, and after another prayer the rite is completed.

West Syrian Tradition

According to St. Ephrem, the Fraction was made just before Holy Communion, but its present position after the intercessions in the Liturgy is commented on by James of Edessa (708). It should be noted that there was some controversy in the 8th and 9th centuries about the prayer that is said during the Fraction. The prayer finally adopted by the Jacobites is that attributed to Denys Bar Salibi (d. 1171), while the *Syrian Catholics accepted the restored prayer of the *patriarch George (758–790).

The action involves breaking the bread into two equal parts, each of which is dipped into the chalice, then one portion is "anointed" with some of the consecrated wine from the chalice. This accounts for St. Ephrem's reference to the "painting" of the bread in several of his hymns. A small piece of the consecrated bread is put into the chalice for the priest's Communion, after which another piece may be dipped several times into the chalice and used to anoint the remaining portions of bread for use in the Communion of the clergy and people.

See KASYO.

G

GALILAEON (Coptic)

The oil of *catechumens. Like the oil of the sick, it is composed of pure olive oil and should not be confused with the *chrism (*myron).

GAMOS (Byzantine/Greek)

One of the *sacraments of the Church, matrimony is often called "the crowning," or "stephanoma," from the practice of wearing crowns as part of the ceremony. The imposition of crowns is accompanied by the words "The servant of God, N., is crowned unto the handmaid (servant) of God, N., in the name of the Father. . . ." The bridegroom is crowned first, then the bride; additionally, a cup of wine is blessed and given three times to the bride and bridegroom, and sometimes *bread is dipped into the wine and given to the couple. They are then led around the lectern three times to show the enduring nature of their love and in honor of the Trinity.

See BRAK; MARRIAGE.

GAVAZAN (Armenian) (also spelled Gauazan)

The staff of office presented to a *vartabed as part of the ordination ceremony. The type of staff given and its design varies according to the grade of vartabed; for example, a minor vartabed has a staff topped with a cross and one entwined serpent, while a major vartabed's staff has two entwined serpents. The words spoken when the gavazan is presented to the ordinand suggest that it symbolizes the power of recovering sinners from the devil and emphasizes the duty of preaching and comforting those who are sick or in need of comfort. As the ceremony continues, this symbolism of leadership, strength, and anchorage is developed.

GAZOPHYLAKION (Byzantine)

A structure found in a Constantinian basilica where offerings were received for the *Liturgy.

GAZZA (East Syrian)
(also spelled Gezza)

See LITURGICAL BOOKS (East Syrian Tradition).

GEBRA HAWARYAT (Ethiopian)

The *lesson from the Acts of the Apostles, which is read by an assistant *priest, the reading having been introduced by a short prayer: "A pure fountain which is from the pure fountain of the Law, being the history of the Acts of the pure Apostles. The blessing of their prayers be with us. Amen."

GEDEKION (Byzantine/Greek)
(also called *Parathronos)

The seat placed beside the *bishop's *throne but on a lower level and much less ornate. This seat is used by a bishop when he is not assisting pontifically.

GE'EZ (Ethiopian)
(also spelled Gheez)

An old Semitic language still used as the liturgical language of the *Ethiopian Church. According to Salaville, this language was the vernacular until the 17th century, having been imported into Ethiopia by pre-Christian immigrants. Of the twenty-six characters of the alphabet, twenty-two bear similarity to Hebrew and *Syriac. Ge'ez has given rise to three modern dialects, Tigre, spoken in the northern mountains; Tigrinya, spoken around Aksum; and Amharic, the language of government and administration.

See LITURGICAL LANGUAGES, TABLE OF.

GENERAL MENAIA (Byzantine)
(also called *Obschaya Mineya)

The general office, to be used on various types of saints' days, for example, the Common of a virgin martyr.

GENESION (Byzantine/Greek)
(also called Genethlion, Gennesis)

Literally, "birth." Feasts relating to a birth, for example, the Nativity of Our Lord and the Nativity of the Blessed Virgin.

GEORGIAN

See LITURGICAL LANGUAGES, TABLE OF.

GEORGIAN ORTHODOX CHURCH

The Georgians, who live in a mountainous region between Russia and Armenia, were allegedly evangelized around the year 325 by St. Nino, a female slave from Colastri in Cappadocia, and later by Armenian and Syrian missionaries. During the 5th century the evangelization was completed by missionaries from Constantinople. The *Byzantine rite was translated into *Georgian in the 5th and 6th century, and according to some authorities, it was at this later date that the country was evangelized by the Syrians. Despite many difficulties the Georgian Church remained independent with its own *catholicos until the country was annexed to the Russian Empire under Tsar Alexander I in 1811, when the catholicos Antony II was forced to resign.

*Slavonic was then substituted for Georgian in the *Liturgy, and despite Tsar Nicholas II's Decree of Religious

Toleration, the Georgian Church remained part of the *Russian Church under the *exarch appointed by the Russian Holy Synod. When the Bolshevik Revolution took place in 1917, the Georgian Church declared its *autocephalous status and elected its own catholicos on May 18, 1918. Georgia became a Soviet Socialist Republic in 1921, when a council of the Church surrendered itself to the Bolsheviks; since then the Georgian Church has been allowed to function fairly calmly and to use Georgian as a *liturgical language. In 1980 the total Georgian Orthodox population was estimated to be about 895,000.

GERON (Byzantine/Greek)

See IDIORRHYTHMIC SKETE.

GERONTAS (Byzantine/Greek)

See SPONSOR; STARETZ.

G'HANTHA (Syrian)
(also spelled G'hontho; *Ghont(h)o; Khudu)

Either (1) a deep bow made while saying a prayer or (2) a prayer that is said with the head deeply inclined. When the g'hantha concludes with an *ecphonesis, this may indicate a *Byzantine origin.

GHELAB (Ethiopian)

See HEBANIE; KESELA; WEGHERET.

GHONT(H)O

See G'HANTHA.

GIASCHOTZ (Armenian)

See DJACHOTZ.

GIRDLE

An ecclesiastical vestment, it is a narrow belt usually of the same color as the *phelonion, or *Byzantine chasuble. Its use in the *Eastern Church is generally confined to *bishops and *priests, with the *deacon wearing an ungirdled *alb. In the *Ethiopian Church a *taperer wears a silk cincture over the alb with its free ends thrown over his back, while in the *East Syrian (*Chaldean) rite, a *reader, *subdeacon, and deacon may all wear girdles (*zunnar).

According to Renaudot, Al Hakim (996–1021) imposed the wearing of the girdle on *Coptic Christians in order to distinguish them from the Muslims, but Butler claimed that it was imposed some 150 years earlier by Khalif Mutawakkil.

The garment's first unambiguous mention as an ecclesiastical vestment was, reputedly, made in the 8th century by St. Germanus of Constantinople. It is thought to have been worn only as part of the ceremonial dress on great occasions and was secured with a highly decorated clasp. As a liturgical vestment the girdle is thought to typify priestly charity, but it may refer to Luke 12:35-38, with its notion of spiritual watchfulness.

See GOTI; POYAS; VESTMENTS, TABLE OF; ZENAR; ZONE; ZOUNARION; ZUNARION; ZUNNAR; ZUNNARO.

GITA (Maronite)

A general term to describe the silk veils used to cover the oblation in the *Liturgy.

See VEILS.

GITA ABSAINIYAK (Maronite)

The silk *veil used to cover the *paten during the *Liturgy.

GITA ALCAS (Maronite)

The silk *veil used to cover the *chalice during the *Liturgy.

GIUTA (East Syrian)

See MALCA.

GIYURA (East Syrian/Chaldean)

See EAST SYRIAN CHURCH, DIVINE OFFICE OF.

GLAGOLITIC

The ancient Slavonic alphabet, which is still used by Catholics of Dalmatia. It was devised by St. Cyril, the Apostle to the Slavs, in the 9th century and wrongly attributed to St. Jerome.

GLASY (Byzantine/Slavonic)

See ECHOS; TONES.

GLORIA

See DOXOLOGIA.

GLUSQOMO (Syro-Jacobite)

An oblong stone container used by the *Syro-Jacobites to house *relics. These *Syrians do not have a tradition of placing relics under the *altar but keep them in a glusqomo, which is kept safe in a cupboard.

GMURIATI (East Syrian)

See FRACTION (East Syrian/Nestorian Tradition).

G'MURTHO (East Syrian)

The particles set aside for the *Communion of the faithful. The laity receive the consecrated particles as the *priest says, "The Body of Our Lord to the pious believer, N., for the pardon of offenses." *Nestorians receive Communion from the *chalice as well, but normally only at Easter and Christmas. Adults receive the *bread in their right hand, while a child under twelve years of age receives on the tongue.

See COAL.

GOLGOTHA (West Syrian)

The stand on which the *Gospel book rests; it stands outside the central *door on the top of the steps leading to the *altar and slightly toward the north. It is usual to find candlesticks on either side of this lectern.

GOMURO (Syrian)

Literally, "perfecter." The small cushion on which the *spoon (*tarwodho) rests. It may be used to wipe the fingers and mouth as well as to purify the *paten after its use.

GONUKLISIA (Byzantine/Greek)

The act of profound kneeling, which involves the getting down on both hands and knees accompanied by the making of the *sign of the cross. It may be a special feature of *Vespers of Pentecost. The *priest reads long prayers while those present remain kneeling.

See METANY; PROSKYNESIS.

GORNOYE MYESTO
(Byzantine/Slavonic)

The elevated place behind the *altar upon which the *bishop's *throne stands. When sitting there, the bishop is said to symbolize the King of Glory. On either side are the seats for the *concelebrants, who represent the apostles and their successors.

GORPHOURAH (Armenian)

See MARMNAKAL; SCHOUSCHPHAH.

GOSPEL

Either (1) the *lesson read from the *Gospel at the *Liturgy or in the Office, or (2) the Gospel book from which the lessons are taken.

The use of the Gospels is universal in all Liturgies, but there are many and varied ceremonies surrounding its reading. The use of ceremonies is ancient, for when St. Jerome was writing from Bethlehem in 406, he mentioned the universal use of lights that were held when the Gospel was read. In the *Peregrinatio S. Silviae*, an account of a pilgrimage by a lady of Aquitaine to Jerusalem in 385, there is mention of *incense being lighted before the Gospel at the Sunday *vigil service, and this may well have been the practice with the liturgical Gospel as well. There is evidence from the writings of Philostorg in the 5th century that it was the custom for those present to stand during the reading of the Gospel.

See ANJIL; AVAT(H)RAN; EVANGELIE; EVANGELION; EWANGELIYUN; LECTIONS; WANGEL.

GOTI (Armenian)

The richly embroidered cincture, or *girdle, designed to secure the *stole to the *alb. A large white napkin is attached to the left side of the goti and is used to cleanse the fingers or sacred vessels in the event of any accident or defilement. As the goti is put on, the *priest recites the prayer "Let the girdle of faith bound in the midst of my heart and of my mind quench in them the thought of impurity, and may the power of your grace abide in them at all times."

See VESTMENTS, TABLE OF.

GOUBA (Byzantine/Slavonic)

See SPONGE.

GREAT CHURCH, THE

The official name of the *Orthodox Church of Constantinople with reference to the Church of the Holy Wisdom (Hagia Sophia), which is mistakenly referred to as that of Saint Sophia, now a mosque.

GREAT (OR GRAND) COMPLINE
(Byzantine)

This Office may be said singly, but it is also said together with *Matins to form the all-night *vigil on the eve of a major feast such as Christmas, Epiphany, or the Annunciation.

It commences with the blessing by the *priest and the prayer "O Heavenly King, the Comforter, Spirit of Truth, who is present everywhere and fills all things, Treasury of good gifts and Giver of life, come and abide in us and cleanse us of all impurity and save our souls, O Good One.'' The *Trisagion, Lord's Prayer, and Psalms 4, 6, 12, 24, 30, and 90 (LXX) are followed by three *troparia, a hymn to the angels and saints, the Nicene Creed, a hymn to the saints, the Trisagion, and Lord's Prayer. A troparion and prayer, Psalms 50 and 101 (LXX), the Prayer of Manasses (king of Judah), the Trisagion, Lord's Prayer, a *kontakion and prayer, precede Psalms 69 and 142 (LXX), all of which are followed by the small doxology.

If it is the eve of a major feast, the *Canon of the saint of the day or of the *Theotokos, together with Psalm 150, is sung next. Further prayers and a short *Litany conclude this lengthy service.

GREAT ENTRANCE (Byzantine)

The ceremony of the Great Entrance derives from the early Church practice of receiving the oblation in a place separate from the sanctuary so that the *bread and wine had to be brought to the *altar for consecration. The movement of the bread and wine, according to the *Apostolic Constitutions*, was performed by the *deacons. St. Euthychius, *patriarch of Constantinople in the 6th century, in his *Homily on Easter and the Liturgy* quotes St. Athanasius the Great (ca. 296–373) in saying that a function of all deacons was to carry the bread and the wine in the *chalice and to place them on the altar. Certainly by the 16th and 17th centuries in both Byzantium and Russia the ceremony of the Great Entrance was performed with great solemnity. Most of our present-day ceremonial

dates from the 17th-century service books.

See ENTRANCE; MEGALE EISODOS.

GREAT FAST

An *Eastern Orthodox term for Lent, which begins on a Monday known as ''Clean Monday'' (or more properly on the preceding Sunday evening, the day known as ''the Sunday of Forgiveness'') and lasts forty-eight days. From the 6th or 7th centuries an eighth or preliminary week of modified fasting has been observed known as ''*Cheese Week'' because no meat is eaten but cheese and other dairy products may be taken. For the *Coptic Orthodox, the Great Fast is a fifty-five-day season and includes a preliminary week of modified fasting. No meat, fish, eggs, or milk are supposed to be eaten, although in practice people often fast only until midday at the start of the Lenten season. As Lent continues they observe a stricter fast, so that by Holy Week the Coptic faithful may be eating only vegetables and pulses.

GREAT FEASTS

The important feasts of the *Orthodox calendar are divided into great, lesser, and little feasts. The most important feast is Easter, ''the Feast of Feasts,'' after which come two groups of great feasts, those of the Mother of God and those of our Lord. Each feast is preceded by a period of preparation known as a forefeast, which may involve fasting, while some may be followed by *synaxis, or *sobor. Most feasts are concluded by an afterfeast, the last day of which is known as the *apodosis, or *otdanie (Slavonic).

See FEASTS OF OUR LORD; FEASTS OF THE THEOTOKOS; TWELVE GREAT FEASTS.

GREAT FESTIVAL, THE (Coptic)

On Easter Sunday morning, psalms and hymns of the Resurrection are sung, the *altar is censed, and *Matins are celebrated. The *Liturgy then commences, and at the end of the Epistle and before the *Gospel, the *door of the *haikal (sanctuary) is closed. Then, with the *priests standing inside and the *deacons outside, all sing a liturgical hymn. The cross and a picture of the Resurrection are taken from beneath the altar where they have been laid as part of the Holy Week ceremonies, and at the opening of the door of the haikal, the clergy process around the church carrying the picture of the Resurrection with them. On returning to the choir, the picture is restored to its usual position and the Liturgy continues as normal for Sundays.

GREAT INTERCESSION

The prayers for the whole Church, which are recited within the *Anaphora. James of Edessa (writing in 708), in his commentary on the *Liturgy, compared the respective positions of the intercessions in the *Antiochene and *Alexandrian rites. He wrote, "In the Imperial City and in Greece, the Liturgy is celebrated . . . first the rite of sacrifice which consecrates and then the commemorations. However . . . Alexandria celebrate[s] the Liturgy differently, first the commemorations and then the consecration and oblation." So it is that the Alexandrian intercessions are inserted into the opening of the prayer before the Sanctus.

In the *Syrian rite, for example, the Great Intercession comprises six prayers, three for the living—the Fathers, brethren, and faithful kings—and three for the dead. Each prayer is in turn made up of two parts, the first part, the *g'hontho, being recited secretly by the *priest bowing down with his hands folded, while the *diptych is said aloud by the *deacon with the people responding "*Kyrie eleison" or "Amen." The second part, of *t'litho, is said by the priest standing with outstretched arms and is known as the *p'shto. At its conclusion the people respond "Amen."

At the g'hontho of the dead Fathers and Doctors the priest makes the *sign of the cross with his thumb over the consecrated *bread, and then on a page of the Book of Life (a list placed upon the *altar containing the names of the departed) he makes the sign of the cross again over the names of the deceased *bishops. With the next prayer he makes the same movement over the names of the departed priests and others. This procedure is reminiscent of St. Cyril of Jerusalem's recollection (348) of the special efficacy of prayer in the presence of the consecrated sacrament: ". . . this is the greatest aid to their souls for whom the entreaty is made in the presence of the holy and most dread sacrifice."

GREAT LITANY (Byzantine)

See VELIKAYA EKTENIYA.

GREAT MARTYR, THE

St. George of Cappadocia, who probably lived in the 4th century and about whom many legends abound. He may have served in the Roman army and was martyred for his Christian beliefs under the emperor Diocletian. As early as the start of the 6th century he was referred to as a good man "whose deeds are known only to God."

GREAT THURSDAY (Byzantine)

Holy Thursday, or Thursday in Holy Week. On this day in some major cathedrals and churches, the washing of the feet ceremony takes place. In the Cathedral of the Dormition of the *Theotokos in Russia and in the Monastery of the Caves in Kiev it is customary, every few years, to consecrate the Holy *Chrism on this day.

See MYRON.

GREAT VESPERS (Byzantine)

(also called *Hesperinos; Vetchernya [Slavonic])

The outline of Great Vespers varies according to whether it is celebrated as a *vigil or not.

1. Great Vespers as a vigil:
   A blessing by the *priest.
   Psalm 103, Great *Litany, and Psalter readings.
   Small Litany.
   "Lord I have cried," sung with its verses appropriate to the *tone.
   Hymn to the Birth-Giver of God (*icons are censed by a *deacon).
   Hymn "O Joyful Light" (composed by Sophronius of Jerusalem).
   A *prokeimenon or gradual (a verse that precedes the *lesson from Holy Scripture, called the "parables," or "paremii" whose relevance concerns their connection with the feast to be celebrated).
   Augmented litany and stichera.
   Nunc dimittis, *Trisagion, and *Lord's Prayer.
   *Troparion of the day.
   Blessing of the *bread, wine, and oil (if a *lity has been celebrated).
   Psalm 33:1-10.
   Priest's blessing.
2. Great Vespers when not a vigil is similar to the above except that the prayer for *Orthodox Christians is added. Great Vespers may be followed by a *Liturgy on the eve of Christmas and Theophany and on the eve of the feast of the Annunciation.

GREEK

See LITURGICAL LANGUAGES, TABLE OF.

GREEK CATHOLICS

A misused and general term describing *Ruthenians, Catholic *Romanians, *Melchites, *Italo-Greeks, and *Byzantine-rite Catholics. This term is misleading; with the exception of the Italo-Greeks the *liturgical languages used by these Churches is not Greek.

GREEK ORTHODOX CHURCH

St. Paul came to Greece in the 1st century and established Christianity there. In the early 4th century the emperor Constantine the Great became ruler of the whole Roman Empire (312), and in 330 he moved his capital from Rome to the site of the ancient city of Byzantium, where he built Constantinople (modern Istanbul). It was from here that missionaries spread throughout eastern Europe. Constantinople became the center of *Eastern Christian civilization, while Rome remained the center of Western Christianity. Relations between the two were tense, and in 858 the *patriarch of Constantinople, St. Photius, challenged Rome. With increased papal claims and the *Filioque controversy, it all came to a head on July 16, 1054, when three papal legates placed a bull of excommunication on the *altar of Hagia Sophia in Constantinople. This marked the start of the Great Schism, which separated the Churches of Rome and Constantinople. After 1054, what is now Greece was involved on the side of Constantinople and was part of its patriarchate. With the Greek War of Independence in 1821, the relations between the Church of Greece and the *ecumenical patriarch of Constantinople broke down, and in a spirit of self-determination, the Greek government declared, among other things, that the Greek Church was *autocephalous. The autocephality was conceded eventually by the patriarch Anthimos in 1850, but the decree insisted that the state should not interfere in Church affairs and that the Holy *Chrism should be sent from Constantinople.

The holy synod of the Greek Church has had a rough passage over the years and has obtained greater freedom from Constantinople. Recently many innovations have been evident in the life of the Greek Church, especially missionary movements concerned with evangelism and education; for example, Apostolic Service, the official organization for home mission activity, has been set up. Other movements are private and include Zoe (Life), Sotir (Savior), and Orthodox Christian unions.

Zoe is fairly controversial, beginning as a movement in 1907 and becoming associated with a weekly paper founded by the late *archimandrite Eusebius Matthopoulos in an attempt to harmonize *Byzantine culture as reflected in its religious life with the modern Western civilization in which society operated. This movement became most vigorous following World War I and was again invigorated following World War II when many deserted parishes became resettled and established with *priests. Zoe is concerned with publishing liturgical and patristic literature and even an edition of the New Testament. Its members are usually unmarried, semi*monastic but with the freedom to leave at any time, and they concern themselves with preaching and the regular reception of the *sacraments.

In 1980 the total *Greek Orthodox community numbered 13,055,760.

GREEK RITE

This term is inaccurate and is used to distinguish the *Byzantine rite from the Roman or *Latin rite, since the Byzantine rite uses many languages other than Greek in its liturgical celebration.

GREGORIAN CALENDAR
(also called New Calendar; New Style)

The *Julian Calendar as adjusted by Pope Gregory XIII in 1582 to make it more accurate. It was adopted in England in 1752 and was accepted in 1924 by most *Orthodox Churches except those of Jerusalem, Russia, and Serbia.

GREGORIANS (Armenian)

Also known as Armenian Apostolics or Armenian Orthodox, they may be called Gregorians because it is believed that Armenia's conversion to Christianity was the work of St. Gregory the Enlightener, or Illuminator, who was a Parthian born around 240. He was consecrated a *bishop by the *metropolitan of Caesarea in Cappadocia in 294 and converted the Armenian monarch, King Tiridates (Tradt) III, to Christianity. St. Gregory appointed his son, Aristakes, to be the *catholicos of the *Armenian Church when he resigned his office.

GUBKA (Byzantine/Slavonic)

See SPONGE.

GURNA (East Syrian/Nestorian)

The font.

See BAPTISM (East Syrian Tradition); BIT QANKI.

GYNAECEUM (Byzantine)

That part of a *Byzantine or *Eastern-rite church that is restricted to women alone. It may be a partitioned and latticed area usually found at the west end of a church, or it may be an area specifically identified for the use of women during the services.

GYNAIKITES (Byzantine/Greek)

The side aisle, or separate gallery, which is reserved specifically for women worshipers. In those churches that do not have a specific aisle, the back of the *nave is usually reserved for the women, while the men customarily occupy the part nearest the front of the church.

See GYNAECEUM.

H

HABITS, COMPARATIVE TABLES OF (Byzantine)

Monastic garments. In the *Byzantine tradition there is some confusion about the garments that constitute the habit. The table on page 329 shows the different garments worn by *monks of various degrees. For further information, consult the entries for the individual garments or respective grades of *monasticism.

See Table 1, page 329.

See DEGREES OF MONASTICISM, HABITS OF.

HAGIA (Byzantine/Greek)

The consecrated *bread and wine, often referred to as the "Holy Thing" before and after the consecration; some authorities think that the term refers to the bread and wine only after they have been consecrated.

See SVATEA.

HAGIA THEOTOKOS (Byzantine/Greek)

The Holy Mother of God.

See THEOTOKOS.

HAGIA TRAPEZA (Byzantine/Greek)

See TRAPEZA.

HAGIASMA (Byzantine/Greek)

An all-embracing term referring to anything that has been blessed or consecrated; for example, holy water, blessed *bread, and even the bread and wine after they have been consecrated in the *Liturgy.

HAGIASMATERION (Byzantine/Greek)

An abridged version of the *Euchologion (benedictional) containing the prayers, Offices, and blessings that a

116

*priest uses most frequently in the course of his parish duties.

See MOLITVENIK.

HAGIASTER (Byzantine/Greek)
(also spelled Hagiastera)

An aspergil, used for the aspersion of holy water.

See KROPELO.

HAGIOLOGY (Armenian)

The Proper hymn, which is sung during the Great *Entrance of the *Armenian *Liturgy. During the singing of the hagiology, the *priest takes off his *saghavart, or if he is a *bishop he removes his *Emiphoron, bows before the *altar, and prays silently.

See SRBASATHSOUTHIUM.

HAGION OROS (Byzantine/Greek)

Literally, "Holy Mountain." An alternative name for Mount *Athos.

HAIKAL (Coptic)

A *Coptic sanctuary.

See ERPHEI.

HAIKLA(O) (Syrian)

Literally, "temple." The *nave within the church, where it is usual to find a separation of the men from the women in such a way that the women may be accommodated in galleries at the west end of the church or behind a screen in the aisle. In Catholic-rite churches an *icon of the Mother of God (*yuqno) is always found here, a practice also common in *Jacobite churches.

HAIR-MER (Armenian)

The *Lord's Prayer.

HAITNUTHIUN (Armenian)

The Epiphany. After the *Liturgy a large metal vessel containing water is set up in the choir and a procession goes around the church accompanied by lighted tapers and *incense. The principal celebrant carries a cross, and on returning to the choir he blesses the water, dividing it crosswise with the cross and pouring Holy *Chrism into it. The congregation may take some of the blessed water home with them. This same ceremony is performed in all the rivers of the parish.

HAIYIMONUTHO (Syrian)

The *Creed.

HAMNIKHO (Syrian)

See URORO; VESTMENTS, TABLE OF.

HAMPUIR SRBOUTIAN (Armenian)

In the *Armenian rite the kiss of peace is given just before the *Anaphora. During this ceremony the *deacon usually censes the *priest, then kisses the *altar, the arm or hand of the priest, and finally the altar again. The deacon subsequently brings the peace to the other clergy and choir, who kiss shoulders. A member of the congregation may participate in the ceremony by placing his hand on his heart and bowing to his neighbor.

See PEACE, KISS OF.

HAOU INOURONE (Syro-Jacobite)

A short hymn, which may be sung in honor of the Blessed Sacrament following its reception in *Communion. An example could be "Come in Peace, O *Priest, who bears the *sacraments of the Lord and who distributes life to men with your hand."

HASIRAH (Coptic/Arabic)

Circular mats about 5" or 6" in diameter, made of silk but with a base of coarser material. Each mat has a small cross embroidered on it and may also have smaller crosses set into the branches of the main cross. There is no strict convention concerning the colors used, but the most usual are red, pink, or green.

See TABAK; THOM.

HAYASTANIAITZ (Armenian)

Literally, "Church of Armenia."

See ARMENIAN CHURCH.

HAYOTZ EKEGHETZI (Armenian)

Literally, "Church of the Armenians."

See ARMENIAN CHURCH.

HAYRAPET (Armenian)
(also called *Hayrik)

An alternative name for the *Armenian *patriarch, or *catholicos.

HAYRIK (Armenian)

See HAYRAPET.

HAYSMAVURK (Armenian)

Literally, "this very day." A shortened version of the *Lives of the Saints* and various homilies, which may be read to the congregation on Sundays before *Vespers.

H'BST (Ethiopian)

Literally, "bread." Specifically, the Eucharist bread, which in the *Ethiopian rite is leavened, flat and round, and imprinted with a cross made up of nine squares. The preparation of this bread is the responsibility of the *deacons, and it must be prepared on the day of the *Liturgy. If it is a large church twelve breads are baked, three of which are sent to the church, but of these only one bread is selected, the others being shared among the clergy.

Non-Catholic Ethiopians use unleavened bread only on Holy Thursday, whereas *Ethiopian Catholics use the unleavened bread at so-called low celebrations and have been known to use leavened bread at all other Liturgies.

See BREAD (Ethiopian Tradition); KORBAN; KURBAN.

HEARERS (Byzantine)

Otherwise known as "audientes," the hearers represent a class of *catechumen, or second order of *penitents.

HEBANIE (Ethiopian)

A garment roughly the equivalent of the Western *amice, made of linen and sewn to the *cappa, or kaba. It is thought that it may be able to serve as a head cover, or if the cleric is a religious, it should serve to cover the hood (kob'e) of the habit.

See GHELBAB; KESELA; WEGHERET.

HEGOUMENISSA (Byzantine/Greek)

The abbess of a *cenobitic monastery.

HEGOUMENOS (Byzantine/Greek)

See ARCHIMANDRITE; HEGUMENOS.

HEGUMEN (Byzantine/Slavonic)

See ARCHIMANDRITE; HEGUMENOS.

HEGUMENOS (Byzantine and Coptic)

Literally, "leader." In the *Byzantine sense, the hegumenos may be the abbot of a *cenobitic monastery and is usually elected for life by the *monks, although confirmation of the appointment is required from the *patriarch, synod, or *metropolitan. Once the election is approved, he is blessed and then enthroned. The hegumenos is assisted in his work of administering the monastery by a council of monks. The term does not necessarily imply that he has charge of a religious community.

Among the *Copts the title may be applied to an *archpriest who is in charge of a church or a cathedral to which other *priests and *deacons may be attached, but it may also be applied to one who is the abbot of a monastery.

See ARCHPRIEST; KUMMUS; HEGUMEN.

HEILETON (Byzantine/Greek)

A large cloth used to fold over and enclose the *antimension.

See EILETON; ILITON.

HEIRMOS

(also spelled *Hirmos).

See IRMOS; TROPARION.

HEMNICHO (Syro-Jacobite)

The pallium, or *omophorion, worn by *bishops of this rite. It is made of white silk and is much the same shape as a *priest's *stole, with a hole for the head, but the hemnicho is wider than the stole and hangs down in front and behind. It may also be heavily ornamented with embroidered crosses. The color is usually that of the chasuble (*faino; phaino).

See HOMOPHORION.

HENANA (East Syrian/Nestorian)

Literally, "holy dust." The dust taken from the tombs of reputed saints and used as a sacramental by the *Nestorians, as a potion for the sick. The same dust may occasionally be mixed with wine and given to bridal couples.

See UNCTION OF THE SICK (Coptic Tradition).

HENOSIS (Byzantine/Greek)
(also spelled *Enosis)

See COMMIXTURE; ISPOLNENIE; KHARRNOUMN; SMIESHEVANIE.

HEORTI DESPOTIKI
(Byzantine/Greek)

*Feasts of our Lord.

HEORTI THEOMETRIKI
(Byzantine/Greek)

*Feasts of the Mother of God.

HEORTI TON AGION
(Byzantine/Greek)

Feasts of the Saints.

HEORTOLOGION (Byzantine/Greek)

Either (1) a table of the feasts or (2) the collection of *troparia that are proper to the feasts.

HEOTHINON (Byzantine/Greek)

A *troparion sung at the end of *Lauds that serves to reintroduce the main theme of the *Gospel read at Lauds.

HERACLIUS, FAST OF (Coptic)

This unusual *fast is observed during the first week of Lent, allegedly because the Christians in Jerusalem had promised the emperor Heraclius (610–641) that if he would massacre the Jews in that city the Christians would fast one week every year for his benefit until the end of the world. Since Heraclius carried out their "pious" wish, they have ostensibly kept their side of the deal.

HESPERINOS (Byzantine/Greek)
(also spelled (H)espernos)

See GREAT VESPERS.

HESYCHASM (Byzantine)

Literally, "quiet." A form of mysticism that involves a form of meditation allegedly first practiced by fourteenth-century *Athonite monks. According to tradition, this method of meditation leads to the experience of the uncreated light of God, or Light of Tabor. The doctrinal basis of Hesychasm was approved by a synod in 1351.

See JESUS PRAYER.

HESYCHAST (Byzantine)

An *Orthodox religious who has reached a high degree of contemplation and mysticism.

HEXAPTERYGON
(Byzantine/Greek)
(also spelled Exapteryga)

See RIPIDIA.

HHAVATATHSEAL (Armenian)

See FAITHFUL.

HIERA TRAPEZA (Byzantine/Greek)

Literally, "holy table."

See TRAPEZA.

HIERATEION (Byzantine/Greek)

The sanctuary, found in the eastern section of the church and containing the *altar (*trapeza) and a table of the *prothesis. In a *Byzantine-rite church the sanctuary is separated from the rest of the church by an *icon screen (*iconostasis), which has three *doors set into it through which the clergy may enter and leave according to strict conventions.

HIERATIKE (Byzantine/Slavonic)

A clerical tonsure.

See KOURA; TONSURE.

HIERATIKON (Byzantine/Greek)
(also spelled *Ieratikon)

An alternative name for Little Euchologion, a manual of prayers used by the *priest for *Vespers, *Matins, and the *Liturgy, together with other occasional prayers.

See LITURGICAL BOOKS (Byzantine Tradition); SLUZHEBNIK.

HIERODEACON (Byzantine)

A *monastic *deacon.

See ORDERS, HOLY (Byzantine Tradition).

HIEROMONK (Byzantine)

A *monk who is in *priest's *orders.

See ORDERS, HOLY (Byzantine Tradition).

HIEROPHYLAKION
(Byzantine/Greek)

An Eastern-style tabernacle.

See ARTOPHORION; RESERVED SACRAMENT.

HIEROSYNE (Byzantine/Greek)
(also called Svyastchenstvo [Slavonic])

See ORDERS, HOLY (Byzantine Tradition)

HIEROTELESTIKON
(Byzantine/Greek)

See HIERATIKON; IERATIKON; LITURGICAL BOOKS (Byzantine Tradition).

HIGRAH (Coptic)

The *Gregorian Calendar. It is used by the Catholic *Copts of Lower Egypt to calculate Easter, whereas the Copts of Upper Egypt use the *Julian Calendar. In civil matters all make use of the Higrah.

HIJAB (Coptic)

See KATAPETASMA; SITARAH.

HIRMOS (Byzantine)
(also spelled Heirmos)

See IRMOS; TROPARION.

HIUPATH'AQNA
(East Syrian/Nestorian)

A *subdeacon; none are ordained at present. In the past such a cleric wore the *stole from his left shoulder, but looped under the right arm.

See ORDERS, HOLY (East Syrian Tradition).

H'MIRA (East Syrian/Nestorian)

A portion of the dough left over from the last preparation of the Eucharistic *bread and preserved as a leaven for the new baking; it should not be confused with the Holy Leaven, or *Malca (Malka).

See BREAD (East Syrian/Nestorian Tradition).

HOLY ATCH (Armenian)

The right arm of St. Gregory the Illuminator (ca. 240–332), which is laid on the head of the *patriarch-elect during his ordination. St. Gregory the Illuminator, or Enlightener, is so called because he illumined the hearts and minds of the people of Armenia with the Gospel story. Many legends and stories about him abound and many details of his life are obscure.

See ETSCHMIADZIN.

HOLY DOORS (Byzantine)

See ICONOSTASIS; ROYAL DOORS.

HOLY OF HOLIES
(Syrian and Ethiopian)
(also called Qdhosh Qudhshe [Syro-Jacobite and Nestorian])

Either (1) the space under the canopy (baldakyn) of the *altar, which is generally the *Syrian understanding of the expression, or (2) the Holy Sacrament itself.

See KEDEST.

HOLY THING

The Holy Sacrament.

See KEDSAT; QUDHSHA.

HOMOLOGETES (Byzantine/Greek)
(also called *Espovieednie [Slavonic])

One who has suffered for the faith, somewhat equivalent to the Western Confessor.

HOMOPHORION (Byzantine/Greek)
(also spelled Homophoryon)

See HEMNICHO; OMOPHORION; URORO RABBO.

HORARIUM (Coptic)
(also called Egbiyah)

A type of breviary.

See LITURGICAL BOOKS (Coptic Tradition).

HORN

A general liturgical term referring to the corners of an *altar, which may be kissed during a *Liturgy. For example, in the Syro-*Jacobite rite the celebrant kisses the corners of the altar upon entering the sanctuary prior to celebrating the Liturgy. He says aloud, "Bind our solemnities in chains, O Lord, even to the Horns of the Altar. My God, I will confess and glorify you." Similarly, a *Nestorian *priest kisses the right and then the left corners of the altar as part of the preparatory rites.

HOROLOGION (Byzantine/Greek)

A liturgical book resembling a Western breviary; it contains the Ordinary, or fixed parts, of the Office with the Proper hymns of the *Liturgy; thus it includes the *Midnight Office, *Matins, the *Hours, the *typika, *Vespers, and *Compline as well as the blessings before and after meals. The choir's part is given in full, omitting those parts reserved for the *priest and *deacon. The book also contains the ordo (*acolouthia), the calendar, the *apolytikion, and the *kontakiona (collect hymn) for each day as well as some *Canons.

In the Slavonic edition, however, the list of feasts and saints together with assorted Canons and occasional services found in the Greek edition may be omitted. Also found as an appendix to the book is the *paschalion, which calculates the dates for future Easters and other movable feasts.

See LITURGICAL BOOKS (Byzantine Tradition); TCHASOSLOV.

HOUPODIACONO (Syrian)

A *subdeacon, who functions not only as an *acolyte but as a *doorkeeper, and therefore as part of his ordination ceremony he is given a taper, since he is expected to light the lamps of the church.

See ORDERS, HOLY (Syrian Tradition).

HOURS (DIVINE OFFICE), COMPARATIVE TABLE OF (Byzantine)

See Table 2, page 330.

HOURS (DIVINE OFFICE), PLAN OF (Byzantine)

The sequence that follows is that used for the First, Third, Sixth, and Ninth Hours on Ordinary days, since the

*Royal Hours celebrated on the eve of Christmas and Theophany are slightly different.

The form used on Ordinary days is as follows: The blessing of the *priest, "O Heavenly King," the *Trisagion, and the Lord's Prayer are followed by psalms, the text of which varies according to the Hour. For example, in the First Hour, psalms 5, 89, and 100 are recited. Third-Hour psalms are 16, 24, and 50; Sixth-Hour psalms are 53, 54, and 90; Ninth-Hour psalms are 83, 84, and 85.

These psalms are followed by the *troparion of the day, the *Theotokion, some scriptural verses, the Trisagion, and the *Lord's Prayer.

The Hours conclude with the *kontakion, a collect hymn, the Prayer of the Hours, and a *Dismissal.

HOZOH (Armenian)

A garment that is put around the shoulders of the dead.

HUDRA (East Syrian)
(also spelled Hudhra, *Kudra)

A liturgical book that contains the Proper of the *Liturgy as well as the Office for Sundays, *feasts of our Lord, and principal saints' days.

See LITURGICAL BOOKS (East Syrian Tradition).

HUFADYAKNA
(East Syrian/Nestorian)

The obsolete order of *subdeacon.

See HIUPATH'AQNA; ORDERS, HOLY (Syrian Tradition).

HULAKI (Coptic)
(also spelled *Kulagi)

The *Euchologion (Missal), used by the prelate during the celebration of the *Liturgy.

See LITURGICAL BOOKS (Coptic Tradition).

HULALI (East Syrian)

The twenty-one divisions of the Psalter, known collectively by the plural, hulali. Each hulala is composed of nine psalms, and each hulali is further divided into three *marmitha.

See EAST SYRIAN CHURCH, DIVINE OFFICE OF.

HULOLO (West Syrian)

An *antiphon, the wording of which varies according to the Proper of the day and which is sung before the *Gospel. The verse is preceded and followed by the word "Alleluia."

See ZUMARA.

HUPP(A)OYO (Syro-Jacobite)

The veil that is specifically used to cover the *chalice.

See SHUSHEPO; VEILS.

HUSSOYA (West Syrian)

A solemn liturgical prayer of propitiation recited during censing.

See CATASTROMA; PROEM.

HUTRO (Syro-Jacobite)

A pastoral staff.

See MURONITHA; SHABBUQTO.

HUTTOMO (Syrian)

Literally, "the seal." The final prayer recited at the close of the *Liturgy and the Office.

See EAST AND WEST SYRIAN CHURCH, DIVINE OFFICE OF; KHUTHAMA.

HYMNS OF LIGHT (Byzantine)

See EXAPOSTILARION.

HYPAKOE (Byzantine/Greek)

A *troparion that was introduced into certain *Canons after the third ode; originally it was sung by all the singers.

HYPAPANTE (Byzantine/Greek)

Literally, "the meeting." The feast of the Purification of the Virgin Mary, also known as Candlemas Day. *Copts refer to this feast as the Presentation, while *Armenians call it the Entry of Our Lord into the Temple.

HYPHASMA (Byzantine/Greek)

The four linen strips on each of which is embroidered or stitched the names and even the images of one of the Four Evangelists. These are attached to the four corners of the altar by the *bishop when he consecrates it. The attachment is made secure with *keromastikos.

HYPODIAKONOS (Byzantine/Greek)

The minor order of *subdeacon; in the Western Church this order was promoted to a major order in 1207 under Pope Innocent III.

See EEPODIACON; ORDERS, HOLY (Byzantine Tradition); SUBDEACON.

HYPOGONATION (Byzantine/Greek)

See EPIGONATION; VESTMENTS, TABLE OF.

HYPOGRAMMATEUS

The undersecretary of a patriarchal council.

HYPOMANIKA (Byzantine/Greek)

See CUFFS; EPIMANIKA.

HYPSOSIS (Byzantine/Greek)

The liturgical elevation of any sacred object; specifically it refers to the Holy Sacrament during the *Liturgy. On Holy Cross Day (September 14/27) the term is applied to the raising and veneration of the cross at the Morning Office before the *Liturgy commences.

See VOZDNOSHT SHENIE.

I

IBRUSFARIN (Coptic/Arabic)
(also called Iufafah)

A white or colored silk *veil or corporal used to cover the bread and wine at the start of the *Liturgy; it is about 18″ square with a cross embroidered in the middle and may sometimes have tiny bells attached either to the center or to the corners of the veil.

See PROSFARIN.

ICON (Byzantine)
(also spelled *Ikon)

A flat, painted representation on wood of Christ, the Virgin Mary, or the saints, the face and hands of which may be left uncovered while the rest of the painting may be overlaid with precious metals. These icons may be found in the *Eastern-rite churches placed upon the walls of the church and on the *iconostasis, or screen, which in *Byzantine churches separates the sanctuary from the body of the church, or *nave.

The painter of the icon is usually a *priest or a *monk, who must prepare himself very carefully through fasting, prayer, confession, and *Communion before beginning work. The icon is painted on a small panel of birch, pine, lime, or cypress, which is smoothed in the center with a plane, leaving the border to serve as a natural frame, thus separating the image from the outside world. Thin tissue is stuck over the wood to form a key, and a layer of gesso is applied to form the painting surface. The pigments used in the painting are often ground with holy water, and sometimes with saints' *relics. When the painting is finished, the icon is blessed.

The Iconoclast controversy, which lasted for a period of 120 years in the 8th and 9th centuries, was not simply a dispute over the art but reflected the theological controversies of the times, such as the question of Christ's humanity and the nature of Christian redemption. Iconoclasts demanded the destruction of any religious art that represented either human beings or God, and in this they had the support of the emperors Leo III and Leo V. Iconodules, or supporters of the icons, had official approval through the conclusions of the Council of Nicea II as well as the active support of St. John Damascene, who wrote and published a defense of the icons under the protection of the Muslim Arab ruler at a time when the Iconoclast Emperor Leo III was attacking the icons.

The icons of the Orthodox Christians are venerated most piously with burning tapers, *incense, and flowers. They represent the point at which heaven and earth meet and serve as a pious reminder of the lives and exploits of the saints of the Church.

See EIKON.

ICONOCLAST (Byzantine)

See ICON.

ICONOSTASIS (Byzantine)
(also spelled Eikonostasion; Eikonostasis; Ikonostasis)

Literally, "a picture stand." The screen separating the *nave of the church from the sanctuary in many *Eastern-rite churches. It is likely that the 4th-century *Syrian sanctuary veil was the forerunner of the 6th-century Constantinopolitan screen, behind which the consecration of the *bread and wine was secretly performed. This had the effect of emphasizing the spirit of awe and mystery that had appeared in the *Catecheses* of St. Cyril of Jerusalem (ca. 349–386) in his "Lectures to Candidates for *Baptism."

In early times, as Codinus describes

events, there were pedestals upon which were conventionally hung likenesses of Christ and other sacred paintings, while Brockhaus, in *Die Kunst in den Athos* (1891), contends that the progressive accumulation of paintings on the separating wall between the sanctuary and the body of the church led to the term "iconostasis" being applied to a permanent screen. The *Greeks applied the term more specifically to the barrier's decorated panels. In early *Russian churches a low type of grille served to separate the nave from the *altar, and this evolved into a perforated barrier, rather like a sculptured colonnade. It was then quite natural to place portable *icons at head level upon the pillars of this colonnade.

The early *Orthodox screen was made from either stone or marble, with the more familiar solid wooden screen being a Russian development in the late 14th and 15th centuries. It was with the easy availability of wood, especially around Novgorod, together with the great flowering of icons, that the barrier grew in height and the wooden screen replaced the stone barrier in Russia. However, the use of stone and marble continued as a feature of Byzantium and the East, and it was probably through the influences of travelers and artists from Russia that the use of a wooden iconostasis spread outside Russia.

In *Byzantine-rite churches, the iconostasis may have as many as four or five rows of icons, and there is a general convention concerning their arrangement on the screen. On the *royal doors may be placed a representation of the Annunciation, to highlight the significance of the Incarnation, and at its four angles there may be smaller medallions or plaques of the Four Evangelists. The side doors have either a painting of a *deacon holding the *orarion (deacon's stole) in his hand, or a representation of a holy angel. Between the royal doors and the south or deacon's door is the icon of Christ, while between the royal doors and the north door is the icon of the *Theotokos, or Mother of God. Further to the right is an icon of the patron of the church, while in the direction of the north door may be an icon of a saint who enjoys a special or local popularity.

The second row of icons is devoted to those representing the *twelve great feasts, with an icon of the Last Supper in the center. The third row has the icons of the apostles with Christ as *Pantokrator in the middle and the Theotokos on one side and St. John the Baptist on the other. This last row is often called *deesis, literally, "supplication," because of the expression of entreaty that is conventionally portrayed in the icons of the Virgin Mary and St. John the Baptist.

In the fourth row there may be the choir of prophets presided over by the Theotokos holding the infant Jesus in her arms. At the top of the iconostasis there may be an icon of the Crucifixion, again with the Theotokos on one side but with St. John the Disciple on the other.

It should be noted that in *Armenian and *Coptic-rite Churches a veil is used to conceal the sanctuary at certain moments in the *Liturgy.

IDIOMELON (Byzantine/Greek)
(also spelled *Automelon)

A *troparion with a special melody of its own, which does not follow the melody set out by the *irmos.

IDIORRHYTHMIC (Byzantine)

Literally, "on one's own." A general *monastic term referring to certain monasteries on Mount *Athos and elsewhere, which, unlike *cenobitic houses, allow considerable freedom with respect to personal property; each monk receives fuel, wine, food, and some money. The *monks meet in the church for various Offices and dine together at Christmas, Easter, and patronal feasts.

IDIORRHYTHMIC SKETE
(Byzantine)

A *monastic arrangement, comprised of a community of cottages (*kalyba) grouped around a *kyriakon (skete church). In each cottage there may be three *monks, one being the elder (*geron), who, together with the other elders, chooses annually the superior of the community. The monks attend the *Liturgy in the kyriakon on Sundays and feast days, with the Office otherwise being said in each kalybai.

IERATIKON (Byzantine/Greek)
(also spelled *Hieratikon)

A shorter book than the *Euchologion; it contains the priest's part at *Vespers, *Matins, and the *Liturgy.

See LITURGICAL BOOKS (Byzantine Tradition); SLUZHEBNIK.

IEREUS (Byzantine/Greek)

A *priest.

See BATOUSHKA; ORDERS, HOLY (Byzantine Tradition); PAPAS.

IESOUS CHRISTOS NIKA

This means "Jesus Christ conquers" and is usually abbreviated IC, XC, NI, KA.

IKON (Byzantine)
(also called *Eikon; Ikona [Slavonic]; Lymen [Coptic]; *Nkar; Surah [Coptic/Arabic])

See ICON.

IKOS (Byzantine/Greek)
(also spelled *Oikos)

A stanza inserted after the *kontakion between *Canticles 6 and 7 during the *Canon at *Orthros or Matins.

ILITON (Byzantine/Slavonic)
(also called *Eileton)

See ALTAR CLOTHS.

IMASKAAM (Ethiopian)

This marks the start of the *Ethiopian Church Year and is equivalent to September 11 or 12 in *Gregorian reckoning.

IMPOSITION OF HANDS, PRAYER OF

(also called Anbero Ed [Ethiopian]; Cha-djidj [Coptic]; S'yomoidho [Syro-Jacobite and Nestorian])

In the *Epistle* of James of Edessa to Thomas the Presbyter (708) mention is made of the three prayers of the faithful "with closed doors"; these are of the Peace, the Imposition of the Hand, and when the Table is Uncovered.

In the *Syrian rite the Prayer of Peace is at the start of the *Anaphora of St. James, and after the *peace is given it is followed by the Prayer of the Imposition of the Hand, or Prayer of Inclination, which is followed then by the Prayer of the Veil. These prayers are enjoined by the Council of Laodicea (370).

In the Syro-*Jacobite rite, the Prayer of the Imposition of the Hand, or of Inclination, (the S'yomoidho) is prefaced by the *deacon saying, "Let us bow down our head before the Lord," to which the *priest replies, "Before you, O Lord." The prayer that follows is said by the priest as he stretches out his right hand over the congregation, whose heads are inclined.

In the *Coptic rite the Cha-djidj is found at the start of the *dismissal at the close of the *Liturgy, but among the *Ethiopians, the Anbero Ed, or Prayer of Blessing (which dates from the ordinances of Zara Jacob 1434–1468), is likewise given at the close of the Liturgy.

The text of the prayer reads, "Lord eternal, light of life, unquenchable . . . . Let your hand be upon them that have bowed their heads before you. . . ."

INCENSE

(also called *Ladan; *Thymiama)

Incense is frequently used throughout the *Orthodox Church. It is based on the gum olibanum, which is mixed with other resinous additions. When placed on hot charcoal in a thurible, or *censer, a very rich perfumed fragrance is produced.

INDIAN CATHOLICS

See SYRO-MALABARESE;
SYRO-MALANKARESE.

INDITIA (Byzantine/Slavonic)
(also called *Endyte; *Ependytes; Ephaploma)

The second altar cloth.

See ALTAR CLOTHS.

INTERPRETERS
(also called Ermeneutai [Byzantine]; m'phashkone [Syrian])

A minor *order intermediate between *readers and exorcists whose job it was to translate *lessons and sermons for congregations of mixed linguistic backgrounds and for the benefit of those who may be unfamiliar with the language of the rite. This order seems to be almost exclusively Syrian, as it receives special prominence in the Syro-*Jacobite Liturgy, where there is a special remembrance of the interpreters in a *g'hantha recited by the *priest during the *Anaphora.

INTINCTION

A common method of administering Holy *Communion that involves dipping the consecrated *bread into the consecrated wine and giving the intincted particle to the communicant, usually by means of a *spoon. This custom has been prevalent since the 5th century.

See COMMUNION.

INVOCATION
(also called *Da'wah; Epiklesis [Coptic]; *Kothschoumn; *K'royotho; *Prizivanie)

The petition for the descent of the Holy Spirit to change and consecrate the Eucharistic oblation. It is generally introduced by a paragraph that takes up the *anamnesis of the institution. The position of the *Epiclesis varies according to the liturgical family to which a particular Anaphora belongs. The text of the *Byzantine Epiclesis illustrates the nature of the prayer, which is said in a low voice: "Send down your Holy Spirit upon us and upon these gifts set out here. And make this bread the Precious Body of your Christ, and that which is in this cup, the Precious Blood of your Christ, changing them by your Holy Spirit. Amen. Amen. Amen."

In common with the Catholic tradition, the *Orthodox believe that Christ is truly present in the consecrated *bread and wine, but unlike the Catholic tradition, the Orthodox do not regard the act of Consecration as being effected solely by the words of institution and take the view that the entire Eucharistic Prayer forms the entire act of Consecration and that if there is a single moment of Consecration, it comes about only at the end of the Epiclesis.

See ANAPHORA; EPICLESIS.

IRMOLOGION (Byzantine)
(also spelled Heirmologion)

A liturgical book that contains the text of words and music or of words alone of the irmoi (*irmos), or theme songs of the *Canons, as well as the service sung in honor of our Lord, the *Theotokos, and other major saints. This collection probably owes its origin to a time when, since the Canons were not sung in their entirety, most of the *troparia eothina were simply read, and the irmos, or model, of each ode was sung. Because the cantors knew the tune of the irmos very well, they did not need to have access to the great volumes that contained the Canon in its entirety.

See LITURGICAL BOOKS (Byzantine Tradition).

IRMOS (Byzantine/Greek)
(also spelled Eermos [Slavonic])

Literally, "chain." The opening stanza in each of the *canticles of the *Canon, which serves as a model for all of the remaining *troparia in the canticle. It acts as a link in a chain by coordinating the message of the biblical canticle that the Canon is expected to accompany and the theme of the feast or celebration that is the subject of the troparia that follow.

IS CHS (Byzantine/Greek)

These letters often appear on *icons and are an abbreviation of "Jesus Christ."

ISON

The dominant of the mode, which is maintained by one singer while the rest execute their elaborate melodies, or pneums.

ISOPOLNENIE (Byzantine/Slavonic)

See COMMIXTURE.

ISTOTCHNIKI (Byzantine/Slavonic)

Literally, "fountains." Red and white ribbons sewn horizontally around a *bishop's mantiya (mandyas), arising from four squares positioned where the mantle fastens. These four squares (skrizhali [Slavonic]; pomata [Greek]) represent the sources of the "fountains," or streams. These sources are sometimes thought of as being the Old and New Testament or the Four Evangelists. The mandyas of an *archimandrite is without these streams.

See MANDYAS; MANTIYA; POTAMOI.

ITALO-GREEK CATHOLIC BYZANTINE RITE
(also called Italo-Albanians)

Byzantine Catholics originally from southern Italy and Sicily who were in communion with Rome before the Great Schism of 1054. Their connection with Albania is the historical association with immigrants and refugees who came to Italy in the 15th and 16th centuries. Their *Liturgy is of the *Byzantine rite, in Greek with a highly individualistic chant. Members of this rite have retained the *Filioque phrase in the Creed and observe the *Gregorian Calendar. One peculiar custom is that Holy *Communion is received by men standing whereas women are required to kneel.

IWANGALLYUNA (East Syrian)

The *Gospel book.

See LITURGICAL BOOKS (East Syrian Tradition).

IZHITZA (Byzantine/Slavonic)
(also spelled Ljitza)

See SPOON.

IZOBRAZITELNAYA
(Byzantine/Slavonic)

The services that are sometimes recited after the *Hours on those days when the *Liturgy is not celebrated. They may also precede the celebration of the Liturgy, for example, on the eves of Christmas and Theophany. The Office consists of hymns, prayers, and readings from the Liturgy. The typika are always said when there is a Liturgy of the *Presanctified.

See TYPIKA.

J

JACOBITES

The name identifies the *Monophysite Church of Syria and derives from Jacob, or James, Baradaeus, a *monk of Phasilta near Nisibis, who was a disciple of the Monophysite *patriarch Severus of Antioch. Jacobites do not recognize the authority of the fourth general council held at Chalcedon in 451 and deny the two natures in Christ.

See DYOPHYSITES.

JAMAGARKUTIAN (Armenian)

Literally, "arrangement of the Hours." A book designed to collate all the requisite prayers necessary for the private recitation of the Office. The book is usually arranged in two main parts, (1) the Common of the Office, as in the *Jamarkik, and (2) the Proper of the Office. The book was published by the *Mechitarists of Venice in 1889.

See LITURGICAL BOOKS (Armenian Tradition).

JAMARKIK (Armenian)

The Book of *Hours, which contains the invariable part of the Office. This book is now incorporated into the single volume *Jamagarkutian, which also contains the variable, or Proper, of the Season. It is customary to distinguish between the ordinary Jamarkik and the Great Jamarkik, which contains many of the chants sung during the *Liturgy. The Great Jamarkik is also known as the Adiani Jamarkik, since some of the chants in this book are sung from the gradines, or adian, which are at the side of the altar.

See LITURGICAL BOOKS (Armenian Tradition).

JAPANESE ORTHODOX CHURCH (also called the Autonomous Orthodox Church of Japan)

The first Christian mission to Japan was that of St. Francis Xavier to Kagoshima in 1549, but the founda-

132

tions of an *Orthodox presence in Japan came much later, in 1871, when Fr. Nicholas Kasatkin (now saint), a chaplain from Smolensk, was appointed to the Russian consulate. Father Nicholas died in 1912, but not before he saw Orthodoxy firmly established in Japan, with most of the clergy being Japanese.

During the 1930s, with the growth of Japanese militarism, the government required subservience to the Shinto religion in an effort to unite the country, and the Japanese Orthodox Church found its constitution so altered that a decision was taken by the then *metropolitan, Sergius, to make the Church fully *autonomous. The constitution insisted that all clergy were to be Japanese, and the appointment of *bishops had to be confirmed by the government. Today, the Japanese Orthodox Church, which celebrates its Liturgy in Japanese, has three dioceses, Tokyo, Kyoto, and Sendai, serving a population of about 25,000. There is still a strong link between the Japanese Orthodox Church and the *Russian Orthodox Church, as evidenced by the frequent and cordial exchange visits.

JASCHOTHSGIRCH (Armenian)

A lectionary.

See DJACHOTZ.

JEBS-JOF (Coptic)
(also called Khudu)

The Prayer of Inclination, which is recited by the *priest at the end of *Communion. Following its recitation, the priest may come outside the sanctuary screen, and with his hand outstretched give the final blessing. The word "inclination" derives from the diaconal warning "Bow down your heads before the Lord," which precedes the prayer.

JEREUNDIR (Armenian)

A book of homilies or discourses, but unlike the *Yaysmavurk, which it resembles, it does not contain the lives of the saints.

JERUSALEM

One of the four original patriarchates of the early Church. It is now the See for four rival *patriarchs: *Greek Orthodox, *Armenian, *Mclkite, and *Latin.

JESUS PRAYER

Also known as the "Prayer of the Heart." This prayer probably had its origin in the early 5th century when such Greek writers as Diadochus of Photice and St. John Climacus of Mount Sinai (d. 649) recommended that the name of Jesus should be repeated constantly, as it was an efficacious form of prayer. This repetition became encapsulated in a short sentence, now known as the Jesus Prayer: "Lord Jesus Christ, Son of God, have mercy on me," to which the words "a sinner" are often added. This prayer is especially associated with the ascetical tradition of the *Hesychasts, also called *Palamites, a name derived from their leader, St. Gregory Palamas (ca. 1296–1359).

JHAMAMOUT (Armenian)

This is roughly equivalent to the western introit, which on Ordinary Sundays is the *Monogenes as found in the *Byzantine rite.

JIN-TSCHI (Coptic)

See TSCHI.

JUBBA (Syro-Jacobite)

A wide-sleeved, open gown worn by *Jacobite *monks.

See ABA.

JULIAN CALENDAR
(also called *Old Calendar; Old Style)

The calendar laid down by Julius Caesar in 45 B.C. was based on the understanding that the solar year lasted for exactly 365¼ days, but this was not quite correct. In fact, the year was shorter than the Julian calculation by eleven minutes and fourteen seconds, and therefore a correction was needed, which was made by Pope Gregory XIII in 1582, with the result that a thirteen-day difference now exists between the Julian and *Gregorian Calendars.

The Gregorian Calendar was not accepted by many *Eastern Orthodox Christians until the 19th century, and its acceptance now is by no means universal. This leads to misunderstandings and confusion; for example, both *Russian jurisdictions, the *Serbian Church, the *Byelorussians, the *Ukrainians, most of the *Athonite monasteries, and the *Old Calendarists use the Julian Calendar, and therefore the feast of Christmas, falls on the day that in the civil calendar is January 7. The observance of Easter and its dependent feasts, Ascension Day and Pentecost, are observed according to the strict rules of the first ecumenical Council of Nicea, so it rarely coincides with the Western reckoning.

K

KABA (Ethiopian)
(also called Kaba Lanka; Kabba)

The principal Eucharistic vestment, or chasuble, resembling an ample hooded cloak that reaches to the feet and is secured at the neck. It is highly ornamented and decorated around its upper part with gold and silver balls. Over the top of the kaba there may be a circular five-pointed vestment called a *lanka. Those clergy in lesser *orders than that of *deacon wear a shortened kaba.

See CAPPA; FELONION; PHELONION; VESTMENTS, TABLE OF.

KACHICHO (Syrian)

A *priest. It should be noted that the newly ordained priest does not *concelebrate the ordination *Liturgy with the ordaining *bishop.

See ORDERS, HOLY (Syrian Tradition).

KADILNITZA (Byzantine/Slavonic)
(also called Kadilo)

See CENSER; THYMATERION.

KADISAE (Syro-Malabarese)

The saints, or people of blessed memory.

KADISHAT ALOHO (Maronite)
(also spelled *Qadisat Alcho)

The *Trisagion, "You are Holy; you are Holy and Mighty; you are Holy and Immortal," is recited three times, to which the choir responds, "Have mercy on us." During the singing the offerings at the *Liturgy are censed with three circular swings of the *censer.

KAFILA (East Syrian/Nestorian)
(also called *Paina; *Pakila; *Ma'pra)

A hoodless cope, the chief Eucharistic *vestment in this rite. Unlike the *Byzantine *Phelonion, it is not joined in front.

See KAHNA.

KAHANA (Armenian)

A *priest who, following his ordination, is obliged to fast most rigorously (*karasoonk). If he is married, the priest's wife is called an *eretzkin, and she enjoys certain privileges in the parish. For a period of three days before the celebration of the *Liturgy, the priest must live away from home and is expected to be continent. Celibate clergy take precedence over married clergy regardless of what orders the married cleric has, but from outward appearances there is nothing to distinguish a celibate from a married priest.

In church the priest may wear a black woolen cloak (*philon). The liturgical *vestments include the *schoorchar (chasuble), below which is the *shapik (an alb of white linen), and the *porurar (stole). With these he wears cuffs (*bazpan) and a girdle (*goti). The bazpan is made from two strips of brocade that are attached to the forearm, like maniples were in the West. A distinctive vestment called the *varkas is placed around the shoulders and stands upright like a stiff collar. All priests wear a round *miter decorated with a small cross on its top.

See ERETZ; ORDERS, HOLY (Armenian Tradition).

KAHANAYAPET (Armenian)

The title of an *archpriest, the principal priest in a diocese.

KAHENAT (Ethiopian)

A general term used to describe the *Ethiopian clergy; the term is not applied to any specific type of cleric.

KAHNA (East Syrian/Nestorian) (also spelled Kahuna)

A *priest. While the candidate for the priesthood is chosen by the community, he must be accepted and ordained by the *bishop. Ideally, he should be married, and unlike the custom in other *Eastern Christian jurisdictions, the priest in the *Nestorian rite may marry after ordination.

In church, the Nestorian priest wears the following *vestments: the *kuthina, an alb-like garment like a *stoicharion, girded about with a *zunnara (belt), and a stole, which like the *Byzantine *epitrachelion hangs down in front and may simply be one piece of material with a hole for the head, or it may be two pieces of material joined together. Lastly, he wears the *kafila, the principal Eucharistic vestment, which resembles a hoodless cope but is not joined in front like the Byzantine *phelonion.

See KASHA; KASHISHA; ORDERS, HOLY (Nestorian Tradition).

KAHNUTHA (East Syrian/Nestorian)

The book containing the burial rites for the clergy.

See LITURGICAL BOOKS (Nestorian Tradition).

KALASIRIS (Byzantine/Greek)

A cassock.

See ANTERION; RASON.

KALB'THO (Syro-Jacobite)

See COMMUNION; SPOON; TARWODHO.

KALEMAVKION (Byzantine) (also spelled Kamelaukion)

See KALIMAVKION; KAMILAFKA.

KALIMAVKION (Ethiopian)

A white turban, part of the outdoor headwear of the *Ethiopian clergy.

KALLOSA (Syrian)

The outdoor headwear of the clergy. All *Syrian *Catholic clergy (and some *Jacobite clergy) wear the *Byzantine-style *kamilafka (kalimavkion). *Bishops may have a small gold button sewn on the crown of the kallosa.

KALOGEROS (Byzantine/Greek)

Literally, "good old man." A term often used to describe individual *monks, usually those of Mount *Athos.

KALUTO (West Syrian)

The vessels in which the Holy *Chrism may be kept; they are usually made from silver, but tin and even glass are sometimes used. These vessels, together with the baptismal oils, are kept in the north apse.

KALYBA (Byzantine/Greek)
(also called Kalybe; Kelya [Slavonic])

A *monastic dwelling that may be one of a group and is usually leased by three *monks, although some such dwellings may be isolated and inhabited only by one or two monks who live a semi-eremitical life.

See IDIORRHYTHMIC SKETE; KELLION.

KALYMMATA (Byzantine/Greek).

A general term describing the veils covering the Eucharistic vessels. These are (1) the proton kalymma, also known as the *diskokalymma, a veil that covers the *paten and is supported by the *asterisk so that it does not touch the *bread on the paten; (2) the *deuteron kalymma, or *chalice veil; and (3) the *aer, or *nephele, which is the outer veil that covers both the chalice and paten. According to St. Germanus of Constantinople, the chalice veil represents the shroud of Christ's body, the paten veil symbolizes the cloth used to cover the Holy Face, and the aer symbolizes the stone that sealed off the Holy Sepulcher. The term "kalymma" is used occasionally to describe the veil worn by a *monk or nun.

See POKROVY; VEILS.

KAMAN (Coptic/Arabic)

Liturgical cuffs worn now only by the Catholic clergy, the non-Catholics having long since discarded them except as part of the ordination rite.

See CUFFS; CUMM; CUMMAN; KAMAN; ORDERS, HOLY (Coptic Tradition); VESTMENTS, TABLE OF.

KAMILAFKA (Byzantine/Slavonic)

A headdress. The term is derived from two words meaning "camel" and "the nape of the neck." It may originally have been some sort of headwear made from camel skin that extended to cover the back of the neck.

It is usually black, but in *Russia and *Romania violet is used by secular clergy. The kamilafka is best described as a cylindrical hat, about 6″ or 7″ in height with either a flat brim at the top, as worn by the *Greek clergy, or brimless, as used by the Russian clergy. A *bishop wears it covered

with a *monastic veil (*epanokalemavchion), which is usually black but may
be white and which extends to below
the shoulder line. A bishop assisting at
the *Liturgy may retain his kamilafka
until the *Epiclesis, but it is usually removed at the Little and Great *Entrances, the *Gospel, and from the
Great Entrance until *Communion.
The term *skouphos, which is often
used in connection with clerical headwear, is only applied to the monastic
kamilafka, which is made from felt.
Greek clergy, both secular and religious, may wear the kalemavkion as
part of their outdoor dress. The veil
(epanokalemavchion [Greek]; *klobuk
[Slavonic]) is not worn by a secular
cleric, or *rasophore, unless he is an
*archimandrite, and it has no decora-
tions, unlike the veil of the *koukoulion. This privilege is probably due
to its monastic origin.

See KALEMAVKION.

KAMIS (Ethiopian and Syrian)

A vestment equivalent to a Western
*alb that extends to the ankles. It may
be made of white or colored silk.

See KUTHINO; VESTMENTS, TABLE OF.

KAMISION (Byzantine)

A long ungirdled tunic of white or colored linen or satin worn by minor
clerics and assistants in the *Byzantine
rite. This tunic has an embroidered
cross on the bottom, neck, and sleeves.

KANION (Byzantine/Greek)

A small glass or metal bottle that has
a sieve-like stopper at one end. It is
used for sprinkling liquids, for example, rosewater during the Holy
Week ceremonies when the *epitaphion is asperged at *Lauds on Holy
Saturday. The fingers of an almsgiver
may also be sprinkled by means of the
kanion. The vessel is sometimes mistakenly called a *bikion.

See HAGIASTER; RHODOSTAGMA.

KANON (Byzantine)

See CANON.

KANONARIA (Byzantine)

See TYPIKON.

KANUNO (Syrian)
(also spelled Kanuna [Nestorian])

In the *Nestorian rite, the equivalent
of the *ekphonesis, or audible conclusion to an inaudible prayer (*g'hantha). Alternatively, the word may be
used of a blessing, which is said in a
loud voice. In the Nestorian *Liturgy,
near the start of the *Anaphora, the
*thanksgiving starts with a kanuna:
''The grace of Our Lord Jesus Christ
and the love of God, the Father . . .,''
which serves to introduce the preface.

See DIPHTUCHO; GREAT INTERCESSION;
QANUNO.

KAPHILA (East Syrian/Nestorian)

The colored headwear worn by a
*Nestorian *patriarch instead of a
*birun.

KAPRANA (East Syrian/Nestorian)

See BREAD (East Syrian/Nestorian
Tradition).

KARASNORTH (Armenian)
(also spelled Karasnortk)

The Great Lent, lasting forty-eight days before Easter, in which abstinence is observed every day excluding Saturdays, Sundays, and the feast of the Annunciation. During the first two weekdays the faithful are excused from fasting.

See DZOUM.

KARASOONK (Armenian)

The obligatory forty-day fast that is most rigorously observed by a newly ordained priest.

See KAHANA.

KARIANJILI (Coptic/Arabic)

A candidate who is to receive this order, which is roughly equivalent to a *reader in the Western Church, is brought before the sanctuary unvested and with his head uncovered. He makes a low bow, after which the ordination ceremony proceeds with the *bishop standing in the doorway of the sanctuary and asking, "Do you affirm that this person is worthy of the order?" When this is affirmed the bishop takes a pair of scissors and cuts a large cross through the hair of the candidate and a smaller cross in each of the angles of the large cross. After prayers, the bishop turns to the west and holds the temples of the candidate during the recitation of another prayer. He then hands a book of the Holy Scriptures to the newly ordained reader.

See ANAGNOSTES; ORDERS, HOLY (Coptic Tradition); READER.

KARSHUNI (West Syrian)

Arabic written in *Syriac script, as used for the rubrics in the *Maronite rite, in which the *Liturgy is celebrated in both Arabic and Syriac. This language seems to be derived from the Syrians' hearing and talking Arabic but being unable to write it.

See SYRIAN RITE, WEST.

KARUYA (East Syrian/Nestorian)
(also spelled Koruya)

A reader.

See AMURA; ORDERS, HOLY (East Syrian Tradition); READER.

KARUZUTHA (East Syrian)

A *litany that is read on Sundays and some feasts, during the recitation of which the *incensed vessels are placed on the *beth gazza or *beth kudsha, a table that is recessed into the north wall of the sanctuary. At the noon Liturgies of the first, fourth, and seventh weeks of Lent, the karuzutha is recited outside on the *bema. Lenten observances, which commence on Quinquagesima, known as "The Entry of Lent," are maintained for seven weeks including Holy Week.

KAS (Syro-Jacobite)

The Latin-shaped *chalice used in this rite; both *paten and chalice have to be consecrated with *chrism by a *bishop before they may be used in the celebration of the *Liturgy.

See KOSO.

KASHA (East Syrian/Nestorian)

A *priest.

See KAHNA; KASHISHA; ORDERS, HOLY (East Syrian Tradition).

KASHISHA (East Syrian/Chaldean)

A *priest.

See ORDERS, HOLY (East Syrian Tradition).

KASHKUL (East Syrian/Chaldean)

A liturgical book that contains the selected prayers and *antiphons for the weekday celebrations.

See LITURGICAL BOOKS (East Syrian Tradition).

KASIS ZAYETRADA'E (Ethiopian)

The Prayer over the Cross Spoon, which is recited over a liturgical *spoon known as the cross spoon because its handle ends in a cross. The spoon is used during the *Liturgy to communicate the faithful from the *chalice. Part of the text of this prayer is "O Lord . . . place your Holy Hand upon this cross spoon for the administering of the Holy Body and Blood of your only Son." This prayer is recited at the start of the Liturgy before the *enarxis.

See ERFA MASKAL.

KASR (Coptic)

The tower of a *dair in the desert.

KASSA (East Syrian/Chaldean)

A traditionally Western-shaped *chalice used by the *Chaldeans.

KASSIS (Coptic)
(also spelled *Kess)

A *priest.

See ORDERS, HOLY (Coptic Tradition).

KASYO (West Syrian)

The Fraction of the consecrated *bread. During the 8th and 9th centuries there was a controversy about which prayer was to be said during the Fraction, and eventually the prayer upon which there was agreement was that ascribed by the *Jacobites to Denys Bar Salibi.

See FRACTION (West Syrian Tradition).

KATABASIS (Byzantine)
(also spelled *Katavasia)

Literally, "a descent." A *troparion that follows an ode of a *Canon on great feasts; this is the model (irmos) of the whole ode. It is called "the descent" because the two sides of the choir used to descend from their places to sing the troparion from the middle of the church.

See IRMOS.

KATAMEROS (Coptic)
(also spelled *Kotmarus)

A lectionary used in the *Coptic rite. The arrangement of the *lessons are attributed to Gabriel II ibn Tarik, *patriarch of Alexandria (1132–1145).

See LITURGICAL BOOKS (Coptic Tradition).

KATANYKTIKON (Byzantine)

A penitential *troparion seeking pardon for sins.

KATAPETASMA
(Byzantine/Greek and Coptic)

The furnishing that separates the apse from the body of the church. The term is used chiefly to describe the parokheth, or veil of the holy of holies, referred to in the Septuagint (Exod 26:31), but scripturally the term was used for the masak, or outer veil (cf. Exod 36:12). It is possible that this older term refers to those days when the separation of the apse of the church was effected by a curtain, which practice is retained by the *Armenians.

In the *Coptic tradition the katapetasma is the veil of the *holy doors, but the word is sometimes used to refer to the veil over the canopy of an *altar. Among the Copts the curtain, or curtains, may be decorated with a cross and are hung across any of the openings in the sanctuary screen. The cross on the curtains is kissed by the clergy after prostrating themselves on entering the church.

See DRYPHAKTA; HIJAB; SITARAH.

KATASARKION (Byzantine/Greek)

See ALTAR; ALTAR CLOTHS; STRATCHITZA.

KATATHESIS (Byzantine)

The act of depositing a *relic in a church.

KATAVASIA (Byzantine/Greek)

See KATABASIS.

KATECHOUMENOS (Coptic)

See CATECHUMEN.

KATEGORIARES

An official whose function it is to announce the forthcoming major feasts and festivals.

KATHEDRA (Byzantine/Slavonic)

A raised dais where the *bishop may vest and perform part of a pontifical service. It is placed in that part of the church that lies between the sanctuary platform and the porch.

KATHEGOUMENOS
(Byzantine/Greek)

The abbot of an *idiorrhythmic monastery. As nominal head he is appointed annually by a council of members who form the *synaxis and in whose hands the real government of the monastery lies.

KATHIEROSIS (Byzantine/Greek)

See ANTIMENSION; THRONOS.

KATHISMA (Byzantine/Greek)

Literally, "to be seated." This term has several meanings. It may be used to describe a *troparion, either read or sung at the end of each kathisma, or division of the Psalter, during *Matins and during which one may be seated, hence its literal meaning. The term may also be applied to the twenty divisions of the Psalter, each one of which is made up of three sections (*stasis). The *Divine Office of the *Byzantine Church is so designed that the entire Psalter may be recited in one week. The term "kathisma" is usually applied in the latter sense, while the former meaning is often designated the sessional hymn.

The term has also been applied to a small *Athonite monastic settlement made up of rented houses but independent of a ruling monastery; however, usually the *Syrian Jacobites have used the term to refer to the *catholic (b'rudiki), an intercession for all people recited during the *Anaphora.

See SEDALEN.

KATHOLIKON

The main church of a monastery in the *Byzantine rite.

See CATHOLICON.

KATHOLIKOS

The title used at one time for the vicar-general of a *patriarch but now the title of the *Nestorian, *Armenian, and *Georgian Church leaders, who are equivalent to a *patriarch.

See CATHOLICOS.

KATHSCHOUMN (Armenian)
(also spelled Kothschoumn)

The text used in this rite varies according to whether the congregation is Catholic or not, for the Catholics make it clear that they consider the Consecration of the *bread and wine to be effected by the words of institution. The text of the *Armenian Catholics refers to the Holy Spirit having already made "the consecrated bread to become truly the Body of Our Lord Jesus Christ"; whereas the *Gregorian, or non-Catholic, Armenian celebrant prays that by "blessing this bread, you will make it truly the Body of Our Lord and Savior, Jesus

Christ." In both rites, the *Epiclesis is accompanied by much signing of both bread and wine, separately and jointly. During the ceremony the *deacon censes the bread and wine continuously.

See EPICLESIS; INVOCATION.

KATHULIKA D'MADHN'HA
(Syrian)

See CATHOLICOS.

KATHULIKI (Syro-Jacobite)

The *Jacobites recite a lengthy prayer of general intercession for all the faithful, living and dead, during the *tukkoso dh'-q'soyo w'rushmo (*Fraction), and its recitation is followed by a *litany. The prayer's origin seems to be quite ancient.

See BRODIKI; CATHOLIC.

KATZION (Byzantine/Greek)

A perfume pan often used in processions and funeral rites that take place in a deceased person's home as well as during the *Liturgy of the Presanctified. The pan is fitted with a support, but it has no chains.

KATZTO (Syro-Jacobite)

A cover similar to the *Byzantine asterisk, whose function is to provide a support for the *veil over the *paten in order to prevent the veil from touching the consecrated *bread. It is made from two intersecting and collapsible loops of metal. Some patens in the Syro-*Jacobite rite have covers bearing crosses.

See ASTERISK.

KAWOK (Syro-Jacobite)

A black silk turban worn as part of the outdoor dress of *Jacobite secular *priests.

KDAM WADATHAR
(East Syrian/Nestorian)

Literally, "before and after." A liturgical book containing some extracts from the Psalter together with some prayers.

See LITURGICAL BOOKS (East Syrian Tradition).

KEDDASE (Ethiopian)

Literally, "hallowing" or "sanctification." A term that means either (1) the *Liturgy of this rite or (2) the *Anaphora used at the Liturgy. The term is used interchangeably throughout the literature of this rite. The Liturgy of the *Ethiopian rite is known variously as the "Sanctification," "Oblation," "Eucharist," or "Consecration." The Missal, which was published for the use of *Ethiopian Catholics, is known as the "Book of the Oblation," so "Keddase" could simply mean the book that contains the full text of the Liturgy.

See ANAPHORA; ENFORA; ZAMESHTIR.

KEDEST (Ethiopian)
(also called Holy of Holies; Kedesta Kedusan; Makedes)

The sanctuary, which is the innermost center of *Ethiopian churches. It is surrounded by the *kene mahelet, used by the choir. Entry to the kedest is forbidden to the laity, and it should be noted that there is an ancient tradition that continence for the preceding twenty-four hours is required of those entering the sanctuary.

KEDSAT (Ethiopian)

See HOLY THING.

KEDUSH (East Syrian/Chaldean)
(also called Kdush Kudshe; *Qanke)

Literally, "holy of holies." The sanctuary, which in both *Nestorian and *Chaldean churches is separated from the *nave by being elevated at the east end of the church and cut off from the nave by a brick wall or arch over which it is customary to suspend a curtain. This screen usually has three plain crosses at its top. On either side of the sanctuary are partitions leading to the treasury, which is to the north, and the baptistery, which lies to the south. It is in the treasury that the *vestments are kept, while the baptistery houses the baptismal font and is the place where the *bread for the *altar is prepared.

KELLION (Byzantine/Greek)

This may be a single dwelling with a chapel (*naidrion) and may be inhabited by three to six *monks, the most senior of whom leases the kellion from the monastery. It is usual to have three lay brothers attached to a kellion except in Russia where lay brothers are not permitted. Sometimes the term is applied to a *priest's house if monastic clergy serve the parish. A *skete is made up of several kellia grouped around a shared church.

See KALYBA; MONASTICISM, HABITS OF (Byzantine Tradition).

KENE MAHELET (Ethiopian)

The passage that separates the two inner circular divisions of an *Ethiopian-rite church. This passage is reserved for the use of the choir, the innermost circle being the sanctuary (*kedest).

KENFO (Syro-Jacobite)

Side-altars, which may be used for holding the accessories required in any liturgical ceremony.

KERION (Byzantine/Greek)

A candlestick; specifically, one designed to hold several candles.

KEROMASTIKOS (Byzantine/Greek)

The paste used as a cement to secure the table of an *altar to its support at the time of its consecration. The paste is a mixture of powdered marble chips, dust from *relics, wax, and putty.

See TRAPEZA.

KEROPEGIA (Byzantine/Greek)

A candlestick that holds several candles.

See KERION.

KEROSTATES (Byzantine/Greek)

Typically a large and usually ornate candlestick found on either side of the *royal doors of an *iconostasis and standing in front of the *icons of Christ and of the *Theotokos. The single candle that is supported in the kerostates is known as the *lampas.

KERYANA (East Syrian/Nestorian)
(also spelled Keryono)

The books of the Old Testament and the Acts of the Apostles; this is one of the books that provides the *lessons to be read during the *Liturgy.

See LITURGICAL BOOKS (East Syrian Tradition); QARYANA; QIRYANA.

KERYTHO (Syro-Jacobite)
(also spelled *K'royotho)

The Epiclesis, which in the Syro-*Jacobite rite is said aloud. During its recitation the *priest waves or flutters his right hand three times over the *bread and makes a deep bow, which according to St. Ephrem (ca. 306–373) should involve the bending of both knees, but Narsai of Nisibis (late 5th century) forbade the bending of the knees during the *Liturgy. The priest continues the prayer and flutters or waves his right hand three times over the *chalice. The *deacon, meanwhile, stands to the right of the *altar and censes the consecrated bread and wine while *fans are shaken and bells may be rung.

See DA'WAH; EPICLESIS.

KESELA (Ethiopian)

A collar-like garment that some *Ethiopian *priests place on their heads. The kesela should not be confused with the *hebanie.

KESHOTZ (Armenian)
(also spelled *Chschoths)

The liturgical *fans to which little bells are attached. These fans are shaken at solemn moments during the *Liturgy.

KESS (Coptic)
(also spelled *Kassis)

A *priest.

See ORDERS, HOLY (Coptic Tradition).

KETHONS (Syro-Jacobite)

The cloth used by *Jacobites always, and Catholics sometimes, to cover the *altar stone (*tablith). This cloth, which is usually heavily embroidered, is folded in four, and without it the *Liturgy should not be celebrated. *Syrian Catholics frequently substitute three cloths for the kethons and celebrate their Liturgy on these.

See ANDIMISI; MANDIL.

KHAGHORDOUTHIUN (Armenian)

Holy *Communion, which is received as part of the *Liturgy. Among non-Catholic *Armenians where the frequent reception of Communion is unusual, it is received by intinction with the words "The Body and Blood of Our Lord and Savior Jesus Christ be to you for salvation and for a guide to eternal life." For *Armenian Catholics Communion is administered with the standard Catholic formula of administration.

Very often a *baptism occurs during a Liturgy, in which case the child may receive Communion immediately. This is done by the *priest dipping his finger into the *chalice and putting it into the child's mouth as he says, "The fullness of the Holy Spirit"; but if baptism has been administered outside the Liturgy, the priest takes the *reserved Sacrament, and with it he makes the *sign of the cross on the lips of the child, saying the same words as before. This is known as "Communion of the lips."

See COMMUNION (Armenian Tradition).

KHARRNOUMN (Armenian)

See COMMIXTURE; ENOSIS.

KHASVO (Syrian/Maronite)

Literally, "venerable." A *bishop.

See EPISQUPO.

KHAVATAMCH (Armenian)

The Creed, which is said to date from the 6th century, includes the anathemas of Nicea, which are found in the Creed of St. Gregory of Tours (538–593) and are uniquely recited in this rite. The Creed is recited immediately following the reading of the *Gospel, and during its recitation the *altar, clergy, and congregation are censed. The recital is performed by the *deacon while holding the Gospel book and standing at the altar with the *priest. At the Creed's conclusion the deacon presents the book to be kissed by the priest.

See CREED.

KHAZRANION (Turkish)

A straight ebony walking stick used by some clergy.

KHERNIBOXESTON
(Byzantine/Greek)

The basin and bowl that are offered to a *bishop by a *subdeacon so that he may wash his hands.

KHITONISKOS (Byzantine/Greek)

An ancient name for a *vestment now called the *stikharion; this term was used by St. John Chrysostom.

KHONEUTERION
(Byzantine/Greek)
(also called Khoneion, khoni)

The drain (*piscina) into which water left from baptism, the ablutions, and ashes from destroyed *icons, *vestments, and *liturgical books may be poured. It is usually positioned beneath the *altar, but it may instead be close by and thus can serve as a shelf upon which the *angelic habit is laid overnight when the profession of a *megaloschemos or *skhimnik is to take place the next day.

See THALASSA.

KHORAN (Armenian)

In the *Armenian rite the *altar is oblong and Western in style, set into a screen positioned across the apse with a *door on either side leading into the space behind, which may serve as a *sacristy. There are gradines set into the back of the altar.

See ALTAR; AVANDATOUN.

KHORUG (Byzantine/Slavonic)

A holy banner, or picture, mounted on a staff and usually to be found in each part of the choir.

KHUBZ MOUBARAK (Arabic)

Literally, "blessed bread."

See BURC'THO; EULOGIA.

KHUDOTO (Syrian/Maronite)

The feast of the Dedication of the Church. This feast is celebrated on one of the Sundays preceding the Sundays of the Annunciation.

KHUTHAMA (Syro-Jacobite)
(also spelled Huttomo)

A liturgical prayer.

See EAST SYRIAN CHURCH; DIVINE OFFICE OF.

KHVALITNYI (Byzantine/Slavonic)

See AINOI; LAUDS.

KIBORION (Byzantine)

A dome or canopy supported on four pillars, which forms a roof over the *altar. Between the columns of this dome curtains were once hung and closed at various moments during the *Liturgy, but this practice has fallen into disuse among *Eastern Christians except in the *Armenian rite. The curtains were known as *tetravela.

KIDAN (Ethiopian)

The "Testament," which is read in the morning and evening; it may be found in the introductory section of the Catholic *Ethiopian Missal, the *Sherata Keddase.

KIDARIS (Coptic)

See TAILASAN; VESTMENTS, TABLE OF.

KIMESIS (Byzantine/Greek)

The Dormition, or Falling Asleep, of the *Theotokos, or Mother of God. The feast is celebrated August 15.

KINDAK (Byzantine/Arabic)

See KONTAKION.

KIRIOPASHKA (Byzantine/Slavonic)

The feast of the Annunciation, which is known as the Kiriopashka if its celebration should coincide with Easter Day.

KISARKAVAG (Armenian)

A *subdeacon, who is presented with

a broom by the *bishop as part of the ordination ceremony.

See ORDERS, HOLY (Armenian Tradition).

KISM (Coptic/Arabic)
(also spelled Kismah)

See FOSH; FRACTION (Coptic Tradition).

KISS OF PEACE

See PEACE, KISS OF.

KITAB ASH-SHAMAMISAH
(Coptic/Arabic)
(also called *Diakonikon)

See LITURGICAL BOOKS (Coptic Tradition).

KITAB IL PASCA (Coptic)

The Psalter, which is used in the *Coptic rite during the Paschal Offices.

KLAM (Coptic)

A miter. Among the *Copts the miter is worn by both *bishops and *patriarchs. According to tradition, the use of the miter by the patriarch of Alexandria dates from St. Cyril's presidency at the Council of Ephesus in 431. Both the *Melchites and the so-called dissident branches of the Church retained the miter, suggesting that the headdress was distinctive and in vogue for the patriarch of Alexandria as early as the first half of the 5th century, prior to the separations and schisms that followed soon after.

There is no set form for the use of a miter among Coptic bishops. The term "taj" is sometimes used, but this is more like a crown; there does not seem to be any difference between the miter worn by a bishop and that worn by a patriarch except in usage. For example, a bishop may not wear his miter or hold his pastoral staff outside his own diocese or when the patriarch is in the bishop's diocese. When this happens the bishop may wear on his head a colored silk *amice decorated with texts, which is also the custom on Good Friday.

The Melchites call the patriarchal miter a tiara, while the Episcopal miter is simply a mitra, the difference being that the tiara is tall and conical whereas the mitra is low and rather globular. The tiara may be made from a ring of silver or gold, from which four bands rise to meet at the apex of the cone, upon which stands a jeweled cross, the whole enclosing a crimson velvet covering. The four bands support porcelain medallions painted with sacred figures and set with gems. In contrast, the mitra may be made of silver gilt or velvet embroidered with gold and jewels.

See METRA; MITER; TAJ; TSCHREPI; VESTMENTS, TABLE OF.

KLEPALA (Byzantine/Slavonic)

See BELA; SEMANTRON.

KLIROS (Byzantine/Greek)

Those parts of the *amvon (*ambo), reserved for the use of the choir.

See SOLEAS.

KLITOS (Byzantine/Greek)
(also called *Gynaeceum)

A term referring to one of the side aisles in a church.

KLOB(O)UK (Byzantine/Slavonic)

The veil that is fitted and fastened to the *koukoulion, which is a thimble-shaped cap that serves as a monastic cowl. On the eighth day after profession the *megaloschemos or *skhimnik lays aside the koukoulion during a brief service and takes up the skouphos and veil for ordinary use. In church, however, the koukoulion and its veil may still be worn. The epanokalemavchion, or klob(o)uk, may be used to designate the veil for both the koukoulion and skouphos alike.

See DEGREES OF MONASTICISM, HABITS OF; HABITS, COMPARATIVE TABLE OF; EPANOKALEMAVCHION; SKOUPHOS.

KNOQ (Armenian)

Literally, "seal." The *sign of the cross, made on any person or object.

KOB'E (Ethiopian)

The hood worn as part of the outdoor dress of an *Ethiopian cleric.

KOBORO (Ethiopian)

The drums used as an accompaniment to the enharmonic *Ethiopian chant.

See COE'NATA.

KODI (Armenian)

A *girdle worn as a regular vestment by a *priest and used to contain the *stole.

See VESTMENTS, TABLE OF.

KODON (Byzantine/Greek)

A cup-shaped bell used at Mount *Athos, where it is placed in the sanctuary. It may be struck three times with a hammer: (1) when the end of the *prothesis approaches in order to give warning that the *Liturgy proper is about to start; (2) before the end of the *Great Entrance; and (3) during the *Liturgy of the Presanctified.

KODONASTASION (Byzantine)

See CAMPANARION.

KOGH (Armenian)

This refers to either (1) the silk *veil that is placed over the prepared *chalice and veil during the offertory ceremonies; the offertory takes place behind closed curtains, and while the veil is being placed over the chalice and *paten, Psalm 92 (LXX), "The Lord reigns and is robed with beauty," is recited and the oblation is censed three times; or (2) the great veil, which is decorated with a golden fringe and which is used to cover the head of the *catholicos during his consecration. On subsequent occasions the kogh may be carried before him on great festivals.

KOHNO (Maronite)

A *priest.

See KUMRO; QASHISHO.

KOIMESIS (Byzantine/Greek)

Literally, "the falling asleep." The Dormition, or Falling Asleep, of the *Theotokos, or Mother of God. This feast is observed August 15.

See KIMESIS; USPLENIE.

KOINONIA (Byzantine/Greek)

See ANAPHORA; COMMUNION; LITURGY.

KOINONIKON (Byzantine/Greek)

A *troparion resembling a Western *Communion anthem and sung during the *priest's and *deacon's Communion. If there is a concurrence of feasts, two of these may be sung.

See PRICHASTEN.

KOKLIARION (Coptic)
(also called *Myster; *Mystheri)

The Communion *spoon. According to Vansleb, it is handed to a candidate being ordained to the diaconate and is held by him during the ordination *Liturgy. The spoon is used ordinarily to administer Holy Communion when the wine and the *bread are administered together. The bowl of the spoon is hemispherical, the handle being a straight strip of metal usually with a dedicatory inscription written or engraved in Arabic characters.

See COMMUNION (Coptic Tradition).

KOLIVA (Byzantine/Slavonic)

See KOLYVA.

KOLYMBETHRA (Byzantine/Greek)

See BAPTISTERION.

KOLYVA (Byzantine/Slavonic)
(also spelled *Koliva; Kolyba [Greek]; *Kutiya)

Blessed *bread, which is a sacramental, prepared and eaten in honor of some saint or in memory of the dead. It is customarily a cake made from wheat grains or from rice and is covered with sugar. It is blessed during a memorial service for the dead, or panikhidi.

KOMBOLOGION (Byzantine/Greek)

A string of beads that should not be confused with the *komboschoinion, although the terms are often used synonymously.

See CHOTKI.

KOMBOSCHOINION
(Byzantine/Greek)
(also spelled Komvoschinion)

Literally, "knotted cord." The knotted cord that is specifically handed to a *monk or nun as part of the ceremony of the reception of the little or great habit. As part of the clothing with the little habit ceremony, the superior takes the vervitza, or lestovka, as it is sometimes called, and holds it in his left hand, saying, "Take brother N., the sword of the Spirit, which is the Word of God, for continued prayers to Jesus: for you must always have the name of the Lord Jesus in mind, in heart and on your lips, saying, Lord Jesus Christ, Son of God, have mercy on me a sinner. . . ." The cord is then blessed and given to the candidate. The komboschoinion used at Mount *Athos has a hundred knots; these are divided into four equal parts by four larger knots or beads, with three additional knots forming a cruciform terminal tassel.

The *megaloschemos is expected to make 12 x 100 great metanies (*metany) and 300 similar ones in the evening, accompanied by prayers. The komboschoinion is otherwise used to count 10 great metanies (to the ground), 30 little metanies (to the hips), and 60 recitations of the *Jesus Prayer. The number of knots (100 + 3) was adopted so as to correspond to the number of psalms and little doxologies that are recited at the Canonical *Hours. The Slavonic knotted cord (*vervitza) is made up of 103 knots divided by 4 larger knots or beads: the first knot is followed by 17 smaller knots, the second knot is followed by 33 smaller knots, the third knot by 40 smaller knots, and the fourth knot by 12 smaller knots, with an additional small knot at the end.

If a monk cannot say the psalms at certain Offices, he makes 700 metanies. If he missed *Vespers, he can substitute 500 metanies. Instead of *Apodeipnon (*Compline), he can make 200 metanies, and for a missed *Orthros he can make 500 metanies.

See VERVITZA.

KONTAKION (Byzantine/Greek)
(also called Kondak [Slavonic])

A collect hymn which recalls the subject of the day's feast and is sung after the sixth ode of the *Canon at the Little Hours and during the *Liturgy.

KORBAN (Coptic/Ethiopian)
(also called *H'bst)

Literally, "oblation." The word may mean either the bread used in the *Liturgy or the Liturgy itself.

See BREAD (Coptic Tradition); KURBAN; PROSPHORA.

KORHRTADEDR (Armenian)

The veil upon which, occasionally, a *bishop kneels during a *Liturgy.

See BADARAKAMADUITZ.

KORUYO (West Syrian)

See ORDERS, HOLY (West Syrian Tradition); READER.

KOSO (West Syrian)

See KAS.

KOTHINA (East Syrian)

See KOTINA.

KOTHSCHOUMN (Armenian)

See EPICLESIS; INVOCATION.

KOTINA (East Syrian)
(also spelled *Kuthina)

The *alb-like garment worn by clerics of this rite. It is the principal *vestment apart from the *zunnara (*girdle) worn by a *reader.

KOTMARUS (Coptic/Arabic)

See KATAMEROS; LITURGICAL BOOKS (Coptic Tradition).

KOUBOUKLION (Byzantine)

The monument in the Church of the Resurrection in Jerusalem, which covers the tomb of Christ in that church. The term also refers to a monument used in *Byzantine-rite churches on Good Friday (Great Friday) and upon which the *epitaphion is placed, censed three times, and venerated by all those present.

KOUCHEG (Byzantine/Slavonic)

See KOVTCHEG.

KOUKLION (Coptic)

See FELONION; VESTMENTS, TABLE OF.

KOUKOULION (Byzantine/Greek)
(also called Cowl; Koukoul [Slavonic])

A cap, to which is secured a black veil (*epanokalemavchion [Greek]; *klobuk

[Slavonic]). When a *megaloschemos or *skhimnik has made his profession, the koukoulion is worn for the eight days following that profession, after which it is removed and the ordinary *kalemavkion (*kamila(v)fka [Slavonic]; *skouphos [Greek]) with veil is worn. The skouphos and veil in the profession ceremony are called the *perikephalais (Greek) or *shlem (Slavonic), literally, "helmet," which is explained by the prayer that accompanies the presentation of the koukoulion in "the Tradition of the Great Habit," for the *priest says, "Our brother, N., is clothed with the cowl of innocency, for a helmet of the hope of salvation, in the name of the Father. . . ." An almost identical prayer is said when the little habit is being presented.

See DEGREES OF MONASTICISM, HABITS OF.

KOUKOULLA (Byzantine)

A baptismal veil.

See BAPTISM.

KOURA (Byzantine/Greek)
(also called Koura Klerike [Greek])

See TONSURE.

KOVSH (Byzantine/Slavonic)

The ladle in which the tepid wine and water, together with portions of *bread, are presented to the communicants after they have received Holy *Communion.

KOVTCHEG (Byzantine/Slavonic)
(also spelled Koucheg)

Literally, "the ark." The equivalent of

the Western tabernacle, in which the reserved Sacrament is placed.

See ARTOPHORION; RESERVED SACRAMENT (Byzantine Tradition).

KRESTNAYA ATIETS
(Byzantine/Slavonic)

A female *sponsor.

See BAPTISM (Byzantine Tradition); SPONSOR.

KRESTOBOGORODITCHEN
(Byzantine/Slavonic)

See STAVROTHEOTOKION.

KRESTONOSETS
(Byzantine/Slavonic)

See DEGREES OF MONASTICISM, HABITS OF.

KRETSHENIA (Byzantine/Slavonic)
(also spelled Krestshenie)

See BAPTISM (Byzantine Tradition).

KROPELO (Byzantine/Slavonic)

See HAGIASTER.

K'ROYOTHO (West Syrian)

The *Epiclesis.

See KERYTHO.

KSHOTZ (Armenian)

Liturgical fans to which little bells are attached. When shaken, the bells provide an accompaniment to the singing.

See FANS; RIPIDIA.

KTHAWA DAGDHAM WADHWATHAR
(East Syrian/Chaldean)

Literally, "Book of Before and After."

See EAST SYRIAN CHURCH, DIVINE OFFICE OF.

KTHOBO DKHOUROBO (Syrian)

The *Syrian Missal, also known as the Book of the Sacrifice, in which it is usual to find the text of seven *Anaphoras. In the Catholic edition of the Missal published in Rome in 1843, the audible prayers are written in *Syriac and *Karshuni while the rubrics are only in Karshuni.

See ANNAPHURA; LITURGICAL BOOKS (West Syrian Tradition).

KTZORD (Armenian)

An antiphonal refrain.

See ANTIPHON; PHOKH.

KUBBAH (Coptic/Arabic)

The dome used by non-Catholic *Copts to place on the *paten to keep the *veils from touching the *bread. It is usually made from two half loops of silver that intersect and are riveted together.

See ASTERISK.

KUBHTHA (East Syrian/Nestorian)

See PROTHESIS.

KUDDAS (Arabic)

See ANAPHORA.

KUDDASHA (East Syrian/Nestorian)
(also spelled Kudasha)

In usage this term is similar to the *Ethiopian use of the word *Keddase." The *Nestorians use three Anaphoras: the Liturgy of the Holy Apostles Adai and Mari; the Liturgy of Theodore of Mopsuestia, or the Second Hallowing; and the Liturgy of Mar Nestorius, or the Third Hallowing. The most ancient of these Anaphoras is probably that of the Holy Apostles. Narsai, who is described as a Nestorian Doctor of the Persian school at Edessa (d. 502), shows in his *Homily on the Mysteries* that this Anaphora dates from at least the end of the 5th century. Doubtlessly it was revised by the *patriarch Jesu Yab III of Adiabene (650–661), and this revision was confirmed by Abdulla Ibn Attayeb in the 11th century. According to Duchesne (1904) and *Liturgia* (Paris, 1930), the *Chaldeans use only one Liturgy, that of the Holy Apostles, but in the official Catholic Chaldean Missal (1901) there is provision for three Anaphoras.

The Liturgy of the Holy Apostles is used from Holy Saturday until Advent on saints' days, requiems, and so-called Ordinary occasions, but the text lacks the words of institution. When the Anglicans printed the Liturgy at Urmi (1890), the words of institution, using 1 Corinthians 11:23-25, were uneasily inserted. The archbishop of Canterbury's Mission found that though the words were missing from the text, they were always pronounced. Why the words were missing is unclear; one suggestion is that the Church Fathers feared that the text would be profaned, but this fear was groundless. Dom Botte suggested that this Anaphora had the words of institution and that the form resembled that found in the Anaphora of Theodore. Duchesne confirmed that the words were certainly in the text, since they served as the basis of the corrections undertaken at the Synod of Diamper in 1599.

The Liturgy of Mar Theodore of Mopsuestia is often called that of Theodore the Interpreter (ca. 350–428) because of his *Commentaries,* which were used by the Persian school as an exegesis of Holy Scripture. Both Anglicans and Catholics refer to this Anaphora as the Second Hallowing, and it is used from Advent Until Palm Sunday.

The Liturgy of Mar Nestorius, or the Third Hallowing, is only used five times a year: Epiphany, the feast of St. John the Baptist and of the Greek Doctors, the Wednesday of the Supplication of *Nineveh, and Holy Thursday.

See ANAPHORA; LITURGY (East Syrian Tradition).

KUDRA (East Syrian)

See HUDRA; LITURGICAL BOOKS (East Syrian Tradition).

KUDSHE (Syro-Jacobite)

The prayer that is recited at the *elevation of the *paten and *chalice during the *Liturgy.

See ZUYOHO.

KUDSHE IKADDISHE
(Syro-Jacobite)

The formula for the administration of Holy *Communion to the clergy is given as "The propitiatory Coal of the Body and Blood of Christ, our God, is given to N. for the pardon of his offenses and the remission of his sins; his prayers be with us. Amen."

See COMMUNION.

KULAGI (Coptic)

A liturgical book used as a missal.

See EUCHOLOGION; HULAKI; LITURGICAL BOOKS (Coptic Tradition).

KULICH (Byzantine/Slavonic)

The rich, spicy cake traditionally baked for Easter.

KUMMUS (Coptic)
(also spelled Qummus)

While the term "hegumenos" has a distinctly *monastic flavor, "kummus" can simply mean the superior of a cathedral. Otherwise, kummus refers to the senior *priest in charge of a church to which other clergy may be attached or to the abbot in charge of a monastery.

When a priest is to be ordained a kummus, he is vested in his priestly *vestments and is led between two archpriests, brought in procession around the church and finally to the *door of the sanctuary, in front of which the *bishop stands. All bow before the *altar, and the bishop says the Prayer of *Incense as he lays his hands on the priest's head and signs his head three times with the *sign of the cross. The priest then kisses the altar and the *Liturgy is celebrated as usual.

See ARCHPRIEST; HEGUMENOS.

KUMRO (Maronite)

A *priest.

See KOHNO; QASHISHO.

KURBAN (Coptic/Arabic)
(also spelled Korban)

Literally, "oblation."

See BREAD (Coptic Tradition); H'BST;
PROSPHORA.

KURBONO (Syrian)

The offering. In the sense of oblation
it may mean either the sacrifice of the
Eucharist or the actual offering, as is
suggested in the following liturgical
words, ". . . on whose behalf this
Kurbono is offered."

KUREPISQUPO (Maronite)

See CHOREPISCOPUS.

KUROBHO (Syro-Jacobite)

James of Edessa seems to use this term
interchangeably with *kurbono when
he writes, "As touching this . . .
reasonable and unbloody sacrifice . . .
the kuobho or kurbono. . . ."

See ANAFORA; ANAPHORA; ANNAPHURA.

KURRILISON (Maronite)

The *Kyrie eleison, which in the
*Maronite rite is said three times in the
*Liturgy of the *Catechumens, which
it serves to introduce. After the recitation of the Kyrie, the *Trisagion is
sung.

KUSHAPA (East Syrian/Nestorian)

See CUSHAPA.

KUTHINA (East Syrian)

See SUDRA.

KUTHINO (West Syrian)

Either the black woolen robe of a
*Jacobite *monk or, more usually, the
*alb worn by the clergy. This vestment
is long and ample, made from cotton,
linen, or silk and with no strict color
convention. It is usually embroidered
with many crosses.

See CITUNAH; KAMIS; KOTINA;
VESTMENTS, TABLE OF.

KUTIYA (Byzantine/Slavonic)

A dish of boiled wheat mixed with
honey and sometimes raisins, placed
on a small table in the church during
a requiem (panikhidi). The wheat
grains are boiled until tender and prepared in such a way that the grains,
softened by careful working, remain
separate. When sufficiently sweetened,
the outside is sprinkled with sesame
seeds and lightly toasted flour. The letters IC, XC, NI, KA (Jesus Christ conquers) may be traced on the surface.
Around the edge of the dish are arranged sugared almonds. It is eaten
communally on the day of burial,
usually at the graveside.

Traditionally, the dish should be
prepared and eaten, again communally, at intervals of nine and forty
days following the death, and again on
the anniversary of the deceased. It
serves to remind the congregation of
the resurrection of the dead, since the
wheat typifies the burial of the body
in order that it may arise, while the
honey symbolizes the sweetness of the
joy of the future life.

See KOLIVA.

KUTMARUS (Coptic/Arabic)

A liturgical lectionary containing the

*lessons of the day, arranged on a daily basis. It contains the lessons from the apostle (the Epistle of St. Paul), the *Catholicon, or Catholic Epistle, and the Praxis (the Acts of the Apostles), as well as some psalms and *Gospel readings for all of the *Liturgies and Offices of the Church Year.

See KATAMEROS; LITURGICAL BOOKS (Coptic Tradition).

KYRIAKON (Byzantine/Greek)

Literally, "The Lord's House." A term to describe a church building.

See CENOBITIC SKETE.

KYRIE ELEISON (Greek)

Literally, "Lord have mercy." This short repeated prayer is sometimes known as the Lesser *Litany, and the words are to be found in the *Apostolic Constitutions*, Book 8 (ca. 375), which contains a *Liturgy of the *Antiochene type attributed to St. Clement of Rome, commonly referred to as the Clementine Liturgy, and which appears to use the *Anaphora of the *Apostolic Tradition* of Hippolytus (ca. 215). The Kyrie Eleison in the Clementine Liturgy serves as the people's response to the diaconal petitions.

L

LABIS (Byzantine/Greek)

The Communion *spoon, used by the *priest to distribute Holy Communion under both species to the faithful. The spoon is made of precious metal and was probably introduced in the 8th century, since the Council of Trullo (691) had reaffirmed the practice of receiving Communion in the right hand, placed crosswise over the left, the *chalice from which the consecrated wine was drunk being presented to the communicant by the priest or *deacon. The spoon was probably introduced into Syria, but the old way of receiving Communion persisted well into the 9th and even 10th centuries.

See COMMUNION; IZHITZA.

LACHUMARA
(East Syrian/Nestorian)
(also spelled Lakhumara)

A prayer that receives its name from the opening words, "To you, O Lord, we give thanks and glorify Our Lord Jesus Christ, for you are the quickener of our bodies and the savior of our souls." This prayer corresponds to the *Byzantine *Monogenes attributed to St. Simon Bar Sabba'e (323–341) and is recited by everybody at the start of the *East Syrian *Liturgy of the *Catechumens.

LADAN (Byzantine/Slavonic)

See INCENSE.

LAFAFAH (Coptic/Arabic)

The veil or large corporal that is spread over the *bread and wine at the start of the *Liturgy. It may be made from white or colored silk and is about 18" square with an embroidered cross at its center. Tiny bells may be attached at the corners of the veil. In desert churches another veil is used to wave over the bread and wine.

See IBRUSFARIN; PROSFARIN; VEILS.

LAHMA DKUDASHA
(East Syrian/Nestorian)

Literally, "bread of holiness." The consecrated *bread, or Blessed Sacrament.

LAHN (Coptic/Arabic)
(also called Tariq)

The eight *tones used in the *Coptic Liturgy.

LAMB

See AGNETZ.

LAMPADARY

An obsolete office of the ancient Church of Constantinople. It was so called because it was the function of the lampadary to see that the lamps of the church were lighted. He had the further privilege of carrying the lighted tapers before the emperor, empress, and *patriarch when they were in procession.

LAMPAS (Byzantine)

A large candle supported in the kerostates.

See KEROSTATES.

LANCE (Byzantine)
(also called Kopyo [Slavonic])

A liturgical instrument used as part of the *Byzantine rite of the prothesis; no other *Eastern rite makes use of such an article. The lance is used in the *Greek rite for the removal of the *amnos, or lamb, from the *bread and for detaching particles of bread in honor of the *Theotokos and the saints. The rest of the bread is then laid aside as the *antidoron.

In the *Russian rite, separate breads are taken from which particles are removed with the lance, then laid aside on the *paten in commemoration of the Theotokos and saints. There has been some speculation as to the date of the lance's introduction into the rite; some authorities claim that it was introduced as early as the 8th century. It is alluded to by Cardinal Humbert in the 11th century, but it was known to St. Germanus of Constantinople (634–733) and to St. Theodore the Studite (759–826). It may be more recent, however, certainly since the 12th or 13th century. According to a *Euchologion published in Venice in 1730 the lance may not be touched by anyone below the order of *subdeacon.

See LOGCHI.

LANKA (Ethiopian)

A circular shoulder cape cut with five points in the form of a cross. This garment is sometimes sewn on the *kaba, or *cappa. It has been suggested that it owes its origin to a *Coptic turban, which used to have flaps that reached to the upper thighs. The five points of the garment are said to represent the five wounds of Christ.

LATIN RITE

That part of the Roman Catholic Church that uses Latin *Liturgies; in 1970 their numbers were 665,235,000.

LAUDS

That part of the *Divine Office at the end of *Matins when Psalm 148, 149, and 150 are recited. On major feasts *stichera are inserted into the closing verses of Lauds.

See AINOI; KHVALITNYI.

LAUH (Coptic/Arabic)

Literally, "slab."

See LAX.

LAVRA (Byzantine/Slavonic)

(also spelled Laura)

A large monastery, but ordinarily it refers to a collection of small, detached monastic cells in close proximity and usually clustered around a church.

See RULE OF ST. ANTONY.

LAX (Coptic)

This consecrated *altar "stone" is a board that fits into the 1" deep rectangular well that is set into the *trapeza, or altar table. The lax has a cross in the middle, an Alpha symbol inscribed on the north side, and an Omega symbol on the south side. The letters IC, XC, YC, and ΘC are set into the four corners of the slab. Not all slabs are rectangular, some being horseshoe in shape or even semicircular, possibly in imitation of the table used at the Last Supper. The lax is covered with a silk or cotton cover.

See LAUH; NAKIS.

LBAITOKH (Maronite)

The *entrance chant sung during the *Liturgy. It is equivalent to a Western introit.

LECTIONS

(also called Entherthsovats; Keryono; *Lexis; Tshtenie)

Before the close of the 4th century, the number of lessons in most churches had been settled at three, one coming from the Old Testament, one from the apostolic writings, and one from the *Gospel. By the 5th century the number of lessons had been reduced to two by the elimination of the Old Testament lesson. This format is not true throughout the *Eastern Church.

Armenian Tradition

The Old Testament lessons (*margarech), which are omitted on the Ordinary days of the calendar, are the first to be read, followed by the Apostle (*Arrachealch). The Old Testament lesson is preceded by the Psalm of Dinner Time (*Saghmos Jaschou), whose text varies according to the day. If a *bishop is present he goes to the *throne with his *deacon at this time and remains there until the conclusion of the Gospel. The Apostle is preceded by the *mesedi and is read on the north side of the footpace of the *altar while facing west. After a blessing of *incense, the Gospel (*Avat(h)ran) is read by a deacon; if, however, the celebrant is the *patriarch, the Gospel is read by an assistant bishop, during which the Gospel book is held in a veil by the deacon and is incensed at the end of each sentence. In Ordinary *Liturgies, the Gospel is read from the center of the altar, facing the congregation and flanked by lighted tapers.

Byzantine Tradition

After the *Trisagion the Epistle is

read as the deacon censes the altar, sanctuary, *priest, and congregation. If it is a pontifical Liturgy, the bishop blesses the incense and sits on the throne during the reading. At the Epistle's conclusion, the Prayer before the Gospel follows immediately. When the deacon has received either the priest's or bishop's blessing, he leaves the sanctuary by way of the *royal doors, preceded by a *taperer, and stands before the congregation while the priest stands in front of the altar facing west. The Gospel is then read by the deacon.

At a pontifical Liturgy, when the reading is concluded the bishop blesses the people with the *dikerion and *trikerion.

Coptic Tradition

In this rite, there is provision for four lessons, three of which are recited outside the sanctuary by a layman, if necessary in both Coptic and Arabic. Curiously, the Coptic Epistle is read facing east, while the Arabic Epistle is read facing west. During the reading of the Coptic Epistle of St. Paul, the priest censes the choir and congregation, while the Catholic Epistle (*Catholicon) is read first in Coptic and then in Arabic, following which either the reader or the people say, "Love not the world" (1 John 2:15, 17). A lesson from Acts (*Praxis) follows, at the conclusion of which the priest puts incense into the thurible, stands at the altar, and says the Prayer of the Acts and then censes the altar, choir, and congregation. The Gospel book is then carried around the altar, and after many ceremonies, the Gospel

is read or sung by a senior cleric while facing the people.

See EVANGELION; ANJIL.

Ethiopian Tradition

Four readings from the Scriptures, called the *menbab, are, as in the *Coptic rite, read only at a solemn Liturgy, while at Ordinary *Ethiopian Catholic Liturgies two lessons only are read. Censing and a special prayer recited by an assistant priest precede the reading of the Epistle by a deacon facing the people. At its conclusion, the deacon enters the sanctuary and a *subdeacon emerges to read the Catholic Epistle, at the end of which an assistant priest announces the reading of the Acts of the Apostles. The recitation of the Trisagion precedes the procession of the Gospel book, which is carried by the deacon preceded by a taperer; after this the Prayer of the Gospel is recited before the sanctuary veil and is followed by further prayers and censings. The priest then reads the Gospel, as he stands facing east between two deacons who bear lighted tapers. Next a short verse is recited, the text of which varies according to the authorship of the Gospel that was read; for example, if St. Mark, "He that has ears to hear, let him hear," to which the people make a response.

East Syrian Tradition

Two lessons from the Old and two from the New Testament are read; the first two are read from the left side of the *bema by successive *readers. The reading of the Epistle is preceded by an introduction (*shuraya), and the reader or subdeacon, having kissed the altar and hand of the priest, comes to the sanctuary door bearing the Book of Epistles, and facing the people, he reads the Epistle. During this reading the priest prays and places incense into the thurible; then, holding the Book of Gospels above his head and accompanied by two taperers, he comes to the sanctuary door and places the Gospels on a portable lectern. He then raises the Gospel book, blesses the people with it, and reads the Gospel.

West Syrian Tradition

The number of Lessons is usually reduced to two, the Apostle (from the Epistles of St. Paul) and the Gospel, each preceded by a secret prayer. Before the Apostle is sung, a gradual is sung by a deacon from the side of the screen. The Gospel is then brought from the altar to the main *door of the screen, but if there is no screen the Gospel is read by a priest using a portable lectern facing west; alternatively the Gospel book may be held by assistants. The Gospel is introduced by a short verse (*hulolo). If a bishop is present he removes his *miter and places it on the altar. The reading, which may be in Arabic, is accompanied by lights, *fans, and incense, and at the end of each sentence, as in the *Armenian rite, the book is incensed by a deacon. On certain major festivals such as Christmas, the Presentation, and Palm Sunday, the Gospel may be interrupted by the chanting of a verse relevant to the feast. At the conclusion the priest bows and says the Prayer after the Gospel. Among *Syrian Catholics a homily often follows at this point.

LEIPSANA (Byzantine/Greek)

Holy *relics.

See MOS(T)CHE.

LEITOURGIKON (Byzantine/Greek)

A liturgical book containing the texts of the Ordinary of the three *Liturgies used in the *Byzantine rite.

See LITURGICAL BOOKS (Byzantine Tradition); SLUZHEBNIK.

LEKANE (Byzantine/Greek)

The basin used in conjunction with the *teston and with which the *altar is washed on Holy Thursday; it may also be used to wash the altar linens.

LESSONS

See LECTIONS.

LEXIS (Coptic)

See LECTIONS.

L(I)ESTOVKA (Byzantine/Slavonic)

See KOMBOSCHOINION.

LIGHTS ON ALTAR, THE

In the *Byzantine tradition it is customary to have only two lights but more are used frequently, and lights are always used in the Little and Great *Entrances. The use of lights in conjunction with the reading from the *Gospels is alluded to in the writings of St. Jerome (342–420), which he wrote from Bethlehem in 406. In the past *Copts commonly used a pair of lights close to but not on the *altar, one at the north side, the other at the south side. Today it is permissible to have the candles standing on the altar with any number of candles and lamps around them. The *Ethiopians normally use three candles that are set on the altar (*meshwa'e) so that two candles are set at the western angles and one is placed in the middle of the eastern side. For Ethiopian Catholics, Rome confirmed in 1939 that it was quite in order to celebrate the *Liturgy without any candles at all. Both the *Nestorians and West *Syrians use two lights only, although the Syrians use the gradines of their characteristic altars and place lights upon these.

See POTHURHAYE.

LIJKANEAT (Ethiopian)

A judge in ecclesiastical matters.

LILIA (East Syrian)
(also spelled Lelya)

The *Midnight office.

See EAST SYRIAN CHURCH, DIVINE OFFICE OF.

LINOBAMBAKOI (Byzantine/Greek)

A description of the crypto *Orthodox in Cyprus, who throughout the Ottoman period concealed their Orthodoxy by adopting Muslim names and externally observing Muslim practices while secretly maintaining their Orthodox faith.

LITANEIA (Byzantine/Greek)

See LITANY.

LITANY (Byzantine)

Literally, "a supplication." A prayer composed of a series of petitions, sung or said by the *priest or *deacon. To each petition the congregation makes some response, for example, "We beseech you, hear us." As a form of prayer it may have originated in Antioch in the 4th century and passed to Constantinople; it is now a common feature of *Eastern Liturgies. In the *Byzantine rite there are several types of litany:

1. The Great Litany (*Velikaya Ekteniya), whose start is signaled by the deacon exclaiming, "In peace, let us pray to the Lord." This litany is found near the start of the *Liturgy and at *Vespers and *Matins.

2. The Little Litany (*Malaya Ekteniya), which is introduced by the deacon when he says, "Again and again in peace, let us pray to the Lord."

3. The Litany of Fervent Intercession, which follows the reading of the *Gospel in the Liturgy and is introduced by the deacon saying, "Let us all say, with all our soul and with all our mind."

See ECTENE; EKTENE; LITANEIA.

LITIYA (Byzantine/Slavonic)

See LITY.

LITTLE ENTRANCE

See ENTRANCE; MIKRA EISODOSIS.

LITTLE EUCHOLOGION
(Byzantine/Greek)

A liturgical book.

See LITURGICAL BOOKS (Byzantine Tradition); SLUZHEBNIK.

LITTLE MONTH (Coptic)

The five or six days in a leap year that precede August 29.

See COPTIC CALENDAR.

LITURGICAL BOOKS

Armenian Tradition

1. Badarakamaduitz, or Korhrtadedr (The Book of the Oblation): contains the text of the *Liturgy used by the *priest; some editions contain also the parts spoken by the *deacon.

2. Book of Ordinations: this book is self-explanatory and is often found together with the Badarakamaduitz.

3. Djachotz, or Tschaschotz (The Book of Noon): a lectionary containing the Epistles and *Gospels used in the Liturgy and Office as well as those parts sung by the clergy including deacons and servers.

4. Donatsoitz (The Indicator of Feasts): a calendar with directions, resembling a *Byzantine Typikon but more detailed, since all cases of concurrence and occurrence are foreseen and for each entry there is full information about the hymns, reading, and psalms that are to be read.

5. Haysmavurk ("This Very Day"): corresponds to the Byzantine Synaxary but is not used extensively by *Armenian Catholics; contains the abridged lives of saints as well as the homilies read to the congregation on Sundays before *Vespers are celebrated.

6. Jamarkik, or Breviary: a book of *Hours, but the Great Jamarkik additionally contains various hymns sung at the Liturgy from the top of the gradines, which rise alongside the Armenian *altar; sometimes this Great

Jamarkik is called the Adianijamarkik. The Ordinary hymns used for the Office may be found in the Sharagan or Terbroutiun. Catholic Armenians use a complete breviary called the Jamagarkuthiun, a single volume first published in 1842.

7. Mashdotz: a Ritual containing the text and rubrics for the administration of the *sacraments and blessings as well as the various funeral ceremonies. Tradition attributes this book to St. Mesrob (345–439), famed for his Armenian version of the New Testament and Book of Proverbs; another claim attributes its composition in the 9th century to the *catholicos Mashdotz. An even later date of composition, the 12th century, has also been claimed.

8. Sharagan, or Terbroutiun (The Book of Choir Boys): contains *canticles with Office hymns not found in the Jamarkik unless they are common to the Liturgy and Office.

Byzantine Tradition

1. Euchologion (Greek) (Book of Prayer): contains the forms for the sacraments and minor ceremonies with the various prayers and blessings used on different occasions. There are two types:

a) The Great Euchologion (Greek) or Bolshoi Iereisky Molitvoslov (Slavonic): contains the priest's prayers and responses together with the truncated parts said by the deacon, choir, or *reader for Vespers, *Matins, and the Liturgy. Other contents include the text for the remaining sacraments as well as the prayers and blessings for other services such as funerals and the reception of the *habit by a religious.

b) The Small Euchologion (Greek) (Book of Needs) or Trebnik (Slavonic): sets out the details of the prayers and forms for five of the sacraments, since the text of the Liturgy is individually treated in the Hieratikon (Greek) or Skuz(h)ebnik (Slavonic), while the ordination rites are found in the Archieratikon (Greek) or Tchinovnik (Slavonic). The Small Euchologion sometimes contains the priest's part at Vespers, Matins, and the Liturgy.

2. Hieratikon, or Ieratikon, sometimes called the Leitourgikon (Greek) or Sluz(h)ebnik (Slavonic): contains the text of the Liturgies of St. John Chrysostom, St. Basil, and the *Presanctified. An abridged Ritual may be found as a supplement in this book, Catholic editions have included some final *dismissal forms (*apolysis) to be used in the Liturgy and Offices on major feasts throughout the year.

3. Archieratikon (Greek) or Tchinovnik (Slavonic): contains the text of the three Liturgies as in the Hieratikon but additionally contains the prayers and forms for purely episcopal ceremonies such as ordination rites.

4. *Horologion (Greek) or Tchasoslov (Slavonic).

5. Octoechos (Greek) or Oktoikh (Slavonic): commonly known as the Parakletike, literally, "The Book of Eight *Tones." A distinction should be made between the Great and Little Octoechos. The former includes not only the contents of the Little Octoechos but also the Office of the eight tones for every day of the week, whereas the Little Octoechos contains the eight Sunday Offices, one for each tone, because variable parts of the services from the first Sunday after Whitsun until the tenth Sunday before Easter recur every eight weeks in the same order, so only eight sets of tones, one for each week, are needed.

6. Triodion (Greek), literally, "Book of the Three Odes." Postnaya Triod (Slavonic), literally, the "Penitential" or "Fasting" Triod: supplies the texts used from the Sunday of the Pharisee and the Publican (the tenth Sunday before Easter) until Holy Saturday— texts for the *Great Fast of Lent. The name is derived from the fact that most of the *Canons in this book have only three odes instead of nine. Pargoire (1905) has suggested that the Triodion is the work of the Studites, but there have been some later additions by Philotheca of Constantinople (1354–1355 and 1361–1375) that were unsympathetic to Catholics.

7. Pentekostarion (Greek) or Tzvyetnaya Triod (Slavonic), literally, "Flowering" or "Festal" Triod: contains the services of the Paschal season, that is, from Easter until the Sunday after Pentecost. This also was probably the work of the Studites, especially those of the 9th century.

8. Menaia (Greek) or Mineya (Slavonic): a collection of twelve books, one for each month of the year, gathered into a single volume. It is the Office of all the fixed feasts, commencing on September 1 (the start of the Byzantine Church Year and known as the Day of Indiction) and ending August 31. Some editions include prayers for the Little Hours, the Lit-

urgy, and the texts for *Compline and the *Midnight Office.

See MENAION.

9. Heirmologion (Greek) or Irmologion (Slavonic): contains the theme songs, or irmoi, which are sung at the start of the canticles of a Canon. Additionally, it may contain smaller, informal services in honor of our Lord, the *Theotokos, or some other saints.

See IRMOS.

10. *Evangelion (Greek) or Evangelie (Slavonic): the Gospels, which are arranged in sections (pericopes [Greek]; zachala [Slavonic]) according to the order in which they are read during the liturgical year. The Tetraevangelion is an abridged New Testament with the text of the four Gospels divided into chapters and verses.

11. Apostolos (Greek), sometimes Praxapostolos, or Apostol (Slavonic): the Book of Epistles, called the Apostle because the greater part of its sections are taken from St. Paul. The Apostolos also includes the texts of the *prokeimenon that precede an Epistle as well as the variable verse that concludes the reading of the Epistle.

12. Psalterion (Greek) or Psaltir (Slavonic): the psalms, divided into groups called kathismata and bound together with the nine biblical canticles, or odes, which are used at *Orthros.

See KATHISMA.

13. Typikon (Greek) or Ustav (Slavonic): sets out the rules concerning the proper conduct of the Church services throughout any year.

14. Menology, or Synaxary. These terms are interchangeable. In the Byzantine Church (*Greek rite) at Orthros between Canticles 6 and 7, the *kontakion and the *ikos are followed by a reading from the Synaxary. This provides a brief overview of the life of the saint or gives an account of the feast being celebrated on that day. Sometimes the term "Synaxary" or "Synaxarion" refers to "Lives of the Saints" arranged according to the Church calendar. A Lesser Synaxarion lists the scriptural *lessons to be read according to a sequence determined by the Church calendar, with its feasts and commemorations, during a year.

15. Theotakarion: provides the Canons of the Theotokos, or Mother of God, for use in the festal offices.

16. *Anthologion (Greek) or Prazditchnaya Mineya (Slavonic).

Summary of Byzantine Liturgical Books. The table on page 330 is a list only; details are under individual headings.

See Table 3, page 330.

Coptic Tradition

1. Euchologion, or Hulaki: divided into three separate parts and edited by Raphael Tuki (18th century) under both Coptic and Arabic titles.

a) Part I: Book of the Three *Anaphoras, that is, of St. Basil, St. Gregory the Theologian, and St. Cyril.

b) Part II: Book Containing All the Holy Prayers includes ordinations, blessing of religious habits, enthroning of *bishops, consecration of *chrism, churches, and altars as well as vessels and vestments. There are also special services for the Epiphany and Holy Thursday celebrations and even the blessing of the oil, water, and bread for one bitten by a mad dog.

c) Part III: Book of the Services of the Holy *Mysteries, Funerals, and assorted Canticles.

2. The Diakonikon: a book exclusively designed for the deacon's use.

3. The Synaxar, or Martyrology: set out along the lines of the Greek Synaxary, with abridged summaries of the lives of the saints together with appropriate commentaries on them. These homilies, or commentaries, often replace the Acts of the Apostles in the Liturgy, and they are read as part of the Morning Office.

4. Difnari, or Antiphonary (sometimes Andifnari): a collection attributed to the *patriarch Gabriel (1131-1145); it provides two alternative hymns and chants for each saint's day.

5. Kutmarus, or Katameros: a lectionary containing the lessons from Holy Scripture as well as the lessons from the Apostle, the *Catholicon, and the Praxis (Acts of the Apostles). It may also include some psalms and Gospels used in the Offices and Liturgies throughout the year. The book is attributed to Patriarch Gabriel.

6. The Pontifical (The Books of Priestly Offices): a combination of the Roman Pontificale and Ritual.

7. The Horarium, or Egbiyah: serves as a breviary, is generally restricted to Catholic Coptic clergy. It was edited by Tuki (1750) under the title *A Book of the Seven Prayers of the Day and of the Night.*

8. Psalmodia: contains the odes, or four canticles from the Old Testament,

together with the Theotokia (Office of our Lady). This Office is Syrian in origin and was composed for the Coptic month of Mary (Choiac) in anticipation of Christmas. The book also contains a collection of hymns in honor of the saints and a doxology that extends to all saints. In 1746 Tuki published a compendium of this book under the Coptic and Arabic title *Book of the Theotokia and Katataxis of the Month of Choiac.*

9. The Office of Holy Week (Kitab il Pasca): a collection attributed to Patriarch Gabriel (1131-1145).

Ethiopian Tradition

1. Sher'ata Keddase, or Mashafa Keddase: a missal containing the text of the many Anaphoras that are available, some of which may be the oldest in existence and one of which, that of the Apostles (Zahawariat) is undoubtedly an expansion of the *Apostolic Tradition* of Hippolytus. In 1945 the Vatican Press published a missal with seventeen Anaphoras called *The Book of the Oblation.* While there is no regulation as to which Anaphora is to be recited, the most usual one employed is that of the Apostles.

2. Mawase'et, or Antiphonary: literally, "the answers."

3. Sher'ata Gecawe: a lectionary containing the psalms and Gospels for Vespers as well as the four lessons and psalms used in the Liturgy.

4. The Pontifical: originally Coptic in this rite because the ordaining bishop was always a Copt, but under the late emperor Hailie Selassie the Pontifical was translated into *Ge'ez for the non-Catholic Ethiopian Church,

Catholic Ethiopians use a Roman Pontifical translated into Ge'ez.

5. Ritual: The one used for the non-Catholics is largely Coptic, being based on an edition by the Coptic Patriarch Gabriel V (1401–1418); Catholics use a Roman Ritual translated into Ge'ez.

6. Mashafa Sa'atat: a breviary used by non-Catholic clergy. Catholics use a Vatican edition published in 1940.

East Syrian Tradition

1. The Taksa: equivalent to the Byzantine Euchologion and containing the text of the three Anaphoras commonly used, those of Sts. Addai and Mari, Theodore of Mopsuestia the Interpreter, and Nestorius. The Chaldeans repeatedly use one Anaphora, that of Sts. Addai and Mari, while the other Anaphoras are called the Second and Third Hallowing respectively. These last two Anaphoras originated in Antioch but were revised with East Syrian overtones, while the former Anaphora of Sts. Addai and Mari probably originated in Edessa, some parts dating from the 3rd century. The book may be bound with the Taksa d'mada (baptismal rite) and the Taksa d'syamida (ordination rite); both of these owe their form to Ishu'yabb III (650–658).

2. The Shamashutha: like a diaconal, providing the text for a deacon's responses.

3. The Karyane (Keryana; Keryono): is like a lectionary, containing either the Epistle, in which case it is called the *Shlika* or *Shliha*, or the Gospel text, when it is known as the *Iwangaliyuna*. This latter book is divided into two volumes; the arrangement of the content differs for *Chaldeans and *Nestorians.

4. The Turgama, literally, "interpretation": a collection of verses sung in the form of hymns between the lessons on Sundays and great feasts, reputedly the work of Ebed Jesu to Barsauma (d. 489). The Chaldeans' responsorial recitation is the responsibility of the deacons.

5. The Kashkul, literally, "containing all": a choir book containing the variable chants sung on weekdays.

6. The Gazza (Gezza/Gaza): contains the variable hymns, antiphons, and collects for those feasts that do not fall on Sundays. The book is attributed to Yaballaha II (1190–1222).

7. The Warda: a hymnbook used by Nestorians and Chaldeans alike, providing the text for those hymns sung during the *Communion and after the Gospel. It dates possibly from the 12th century.

8. The Baootha d' Ninwaye (Ba'utha d' Ninwayi), or *Nocturn of the Ninevites: a collection of hymns used specifically during the *Ninevite Fast. The collection is attributed to St. Ephrem.

9. The Hudra, or Kudra, literally, "circle": contains the variable chants for the Office on *Feasts of our Lord and during the Ninevite Fast. The arrangement is attributed to Ishu'Yabb III (650–658).

10. The Sunhadus: a breviary providing the text for Vespers (Ramcha), Compline, The Midnight Office (Lilia), and the Morning Office (Sapra).

11. The Dauida, or Psalter: provides the text of the psalms that are sung at the services.

12. The Kthawa d'burrakha, literally, "the blessing": contains the rites

to be observed during the *marriage service.

13. The Taksa d'kahnutha: used for the burial of clergy. An alternate book, the Taksa d'anida, is used for the burial of laity.

14. The Taksa d'husaya, literally, "rite of mercy": provides the service for the reconciliation of *penitents.

Other books used by the Nestorians include the Kdam Wadathar, or the Before and After, which contains extracts from the Psalter as well as prayers for use on Sundays and Weekdays, and the Abu-Halim, which provides the concluding prayers at nighttime on Sundays and is named after its composer.

West Syrian Tradition

1. The Annafura, or Kthobo Dkhourobo: the Missal. While the Syro-*Jacobites' Missal is reputed to contain sixty-four Anaphoras, the principal one used is that of St. James. The Catholic Missal (1843) contains seven Anaphoras.

2. The K'tobo d'teshmeshto: equivalent to a diaconal or, as it may be described, "The Book of the Clerks Used in the Ecclesiastical Ministries."

3. The Ewanghelion: Book of Gospels.

4. The Egroto Dashlihe, literally, "The Epistles of the Apostles": contains the other lessons used in the Liturgy.

5. The Penqitho: contains the Offices of Vespers, Matins, and Terce for Sundays, great feasts, and during Lent.

6. The Shehimo: the Office book used for ordinary commemorations.

LITURGICAL LANGUAGES

Armenian. A language of Indo-European origin; the followers of St. Mesrob translated the Scriptures and other patristic writings into Armenian between 400 and 450, so that by the end of the 5th century both the Office and *Liturgy were celebrated in Armenian. St. Mesrob is credited with having invented the Armenian alphabet of thirty-six letters, which, it is claimed, was followed by a considerable growth in national literature.

Greek. While it was Aramaic, a Semitic dialect, that was used at the Last Supper, around A.D. 50 Greek came to be used at Antioch for celebrating the Liturgy in the form known as Koine, or New Testament Greek, which was the common language of the day. This Greek usage in the *Byzantine Liturgy spread from Constantinople to the Near East and from there to other Christian centers.

Georgian. The original liturgical language for Georgia was Greek, having been introduced in the 4th century by missionaries from Constantinople; the use of Georgian was a later development. The liturgical books were translated into Georgian in the 10th and 11th centuries, probably by *Athonite *monks.

Staroslav/Old or Church Slavonic, also Palaeo-Slavonic. Through the efforts of Sts. Cyril and Methodius in the 9th century the Slavs were given the Scriptures and the Byzantine Liturgy was translated into Old Slavonic, and Pope John VIII, despite opposition by some German bishops, gave permission for St. Methodius' clergy to celebrate the Liturgy in Slavonic. St. Cyril, who died in 869, probably worked out the Glagolitic alphabet, which lies at the foundation of Slavonic literature. The so-called Cyrillic alphabet may have been designed by St. Cyril and his followers.

Romanian. Romania was probably Christianized at the start of the 3rd century, allegedly through the efforts of St. Nicetas, *bishop of Remesiana (ca. 335–414). This language had its origins in Latin but was later influenced by Slavonic, Greek, and Turkish and finally was established as a liturgical language in the 16th and 17th centuries. When many Transylvanian Romanians united with Rome in 1697, the language was confirmed by Rome as an acceptable liturgical language, and these Catholics adopted the Latin alphabet and reprinted all the liturgical books. This led to the abandonment of Slavonic or Cyrillic script by the Romanian *Orthodox as well.

Coptic. There is considerable evidence that from the 3rd century the Coptic language was used in the Liturgy, for it was St. Antony the Hermit (ca. 251–356), whose only language was Coptic, who decided upon his vocation as a hermit after hearing the reading from the nineteenth chapter of St. Matthew's Gospel. The dialect, being from Upper Egypt, was Sahidic or Theban, as distinct from Lower Egypt's Boheiric dialect. The Coptic alphabet is like the Greek, and many words are adapted from the Greek vocabulary. Following the Arab conquest of 641, Coptic became a disused language, and the Christians found that they needed an Arabic translation

of the Liturgy. This linguistic duality persists.

Ethiopian or Ge'ez, also Lesana Ge'ez. This Semitic language was originally spoken by a group of pre-Christian immigrants from Yemen and persisted well into the 17th century, when it was supplanted by Tigre, Tigrina, and Amharic. Ludolf (17th century) and Dillmann (late 19th century) awoke fresh interest in the language. The alphabet numbers twenty-six characters of which twenty-two are similar to Hebrew and Syriac characters.

Arabic. For centuries Arabic had been the liturgical language of the Syrians, Copts, Maronites, and Melchites of the Near East. For the Melchites, the Syriac originally used by them was replaced by Greek, which has been almost entirely supplanted by Arabic, certainly since the 17th century. The Maronite Liturgy is based on the Syriac Liturgy of St. James of Jerusalem. While the Bible is written in Arabic, the rubrics to be observed during the Liturgy are written in Karshuni, that is, Arabic written in Syriac characters.

Syriac. This liturgical language is probably a derivative from the early Greek used in the Liturgy; evidence for this is found in the Greek Liturgy of St. James and in the *Canons of St. John Damascene. During the 3rd century St. Procopius, at Scythopolis, had acted as a translator of some of the *lections from Greek into Syriac for the use of the faithful attending the Liturgy. The hellenization of Antioch established the strength of the Greek language, especially among the educated classes, while Syriac remained the language of the lower classes, and this persevered well into the 13th and 14th centuries.

Church Syriac is divided into (1) West Syriac, as used by Antiochene Syrians, and (2) East Syriac, or Chaldean, as used by the Chaldeans, Nestorians, and Syro-Malabarese Churches. The difference is not only one of pronunciation but script; the West Syrians use Serto script while the East Syrians use the Nestorian script, perhaps because of its decorative appearance.

LITURGICAL LANGUAGES, TABLE OF

(for details, see preceding entry)

See Table 4, page 331.

LITURGIKON (Byzantine/Greek)

(also called Leitourgikon; Leitourgiarion)

A book containing the text of the three *Byzantine *Liturgies as well as an abridged version of the Ritual.

See HIERATIKON; LITURGICAL BOOKS (Byzantine Tradition); SLUZ(H)EBNIK.

LITURGY

A general term, difficult to define, but according to Crichton (1987) "it is the communal celebration by the Church, which is Christ's body and in which he with the Holy Spirit is active, of the Paschal mystery. Through this celebration . . . Christ . . . makes present and available to men and women . . . the reality of his salvation." Most often it refers to the celebration of the Holy Eucharist, but it may represent different meanings: (1) as Leitourgia (Greek) or Litourgiya (Slavonic), which suggests a sense of ministry or service. The word does appear in the New Testament: "As they ministered to the Lord and fasted. . . ." (Acts 13:2). But by the 4th century the word described priestly ministrations and was fully recognized by Canon 1 of the Council of Ancyra (314); it was not used exclusively to describe the Eucharist but could be used of any solemn service, such as *baptism; (2) as *Kurbono or Qurbono (Syro-Jacobite) or *Prosfora (Coptic), where the notion of sacrifice is implied; (3) as *Keddase (Ethiopian) or *Kuddasha (East Syrian/Nestorian), which suggests a sense of consecration.

Armenian Tradition

In the past there were at least ten Anaphoras, including those of St. Gregory the Illuminator and St. Isaac the Great, but the Liturgy now celebrated appears to be a local modification of the *Liturgy of St. Basil. According to Salaville, the *Armenian Liturgy now presented as the Anaphora of St. Athanasius of Alexandria is "a compilation made from the Greek *Liturgy of St. James and the *Liturgy of St. John Chrysostom." It was St. Nerses of Lampron, archbishop of Tarsus (12th century), who spoke of the Armenian rite as being that of St. John Chrysostom. The Catholic Liturgy of this rite owed its form to Basil Barsegh and John Agop, two 17th-century Armenian *priests who had become Latinized, but this trend was halted in the early 19th century through the work of the *Mechitarist Gabriel Avedikian (1750–1827). The Liturgy is not supposed to be celebrated from Mondays to Fridays during Lent or during the Fast of *Nineveh. Among the *Georgians, following St. Nerses of Ashtarak and the Council of Dvin under John IV Oznetsi (719), the Liturgy is celebrated only on Saturdays and Sundays and major feast days.

Byzantine Tradition

In this liturgical family there is a clear set of influences from both Antioch and Jerusalem. This rite is used extensively by the Catholic *Melchites, *Ruthenians, *Russians, *Romanians, and many other language groups including *Greek, Arabic, and *Staroslav. There are three principal Liturgies, those of St. John Chrysostom, St. Basil the Great, and the *Presanctified, otherwise known as the *Liturgy of St. Gregory of Rome. A fourth Liturgy, that of St. James the Apostle, is rarely celebrated.

The *Liturgy of St. John Chrysostom is the one most often celebrated, while that of St. Basil is celebrated ten times a year and the Liturgy of the Presanctified is restricted to the nonliturgical days of Lent. This has been the situation since the time of Nicephorus, *patriarch of Constantinople (806–815). The Council of Trullo (692) regarded St. Basil of Caesarea as being the author of the Liturgy that bears his name, and it was from Caesarea that it came to Constantinople, where it underwent many changes and additions. The Liturgy was originally *Antiochene, with a distinctive post-Sanctus section, and this most ancient of the three Anaphoras, possibly 6th century, influenced the Liturgy of St. John Chrysostom.

The antiquity of the *Liturgy of St. Basil is supported by correspondence written by Scythian *monks (520) to the African *bishops in exile in which a passage taken from the Liturgy is quoted at length. St. John Chrysostom's Liturgy has been so called since the 7th century, but the earliest manuscript dates from the 8th century; this contains the Anaphora that is similar to the one found in the saint's sermons when he was preaching from 370–397 in which he refers to the Liturgy. It has been suggested that the present liturgical form may be a late 6th-century composition synthesized at Constantinople along Antiochene lines, for its West Syrian origin is suggested by the placing of the *Epiclesis after the institution and before the intercession.

The Liturgy of the Presanctified is clearly derived from the Liturgy of St. John Chrysostom, and while the Council of Laodicea (370) forbade the celebration of St. John's Liturgy on *fast days in Lent, it did not forbid a Presanctified Liturgy. St. Epiphanius of Salamis (310–403) is alleged to have compiled this Liturgy, which suggestion is in part corroborated by the writings of St. Sophronius of Jerusalem (ca. 560–638). Its use was permitted by the Second Council of Trullo in 692 (can. 52), but why it was attributed to St. Gregory the Great (540–604) is unclear. This Liturgy of the Presanctified underwent a subsequent revision and is now celebrated by *Byzantine Catholics and non-Catholics alike on every Wednesday and Friday in Great Lent.

Coptic Tradition

An antecedent of the Coptic Liturgy is the 5th century Greek Liturgy of St. Mark, while Serapion's *Euchologion*, discovered at Mount *Athos in 1895, provides evidence of an early mid-4th-century local Alexandrian Anaphora. Coptic Anaphoras have certain characteristics, notably that the intercessions are inserted into the middle of the preface instead of appearing after the Consecration, while the Epiclesis provides a link between the Sanctus and the institution. The normal Anaphora used by Catholic and non-Catholic Copts alike is that of St. Basil, which is not to be confused with the Byzantine Anaphora of the same name. The others are accredited to St. Gregory of Nazianzus and St. Cyril of Alexandria.

1. *St. Gregory of Nazianzus* (329–389). This Anaphora is unusual because it is addressed to Christ throughout and was probably meant to reflect the definition of Nicea I (325). It is celebrated on the eves of Christmas, Epiphany, and Easter, and it is so timed that the Liturgy is expected to conclude at midnight.

2. *St. Cyril of Alexandria* (d. 444). This is the old Alexandrian Anaphora of St. Mark in its Coptic form and is rarely used. It faithfully retains the text of the old Anaphora of St. Mark. Catholic Copts use it only once a year, on the Friday before Palm Sunday (Hammond and Bute), but non-Catholic Copts are said to use it on the feasts of Sts. Cyril and Mark and when a bishop is to be consecrated. Theoretically, this Anaphora's use is restricted to the fast and month of *Chosiac, or Advent, and during the Lenten fast.

Ethiopian Tradition

The Missal contains the Apostles' Anaphora (*Zahawariat), which closely follows St. Mark's Liturgy and is thought to be an expansion of Hippolytus' *Apostolic Tradition*, but the pre-Anaphora section, the intercession, and post-*Communion prayers are all ascribed to Basil of Antioch. There are seventeen other Anaphoras that may be substituted for the Apostles'. These include those of Our Lord Jesus Christ, Our Lady Mary (by Kyriakos of Behnsa), and many others that often exist only in fragmentary form.

East Syrian Tradition

The Anaphoras used are those of Sts. Addai and Mari, Theodore of Mopsuestia the Interpreter, and Nestorius. The Anaphora of Nestorius is quite different from that of Sts. Addai and Mari, which led Baumstark to demonstrate a close resemblance to the Byzantine St. Basil Anaphora and from which he concluded that the Anaphora was a highly modified rite of Constantinople, the editing having been made by Nestorius himself and translated into *Syriac by Maraba I (536–552).

The Anaphora of Sts. Addai and Mari, unique on account of its addressing Christ and not God, is used by *Chaldeans and *Nestorians alike. This Liturgy, which originated in Edessa, has been the object of speculation, since the oldest parts of the Anaphora go back to the 3rd century, while the Sanctus seems like an awkward interpolation. The absence of the institution and the authenticity of the

Epiclesis have already been commented on (*Anaphora). The definitive presentation of the Anaphora of Sts. Addai and Mari is attributed by the Nestorians to the patriarch Ishu'yab III (7th century).

The Anaphora of St. Theodore, thought to be an adaptation of a Liturgy from Asia Minor, is used on Sundays from Advent until Palm Sunday, excluding those days set aside for the use of Nestorius' Anaphora.

The Anaphora of Nestorius is used at Epiphany, the feast of St. John the Baptist (the Friday after Epiphany), the Greek Doctors (the Friday after the fourth Sunday after Epiphany), Wednesday of the Fast of the Ninevites, and Holy Thursday.

Catholics refer to the Liturgy of St. Theodore as the Second Hallowing, while that of Nestorius is called the Third Hallowing. Nestorians use Syriac as the *liturgical language, while Catholics use pure Syriac with Eastern pronunciation and characters, with the Holy Scriptures read in the vernacular.

West Syrian Tradition

This is the old rite of Jerusalem from where it was imported to Antioch in the 4th century and was called the Liturgy of St. James. This is attested by the account given by St. Cyril of Jerusalem to the newly confirmed, who attended it for the first time in 348. There seems to be some evidence of a conflation of the Liturgies of Jerusalem and Antioch around the start of the 5th century. Doubtless the earlier Liturgy was influenced by the Liturgy of St. Basil, which in turn probably affected the Liturgy of St.

Mark. According to Dionysius Bar Salibi (12th century), the Liturgy originated in the following way. On Whitsunday the apostles received the Holy Spirit, and the next day they consecrated the *chrism. On Tuesday they consecrated an *altar, and on Wednesday St. James, the Lord's brother, celebrated the Liturgy. When he was asked from where he had taken the Liturgy, he is reported as saying, "As the Lord lives, I have neither added nor taken anything from what I heard from our Lord."

There are at least sixty-five more Anaphoras that may be used to substitute for that of St. James, few of which are ever used. Arabic written in *Karshuni (Arabic written in Syriac letters) is now largely used for the *lessons, the Our Father, and various prayers and hymns of the Liturgy.

LITURGY OF APOSTOLIC CONSTITUTIONS

This was found in Books 2 and 8 of the eight books probably compiled in the 4th century. While it may have been designed in the 4th century along the lines of the received liturgical forms of the preceding centuries, it may represent the original rite of *Antioch, from which all *Eastern *Liturgies except those of the *Copts are derived.

LITURGY OF GREGORY THE GREAT (Byzantine)

A name by which the *Liturgy of the Presanctified is known, but there is no evidence to suggest that this *Liturgy owes its composition to St. Gregory.

LITURGY OF ST. BASIL

One of the Liturgies used in the *Byzantine Church; it seems to be an improved or revised version of the early *Anaphora of Basil of Caesarea, the reviser reputedly being St. Basil. The structure of this Liturgy is *Antiochene with a very long postsanctus section. There are many similar words and passages in the *Liturgy of St. John Chrysostom, and it is likely that the *Liturgy of St. Basil influenced the *Liturgy of St. John Chrysostom.

The Liturgy of St. Basil is used by *Eastern-rite Catholics and *Orthodox on Lenten Sundays (except Palm Sunday), Great (or Holy) Thursday, Great (or Holy) Saturday, the *vigils of Christmas and Epiphany, and the feast of St. Basil (January 1).

See LITURGY (Byzantine Tradition).

LITURGY OF ST. JAMES

This *Liturgy, attributed to St. James, the brother of our Lord, came from Jerusalem as a modification of a primitive *Antiochene *Liturgy of the Apostolic Constitutions, which it superseded. Since the *Jacobites used it in *Syriac before their separation from the *Orthodox in 550, it continued to be used in the West and was supplanted in the 13th century by the *Byzantine rite. Catholic and Jacobite Syrians still use the Syriac version, while the *Maronites use a modified version.

LITURGY OF ST. JOHN CHRYSOSTOM

See ANAPHORA; LITURGY (Byzantine Tradition).

LITURGY OF THE PRESANCTIFIED

A *Liturgy that in the *Byzantine rite is celebrated on Wednesdays and Fridays during Lent and on the first three days of Holy Week. This Liturgy does not contain a Consecration prayer and is combined with *Vespers. Holy *Communion may be received from the Sacrament *reserved in the *artophorion from the previous Sunday's Liturgy. The *vestments at this Liturgy may be either red or black. The *antidoron is distributed to the congregation before the *apolysis, since the congregation may make offerings of *bread that has been blessed after the Great Entrance (see ENTRANCE [Byzantine tradition]).

St. Sophronius (ca. 560–638) called it an "apostolic institution," in the sense that its institution was not in anyone's living memory, and certainly the antiquity of this Liturgy's origin is unclear, especially since a Liturgy like that of the Presanctified was used in the West on fast days in pre-Nicene times, which might suggest a mid-fifth-century Byzantine origin.

The Liturgy is sometimes called the Liturgy of St. Gregory Dialogos, that is, of Pope St. Gregory the Great (540–604), who probably revised the earlier form and is allegedly responsible for its present format.

See LITURGY (Byzantine Tradition); PROEGIASMENA.

LITY (Byzantine/Greek)
(also spelled *Litiya)

Literally, "entreaty." On the eves of great feasts a procession with intercessions takes place at the end of the *Litany of Fervent Intercession when the appointed troparia (*troparion) are being sung, during which the clergy go to the *narthex and the church is censed while a *deacon intones the litany for the people's needs. During the lity *bread, wine, and oil are blessed, and when in times past the all-night *vigil lasted until morning, these offerings were distributed to the congregation in order to sustain them. Sometimes the term "lity" refers to a modified Office of the Dead.

LOBSH (Coptic)

Part of the Office of the *Theotokia, which includes hymns to our Lady, used especially in the season before Christmas.

LOGCHI (Byzantine /Greek)

See LANCE.

LORD'S PRAYER

This is found in all *Liturgies except the *Liturgy of the Apostolic Constitutions (375).

In the *Armenian Liturgy preceding the *elevation and *Fraction the celebrant recites the introduction and embolism (*embolismos). Copts recite the Lord's Prayer in Arabic following the Prayer of the Fraction, from which there are six varieties to choose. The prayer is recited by the people with uplifted hands, but in a form different from that recorded in St. Matthew's Gospel, and as in the *Syrian rite, the prayer concludes with an ascription. In the *Ethiopian rite the position of the Lord's Prayer is identical to its position in the *Coptic rite and is recited

by the congregation together, with the usual ascription.

For the *Byzantine faithful this prayer's recitation precedes the ceremony of the Fraction and elevation with the words "Holy Things to the Holy." The *priest concludes the prayer with an ascription.

In the West *Syrian Liturgy this congregational prayer is recited in Arabic, with outstretched arms, after the Fraction. According to St. James of Edessa (708), the priest introduced the prayer, which then was recited entirely by all the people.

*Maronites recite The Lord's Prayer before the Fraction, but it follows the elevation of the consecrated *bread. The position of the Fraction in this rite is said to date from the 16th century.

In the *Chaldean Liturgy the prayer follows the Fraction and is introduced by a *Litany, which seems to be of 4th-century *Antiochene origin. The text concludes with the ascription.

LUBAN (Coptic)

A variety of *incense used by *Copts. Tradition holds it to be the incense offered to Jesus by the Magi.

LUFAFAH (Coptic)
(also spelled Lifafah)

A type of silk or linen corporal.
See VEILS.

LZHITZA (Byzantine/Slavonic)
(also spelled Izhitza)

The *spoon used to distribute the consecrated *bread and wine to the laity during Holy *Communion, when the *priest says to the communicant, "The servant of God, N., partakes of the precious and holy Body and Blood of our Lord and God and Savior Jesus Christ unto the remission of his/her sins and unto everlasting life."

See LABIS.

M

MA'APRA (East Syrian/Nestorian)

The chasuble. It is laid on the *altar until the *Liturgy of the Faithful commences, which is signaled by the close of the Anthem of the Gospel following the reading of the *Gospel. This chasuble is put on after the altar has been incensed, and a blessing is then given by the celebrant. The ma'apra resembles a highly ornamented hoodless cope, but one that is not joined in the front at the neck.

See PAINA; PAKILA; VESTMENTS, TABLE OF.

MACDAN (Ethiopian)

See MACHFAD.

MACDAN KEDUS (Ethiopian)

See KEDEST.

MACHFAD; MACHFADAT
(Ethiopian)
(also called Macdan)

The veils in which the oblation is wrapped during the *Ethiopian *Liturgy. Before the *prothesis commences, a prayer is recited over these veils: "O our God . . . send down your hand and power . . . on the cloths which will cover your Holy Body. . . ." As part of the prothesis, the *priest puts the *bread in a napkin held by an assistant, after which a procession forms around the *altar with the priest holding the veiled bread and preceded by a *taperer while a *deacon may carry the *chalice or vessel of wine.

See VEILS.

MADB'HO (Syrian)
(also spelled Madbkha; Madhbh'ha)

It variously means "table of life" or "sacrificing place" and clearly refers to either a sanctuary or an *altar, which among *Chaldeans should be fixed and made of stone, according to the canon of John Bar Abgar (900–905).

See ALTAR; KEDEST; KEDUSH; PATHORA; POTHURHAYE.

MADROSE (West Syrian)

A hymn thought to have been written by Bar Daysan, a 3rd-century Gnostic, but edited along *Orthodox lines by St. Ephrem (ca. 306–373), who was famed for his metrical homilies and hymns.

MA'ETANT (Ethiopian)

See CENSER.

MAFRIAN (Syro-Jacobite)

Literally, "fructifier." The title of address of the *Syro-Jacobite *patriarch's vicar-general.

MAGDAS (Ethiopian)
(also spelled Makedes)

See KEDEST; MACDAN KEDUS; MAKDAS.

MAGH'LONUTHO (Syro-Jacobite)

The *dismissal prayer, otherwise known as the commendation, which used to be recited in a low voice in *Syriac, but since 1922 it is said aloud in Arabic. During its recitation the *priest slightly turns toward the people and blesses them with an uncustomary single, not triple, *sign of the cross.

MAGHZMAH (Armenian)

The *paten, of *Byzantine design and made of precious metal on which the consecrated *bread is placed in the *Liturgy.

MAIA (Coptic)

A variety of *incense employed by he Copts. Incense figures largely in *Coptic ceremonies, for example, incense is offered at the Prayer of the Morning Incense, a service alternatively known as the Coptic Morning Service for the Lord's Day, which is offered every day by a *priest who is expected to be fasting at the time.

MA'IDAH (Coptic)

See ALTAR; TRAPEZA.

MAKARISMOI (Byzantine/Greek)

See BEATITUDES.

MAKDAS (Ethiopian)
(also spelled *Magdas)

The part of the church that is set aside for the choir and communicants. *Ethiopian churches are often circular and interiorly divided by three concentric circles. These enclose the sanctuary (kedest; kedesta kedusan) in the center, while the second interior division (makdas) is reserved for the choir and communicants, and the third division (kene mahlet) is used by the rest of the congregation. Other styles of Ethiopian church buildings may be quadrangular in form with a square area set aside in the center that has an *altar retained behind a veil and enclosed in a type of domed closet; a third common style of building is basilican in design, with three *naves, and a sanctuary separated from the rest of the church by a veil.

See KEDEST.

MALABAR JACOBITES

See MALABARESE CHRISTIANS.

MALABAR RITE CATHOLICS

Malabar-rite Catholics have been under the jurisdiction of the *Latin-rite archbishop of Goa, and therefore the *pope, since 1599. The system and forms of worship are according to *East Syrian–*Chaldean usage, with the *Anaphora of the Holy Apostles (Sts. Addai and Mari) as revised by the Synod of Diamper in 1599. The *Liturgy is called the Kurbana, or Offering, and while the *Syriac language and general outline of the original Liturgy is preserved, Western influences have appeared.

See SYRO-MALABAR RITE; SYRO-MALABARESE.

MALABARESE CHRISTIANS

This term may refer to (1) Catholics of the *Latin and *Syro-Malabar rites, (2) *Nestorians, known as *Mellusians, or (3) *Malabar Jacobites.

These Christians claim an origin back to the apostle Thomas, but with the arrival of Portuguese Catholics in the 16th century an attempt was made to convert these Syrians to Catholicism. In 1653 a group decided to seek *autonomy and attempted to consecrate the *archdeacon Thomas Palakomatta, using twelve *priests, to become Mar Thoma I. This was clearly unsatisfactory, and the *Syrian Jacobite *patriarch sent Mar Gregorios, a *Monophysite from Diarbekir. For the next hundred years the Jacobite patriarch sent out ordaining *bishops, but the jurisdiction was exercised by priests, all called Thomas, of the Palakomatta family. Eventually one such Thomas was consecrated bishop, taking the title of Dionysius I, but in 1778, six years after his consecration, he requested that he be received into the Catholic Church along with his people. Considerable difficulties presented themselves that frustrated this purpose.

The Mar Thoma Syrian Church of Malabar, or the Reformed Syrian Christians, is a group that has been heavily influenced by Anglican missionary activity and has drifted toward Protestantism.

See MELLUSIANS; SYRO-MALABARESE.

MALAYA EKTENIYA

The Small Litany, led by the *deacon, follows the first *antiphon during the *Liturgy and is said while the Prayer of the Second Antiphon is being recited secretly by the celebrant.

See LITANY.

MALAYALAM

The language used by the Syro-*Jacobite Church at *Malabar and by the *Malankarese Catholics. Like Tamil, it is one of the Dravidic dialects spoken in southern India.

MALCA (East Syrian/Nestorian) (also spelled Malka)

Literally, "king." The Holy Leaven, which is used by the Nestorians in their preparation of the bread for use in the *Liturgy, is kept in a chalice in a small cupboard (*giuta) above the *altar. It consists of a mixture of flour, salt, and powdered fragments of sacramental bread, because at every celebration of the Liturgy, a little piece of consecrated bread is placed into the Malca, and so a link is thought to be established with a succession of Liturgies that extend back, according to tradition, to the Last Supper, when a loaf of bread was given to St. John, who allegedly mixed it with water that fell from Christ's body at his baptism and with the blood and water that followed the piercing of his heart. This doughy mixture was then divided among the apostles, and it has been passed on by a process of leavening ever since. A renewal of this leaven, or Malca, normally occurs as part of the Holy Thursday celebrations.

This renewal is a special and complex service and consists of the *bishop mixing some flour, salt, oil, and water and then after numerous prayers, blessings, and censings, mixing a little of the old Malca with the new mixture on the silver plate, which is then placed on a small table in the sanctuary. After further chants and prayers the new Malca is placed in the *chalice, which is raised and then placed in the cupboard specially set aside for the Malca's safekeeping. If there is any superfluous Malca, it is burned and the ashes mingled with water, then emptied through a *piscina or its equivalent into the foundation of the church building.

See BREAD.

MAMHER (Ethiopian)

The abbot of one of the non-Catholic communities that follow the Rule of St. Antony; he may also be considered to be equivalent to the *Coptic *archpriest, or kummus.

See KUMMUS.

M'AMUDITHO (West Syrian)

Literally, "house of baptism." A baptistery. According to Bar Hebraeus (13th century) it is usually on the south side of the *altar.

MANDARAH (Coptic)

A guest room in a monastery or church building.

MANDELION (Byzantine)
(also spelled Mandilion)

The towel that may be put over a *bishop's arm to protect the *vestments when he is vested for the consecration of a church. Alternatively it may refer to the towel that a *subdeacon places over his left shoulder to be presented to a bishop so that he may dry his hands after washing them during the *Great Entrance ceremonies before the oblation is brought from the *prothesis to the *altar.

MANDIL (Syro-Jacobite)

A liturgical cloth.

See KETHONS.

MANDYAS (Byzantine/Greek)
(also called Mantiya)

See DEGREES OF MONASTICISM, HABITS OF.

MANERSHOOUSHI (Coptic)

This term describes an *altar in the sense of being a sanctuary.

See ALTAR; TRAPEZA.

MANICHAEISM

A 3rd-century Persian, Mani was responsible for the belief named after him, which maintains that there are two eternal and opposing principles, good and evil; humans are seen as a mixture of both, with the highest duty being to eradicate the "darkness," or evil side of their nature, by the rejection of wine, flesh meat, prosperity, and sexual activity.

MANOUALION (Byzantine)

A single candlestick bearing a single candle, or lampas, which is carried in the right hand of a *reader during a procession.

See LAMPAS.

MANTIYA (Byzantine/Slavonic)

Part of the angelic habit, which is designed to cover the whole person. It is called "angelic" because its flowing lines were meant to typify the wings of angels. The mantiya is presented to the *monk during his clothing in either the little habit or the great habit by the superior, who holds it in his left hand and recites a prayer: "Our brother, N., is clothed with the garment of salvation and with the armor of righteousness, that he withdraw from all unrighteousness . . . and that he may have the remembrance of death always in his mind . . . and be dead to every evil deed. . . ." The mantiya is then blessed and the monk is clothed with it. All monks when present at the Divine Services are expected to wear this black mantiya.

Hierarchs, such as *bishops and *archimandrites, may wear a richer mantiya, which is often purple or some other suitable color. This is the choir dress of all bishops, and until the 15th century it was worn outside of church. Upon it are sewn the Tables of the Law (*Pomata, [Greek]; *Skrizhali [Slavonic]), which are squares of velvet at the neck and foot symbolizing the Old and New Testaments. The four squares are sometimes decorated with the symbols of the Four Evangelists, so the Pomata or Skrizhali represent the four Gospels. In addition there are the "streams" of doctrine (Potamoi [Greek]; Istotchniki [Slavonic]), represented by red and white ribbons sewn horizontally around the mantiya. The garment is secured at the neck and bottom. It should be noted that archimandrites and hegumens do not have stripes on their mantiya; a bishop's mantiya sometimes may have small bells attached.

See DEGREES OF MONASTICISM, HABITS OF; HABITS, COMPARATIVE TABLE OF.

MAPHRIAN (Syro-Jacobite)
(also spelled Maphryono)

See MAFRIAN.

MAPPA (Coptic)

See MARPPA; STOICHARION.

MA'PRA (East Syrian)
(also spelled *Ma'apra)

See PAKILA.

MAR (Syrian)

Literally, "Lord." A term applied not only to a male saint but used of a prelate and applied to all *Syrian Orthodox, *Syro-Malabarese, *Syro-Malankarese, *Nestorian, and Catholic *Chaldean *bishops. The term as applied to female saints is *Mart or Martha.

MARGARECH (Armenian)

The Old Testament lessons read during a solemn celebration of the Liturgy.

See LECTIONS.

MARGARITES (Byzantine)

A name referring to the consecrated particles given in holy *Communion.

See PEARL.

MARMITHA (East Syrian/Nestorian)

The section of the Psalter appointed to be read on a particular day; it approximates the Western introit.

See DAWIDHA.

MARMNAKAL (Armenian)
(also called *Gorphourah; *Schouschphah)

The corporal, which is laid out on the *altar prior to the celebration of the *Liturgy. In a sense it is a portable altar; its use as a corporal is reflected in the word for "veil" (schouschphah, from shushepho [Syriac]).

See ANTIMENSION.

MARONITE LITURGY

The early *Antiochene *Liturgy was modified for use at Jerusalem, and its Greek form, the *Liturgy of St. James, was celebrated throughout the patriarchate of Antioch. Inevitably, the *Greek was translated into *Syriac, so the Maronite Liturgy became simply the Syriac Liturgy of St. James of Jerusalem, but with many Latin modifications. The Maronite Liturgy most commonly used, however, is the *Anaphora of the Holy Catholic and Roman Church, the Mother of All Churches. It is celebrated in two languages, Syriac-Aramaic and Arabic, the present-day vernacular of the Maronite people.

MARONITES

Catholics of the *Antiochene rite found mainly in Lebanon. There is some dispute about the origin of the name "Maronite," for allegedly a Syrian anchorite named Maro, a contemporary of St. John Chrysostom (347–407), lived near Cyr, and a monastery was founded on the Orontes River following his death in 410. It is from this foundation at Beit-Marum in the Apamée region in Syria that modern Maronites claim their origin.

Later John Maro, a *monk of this foundation, was nominated *bishop of Botyrs in 676 at the insistence of the *patriarch Macarius; at the Sixth General Council he was subsequently deposed because of his alleged *Monothelitism. He died in 707. Following the destruction of the old monastery of St. Maro by the imperialists, another one was founded at Kefr-Nay in the district of Botyrs, and it was to this foundation that the head of St. Maro was brought. So it is partly from John Maro and partly from St. Maro that the *Monothelite Christians on Mount Lebanon came to be called Maronites.

While the rite's antiquity can certainly be confirmed, its *orthodoxy is questionable, in light of the conversion of forty thousand Maronites to Rome in 1182, which conversion was effected by the Latin patriarch Amaury of Antioch. The Crusades had brought the Maronites into contact with the Western Church, and their conversion came as a result. Under protection of the Crusaders the Maronite Church experienced considerable prosperity and patronage.

Until the 18th century there were many abuses and usages that had to be carefully corrected or modified, and the Council of Lebanon, which was convened at the Monastery of St. Mary of Luweiza in 1736, was seen by the Maronite hierarchy as an attempt to cut back local privileges and to abolish many well-established "abuses." The council's decrees were to take many years to be applied, and the future of the Maronites was by no means destined to be peaceful. In 1860 they suffered dreadfully at the hands of the Turks, and during this massacre the abbot of Deir al-Kkamar was appallingly tortured and in the space of three weeks sixteen thousand Maronites were driven from their homes; some of these martyrs were beatified by *Pope Pius XI in 1926. The massacres were repeated during the Great War, which forced many to flee to the New World, while Lebanon was brought to order and became established as an independent and sovereign state; in the 1980s renewed fighting and death struck at Lebanon again.

MARONITES, LITURGICAL CALENDAR OF

The *Maronite Church Year commences in October, and the six Sundays preceding Christmas are used to recall the events that led to Christ's nativity. An unusual custom has developed in which two hosts are consecrated on December 15; one host is placed in the tabernacle, and on every evening of the nine days preceding Christmas it is removed from the tabernacle and elevated. It is only on the last day of the "novena" that it is finally received in *Communion.

Following the blessing of the waters at Epiphany, the subsequent weeks are called "After Epiphany," while the three weeks that precede Lent are dedicated to the commemoration of the dead. Ashes are imposed on the first Monday in Lent, and during Passiontide the pictures and statues are customarily swathed in sheeting, and a large black curtain decorated with symbols of the Passion is hung so as to conceal the *altar. The weeks following Easter and Pentecost are called "After Pentecost" until September 14, the feast of the Exaltation of the Cross; the weeks that follow are called "After the Exaltation of the Cross." The usual Lenten *fasts and periods of abstinence are observed in this rite as rigorously as with their *Eastern Orthodox brethren; these periods include the Great Lent, or the Lent of the Apostles (June 25–28); the Lent of the Assumption (August 7–15); and the pre-Christmas fast.

Holidays of obligation include the feast of St. Antony on January 17 and the national feast of Mar Marun on February 9, although a commemoration of Mar Marun is observed on the second Sunday of every month.

MARONITES, LITURGICAL LANGUAGE OF

See LITURGICAL LANGUAGE, TABLE OF.

MARONITES, PATRIARCH OF

See ANTIOCH, PATRIARCH OF (Catholic).

MARPPA (Coptic)

See STOICHARION.

MARRIAGE

One of the *sacraments of the Church.

Armenian Tradition

The ceremony is commonly referred to as "the imposition of the crown." Marriages usually take place on Monday or Thursday, when the clergy go to the bride's home and bless the robes and ring, and with the arrival of the bridegroom they form a procession, which makes its way to the church. The wedding service proper is preceded by a betrothal ceremony, which involves a blessing of the bride's dowry. In the past the *Armenians marked the betrothal by the presentation to the bride of a cross, which was to be worn around the neck.

In the church the bride and bridegroom stand side by side at the sanctuary gate, and the *priest places the Bible on their heads and recites the Prayer of the Sacrament. During the singing of Psalm 21 a garland is prepared for the bridegroom, and while Psalm 45 is sung by the choir a similar garland is prepared for the bride. After further prayers the garlands are put on the heads of the bride and bridegroom, after which they receive a blessing and Holy *Communion. The service is shorter for widows and widowers when they remarry.

Byzantine Tradition

This *sacrament is referred to as "the crowning," which reflects the old tradition of the newly married couple wearing their crowns (of olive leaves in Greece) for a week after the ceremony. Since the 11th century the crowning, or marriage service proper, has immediately followed the betrothal ceremony. The betrothal ceremony was designed to be celebrated after the *Liturgy and takes the form of a *litany and a blessing of rings, during which the bride is blessed with the bridegroom's ring and vice versa as the priest says three times, "The servant of God, N., is betrothed to the handmaid of God, NN., in the name of the Father . . . ." The rings are then given to the bridal pair and exchanged as the priest prays.

When the couple have returned from the back of the church accompanied by the clergy to the singing of Psalm 127 (traditional since the 4th century), the priest brings them to the table, which stands before the *iconostasis. Following a scrutiny as to whether both are free to marry, a litany is recited and the bridal couple are crowned with the crowns that are resting on the table as the priest says, "The servant of God, N., is crowned unto the handmaid of God, NN., in the name of the Father . . . ." The words are repeated for the bride. A triple blessing is said, an Epistle and *Gospel are read, and the *Lord's Prayer is recited. The couple are then given a goblet of wine to drink; this they do three times and their hands are joined together beneath the priest's stole. The couple are then led around the table three times with the bridal attendants following them and holding the crowns above their heads. A hymn is sung, the crowns removed, and with a final blessing the ceremony is concluded.

See BRAK; GAMOS.

Coptic Tradition

The marriage contract, which is performed at home accompanied by various prayers and the Lord's Prayer, is an important part of the ceremonies which follow and which include a blessing of the bride's dowry of clothes and jewelry.

The marriage service, not permitted during Lent, normally takes place after *Matins when the couple arrive at the church. The service is quite noisy by Western standards with ululation or zagarit (howls) obscuring the prayers. A veiled tray is placed in the choir, and on it is a gold cross, ring, girdle, and some *incense. Following the recitation of psalms, an Epistle (Eph 5:22–6:3), Gospel (Matt 19:1-6), and prayers, the tray is unveiled and the articles are blessed separately. A ring is put on the groom's ring finger of the right hand, a blessing is given, and he is led to where the bride is waiting and asked to offer her a ring and a small crown. If the bride stretches out her hand this is taken to imply acceptance of the groom as her husband. The couple are then covered with a white silk or linen veil, and after many blessings they are anointed with blessed oil on their foreheads and wrists. When the crowns have been blessed they are held over the couple while the prayer is recited: "With glory and honor, the Father has crowned them, the Son blesses them, and the Holy Spirit crowns them, comes down upon them, and perfects them."

Then with their arms crossed before them, the gold cross is laid on their heads while the priest recites the Absolution over them and, following further prayers, joins the hands of the bride and bridegroom. A procession forms, which precedes the *Anaphora at which the couple receive Communion. After eight days it is traditional to attend a further service, when the crowns are removed and the couple may be blessed again.

See ZIJAH.

East Syrian Tradition

1. *Chaldean. The ceremony in this rite resembles that of the *Byzantine rite except that the drinking from the goblet of wine occurs near the start of the ceremony rather than at the end.

2. *Nestorian. The Nestorians do not consider marriage a sacrament. When the bridegroom is brought to the bride's house at the start of the ceremony, both are crowned with wreaths of intertwined red, blue, and white threads. The ceremony commences with several anthems and prayers, after which the wedding goblet is prayed over and blessed with the wedding ring, which is then placed inside the cup with a small cross and a tiny speck of dust from the tomb of a saint, which is then mixed with the wine. This goblet is blessed three times, and when the bridegroom has drunk about two-thirds of it a *deacon hands it to the bride, who also drinks from it; both bride and bridegroom are then blessed between the eyes. The bride's clothes are then blessed, and she comes to stand at the bridegroom's right side. The blessing (buraka) follows, and

wreaths are placed on their heads to the accompaniment of psalms. The ceremony concludes with a litany, further anthems, and prayers, as well as a long prayer attributed to St. Ephrem of Syria (ca. 306–373) during which the couple are blessed along with the rest of the congregation.

West Syrian Tradition

There seems little difference between the rite observed by the *Jacobites and that used by the *Syrian Catholics; in form, the ceremony resembles the Byzantine rite and consists of two parts, the blessing of the ring and the crowning. Much emphasis is placed on the procession, which follows the crowning ceremony. During these ceremonies a ring is given to both bride and bridegroom; formerly only one ring was given and that to the bride by the bridegroom. The bride and groom are crowned finally with a wreath.

MART (Syrian)

A title for a female saint.

See MAR.

MARTUTA (East Syrian/Nestorian)

A *pallium; its use has now been discontinued.

MARTYRIKON (Byzantine/Greek)

A *troparion in honor of a martyr. Troparia are simply short hymns and a martyrikon is simply a class of troparion, just as an *apolytikon is a troparion preceding the *dismissal ceremony at a *Liturgy.

MARTYRIUM (East Syrian)

A depository for *relics.

See BETH KADDISHE.

MARWAH'THO (Syrian)

Fans that are like small metal discs decorated with a seraph's face and wings to which bells may be attached. The disc is attached to a pole and is shaken at solemn moments during the *Liturgy.

See FANS.

MARWEBE (Syrian)

The *antiphons that are sung whenever the Magnificat is recited.

MASHAFA KEDDASE (Ethiopian)

See LITURGICAL BOOKS (Ethiopian Tradition); SHER'ATA KEDDASE.

MASHAFA SA'ATAT (Ethiopian)

The Book of *Hours used by non-Catholic *Ethiopians.

MASHDOTZ (Armenian)

A Ritual, the contents of which include the forms of administration of the *sacraments, funeral ceremonies, commemorations after death, and blessings of houses at Easter and Epiphany, as well as Western-style blessings now commonly used.

See LITURGICAL BOOKS (Armenian Tradition).

MASN (Armenian)

A particle of the consecrated *bread which has been separated from the rest of the bread and which is to be placed into the *chalice.

See FRACTION.

MASNAPHTHO (Syrian)
(also spelled Masnaftha)

Among Syrian Christians (*Maronites and Syro-*Jacobites), this is the *amice-like hood worn by a bishop as part of his consecration ceremony. Made from quite expensive material, it is worn over the head during the *Liturgy, but during the *Gospel, consecration, and post-Consecration prayers it is worn folded around the neck. If a *bishop is wearing a *miter, the masnaphtho is folded across the shoulders. Among the Maronites, the term is applied to the amice-like garment worn by *priests over their *albs, or *citunah, but the priestly masnaphtho has a central cross embroidered on it, and during vesting it is put on after the *zunnar (girdle).

See BIRUN.

MASOB (Ethiopian)

A round covered metal or wickerwork box about 5″ in diameter and 2″ in depth in which the *bread is brought to the *altar before the *prothesis. To judge from the prayers said over the masob during the preparatory ceremonies of this rite, one may conclude that the masob may have been used as a *paten.

MASSAH WAJH (Coptic/Arabic)

Literally, "wipe the face." At the end of the *Liturgy the *priest sprinkles holy water over the congregation, then passes his now-wet hands over his own face and those of the congregation.

MASTABQU'E (Ethiopian)

Occasional prayers, infrequently used by *Ethiopian Catholics, the texts for which are found in the *Sher'ata Keddase.

MASTYANEETSA
(Byzantine/Slavonic)
(also spelled Mastyanitsa)

See APOKREOS.

MATINS

See ORTHROS.

MATOUTHSARAN (Armenian)

May refer specifically to the *prothesis table at the north side of the sanctuary; more generally it indicates the offertory ceremonies of this rite, during which the great curtain is drawn across the sanctuary.

See ENTSAIARAN.

MATS (Coptic)

See TABAK; THOM.

MATUNIYAS (East Syrian)

A deep bow or even a genuflection.

See METANY.

MAUMYONO (Syrian)

An exorcist, for which there is no special ordination ceremony, but the individual must receive a special license from the *bishop who is authorizing an exorcism.

MAWASE'ET (Ethiopian)

Literally, "answers." A collection of *antiphons used by non–Catholic *Ethiopians.

MAZAMER (Ethiopian)

See DEFTERAS; SINGER.

MAZMAZA KURBANA (Ethiopian)

The rubbing of the *bread at the start of the *Liturgy, similar to the *Coptic usage; this is done to test the soundness of the bread and to remove any loose particles.

MAZMORONO (Maronite)

A *minor order, which in this rite may be conferred on a seven-year-old.

See SINGER.

MAZNAVOR (Armenian)

A minor grade of teaching cleric.

See VARTABED.

M'CAPRANA (East Syrian/Nestorian) (also spelled Mkafrana; *Mkaprana)

The *Nestorian equivalent of the blessed *bread (*eulogia), which is usually distributed at the end of the *Liturgy during the recitation of the Prayer of Mary. The people go forward, kiss the hand cross held by the *priest, and then receive the blessed bread being distributed by one of the *priests or *deacons standing at the *nave entrance to the baptistery. The distribution of the blessed bread is not observed by the *Chaldeans.

MCHAMCHONO (West Syrian) (also called Diacono)

The *deacon, who as part of the ordination ceremony receives a *censer (*pirmo) and makes a signed profession of faith; this signing is repeated if further orders are received. The deacon wears his stole (*uroro) in a distinctive fashion: it is carried on the left shoulder with the overhanging parts falling behind and in front; often the Syrian deacon wears special shoes (m'sone) resembling the *priest's shoes. In addition he wears the alb (*kuthino), which has its sleeves confined by long, narrow, distinctive cuffs (*zende; *pedhitho).

See ORDERS, HOLY (West Syrian Tradition).

MECHIR (Coptic)

The sixth month of the Coptic year, which corresponds to the period from January 26 to February 24.

See COPTIC CALENDAR.

MECHITARISTS

A congregation of *Armenian Catholics residing on the Island of St. Lazzaro near Venice whose apostolate is concerned with publishing. The name of the congregation is derived from Peter Manuk (Mechitar), an Armenian born in 1676 and ordained *priest in 1699, who founded a society in Constantinople in 1701 that had as its aim the education and union of the Armenian and Roman Catholic Churches. Mechitar encountered considerable opposition, and as a result he retreated to St. Lazzaro, where he died in 1749. The *monks, who are usually bearded, wear a black *habit with wide sleeves, a cloak, and a hood.

MEGA EUCHOLOGION (Byzantine)

This liturgical book contains the fixed texts of *Vespers, *Matins, and the *Liturgy as well as the texts of the other *sacraments, other services, and blessings such as *monastic profession, consecration of a church, and funeral rites.

See EUCHOLOGION; LITURGICAL BOOKS (Byzantine Tradition).

MEGALE EISODOS (Byzantine)

See ENTRANCE (Byzantine Tradition).

MEGALOPHONOS
(Byzantine/Greek)

The recitation of the Nicene *Creed in answer to the question concerning belief of a consecrand during his consecration as a *bishop. The consecrator says to the bishop-elect, "And how believest thou?" to which the consecrand recites the symbol of the faith, or Creed. This exchange takes place while the bishop-elect is standing on the *orletz (circular mat), on which is imprinted or embroidered an outstretched eagle. During the Creed's recitation the bishop-elect stands on the tail of the embroidered eagle.

MEGALOSCHEMOS
(Byzantine/Greek)

The highest grade to which an *Eastern *monk may aspire. It is marked by exacting asceticism, and it requires many years of service in the religious life before admission to this grade is granted. If a *bishop attains it he may not celebrate any episcopal function, but a *priest may continue to celebrate the *Liturgy.

See DEGREES OF MONASTICISM, HABITS OF; HABIT, COMPARATIVE TABLE OF; MONASTICISM (Byzantine Tradition); SKHIMNIK.

MEGALYNARION
(Byzantine/Greek)

A *troparion that is sung at *Matins after the *polyelaios (Pss 134; 135), or it may substitute for the Magnificat. It usually begins with the word "magnify." It is known also as the Exaltation, and during its singing, first by a *priest and *deacon together and then by the choir, the *icon of the feast being celebrated is censed.

See VELICHANIE.

MEGHEDI (Armenian)

A hymn, the text of which varies according to the feast day. It is sung specifically during the *prothesis while the *altar veil is drawn.

MEIERAF (Ethiopian)

The common form of the Daily Office.

MEKAMIA (Ethiopian)

Crutches that may be used by clergy and laity alike to support themselves during the long *Ethiopian *Liturgies.

MELCHITE
(also spelled *Melkite)

*Byzantine Catholics of the Middle East, who use Greek or Arabic in their services. The name may be derived from the Syrian "malcoye" (literally, "royal" or "royalists"), because the Council of Chalcedon (451), to whose decrees these Catholics acceded, was thought to have been directed entirely by the emperor Marcian (450–457); the name was applied to those who had remained loyal to the Eastern emperors after the Muslims had taken over Egypt. The name is also applied to those Arabic-speaking Byzantine-rite Catholics of the Near East, who in 1724 came to be so organized when the *Orthodox *patriarch of Antioch, Cyril VI (Cyril Tanas), was elected. As a result, an anti-Catholic party chose Sylvester of Cyprus, who was consecrated at Constantinople and was presented as the true patriarch of Antioch and approved by the Turkish authorities. However, Cyril experienced great difficulty with both the Jesuits and *Maronites, who went to great lengths to induce the Melchites to join the Maronite rite. *Pope Benedict XIV eventually had to intervene to sort out the unpleasantness. During the rule of Maximos II Mazlum (1833–1855) many reforms were introduced, and the Turkish authorities granted civil autonomy for the Melchites under their own patriarch.

MELCHITES, PATRIARCH OF (IN ANTIOCH)

Although his residence is in Damascus, the jurisdiction of the *Melchite *patriarch is extensive. For well over a hundred years he has held the title and jurisdiction of the patriarchates of Jerusalem and Alexandria. Upon election by the *bishops in synod, which election has to be confirmed by the *pope, the patriarch takes the title "Patriarch of Antioch and of All the East" and receives a *pallium from the pope. The patriarch has the right to

consecrate the *chrism for the Melchite community and may bestow the *omophorion on his bishops, whom he may nominate and convene to a synod. Melchite clergy observe *Byzantine traditions, with married clergy in charge of parishes, while the celibate clergy are more usually concerned with education.

MELISMOS (Byzantine/Greek)

See FRACTION.

MELKAITA (East Syrian/Nestorian)

See BREAD (East Syrian Tradition).

MELKITE

See MELCHITE.

MELLUSIANS

An ostensibly *Nestorian sect centered largely in and around Cochin (Southwest India); the present Mellusian population is sparse and insignificant. The sect had its origin through a series of typical disagreements that started when the Catholic *Chaldean *patriarch, Joseph IV Audo (1759–1781), sent *Bishop Rokkos (at the behest of a *Malabarese *priest, Antony Thondanatta) whose function was to represent and assert the Catholic patriarch's jurisdiction in Malabar. Bishop Rokkos was recalled to Rome, and Thondanatta was consecrated bishop by the Nestorian *catholicos at Kudshanes, after which he returned to Malabar. Thondanatta, as Mar Abd-Iso, reconciled with Rome, but Patriarch Joseph IV sent another bishop, Elias Mellos, to Malabar against Rome's advice, and it was in this poor climate that existed between Audo IV and Rome that Mellos' name came to be adapted as the label for this sect, the Mellusians. With Mellos' sudden departure from Malabar, Thondanatta took over the leadership of the sect, and following his death in 1900 the Nestorian catholicos sent another bishop, Mar Timothy, to oversee the congregation. It has since declined dramatically in numbers.

MEMORIAL

In the *Eastern Church, this has several meanings:

1. As an intercession, for which the Syro-*Jacobite term "methdachronutho" referred to in James of Edessa's *Epistle* came to be used. (He comments on the order of commemorations that the "Alexandrine Fathers" make before offering the Holy *Kurobho; whereas others first offer the Kurobho and then make the commemorations.)

2. As an offering in commemoration, as the *Ethiopian term "tazcar" might suggest and as found in the Prayer of the *Enarxis in the Ethiopian *Liturgy.

3. As a commemoration of the dead, as the *Nestorian term "dukrani," or "duchrana," suggests when applied to a saint's day, or for the dead, when a *Cushapa (*Litany of the Departed) is said as part of the *Anaphora: "Lord and our God, may this offering be accepted for all . . . the Church . . . and for all the departed . . . who have gone from among us."

MENAION (Byzantine/Greek) (also called Mineya)

One of the twelve volumes that make up the collection called the Menaia, each volume of which corresponds to a month of the Church Year, which commences on September 1, "The Day of the Indiction." This book contains the variable parts of the *Divine Office for the immovable feasts and special hymns and prayers for each of the feasts being commemorated. Under each date, there are also comments about the life of the particular saint being commemorated as well as a note about any rubrics peculiar to that day. The historical comments are found between the sixth and seventh odes, which are found in the text of the Office, or *Acolouthia. An appendix usually contains the rite to be observed for those saints that have no Proper Office.

See LITURGICAL BOOKS (Byzantine Tradition).

MENBAB (Ethiopian)

The four lessons customarily read at an *Ethiopian *Liturgy.

See LECTIONS (Ethiopian Tradition).

MENOLOGION (Byzantine/Greek)

The Menologion corresponds roughly to the Western, or Roman, Martyrology and is technically an ecclesiastical calendar for the year containing the biographies of saints and martyrs arranged by month. The first compiler of such a book was allegedly St. Eusebius of Caesarea (ca. 260–341); another edition was arranged by Palladius, *bishop of Hierapolis (ca. 368–430).

See LITURGICAL BOOKS (Byzantine Tradition).

MERON (Armenian)

The holy oil, or chrism, that is consecrated for the *Armenians by the *catholicos of Cilicia, *patriarch of *Armenian Catholics. The non-Catholic Armenians receive their chrism from either the Armenian catholicate of Cilicia or from the Catholicos of Etchmiadzin, patriarch of all Armenians.

See CATHOLICOS; CHRISM.

MEROPOMAZANIE
(Byzantine/Slavonic)

See CHRISMATION.

MESEDI (Armenian)

After the Prophet has been read in the *Armenian *Liturgy, the mesedi is the psalm which immediately follows and which precedes the reading of the *Apostle. The term may sometimes refer to a hymn sung at Vespers.

See LECTIONS.

MESHAFA KANDIL (Ethiopian)

A manual used during the anointing (*unction) of the sick.

See LITURGICAL BOOKS (Ethiopian Tradition).

MESHAFA KEDDASE (Ethiopian)

The Missal, which is divided into two parts. Part I contains all the available *Anaphoras (*Keddase), of which there may be as many as twenty. Part II provides the psalmody for the *Liturgy, which is chanted by specially trained choirs (zemmare).

See LITURGICAL BOOKS (Ethiopian Tradition).

MESHAFA NUZAZE (Ethiopian)

A penitential manual. Among the non-Catholic *Ethiopians, the sacrament of *Penance is often administered only where there is danger of death.

See LITURGICAL BOOKS (Ethiopian Tradition).

MESHAFA TAKLIL (Ethiopian)

The book for *marriage ceremonies.

See LITURGICAL BOOKS (Ethiopian Tradition).

MESHWA'E (Ethiopian)

The term suggests the sense of the *altar as being a "sanctuary." An *Ethiopian altar should have a cross and at least two candles, while in an *Ethiopian Catholic Church there should be provision for the reservation of the Blessed Sacrament. It is of interest to note that it is now licit for Catholic Europeans to celebrate the *Liturgy without any candles at all.

See ALTAR.

MESOCHOROS (Byzantine/Greek)

A *Greek cleric who, while positioned in the middle of the choir, conducts and leads the singing.

MESONU(Y)KTIKON
(Byzantine/Greek)

The Midnight Office of the *Eastern Church, for which there is no Western equivalent. It commences with the blessing by the priest followed by the *Trisagion, the *Lord's Prayer, and on Sundays, the *Canon and *troparia to the Holy Trinity; while on other days a psalm, for example Psalm 50, may be recited. The Nicene *Creed follows, but this is omitted on Sundays when the subsequent Trisagion and Lord's Prayer are substituted by forty *Kyries. The next section of the Office, which includes reading from the psalms, the Trisagion, Lord's Prayer, and troparia, are also omitted on Sundays, but the Midnight Office always concludes with the *dismissal by the priest, prayers for mutual forgiveness, and a final *litany. This Office is not sung when there is a great *vigil, on Easter Monday, or during Holy Week.

See MIDNIGHT OFFICE; NOCTURNS; POLUNOSHCHNITSA.

MESORE (Coptic)

The twelfth month of the Coptic year, which corresponds to the period from July 25 to August 23.

See COPTIC CALENDAR.

MESORION (Byzantine/Greek)
(also spelled Meso-ora)

The Short *Hours, which may be inserted or supplemented between the Day Hours and between *Vespers and *Compline.

See MEZHDOCHASIE.

MESSIHAYE

A general term sometimes applied to the *East Syrians, *Syro-Chaldeans, or *Assyrian Christians.

METANOIA (Byzantine/Greek)
(also called *Exomologesis)

Literally, "repentance" or "penance." In the *Byzantine tradition the sacrament of Penance is administered quite infrequently and then usually only when Holy *Communion is to be received, especially at Christmas, Easter, Pentecost, and the Dormition of the Mother of God. There are no confessionals in a Byzantine church as are found in Western churches, and the *pneumatikos, or *priest who is to hear the confession, stands or sits to the side of the lectern on which lies an *icon and a hand cross. This position of the priest serves to emphasize his nonjudgmental role, which is that of a witness and a minister of God. The *penitent may either kneel or stand before the priest, and after the declaration of the sins and some spiritual advice, the penitent should kneel while the priest places the end of his *stole on the penitent's head and pronounces the absolution. The form of absolution varies according to whether it is of the *Greek or *Russian rite.

In the Russian rite the formula is indicative: "May our Lord and God, Jesus Christ . . . forgive you my child, N., . . . and I, . . . through the power given to me by him do forgive and absolve you from all your sins, in the name. . . ."

The formula in the Greek rite is deprecative, and the *sign of the cross is then made on the penitent's head.

See PENANCE, SACRAMENT OF; POKOYANIE.

METANY

This may be either (1) a great metany (megale metanoia), which is a profound prostration on hands and knees while the ground is touched with the head. The ground is then kissed and the *sign of the cross is made while a short prayer is said. (2) A little metany (mikra metanoia), which is a low bow with the fingers of the right hand stretched out so as to nearly touch the floor.

METHTA'BRONO (Syrian)

See ENERGUMEN.

METOCHION (Byzantine/Greek)

A daughter house, or farm, separate from a *lavra, or principal *Byzantine monastery, and administered by *monks sent from the lavra.

METRA (Coptic)

See KLAM; MITER; TAJ; TSCHREPI.

METRAN (Syrian)
(also spelled *Mitran)

See METROPOLITAN.

METROPOLITAN

The head of an ecclesiastical province in the *Eastern Orthodox Church, with his headquarters in the civil capital city. The term is occasionally applied to a Roman Catholic archbishop who has suffragan *bishops or to an Anglican archbishop.

MEZHDOCHASIE
(Byzantine/Slavonic)

An intermediate Office, or "between *Hour," which is recited during periods of *fast and after the recitation of any of the Little *Hours (for example, the Ninth Hour).

See CHASY; MESORION.

M'HAIMNO (Syrian)

See FAITHFUL.

MIDNIGHT OFFICE

See MESONU(Y)KTIKON; NOCTURNS; POLUNOSHCHNITSA.

MIESETESHVIE
(Byzantine/Slavonic)

See MENOLOGION.

MIKRA EISODOS
(Byzantine/Greek)

The Little Entrance.

See ENTRANCE (Byzantine Tradition).

MIKROSCHEMOS
(Byzantine/Greek)
(also spelled Mikroschema)

See DEGREES OF MONASTICISM, HABITS OF; MONASTICISM (Byzantine Tradition).

MINEYA (Byzantine/Slavonic)

See MENAION.

MINOR ORDERS

In the *Eastern Orthodox Church there are now principally two minor orders, that of lector, or reader, and that of subdeacon. The order of reader can be given by an *archimandrite or *archpriest in the *Byzantine rite if necessity warrants it. These two orders emerged and persisted out of the multitude of clerics whose functions were not strictly liturgical and included such "clerics" as gravediggers and notaries.

See ORDERS, HOLY.

MINTAKAH (Coptic/Arabic)

See GIRDLE; VESTMENTS, TABLE OF; ZOUNARION.

MIRWAHAH (Coptic/Arabic)

See CHEROUBIM; FANS; RIPIDION; RIPISTERION.

MISTIKOS (Byzantine/Greek)

The prayers that are recited silently by the *priest.

MITER

(also called Klam [Coptic]; Metra [Coptic and Slavonic]; Mitra [Greek])

The dome-shaped metal crown, which is usually heavily ornamented with precious stones and which is conferred upon all *bishops, *archimandrites, and certain *archpriests in the *Byzantine rite. The miter may have a small cross at the top, the normal custom in the Diocese of Kiev.

The origin of the miter is subject to some controversy among liturgists. It is known that Greek bishops celebrated the *Liturgy with uncovered heads, but the *patriarchs of Alexandria had the privilege of wearing miters because they had succeeded St. Cyril (376–444), who had received the privilege of wearing the miter from *Pope St. Celestine I, whom St. Cyril had represented at the Council of Ephesus in 431. That this privilege came to be extended to all bishops was certainly true from the early 18th century.

As the miter is put on, Ps 20:4-5 is recited: "You have set on his head a crown of precious stone. He asked life of you and you have given him length of days, forever and ever." In the Byzantine rite the miter is removed during the Liturgy of the *prothesis, at the *Great Entrance, just before the *Creed and during its recital, and at the Consecration and *Communion.

MITRAN (Syrian)

See METRAN; METROPOLITAN.

MIXED CHALICE

(also called Ithad [Arabic]; Soedinenie [Slavonic])

The addition of water to the wine in the *chalice was the practice in the early Church, as evidenced by Justin Martyr's *First Apology* (150), when he refers to the "bread and a cup of water and of mixed wine"; it probably reflects the Jewish custom of adding water to wine. Ancient *Liturgies refer to this mixing either discreetly in the rubrics or implied in the prayers of the Liturgy, for example, in the *Apostolic Constitutions* (ca. 375) as part of the narrative of the Institution when the *priest says, "Likewise also he mixed the cup of wine and water and sanctified it, and gave it to them."

This mixing is found in all Liturgies except that of the *Armenians and was the subject of much controversy. The nonobservance of this practice was condemned by the Second Council of Trullo and the subsequent Councils of Sis (1307) and Adana (1313), both of which ordered that water be added, but in 1359 the *catholicos Mesrob condemned the practice. *Pope Eugenius IV (1439), who was much concerned with the union of Rome and the Armenians, ordered that water and wine should be mixed, but his wish was not always complied with, and a decree from Propoganda in 1833 insisted that a little water be added to the wine. In the *Byzantine Liturgy the addition of hot water to the chalice at the *commixture seems to have been firmly established in the 6th century.

See ENOSIS.

MIZMAR (Coptic)

A flute that, together with *cymbals and handbells, may be sounded during the *Coptic *Liturgy.

M'KABLANA
(East Syrian/Nestorian)

See VEILS.

MKAPRANA
(also spelled Mkafrana)

See M'CAPRANA.

M'KHAP RANITHA (East Syrian)

A *purificator, principally used as a *chalice covering and used after the *commixture ceremony to wipe around the brim of the chalice, after which it is placed to the left of the chalice. At the end of the *Liturgy, the purificator is used to gather any crumbs of *bread into the chalice, and it may be used finally to clean both the *paten and chalice at the *altar.

MNEME (Byzantine)

The commemoration of anyone, whether a saint or some other person, living or dead.

MNESTRA (Byzantine/Greek)

The solemn engagement rite, which takes place in the church. During this ceremony lighted tapers are given to the couple and blessed rings are put on their hands by the *priest. Such an engagement may, of course, be subsequently broken; however, it is customary to link this ceremony with the marriage rite itself.

See ARRHABON; ESPOUSALS; MARRIAGE.

MOLEBEN (Byzantine)
See MOLIEBNY.

MOLIEBNY (Byzantine/Slavonic)
(also spelled *Moleben)

The service of prayers, either as thanksgiving or intercession, before a particular *icon. Such a service may also be performed to mark a special occasion. The hymns and *Gospel selected depend on whether the moliebny is a service of intercession to our Lord, to the Mother of God, or to a particular saint. The rest of the service consists of prayers and *litanies. The service concludes with the congregation coming forward to kiss the hand cross, which is held by the *priest.

MOLITVENIK (Byzantine/Slavonic)
Literally, "collection of prayers."

See HAGIASMATERION.

MONACHIKE KOURA
(Byzantine/Greek)
(also called *Apokarsis)
See TONSURE.

MONASTERION
See LAVRA.

MONASTIC HABIT

A general term describing the *habit or garments worn by monks and nuns. The kind of habit worn differs according to the degree to which a monk or nun is admitted, especially in the *Byzantine rite. There are three degrees of the Byzantine monastic state; the full or angelic habit is worn only by those religious who have been admitted to the highest degree. It is called "angelic" because the wearer is assumed to live "the angelic life" of the religious.

See DEGREES OF MONASTICISM, HABITS OF; MONASTICISM; MONKS.

MONASTICISM

See DEGREES OF MONASTICISM, HABITS OF; MONASTIC HABIT; MONK.

Armenian Tradition

The Rule of life for *Armenian Catholic *Mechitarists is that of St. Benedict, which supplanted the original Rule of St. Antony. Among non-Catholic *Armenians the monastic life has been on the decline. There are several types of monk: the *sarkavak (monk *deacon), the abegha (monk *priest), the *vartabed (minor doctor), the dzayragooyn vartabed (supreme doctor), and the episcopos (*bishop). A monk priest is ordained and is invested with the monastic veil (*veghar) when he is at least twenty-two years of age.

See MECHITARISTS.

Byzantine Tradition

There are four distinct types of monk:

1. Eremitic (literally, "solitary"). He may be called a hesychast who lives in a hesychasterion, or hermitage, which is usually some inaccessible cave, and he may rarely if ever be seen. Alternatively, the eremite could live in a cell, or *kellion. The eremitic mode of life is modeled on St. Paul of Thebes (ca. 230–342) and St. Antony (251–356).

2. Semi-eremitic, where the monk lives in a colony but not as a solitary. However, a common Rule of life is not observed, as each follows some individual plan of asceticism under the spiritual direction of an abbot. This way of life is reminiscent of St. Antony. The semi-eremites live in a *skete (literally, "a place of asceticism"), or *lavra. Today the term "lavra" has come to mean a large skete. A skete is really a small monastic village which is internally self-governing but which is dependent on the principal monastery for its legal foundation. While the number of monks that may inhabit a skete is limited, movement from one skete to another is permitted. Sketes may be either *cenobitic or *idiorrhythmic. In the former case, the monks live a common life, taking their meals together in the refectory and saying the Office in the *kyriakon, or church of the skete, where the *Liturgy is also celebrated. The superior, or *dikaios (proestos), holds his office for life and is elected by all the monks and not by the elders (gerontes) alone; however, this election has to be approved by the principal monastery. Idiorrhythmic sketes consist of many separated houses, or kalybai (*kalyba), and these may be leased by three monks, but without any lay brothers

in attendance. It may sometimes happen that a kalyba is assigned to one or two monks for the rest of their lives, but without any right of succession. While the kalybai surround the church of the skete, which is where the Liturgy is celebrated on Sundays and the Office is chanted, each cottage has a small chapel, although the Liturgy is not usually celebrated there. The superior of the skete is elected once each year on May 8, when all the elders of each kalybai gather, and upon election the superior goes to reside in the guest house, or zenon.

3. Cenobitic monks, or monks of the common life, are modeled on the lines of the first cenobium (Greek, "common life"), which was founded by St. Pachomius (292–346) at Tabennisi. Both St. Basil and St. Benedict are said to have been influenced by his Rule, the original text of which no longer exists. St. Basil introduced St. Pachomius' cenobitic ideal into a cenobium at Neocaesarea in Pontus in 360. Under this system, the monks live in different buildings but within the precincts of the monastery. The meals are eaten at different times, but the monks come together for the services; St. Basil established a "common roof, common table, and common prayer." In modern *Orthodox monasteries the monasteriacos (monk) who lives in such a monastery holds all property in common with his fellow monks. The superior (*hegumen) is elected by a ballot of all the monks and holds the office for life, aided and advised by a council of elders.

4. Idiorrhythmic monks who are not semi-eremitic first appeared on Mount *Athos in 1374, when the ascetic ideal had become a little relaxed. Under this system the monks may singly or collectively own, buy, and bequeath property. With their obvious independence of a hegumen, a council of monks is responsible for the corporate control of the monastery, and this council holds office for one year only. The nominal head of an idiorrhythmic monastery is called a "kathegumenos." The inhabitants of an idiorrhythmic monastery receive payment for their work, and no restriction seems to operate as to how many occupants may be accommodated in such a monastery (*stavropegion), which is independent of diocesan control. The church of such a monastery provides the central place for worship, but there is provision for various small chapels.

Two other types of monastic dwelling may be encountered in *Byzantine monasticism, the *kellion (cell) and the *kathisma (hut). The kellion is usually a single building with a chapel (*naidrion) inside it, and it is normally attached to a small tract of land. The responsibility for the kellion devolves on three monk occupants, and there are quite complex rules that govern its working and the leadership of the group. In the deed of trust, which is drawn up by the principal monastery, the first monk (protos) is the elder of the kellion, and it is his responsibility to appoint two other monks to be joint tenants. When the protos dies, his place is taken by the second monk, and another monk joins the kellion. Every time there is a shift in leadership a new lease is drawn up, and a portion of the total valuation of the kellion is paid into the treasury of the main monastery, while the estate of the deceased protos passes to his successor. The assistance of up to three lay brothers is permitted in Greek monasteries, but not so in Russian foundations.

The second type of monastic dwelling, the kathisma, is occupied by an eremitic monk who pays a sum of money to the principal monastery, which in turn provides the monk with a small portion of food, usually bread, each day.

Coptic Tradition

In recent times there has been a rapid growth in Coptic monasticism and a revival of Coptic Christianity. Some thirty years ago in the Wadi Natrun north of Cairo and in the district of Scetis, several monasteries, notably St. Macarius the Great (probably founded by St. Amoun [275–337] but popularized by St. Macarius around 390), came under the guidance of a remarkable priest, Matthew the Poor. Under his guidance there has been an ambitious program of agricultural and horticultural research and publishing. The life is very ascetic, the staple food being dried beans and bread. Provision is made for Coptic nuns, who are less commonly encountered.

Ethiopian Tradition

Ethiopian monasticism is not very regulated, some religious being eremitical while others live in community. Two main observances exist: that of St. Eustathius near Adua and that of St. Takla Haymanot (reputed to have introduced the "angelic life" in 620) at Dabra Libanos in the Salaleh district of Shoa. This latter foundation's superior (itshage) exercises considerable

ecclesiastical control and often rivals the *abuna of the Church. The Observances of St. Antony are followed and the life-style is generally extremely ascetic; few monks are priests, and provision is made for hermits as well as nuns, who may choose either to live the common life or to live under vows in their own homes.

Maronite Tradition

There are three congregations of Maronite Antonians, which are largely contemplative and pursue a very ascetic life of abstinence from flesh meat. These are the Antonians of St. Isaiah, the Aleppine Antonians, and the Baladite Antonians. The Aleppines, also known as Halabiyeh Antonians, later became known as the Lebanese Monks of St. Antony, with headquarters at Luweize near Zuk-Mihail. The Baladites arose from a separation from the Aleppines caused by disagreement between the "mountain" or "country" monks (the Baladites) and the Aleppines in 1770. A missionary order emerged modeled on the lines of the Redemptorists, known as the Lebanese Maronite Missionaries of Kraim. Antonian Maronite nuns are common; their mode of life is strictly contemplative. There are also active orders such as the Visitandes, the Sisters of the Holy Family, and the Sisters of the Sacred Hearts of Jesus and Mary.

East Syrian Tradition

Non-Catholic *Nestorians no longer have a monastic tradition in operation, but among the Catholic *Chaldeans there is the Congregation of St. Hormisdas, which follows an Antonian tradition. This was adapted by Gabriel Dembo in 1808 from the Maronite Antonians and was formally recognized in the mid-19th century by *Pope Gregory XVI. There are Chaldean nuns, belonging to the Institute of the Sisters of the Immaculate Conception (founded in 1922), whose apostolate is largely educational.

West Syrian Tradition

Very few non-Catholic monastic foundations remain; the rule that was observed was an ascetic form of the Antonian type. Catholic Syrian monasticism is more lively, and there are many Catholic Syrian convents.

MONKS

See DEGREES OF MONASTICISM, HABITS OF; HABITS, COMPARATIVE TABLE OF; MONASTICISM.

Armenian Tradition

The *habit worn by *Armenian religious is a black robe with a black hood. In choir a black woolen cloak (*philon) and a cone-shaped hat (*pakegh) may be worn. The pakegh is usually violet in color and is covered with a veil (*veghar).

See MONASTICISM (Armenian Tradition).

Byzantine Tradition

From the *Novels* of Justinian (535), it is evident that a probationer to the religious life was expected to wear lay dress until he received the *tonsure and habit from the *hegumen, or superior of the monastery. A so-called intermediate grade of monk came to be in-troduced toward the end of the 8th century, when St. Theodore the Studite wrote about the little habit, which was given to such an intermediate grade of monk. The so-called lowest grade of monk, thought of as an "imperfect monk" (*rasophore), marks the start of the monastic life. The candidate is tonsured and is given part of the monastic habit to wear, although in practice he may wear a *rason and *skouphos before becoming a rasophore, and he is expected to persevere in the religious life. It should be noted that no one is obliged to proceed beyond the grade of rasophore.

After a period of probation, the rasophore (or archarios) comes to be called a *stavrophore because he wears a wooden cross (stavros); he may also be called a microschemos because of the habit he now wears. He makes his vows before receiving the tonsure and little habit and *cenobitic monks of this grade resemble the cenobitic ideals of St. Pachomius, St. Basil, and St. Theodore the Studite. The vows of stability, chastity, obedience, and poverty are taken in that order, in answer to a series of direct questions asked of them by the superior, whether hegumen or hegumenissa. This intermediate monk was occasionally called a "perfect" monk because he had passed through his probation and affirmed his vows, but as a rule he was called a "proficient" monk.

The highest grade of monk wears the full angelic habit and is called a *megaloschemos (Greek) or skhimnik (Slavonic). Progression from a rasophore to a megaloschemos is possible without first becoming a stavrophore, but such a move requires the approval of the hegumen and elders of the community. Lay brothers technically may pass from being probationers to megaloschemoi without becoming either rasophores or stavrophores because of their many years of service in the monastery. As a megaloschemos, the religious may live his life apart from the others as a *hesychast or as a semi-eremite; his life is marked by much prayer, fasting, and the observance of silence. He is forbidden to eat flesh meat, which may include fish, so his diet is largely vegetarian. If a *priest becomes a megaloschemos he may continue to celebrate the *Liturgy, but if he is a *bishop he may not exercise his episcopal functions.

See MONASTICISM (Byzantine Tradition).

Coptic Tradition

The habit consists of a brown woolen robe, black cloak with ample sleeves, and a leather *girdle. A turban is worn, to which the *shamlah is attached. This is a 1″ band of black serge that extends to the neck and corresponds to the angelic habit. The wearing of the shamlah commits the monk to a most ascetic way of life, with much prayer, fasting, and penance.

See MONASTICISM (Coptic Tradition).

Ethiopian Tradition

There is no fixed shape or color for the habit, which consists of a tunic, belt, cloak, and hood. A postulant becomes a novice when the superior gives him the girdle (*Quenat). He later receives the tunic, or cassock, and an *askema, which is ornamented with twelve crosses. Finally, at solemn profession or its equivalent, the Ethiopian monk receives a tall white hat, or "bonnet of perfection," the yefe'-tsamie qob.

See MONASTICISM (Ethiopian Tradition).

Maronite Tradition

Maronite Antonians traditionally wear a black gown with a small hood, leather belt, and sandals. The Maronite Missionaries of Kraim, founded by Father Habib in 1865 and modeled along the lines of the Redemptorists, wear a black habit, leather girdle, hood, cloak, and sandals.

See MONASTICISM (Maronite Tradition).

East Syrian Tradition

Among Catholic East Syrians, or Chaldeans, the Congregation of St. Hormisdas wear a black habit with hood. There is no non-Catholic East Syrian or Nestorian monasticism.

See MONASTICISM (East Syrian Tradition).

West Syrian Tradition

Admission to the monastic life in this tradition is preceded by a tonsure. The habit is a black woolen robe (*Kuthino), a leather girdle (*Zunnoro), a hood (*Eskhim), and a cloak (*Jubba).

See MONASTICISM (West Syrian Tradition).

MONOGENES

A hymn or anthem traditionally ascribed to the emperor Justinian

(527–565) and addressed to the Triumphant Redeemer. It forms the conclusion of the second *antiphon in the *enarxis of the *Byzantine *Liturgy: "O only begotten Son and Word of God; You who are immortal yet deigned for our salvation to become incarnate, of the Holy Birth-Giver of God and ever Virgin Mary . . . O Christ God trampling down death by death, who are one of the Holy Trinity and are glorified together with the Father and the Holy Spirit. . . ." The hymn is also found in the *Liturgy of St. James and that of St. Mark, where it occurs at the Little *Entrance.

MONOPHYSITE

A pejorative term for *Oriental Christians, also a term applied to those who hold a belief in *Monophysitism. As a heresy it spread throughout the East, especially in Syria and Egypt, in the 5th century; its adherents later came to be called *Jacobites. The heresy affirms that Christ had but one nature, the divine, and not two natures so united as to preserve their distinctness.

See MONOPHYSITISM.

MONOPHYSITISM

Literally, "one nature." A heresy that holds that in Jesus Christ there is only one nature and that his humanity is absorbed in his divinity. The heresy was condemned by the Council of Chalcedon in 451, but the rejection of the council's definition led to the separation of the *Coptic, *Ethiopian, Syro-*Jacobite, and *Armenian Churches from the rest of the *Orthodox community, and these non-Orthodox Churches came to be called *Monophysite.

MONOTHELITE

A heretic who holds that our Lord had two natures but only one will, which was divine. It dates from the 7th century and was condemned by the sixth ecumenical council, held in Constantinople in 681.

See MONOTHELITISM.

MONOTHELITISM

A heresy that states that in Jesus Christ there is one divine energy and one will, which is inconsistent with the reality of Christ's humanity. The heresy was seen as an attempt by the *Byzantine emperor Heraclius in 638, at the suggestion of *Patriarch Sergius of Constantinople, to try to reconcile the *Orthodox and *Monophysites, especially in the face of the seventh-century Arab invasion, which was on the increase and was spreading Islam. Patriarch Sergius had the support of *Pope Honorius, who neither defended nor condemned the heresy and who wrote, "We must not wrest what they say into Church dogmas." Honorius should have condemned this heresy, and his failure to do so resulted in his being anathematized by the sixth ecumenical council in Constantinople in 681. Pope St. Martin I held a synod in Rome in which Catholic doctrine of the two wills in Christ was affirmed; both Sergius and Honorius were condemned. This infuriated the *Byzantine emperor, who arranged to bring Pope Martin to Constantinople. Pope Martin eventually died in exile in 655.

See MONOTHELITE.

MONOVAMPOULOS
(Byzantine/Greek)

An obsolete single-branched candlestick that was carried before a *bishop.

MORNING INCENSE, OFFICE OF
(Coptic)

An Office recited before the celebration of the *Liturgy; it consists of the *Lord's Prayer, a psalm of thanksgiving, offering of *incense throughout the sanctuary and church, hymns, the *Creed, which commences with "We believe," intercession, and the prayer of *Absolution to the Son. The *priest is fully vested during the recitation of this Office, since the *Liturgy immediately follows.

MOS(T)CHE (Byzantine/Slavonic)

See LEIPSANA.

MOTHAT (Ethiopian)

The *stole worn by *Ethiopian clergy; it is *Byzantine in shape, and the pieces are joined together in front with a narrow opening through which the head can pass. It is usually embroidered with many crosses.

MOTWA (East Syrian/Nestorian)

Literally, "seat." An anthem, the text of which varies according to the day of the week. It is taken from the Night Office and may be sung while sitting. As part of the *Liturgy it is recited during the preparation of the *bread as the breads are removed from the *oven and placed on the *paten.

See BREAD (East Syrian/Nestorian Tradition).

MOUNT ATHOS
(also called Holy Mountain)

A promontory of the Chalcidice peninsula in the Aegean Sea. In early times it was inhabited by hermits; around 960 St. Athanasius of Trebizond, a *monk from Mount Kyminas in Bithynia under St. Michael Maleinos, settled at Athos. He founded the first *cenobitic monastery there, which was dedicated in 963. Other foundations soon followed, and in the face of opposition by some of the hermits already there, St. Athanasius appealed to the emperor, who established Athanasius' authority.

While Athos is dependent on the *ecumenical patriarch, it is a sovereign, self-administering region within the Greek state and is governed by a Holy Community, which consists of a representative from each of its twenty monasteries. These representatives are divided into four groups of five, each group serving on the region's Holy Administration, or Iera Epistasia, for one year. With the passage of time there has been a gradual decline in the population. In 1913 there were 7,970 residents; by 1971 the population had fallen to 1,145. The figures increased during the 1980s.

MOUSA (Byzantine/Greek)

See SPONGE.

MR-THOU

These letters stand for "Mother of God" and are frequently found on *icons of the Mother of God.

M'SHAM-SHONO (Maronite)

A *deacon; he must be at least twenty-one years of age at the time of his ordination, after which he is obliged to recite the *Divine Office. The *vestments worn by the deacon, like those of many other *Maronite clergy, are becoming increasingly Western, but properly, he wears a *stole over the left shoulder above an ample *alb and *girdle.

M'SHAM-SHONOITHO
(Maronite and Syro-Jacobite)

In these rites the deaconess refers to a vessel in which the celebrant's fingers may be washed. In the Syro-*Jacobite rite this vessel is also used for mixing the water and wine at the offertory.

See DEACONESS.

M'SONE (Syro-Jacobite)

The special shoes worn by *priests and *deacons as part of their Eucharistic *vestments.

MUNNA-NORBA (Syro-Malabar)

The three-day Fast of *Nineveh observed in the *Syro-Malabar rite, starting on the eighteenth day before the first day of Lent.

MURONITHO (Syro-Jacobite)
(also called *Hutro; *Shabbuqto)

The *crozier, or pastoral staff, designed as two intertwined serpents with a ball surmounted by a cross between them. Occasionally the staff terminates in a curved serpent's head, which is made to arch, resembling a Western crozier. The Catholic *patriarch's staff has a ball at the top which has a cross at its apex, while the *Jacobite patriarch's staff looks rather like an imperial scepter. During the consecration of a *bishop, the consecrand is ceremonially invested with the muronitho, accompanied by the words "The Lord has sent you a rod of strength out of Sion." When a patriarch is being "ordained" every participating bishop grasps the muronitho with his right hand and all hold it together, then the senior bishop present raises the patriarch's hand above the others and rests it at the top of the staff, at which point the ceremony is concluded.

MUSHRABIAH (Coptic)

The fine latticework used for windows.

MYRON

*Bishops who are the heads of *autocephalous Churches can consecrate the chrism, or *myron, for use throughout their Churches; for example, the *patriarch of Moscow consecrates the chrism for use throughout the *Russian Orthodox Church, while the *Coptic patriarch consecrates the chrism for the use of the Coptic community. In the words of the Council of Laodicea (can. 48), the myron makes the recipient a sharer in the kingdom of God. It was probably with this in mind that chrismation was recognized as the means whereby schismatics could be reconciled with the *Orthodox Church. When, for example, Roman Catholics become Orthodox Christians they are often received through chrismation. In the Orthodox Church the chrism is a mixture of pure olive oil and white grape wine, to which is added a number of aromatic substances that symbolize the many graces or gifts conferred through the *sacrament.

In the history of the *Russian Orthodox Church different recipes of the ingredients have been known at different times; for example, in the 17th century, the number of ingredients varied from fifty-three to fifty-five, while in 1894 the published *Office of Preparation of the Chrism* reduced the number of ingredients to thirty. In addition to top-grade olive oil and white grape wine the ingredients include *incense, rose petals, violet and calamus roots, galanga, and oils such as rose, nutmeg, lemon, and cloves.

See CHRISM; CHRISMATION.

MYSTER (Coptic)

See COMMUNION (Coptic Tradition); KOKLIARION.

MYSTERIES

The general term used throughout the *Eastern Church to describe the *sacraments.

MYSTHERI (Ethiopian)

See COMMUNION (Ethiopian Tradition); KOKLIARION.

MYSTIC RECITATION

An expression often used to describe those parts of the *Eastern Orthodox *Liturgy (*Byzantine) said in a low voice or whisper.

MZAMRONO (Syrian)

A *singer. This *minor order is received at the *elevation in the *Liturgy; as part of the ordination ceremony the ordinand receives a Book of Psalms. The function of the mzamrono is to make the responses usually ascribed to the people in the rubrics of the Liturgy.

N

NABEDRENNIK
(Byzantine/Slavonic)
(also spelled Nabedrensk)

An oblong piece of stiffened rich material suspended from the hip of the *priest. This is the first mark of distinction that is granted to *Russian clergy. If a priest earns the right to wear the epigonation, the nabedrennik hangs from the left side. It is thought by some to signify the Sword of the Spirit, which is the Word of God, while others suggest that it represents the towel used by Jesus at the Last Supper when he washed the disciples' feet. The Nabedrennik is identical to the *palitza except that it is suspended by two corners, whereas the palitza hangs from one corner only.

Other distinctions that the Russian clergy may acquire, in addition to the epigonation, include the gold pectoral cross and the title of *archpriest. The silver pectoral cross worn by a Russian priest serves to distinguish him from a *deacon, a privilege granted by the Holy Synod to commemorate the crowning of Tzar Nicholas II in 1894.

See EPIGONATION.

NAFUR (Maronite)

One of the three silk veils used to cover the Eucharistic vessels.

See GITA; VEILS.

NAIDRION (Byzantine/Greek)

A small chapel in a monastic house, which may itself be part of a larger monastic community.

See KELLION; MONASTICISM (Byzantine Tradition).

NAKHARRBEAL (Armenian)

An obsolete rite of the *Presanctified.

NAKIS (Coptic)

See LAX.

NAPQA (East Syrian/Chaldean)

Literally, "one who has left the world." A *Chaldean monk who is probably a member of the Antonian Congregation of St. Hormisdas, reputedly founded by Gabriel Dambo in 1808. The *habit is a black gown and hood as well as the customary black turban.

See MONASTICISM (East Syrian Tradition); MONKS (East Syrian Tradition); RABAN.

NARTHEX (Byzantine/Greek)

In early churches and in some *monastic churches there were two divisions of the narthex, or entrance to the church; these were the outer narthex (exonarthex) and the inner narthex (esonarthex). The esonarthex was where the monks recited the Morning Office of *Orthros and *Ainoi, while the exonarthex was little more than a covered area that gave access to the church, designed to provide shelter during bad weather. The esonarthex was separated from the rest of the church by a small rail; later it was separated from the *nave by a *door sometimes called the *royal doors, although this term is commonly used to describe the central or *holy doors set in the *iconostasis. Various grades of *penitents, such as *hearers, *catechumens and *competentes, stood in the esonarthex during the *Liturgy.

See PRITVOR (Slavonic).

NAVAGADIKH (Armenian)

A mild day of abstinence on which flesh meat is forbidden, as on the *vigil of a feast.

NAVE

(also called Haicla [East Syrian]; Khmbaran [Armenian]; Korabl [Slavonic]; Naos [Greek])

That part of the church in which the faithful gather to hear and attend the *Liturgy and in which the *ambo and *soleas are located. A reserved area for women, the gynaeconitis, is often marked by being separated from the rest of the nave by a small grille, as among the *Copts, or by the use of a small gallery, which may be found in some *Byzantine-rite churches.

NAVECHERIE (Byzantine/Slavonic)

See PARAMONI.

NEBRID (Ethiopian)

An *archdeacon or rector of a cathedral.

NEFEK (Ethiopian)

An assistant *priest.

NEFKA DIYAKON (Ethiopian)

A *subdeacon, of which there are few today, since the liturgical functions are now more often performed by a *deacon. Such functions would include the reading of the Catholic Epistle in the *Liturgy. The customary *vestments of a subdeacon were a linen alb (*kamis) with wide sleeves, a girdle (*zenar), a *stole that sometimes hangs down the back, and a shortened cope-like *cappa, which is fastened at the neck.

See ORDERS, HOLY (Ethiopian Tradition).

NEKROSIMON

A *troparion for the dead, and for those who are living that they may pray for a happy death.

NEPHELE (Byzantine/Greek)

Literally, "cloud."

See AER; KALYMMATA.

NEPOROCHNYI (Byzantine/Slavonic)

See EVLOGITARIA.

NESHKAR (Armenian)

Literally, "wafer." The Eucharistic bread. The same word may be extended to include the *eulogia.

See BREAD (Armenian Tradition).

NESTEIA (Byzantine/Greek)

See FASTS (Byzantine Tradition); POST.

NESTORIAN

See EAST SYRIAN.

NESTORIAN CHURCH, CLERGY OF

The clergy ranks are based on the nine choirs of angels. The *patriarch represents the cherub; the *metropolitans represent the seraphim; the *bishops (*efiskufa) represent the thrones; *archpriests (*rab kumre) represent the dominions; the *chorepiscopus (sa'-aure) represents the virtues; the *priest (*kahna) symbolizes the powers; the *deacons (*shamasha or *dyakna) represent the principalities; the *subdeacons (*hufadyakna) represent the archangels; and the *readers (*karuya) represent the angels.

NESTORIAN CHURCH, DIVINE OFFICE OF

See EAST SYRIAN CHURCH, DIVINE OFFICE OF.

NESTORIAN CHURCH, LITURGICAL BOOKS OF

See LITURGICAL BOOKS (East Syrian Tradition).

NESTORIAN CHURCH, LITURGICAL LANGUAGE OF

See LITURGICAL LANGUAGES, TABLE OF.

NESTORIAN CHURCH, SACRAMENTS OF

According to Joseph Assemani (1710–1782) there were only three *sacraments in the Nestorian Church, *baptism, Holy Eucharist, and orders, but in practice seven seem to be recognized, although there is uncertainty as to which ones they are.

The Nestorian *patriarch Timothy II (1318–1360) suggested the following: holy orders, consecration of a church and *altar, baptism and holy oil, the holy sacrament of the Body and Blood, blessing of *monks, the Office for the dead, and *marriage.

Badger claims that the list is orders, baptism, oil of unction, oblation of the Body and Blood of Christ, absolution, Holy Leaven, and the *sign of the cross. The liturgical books have a form available for *penance and absolution, although it is rarely if ever used.

See also under the headings for individual sacraments: ORDERS, HOLY (East Syrian Tradition), etc.

NE'US CRESTIYAN (Ethiopian)

Literally, "young Christian." The catechumens, who are being dismissed at the start of the *Liturgy of the Faithful.

See CATECHUMEN.

NINEVEH, FAST OF
(also spelled Ninive)

A pre-Lenten fast, normally of three days' duration, which is observed in all *Eastern-rite Churches with the exception of the *Byzantine rite, which substitutes Cheese Week for this fast. Cheese Week is preceded by the Sunday of Meatlessness on the seventh Sunday before Easter. The fast commemorates Jonah's preaching and the penance that followed. Among the *Armenians the fast is called *Aratshavoratz. It lasts five days and is observed in the tenth week before Easter, not only to commemorate the preaching of Jonah but also the preaching of St. Gregory before the nation was converted, and hence the fast's name, that of St. Gregory.

'NKAR (Armenian)

The *Armenian equivalent of an *icon, of which there are very few in Armenian churches; this distrust of pictures may have affected the Iconoclastic controversy at Constantinople in 717 with the accession of an Armenian as Emperor Leo III.

NOCTURNS
See MESONU(Y)KTIKON; MIDNIGHT OFFICE; POLUNOSHCHNITSA.

NOMOCANON (Greek)

Literally, "law, rule."

See SYNTAGMA.

NON-CHALCEDONIAN

A term used to refer to those Churches that did not accept the definition of the Council of Chalcedon in 451 concerning the nature of Christ. This council condemned the teaching of Eutyches, opposed Nestorius, and defined that there was "one and the same Christ the Son, Lord, Only-Begotten, in two natures, without confusion, without change [against Eutyches], without division, without separation [against Nestorius]." Whereas the Council of Ephesus (431) had seen the separation of the *Nestorians, the Council of Chalcedon occasioned the departure of the *Monophysites, who today comprise five *autonomous groups: (1) *Coptic Orthodox Church, (2) Orthodox Church of *Ethiopia, (3) *Armenian Orthodox Church, (4) *Syrian Orthodox Church, and (5) Syrian Orthodox Church in *India.

NOQUSHO (Syrian)

A tongueless bronze cup that is struck by a metal rod at the same time the *cymbals (*sesle) are sounded to mark important moments in the *Liturgy.

NUPTIAL CROWN

An ornament placed on the heads of bride and bridegroom as part of the *marriage ceremonies, hence the alternative name "the crowning" when referring to marriage. The *priest places the crown first on the head of the bridegroom as he says, "The servant of God, N., is crowned unto the handmaid of God, NN., in the name of the Father and of the Son and of the Holy Spirit"; the ceremony is repeated for the bride.

See MARRIAGE.

O

OBLATION OF OIL (Ethiopian)

The service at which the oils of *catechumens and the sick are consecrated and which follows the consecration of the *bread and wine in the *Liturgy. The *Anaphora used is that of the "Ethiopic Church Ordinances," which is related to the *Canons of Hippolytus (ca. 220) and which provides the sources of the offertory rubric and the oblation of the oil after the *invocation. Interestingly, the *Ethiopian *Anaphora of the Apostles is derived from this earlier Anaphora, as well as some Egyptian Anaphoras. The date of the document is uncertain, but Bunsen considered that the second century is probably correct, although the evidence is fairly scant.

OBSCHAYA MINEYA (Byzantine/Slavonic)

See MENAION.

OBSHCHENIYE (Byzantine/Slavonic)

Holy Communion.

See COMMUNION (Byzantine Tradition); PRICHASTIYE.

OCTOECHOS (Byzantine/Greek) (also spelled Octoekhos)

A two-volume *Eastern Christian liturgical book containing the Common of the season. One volume is an abridgment of the other and is known simply as the Little Octoechos, or simply the Octoechos, while the larger and more extensive book has come to be called the Great Octoechos, or Parakletike. The Little Octoechos contains eight Sunday Offices corresponding to each of the eight *tones, hence the name of the book. In each tone, or mode, there are seven sets of services, which correspond to each day of the week, so that when the eighth mode is completed, the first is begun again.

Pargoire (1905) claimed that the *Orthodox Church had a book of eight tones dating from the 6th century to which some writings of St. John

Damascene (ca. 675–749) were added; some additions by the Studites were added in the 9th century, and by the second half of that century Metrophanes of Smyrna was still working on its composition. In the Sunday Office of *Orthros, or Matins, is found a *Canon attributed to St. John Damascene and known as Anastasimos (of the Resurrection); while as part of the *Nocturns, a Canon attributed to Metrophanes of Smyrna, called Triadikos (to the Holy Trinity), is found.

See BOOK OF EIGHT TONES; LITURGICAL BOOKS (Byzantine Tradition); PARAKLETIKE.

ODE (Byzantine)

See CANON; ENNEA ODAI.

OECONOMUS (Greek)

Literally, "house" or "to manage." In *Eastern *Orthodoxy this title refers to an *archdeacon, or *priest who administers the episcopal finances and who may even take over as caretaker of an *eparchy during a vacancy of the title.

OECUMENICAL PATRIARCH

A title of the archbishops or patriarchs of Constantinople since the 6th century, when John IV (the Faster) was patriarch of Constantinople.

See ECUMENICAL PATRIARCH.

OGLASHENNIY
(Byzantine/Slavonic)

See CATECHUMEN.

OIKOS (Byzantine/Greek)

The stanza that immediately follows the *kontakion between *Canticles 6 and 7 at Matins, or *Orthros.

See ORTHROS.

OIKTOIKH (Byzantine/Slavonic)

See LITURGICAL BOOKS (Byzantine Tradition); OCTOECHOS.

OLD BELIEVERS

The Old Believers arose from the 1666 schism started by the *archpriest Avvakum within the *Russian Orthodox Church as a protest against the liturgical reforms of *Patriarch Nikon. These reforms included blessing with three fingers instead of two, minor changes in the Apostles' *Creed, and the triple singing of the Alleluia during Lent instead of the more familiar repeated single response. As a result of a bitter persecution that lasted until the mid-19th century, the community, or sect (raskol), flourished, but many religious excesses became manifest. The Old Believers were dependent upon the ministrations of discontented *priests until 1846, when the deposed *bishop Ambrose of Boznia joined them and set up a hierarchy. Today this group is known as Popovtsy. Another group of Old Believers, the Bezpopovtsy, continues without ordained clergy.

OLD CALENDAR

See JULIAN CALENDAR.

OLD CALENDARISTS

The self-styled "Authentic Orthodox," but in fact they are *Greek Orthodox who rejected the *ecumenical patriarch's recommendation of 1924 that a change be made from the Old or *Julian Calendar to the New or *Gregorian Calendar. In 1980 they numbered around 215,400 adherents.

See PALEOHEMEROLOGITES.

OMOFOR (Byzantine/Slavonic)

See OMOPHORION.

OMOFORION (Coptic)

See OMOPHORION.

OMOLOGIA (Coptic)

Literally, "confession." The profession, or confession, of faith, which precedes the reception of Holy *Communion. In the *Coptic rite it is recited after the ceremony of *consignation and commences with the words "Amen, Amen, Amen, I believe and confess to my dying day. . . ." The wording of the Omologia has been the subject of much controversy, as minute odd insertions have been introduced that suggest an affirmation of *Monophysitism.

In the closely related *Ethiopian rite the *Jacobites exclaim, "This is the True Precious Blood . . . Amen," and "This is the Body and Blood of Emmanuel our True God."

OMOPHORION (Byzantine/Greek) (also spelled *Omofor; *Omoforion)

A pallium. According to Marriot, it has been worn by *patriarchs and *metropolitans as well as most *Eastern *bishops since the 5th century, but curiously there is no evidence of the omophorion being used at the investiture of either a bishop of metropolitan in any known Pontifical. There is, however, an early mention of the omophorion in connection with the patriarch Theophilus of Alexandria in the early 5th century. St. Isidore of Pelusium, an Egyptian (d. 440), wrote in his *Epistle* that it is supposed to symbolize the lost sheep that our Lord went to find and brought back on his shoulders.

As to whether the omophorion arose first in Rome or Alexandria, there is no direct evidence for either conclusion. In the 6th century it was customary for a new Coptic patriarch to take the pall of St. Mark from the neck of his deceased predecessor before burial as part of the solemn ritual in the making of a new patriarch, and he would then place it around his own neck.

According to Brightman, it is a long scarf originally made of lamb's wool marked with crosses and worn by bishops over the chasuble, then passed over the shoulders and tied loosely on the left shoulder with the ends falling nearly to the ground at the back and front.

Among *Coptic Catholics and non-Catholics alike this vestment resembles a Western pallium. It is made of white silk or wool and forms the outline of a broad Y; to that extent it resembles the common Greek omophorion.

The *Byzantine Church recognizes two forms of the omophorion, the great and the little omophorion. In this rite it is usually a long band of rich material embroidered with many crosses that a bishop wears around his neck with one end hanging down in front on the left side and the other end hanging behind.

When the great omophorion is being put on, the following prayer is recited: "You have taken on your shoulders, O Christ, our nature that had gone astray; you have lifted it up on to your shoulders and have offered it to God the Father." This great omophorion is removed during the reading of the Gospel and stays removed until the end of the *Liturgy, while the little omophorion is worn from the *Cherubikon until the end of the Liturgy but is taken off at the Great *Entrance, when it is carried in front of the offerings. It should be noted that the little omophorion is worn at ordination ceremonies.

See HEMNICHO; MARTUTA; URORO; URORO RABBO; VESTMENTS, TABLE OF.

OMPHALOS (Byzantine/Greek)
(also called Mesonaos)

An architectural term referring to the central point of the church. The location of this is supposed to be in the middle of the choir, facing the *royal door.

ONITHA DH'QANKE (East Syrian)
(also spelled *Unitah d'qanki)

Known as the Anthem of the Sanctuary, it consists of verses from psalms and the Gloria, which is sung in the *bema of the church during the *Liturgy. The text for this anthem varies according to the feast being celebrated.

ORAI (Byzantine/Greek)
See CHASY.

ORARION
(Byzantine/Greek and Coptic)
(also called Orar [Slavonic])

In the *Byzantine tradition, a *deacon's stole, which is a long band of material worn over the left shoulder. The significance of wearing it on this shoulder is to demonstrate that because the deacon is a minister to the *priest he has only a secondary place in the hierarchy. During the *Liturgy at the start of the Our Father, which precedes the *Fraction, the deacon normally crosses the stole across his chest and back. According to tradition, the deacon is said to belong to the "angelic order," a minister to the priest in holy things. The deacon's stole sometimes has the words "Holy, Holy, Holy" embroidered upon it; this is affirmed by the writings of St. Simon of Thessalonica.

In the *Coptic tradition there are two forms of orarion (*shordion), and both are confusedly called by the general term patrashil (*batrashil), which according to Butler represents a corruption of the Greek *epitrachelion." In Coptic both are called the orarion.

The orarion was mentioned in the East at least two hundred years before it was mentioned in the West. The Council of Laodicea (ca. 363) forbade the orarion to those in *orders lower than deacon, while in the West it was at the Second Council of Braga (Spain) in 563, that the orarion was mentioned, affirming that deacons were permitted to wear it from the left shoulder. The Laodicean prohibition did not affect the Coptic Church, for we find in the Tukhian Pontifical (1761) the prescription that a *subdeacon may be invested with the orarion at his ordination.

The epitrachelion type of Coptic *stole has an opening at the upper end for the head, and from the neck down it is embroidered with crosses or with figures of the apostles in six pairs. If it should lack any decoration it is called a *sudr. There is often a line down the middle of the front of the stole and not a seam, suggesting that it may owe its origin to an unjoined stole.

The other type of Coptic stole is a long scarf, 9" wide and 6" long, which is worn by deacons. It is passed across the chest, under the arms, then crossed at the back and drawn over the shoulders, so that the end can be tucked in the front under the *zounarion, or colored band; among non-Catholic Copts this band is not usually worn. Subdeacons' stoles are narrow and made of silk or similar material, usually purple, yellow, red, and green, sometimes with three or more colors side by side in longitudinal bands and the whole *vestment embroidered with crosses and flowers. This stole is worn so that the central part is placed on the waist in front, forming a girdle, with the ends drawn behind, crossed over the back, and brought over each shoulder to the front, where they fall straight down and pass under the girdle.

See SHORDION.

ORDERS, HOLY

One of the seven *sacraments recognized throughout the Christian East. In practice, its administration varies according to the rite.

Armenian Tradition

Admission to the clerical state is marked by a *tonsure. When the candidate is admitted to the *minor order of doorkeeper he is presented with the keys of the church, the doors of which he then proceeds to lock and unlock during the singing of a hymn.

When the order of reader is given the ordinand is handed a Book of Epistles by the *bishop, and when the order of exorcist is given the ordinand receives a copy of the Ritual, during which presentations lengthy prayers are recited; for example, to exorcist candidates, the bishop prays, "Take this; treasure in your mind the words written there. I now give authority to place your hand upon the possessed and cause those about to be baptized to renounce the evil one. . . . Amen."

An acolyte is first presented a candle and candlestick, then given an empty flagon by the bishop to emphasize the acolyte's role as a servant in the sanctuary.

The ordination to the subdiaconate takes place during the *Liturgy with the bishop sitting on the *throne. Following several readings, the bishop places his hands on the ordinand's head and, having presented him with an empty *chalice and *paten, prays a prayer peculiar to the order being received, for example, "Take this holy chalice and be authorized to carry it to the holy *altar of the Lord, for the great and precious Mystery of Christ our God, to whom belongs glory, power, and honor now and forever more."

The diaconate is solemnly bestowed by the bishop during the Liturgy when he places his hand on the candidate's head four times accompanied by an acclamation by the congregation that the man is worthy. The ordinand is then vested in his distinctive *stole by the bishop, who also presents him with the Book of the *Gospels. The Liturgy then continues.

Candidates for the priesthood must be at least twenty-six years of age and the laity must have expressed their approval. Following a full confession of faith on Saturday night, the ordination Liturgy is celebrated the following morning. The bishop blesses the ordinand, places his right hand on the ordinand's head, and then vests him in the stole. Following the reading of the Epistle and Gospel, the bishop places his right hand on the ordinand's head again and recites two prayers that invoke the Holy Spirit. A blessing of the priestly *vestments follows and the ordinand is vested in them, after which the bishop places his hands on the ordinand's head and then anoints his hands as well as his forehead. The bishop finally presents a chalice and paten holding unconsecrated *bread and wine and says, "Receive these, because you have received power through the grace of God to consecrate and complete the Holy Sacrifice, in the name of our Lord Jesus Christ. . . ." The new priest is then *incensed three times, and bowing before the altar and the bishop, he gives his first blessing to the congregation.

The consecration to the episcopacy is performed, in the non-Catholic tradition, by the *catholicos, whereas the *patriarch performs the ceremony for the Catholic community. The ceremony is marked by many anointings during the singing of Psalm 132, a profession of faith, and an imposition of the Gospel book. This imposition

during episcopal consecrations seems to date from the *Apostolic Constitutions* and seems general throughout the Eastern Church.

Byzantine Tradition

There are two minor orders of this rite—taperer-reader, or lector (*anagnostes; *tchetz), and subdeacon (*hypodiakonos; *ypodiakon). Both of these orders may be received outside of the Liturgy.

The ordination to the order of lector involves prayers before the Book of Epistles is placed on the head of the ordinand, who is then led into the middle of the church, and facing east, he is handed the book, from which he reads a few passages from where it has fallen open by chance. He is then vested with a simple tunic (*felon), but his usual vestment is the *sticharion, a dalmatic-style vestment.

The Rite of ordination to the subdiaconate includes the presentation of a towel, basin, and bowl to the ordinand, who proceeds to wash the bishop's hands as evidence of the deacon's assisting role in the Liturgy, whereas the subdeacon usually assists the deacon.

The diaconate is conferred in the Liturgy, after the Consecration and before the *Fraction, when the candidate comes to the altar and receives the bishop's blessing. The ordinand then kneels on his right knee before the altar. The bishop lays his right hand on the ordinand's head and says, "The Grace of God . . . appoints the most religious subdeacon, N., to be a deacon. Let us pray for him that the grace of the Holy Spirit may come upon him." The use of this formula is unusual, but the fact that its use can be traced to the 4th century is impressive. Clearly, a declarative form of ordination seems to be preferred to one of petition or *Epiclesis. At the ceremony's close the stole is undone and arranged so as to hang from the left shoulder, then the *cuffs and finally the *ripidion (fan) are presented. At each presentation the congregation affirms that the candidate is worthy.

As part of the ordination to the priesthood, which takes place at the end of the Great *Entrance, the candidate is led around the altar three times following the singing of the *Cherubikon, then, kneeling on both knees before the bishop and with the forehead and hands resting on the altar, he is blessed three times. The bishop then lays his hands upon the ordinand and recites the declarative Prayer of Ordination, followed by two prayers and a *litany led by the *archdeacon. The *epitrachelion and *phelonion are presented to the ordinand, but there is no anointing. The close of the ceremony is marked by the affirmation by the clergy, choir, and people that he is worthy, "axios," and the newly ordained priest concelebrates the Liturgy. A priest is commonly called "Papas" (Greek) or "Batoushka" (Slavonic).

For consecration to the episcopacy at least three bishops are required to be present. Following the three confessions of faith, the Liturgy commences, and during the Liturgy of the *Catechumens until the *Trisagion the bishop-elect stands vested as a priest and is positioned to the south of the altar. After the singing of the Trisagion the bishop-elect kneels on both knees

before the altar, and an open Gospel book is placed on top of the consecrand's head with the writing down, as the principal consecrator says, "The Grace Divine which always heals that which is sick and completes that which is wanting, through the laying on of hands, elevates you, the most Godloving, N., duly elected to be the Bishop of the God-saved cities, NN. . . ." The principal bishop or consecrator then makes the *sign of the cross above the head of the new bishop, while the assistant bishops hold the Book of Gospels. Further prayers are recited, following which the Gospel book is returned to the altar and the new bishop is vested with the *sakkos and other episcopal vestments, then with the pastoral staff, or *crozier. The new bishop concelebrates with the ordaining bishop.

Coptic Tradition

The *Coptic Church recognizes seven orders. The posts of archdeacon and archpriest are not conferred in the same way as the traditional orders of bishop, priest, deacon, subdeacon, reader, cantor, and corbani (breadman). Under *Pope Shenouda III, the functions of the subdeacon, lector, cantor, and corbani are performed by deacons.

When a candidate is to be ordained a reader (*Karianjili), the tonsure is conferred, after which the bishop turns west and holds the candidate's temples while another prayer is recited and the Gospel book is handed to the reader.

During the ordination to the subdiaconate (*abudiyakun), the ordinand stands at the sanctuary *door, and when the bishop has completed the Prayer of the Morning Incense, he places one hand on each of the ordinand's temples so the thumbs meet on the forehead, and the Prayer of Ordination is recited. The sign of the cross is made on the ordinand's forehead once and then repeated three times; the ceremony concludes when the *orarion is placed over the new subdeacon's left shoulder. During the Liturgy, which continues, the ordinand holds a lighted candle in his hand.

The candidate for the diaconate is vested, but he is not supposed to wear the stole (orarion) until the bishop vests him with it during the ordination ceremony. According to Vansleb, the Eucharistic *spoon (*Kokliarion) is presented to the ordinand, who continues to hold it during the Liturgy, at the close of which the bishop breathes on the ordinand's face.

The elevation to the rank of archdeacon (rais a-shamamisah; *Ra'is a-shamamish) involves a ceremony during which special prayers are recited and the orarion is rearranged. In addition, the ordinand is vested with an iron pectoral cross if he is to act as the bishop's vicar-general.

To be ordained a priest in the Coptic Church the candidate must be thirty-three years old, of good character, married, and a deacon. If he is not already a deacon, he must be progressed through the orders of reader and deacon on successive days prior to ordination to the priesthood, or *kassis. The candidate is brought vested as a deacon to the choir and is led in procession around the church. He bows to the altar while the bishop faces east and commences the Prayer of the Morning Incense. Then the bishop faces west and lays his hands on the candidate's head and recites a prayer. Turning east again he recites further prayers, then turning to the west again he signs the ordinand's forehead with a cross. The ordinand is then proclaimed a priest, and the bishop makes three more crosses on the new priest's forehead, then vests him as a priest. There follow some admonitions, and the new priest kisses the threshold of the *haikal as well as the hand of the ordaining bishop. After *Communion has been received by the new priest, the bishop lays his hands on the ordinand's head three times and all shout "Axios" (he is worthy) as the priest is named along with the name of his parish. According to Vansleb, the bishop breathes in the face of the priest and says, "Receive the Holy Spirit." A forty-day *fast follows, which is observed every day from sunset until 3:00 p.m. the next afternoon.

Consecration to the episcopacy is a very lengthy ceremony, and the patriarch alone performs it. The candidate should never have married, and if it should happen that the candidate is only in deacon's order then the intervening orders must be supplied on consecutive days, while if the bishop-elect is a secular cleric, he must receive the *monastic *habit. The Liturgy commences following an all-night *vigil, and at the conclusion of the reading from The Acts the patriarch stands at the door of the haikal; then, accompanied by assistant bishops, the bishop-elect processes around the church, after which a deacon reads the instrument of election. After numerous blessings and prayers, the *peace is given and the senior deacon cries "Lift up your hands, O bishops," upon which all the bishops lay their hands on the shoulders of the new bishop, while the patriarch alone lays his hands on the consecrand's head. The new bishop is vested and the patriarch presents a small cross to him and, following a prayer, raises his hands over the new bishop declaring, "Axios." Taking his seat to the right of the patriarch, the new bishop holds the Gospel book and receives Holy Communion from the patriarch. During the Liturgy when the corporal is placed over the consecrated *bread and wine, the new bishop has the Gospel book placed upon his head and the patriarch says the peace. A reading from John 20 follows, and at the words "Peace be to you" (v. 21) the patriarch holds the Gospels over the head of the new bishop. He repeats this at the words "As the Father has sent me, I also send you." The reading is resumed, and at the words "Receive you the Holy Spirit" (v. 22) the patriarch breathes in the form of a cross on the face of the new bishop, and as the patriarch exclaims "Axios," the bells are rung. Finally, at the words "they are retained" (v. 23) all the congregation shout, "A hundred years." At the conclusion of the Liturgy the patriarch vests the new bishop in a dark-colored processional cope and the new bishop gives a blessing.

Ethiopian Tradition

*Ethiopian Catholics in common with *Syrians do not observe the convention of the newly ordained priest or bishop *concelebrating with the ordaining bishop. Among non-Catholic *Ethiopians, it seems that little preparation is undertaken prior to the reception of orders and a semihereditary, priestly caste appears to have arisen; most clergy are married. Orders are often bestowed in such numbers and circumstances as to cast doubt on the validity and ability of the men being ordained. The episcopacy, since it was derived until recently from the Copts, does not cause such doubts.

East Syrian Tradition

In common with the *Chaldeans, the *Nestorians confer by the laying on of hands without any anointing and after the recitation of an Epiclesis. The Nestorians have doubts as to the sacramental character of ordination, although they admit that the priesthood is "ordained by Christ himself," that grace comes through the laying on of hands, and that it is this that confers priestly ministration and authority.

When a reader is to be ordained he stands on the first step of the *bema, and the bishop blesses him by laying his hand on the candidate's head.

At the ordination to the subdiaconate, the ordinand stands on the middle step of the bema and is blessed by the bishop, who places his right hand on the head while stretching out his left hand and reciting the appropriate prayer.

The diaconate, priesthood, and episcopacy are all conferred by the Nestorians using the same prayers and more or less the same form that used to be followed by the Chaldeans.

When the diaconate is to be conferred, the bishop lays his right hand on the head of the ordinand, and stretching out his left hand, he recites some lengthy prayers, following which the ordinand is blessed and then vested with the stole, which is placed over the left shoulder. The Epistles are handed to the candidate who is then signed between the eyes, from below upward and then from right to left, while the bishop recites the following formula in a loud voice: "N. has been set apart, consecrated, and perfected to the work of the Ministry of the Church and to the Levitical and Stephanite Office in the name of the Father. . . ."

The ordination to the priesthood is similar except that at the beginning some of the ordinand's hair is cut off. Following the presentation of the Gospels, the same formula as that used among the Chaldeans is recited: "N. has been set apart, consecrated, and perfected for the work of the Presbyterate of the Church and for the Office of the Aaronic Priesthood, in the name of the Father. . . ."

Consecration to the episcopacy is preceded by an all-night vigil and is usually performed by the patriarch. During the initial stages of the ceremony the consecrand is vested as a priest. At one stage the open Gospel book is placed on the consecrand's back in such a position that the Gospels may be read, the usual passages being Matthew 16:13-19 and John 21:15-17, at the end of which the book is closed and the assistant bishops place their right hands on the consecrand's side. The Prayer of Consecration follows.

Following several prayers and blessings, the new bishop is vested with the episcopal vestments and is finally blessed between the eyes by the con-

secrating bishop's thumbs, from below upward and then from right to left while the following formula is recited: "N. is set apart, consecrated, and perfected to the great work of the Episcopate in the city of NN., in the name of the Father. . . ."

West Syrian Tradition

The orders conferred in this rite are those of singer, reader, subdeacon, deacon, priest, and bishop. While a special blessing is used for those to be admitted to the order of singer, or psalmodist, the other orders are conferred using a somewhat similar formula: "N. is ordained [reader, subdeacon, etc.] in the Holy Church of Jesus Christ, in the name of the Father . . . ." Before ordination to the diaconate a candidate must sign a solemn profession of faith.

Orders are conferred within the Liturgy, for example, the priesthood and episcopacy are conferred toward the end of the *Anaphora so that the ordaining bishop can touch the consecrated bread and wine before ordaining the ordinands. The Prayer of Ordination stresses the sacrificial powers of the new priest as well as his teaching and preaching authority. The ordination ceremony is accompanied by the laying on of hands and a prorection of instruments but unaccompanied by an anointing; further, there is no concelebration at the ordination and consecration Liturgies of new priests and bishops.

All West-Syrian bishops are celibate and live in monasteries, and the candidates for the episcopacy are named and consecrated by the patriarch, assisted by at least two bishops. While a *miter is not usually worn, the "crowning" of the bishop as part of the consecration rite forms an important part of the ceremonies.

ORIENTAL CATHOLICS

*Eastern-rite Catholics in communion with Rome.

ORKIOLION (Byzantine/Greek)

A vessel for containing the hot water that is added to the contents of the *chalice just after the *Fraction. As the priest pours the hot water into the chalice, he says, "Blessed is the fervor of your saints, always, now and for ever and unto the ages of ages. Amen." The use of the orkiolion probably dates from Justinian (527–565), but it may have been introduced into the *Liturgy after the Council of Chalcedon in 451 and was probably a precaution against the contents of the chalice freezing in very cold climates. According to Nicholas Cabasilas (1371), its symbolism may be seen as the Holy Spirit communicating itself to the faithful. Catholics of the *Byzantine rite are permitted to use the orkiolion (Pope Benedict XIV; 1742).

See THERMARION; ZEON.

ORLETZ (Byzantine/Slavonic)

The "eagle," as this is sometimes called, is a small circular rug on which is a representation of an eagle flying over a battlemented city. A *bishop stands on this rug during various services, and as part of the ceremony of his consecration he is led to stand on certain parts of the rug. For example, during the first profession of faith (*Creed) the consecrand stands on the tail of the eagle; while making the second profession of faith he stands on the center of the eagle; and just before making the third profession, or confession of faith, he stands on the head of the eagle.

ORTHODOX

Literally, "right believing." A name applied to all who accepted the decrees of the Council of Chalcedon (451).

ORTHODOX EASTERN CHURCH

The patriarchates of Constantinople, Alexandria, Antioch, and Jerusalem together with their associated Churches, which became separated from Rome in 1054 and again after 1453. The *patriarch of Constantinople has a primacy of honor. There are eleven other *autocephalous Churches: Albania, Bulgaria, *Cyprus, *Czechoslovakia, *Georgia, *Greece, *Poland, *Romania, *Russia, *Serbia, and Sinai. The heads of the Russian, Romanian, Serbian, and Bulgarian Churches are called patriarchs, while the head of the Georgian Church is called the *catholicos-patriarch. The others are headed by a *metropolitan or archbishop. Two other *Churches, which are *autonomous Orthodox Churches, are those of *Finland and *Japan.

ORTHODOXY

The system of faith, practice, and discipline observed by all *Orthodox believers.

ORTHODOXY, SUNDAY OF

The first Sunday in Lent, or the *Great Fast, in which the victory of the Church over the *Iconoclasts (842) is commemorated. As part of the Office of Orthodoxy, which is celebrated before the *Liturgy, the great teachers and supporters of *Orthodoxy are gratefully commemorated and the opponents condemned.

ORTHROS (Byzantine/Greek)

Literally, "daybreak." After the reading of the *Exapsalmos, or Six Psalms (3, 37, 62, 87, 102, and 142), during which recitation the congregation is expected to stand quietly, the Great *Litany follows succeeded by a *troparion and a Psalter reading, or selection from the psalms (stikhoslovie kafismi [Slavonic]; *Kathisma). When the first selection has been read, the Small Litany (Malaya Ekteniya) is sometimes recited, and with the *incensing of the church, the *polyelaios (Pss 134 and 135) is sung. If the occasion is that of a great feast, then the *Megalynarion is sung by the *priest and *deacon together with the choir in front of the *icon of the feast, which is censed during the singing of the Exaltation. A hymn may follow, succeeded by the Hymn of Degrees or Degrees of the *Antiphon, followed by the *prokeimenon (gradual) according to the *tone. A *Gospel reading is then succeeded by the reading of Psalm 50 and a hymn, during the singing of which the Gospel book is placed on a table in the middle of the church. The *Canon follows and includes the Hymn of Light (*Exapostilarion), which is read, not sung (except on August 15, the Dormition), and the Canon is drawn to a close. *Lauds (*Ainoi) normally follows immediately.

The Canon probably originated at the monastery (*lavra) or Mar Saba near Jerusalem during the 8th century. It was here that some Syrian *monks organized the Canon form of hymnody, by which strophes (troparia) were inserted between the verses of the biblical canticles. This form replaced the older *Syrian *kontakion form, which was made up of a succession of lines of equal length grouped in acrostic stanzas. These kontakion forms were not completely removed, as a few strophes have been inserted between the sixth and seventh odes of the present Canon.

Lauds commences with *stichera (verses) of the feast being celebrated followed by the great doxology and troparion. After this the Litany of Fervent Intercession, the blessing by the priest, and prayers for deceased *Orthodox Christians precede the final *dismissal by the priest.

See MATINS; UTRENYA.

OSANNA SUNDAY (Coptic)

Otherwise known as Palm Sunday. At midnight there is a solemn *Matins during which the *bishop blesses palm branches, after which palms, tapers, and crosses are processed around the church with a stop at every principal picture, reliquary, and *altar. The procession returns to the sanctuary (*haikal) and the *Liturgy is celebrated, the *lessons of which are those appointed for the commemoration of the dead.

OSTRICH EGGS

These are common as part of the church furniture throughout many churches in the East, because it is piously believed that they are a symbol of the Resurrection. An explanation of this favored by the Copts is that they are symbols of faith, since the ostrich is reputed to hatch her eggs simply by gazing at them. A more pragmatic explanation is that they are suspended from the roof to prevent mice from climbing down the cords supporting the lamps and so getting to the oil in the many lamps that abound in *Eastern churches.

OTDANIE (Byzantine/Slavonic)

Literally, "giving back." The last day of the *poprazdnestvo, otherwise called the "after-feast," which follows a major feast. On the otdanie (*apodosis) the festal Office is repeated more or less as it was on the day of celebration.

See APODOSIS.

OTPUST (Byzantine/Slavonic)

A *dismissal hymn sung at the end of *Vespers just before the *bread is blessed and during the censing of the table on which the bread is placed.

See APOLYSIS; DISMISSAL.

OUR FATHER

The prayer taught by our Lord to his apostles (Matt 6:9-13; Luke 11:2-4). It is sung at least once in all *Eastern *Liturgies but twice during the *Chaldean and *Malabarese Liturgies. The *Copts traditionally add "through Jesus Christ our Lord" at the conclusion.

OURAR (Armenian)

The diaconal stole, which is about 10′ x 5″. It has three crosses embroidered on it and is normally worn over the left shoulder with the free ends falling in front and behind. During the ordination ceremony (*see* ORDERS, HOLY [Armenian Tradition]) of an Armenian *deacon, following the imposition of the *bishop's right hand on the ordinand's head for the fourth time the bishop invests the ordinand with the ourar, after which the ordinand is presented with the *Gospel book.

See VESTMENTS, TABLE OF.

OVEN (East Syrian/Nestorian)

A clay-lined cavity that may be set into the floor of the sanctuary or some other, separate area but attached to the church building. This oven is used for baking the loaves for use in the *Liturgy.

See BREAD (East Syrian Tradition).

P

PACHON (Coptic)

The ninth month in the Coptic year, which corresponds to the period from April 26 to May 25.

See COPTIC CALENDAR.

PAHK (Armenian)

A day of abstinence, which rule extends to all Wednesdays and Fridays throughout the year except when a great feast has just been celebrated. On such days of abstinence everything is strictly forbidden except vegetables and honey.

PAINA

See PAKILA.

PAKEGH (Armenian)

A conical hat worn by clerics. It is shorter than a *kamilafka; if the wearer is a religious the pakegh may be purple and have a veil.

See VEGHAR.

PAKILA (East Syrian)
(also called *Paina)

The outermost Eucharistic vestment worn by *Chaldeans and *Nestorians; in design it resembles a hoodless Western cope. Among the Nestorians it may be ornamented with crosses.

See MA'APRA; VESTMENTS, TABLE OF.

PALAMITES

See JESUS PRAYER.

PALEOHEMEROLOGITES

This group is quite widespread and has an extensive structure with a hierarchy, 250 priests, 81 monasteries and convents, and about 250,000 faithful. The most notable convent is the Old Calendarist Convent of Our Lady at Keratea in Attica, founded in 1925 with about 280 nuns.

See OLD CALENDARISTS.

PALIN (Coptic)
(also spelled Pallin)

PALITZA (Byzantine/Slavonic)

A vestment that resembles the epigonation, but unlike the epigonation, it is suspended from one corner only and is always worn on the right hip. If the *priest has the right to wear an epigonation as well as a palitza, the epigonation is moved from the right side and is suspended on the left side.

See EPIGONATION.

PALLIUM

See OMOPHORION.

PANAGARION

See PANAGIA.

PANAGIA (Byzantine/Slavonic)

Literally, "all holy." While this title is often used to describe the Mother of God, it more commonly refers to the circular medallion worn around the neck of *Byzantine-rite *bishops.

It may also mean a triangular loaf of bread eaten by *monks after the morning meal. During the recitation of the grace a monk lifts up this piece of bread while invoking the Holy Trinity and the Mother of God. The bread is kept in a vessel, the panagarion, ornamented with pictures of our Lord and the Mother of God.

See ENCOLPION.

PANAGUE (Armenian)

An *Armenian episcopal pectoral cross, which is now oval in shape and decorated with precious stones.

See EPISCOPOS.

PANIKHIDNIK (Byzantine/Slavonic)

A requiem stand.

PANNYCHIS (Byzantine/Greek) (also called Panikhidi; Pannykhidia [Slavonic])

A term having two meanings: (1) the liturgical preparation for a feast, as referred to by St. Athanasius (*Apostolic Constitutions* 25), which is more correctly a Night Office (*Agrypnia) and which lasts all night; (2) the Office of the Dead, a mournful service of psalms, *litanies, hymns, prayers, and blessings, which are recited or sung as part of the burial service. A table bearing a bowl of rice or wheat grains is placed with some lighted tapers in the church to symbolize the Resurrection.

PANTOKRATOR (Byzantine/Greek)

Literally, "all mighty." The image or *icon of Christ ruling as Christ the King.

PAONI (Coptic)

The tenth month of the Coptic year, which corresponds to the period from May 26 to June 24.

See COPTIC CALENDAR.

PAOPI (Coptic)

The second month of the Coptic year, which corresponds to the period from September 28 to October 27.

See COPTIC CALENDAR.

PAPAS (Byzantine/Greek)

Literally, "a father." The familiar name given by Greeks to a *priest.

See BATOUSHKA; IEREUS.

PAPOUTSIA (Byzantine/Greek)

See EMBADES.

PARABOLANI (Coptic)

In the Ancient Church of Alexandria these were the appointed visitors of the sick.

PARADISCUS (Syro-Jacobite)

Literally, "house of oblation." The place where the Blessed Sacrament may be reserved. *Jacobites reserve the Sacrament in a covered *chalice on one of the gradines of the *altar, while Catholic *Syrians use a Western-style tabernacle in which the intincted and consecrated *bread is reserved. The Sacrament is renewed daily, because although in the past it was customary to reserve for a year part of the Sacrament that had been consecrated on the last Holy Thursday, James of Edessa (707) condemned the practice.

See BEIT QURBAN.

PARAKLETIKE (Byzantine/Greek) (also called Oktoikh [Slavonic])

Literally, "book of supplication." The editing of this book is attributed to St. Joseph the Hymn Writer (9th century), a brother of St. Theodore the Studite (759–826). It contains the Proper of the *lessons for weekday Offices as well as the Sunday collects that are found in the Little Octoechos.

See LITURGICAL BOOKS (Byzantine Tradition); OCTOECHOS.

PARAMAN (Byzantine/Slavonic) (also called *Paramandyas)

Part of the monastic habit. It is a large rectangular piece of cloth on which are embroidered the instruments of the Passion together with the inscription "I bear the wounds of the Lord upon my body."

See HABITS, COMPARATIVE TABLE OF; MONASTICISM (Byzantine Tradition).

PARAMANDYAS (Byzantine/Greek)

See PARAMAN.

PARAMONI (Byzantine/Greek)

Literally, "to wait." The celebrations that are observed on the eves of Christmas and Theophany, in which the Great or Royal *Hours are recited; these Hours are so called because in times past the *Byzantine emperor and his court attended these celebrations.

See NAVECHERIE.

PARASTASA (Byzantine/Slavonic)

The great requiem service, which may be said after the evening service.

PARATHRONOS (Byzantine/Greek)

A less ornate seat than the *thronos. It is used by a *bishop when participating in a ceremony that is neither pontifical nor specifically solemn.

See GEDEKION; THRONOS.

PAREMII (Byzantine/Slavonic)

Otherwise known as the Parables. At *Vespers they are the *lessons from the Old and New Testaments in which prophecies concerning the feast being commemorated are found.

PARISH

See PREHOD.

PARISTO (Maronite and West Syrian)

See BREAD (Syro-Jacobite Tradition); BURSHANAH; KURBONO.

PARTICLE

The portion of consecrated *bread (Tshastitza [Slavonic]) distributed to the faithful during the *Liturgy.

See COMMUNION.

PASBANS (Armenian)
(also spelled *Bazpan)

Small slips of brocade worn on each wrist in addition to the napkin attached to the *zone; these strips are traditionally used for wiping the hands during the *Liturgy.

See VESTMENTS, TABLE OF.

PASCHALION (Byzantine/Greek)

A table used for establishing the date of Easter.

See HOROLOGION.

PASKHA (Byzantine/Slavonic)

An Easter food made of sweetened curds mixed with butter, cream, eggs, and various dried fruits and nuts and prepared in a fairly long, narrow four-sided mold that reduces in size as the mixture rises, making something of a wedge-shape with a hole through which the pressed curds can release their liquid. When it has been pressed and is reasonably dry it is unmolded and decorated with almonds and glace cherries, while the letters XB are outlined on one side, standing for "Christos voskress" (Christ is risen). A paper rose is sometimes placed at the apex of the molded sweet.

PASTOPHORION (Byzantine)

Until the close of the 4th century this was a small *sacristy built adjacent to the apse and was used for the reservation of the Blessed Sacrament.

PASTORAL STAFF

See CROZIER; PATERISSA; POSOKH; RABDOS.

PATARAG (Armenian)

A Liturgy. That which is used by the *Armenians is a modified version of the *Liturgy of St. Basil, but in times past there were ten other *Anaphoras and a rite of the *Presanctified, or *Nakharrbeal (sometimes Nakhasrbeal).

See ANAPHORA; LITURGY.

PATARAGAMADUITZ (Armenian)
(also spelled *Badarakamaduitz)

A book containing the liturgical text.

See LITURGICAL BOOKS (Armenian Tradition).

PATEN

The plate on which the consecrated *bread is placed during the *Liturgy. In the *Armenian rite, the paten (*maghzmah), a *Byzantine-shaped vessel, holds the unleavened bread (*neshkhar); this bread is presented to the celebrant by the *deacon as part of the preparatory rite of the Liturgy, which precedes the Liturgy of the *Catechumens. The paten is not used in conjunction with a Byzantine-style *asterisk.

The Byzantine paten is Western in appearance, while the *Russian paten, or *diskos, has a foot to support it, so the paten is never set into the top of the *chalice as in Western liturgical practice. The paten is used with an *asterisk to support the covering *veil.

The paten (*diskos) used by the *Copts is usually quite plain, flat, and circular, with a vertical raised border, but it lacks a middle depression and is without engravings or supporting foot.

In the *Ethiopian rite the paten (*cachel, literally, "tray") is about 7" long.

The *East Syrian or *Nestorian paten, which is known as the *pilasa or pathura, is a little larger than that used by the Ethiopians and is about 12" long. The paten used by the *Chaldeans is of Western design.

In the West Syrian tradition the paten, being circular, is similar to that used by the Byzantine rite but has an upturned edge.

PATERISSA (Byzantine)

Literally, "father's or old man's staff."

See CROZIER; PASTORAL STAFF; POSOKH; RABDOS.

PATHORA (Syrian)

Literally, "table." According to Narsai (d. 502), this general term refers to an *altar in the sense of sanctuary. *East Syrians, however, use the term to refer to both the *chalice and *paten as well as the table of the altar.

See ALTAR; MADB'HO; PATHURO D'HAIYE.

PATHURO D'HAIYE (West Syrian)
(also spelled Pothurhaye)

A specific reference to the "table of life," or *altar, when at the start of the *Liturgy of the *Catechumens the middle of the altar is censed three times as the celebrant says, "Adoration to the Gracious Father." It is apparent that this part of the altar symbolizes God the Father. When the north side of the altar is censed, the *priest says, "Adoration to the Compassionate Son," while at the censing of the south side, he says, "Adoration to the Holy Spirit, the Giver of Life," a clear indication that this side of the altar represents the Holy Spirit.

PATRIARCH

The supreme *bishop of an autocephalous Church, especially one that is either Catholic or *Orthodox. Among non-Catholics the patriarch is the highest episcopal authority and has the right to call other *metropolitans to a synod. Throughout a patriarch's jurisdiction it is normal for him to ordain all the bishops and to send them the holy *chrism for use in their dioceses.

The five most ancient patriarchates are Rome, Constantinople, Alexandria, Antioch, and Jerusalem. A patriarchate of Moscow was set up in 1589, but on occasion it has been suspended, for example, following Patriarch Tikhon's death in 1925. It was restored under Stalin in September 1943 with the election of Sergius, who was quickly succeeded by Alexis. All patriarchs are assisted by a patriarchal synod.

PATRIARCHAL OFFICIALS

The following is just a selection:

1. Mega sakellarios, or great treasurer, who is the visitor to the monas-

teries. The visitor to the convents is called the tes sakelles.

2. Chartophylax, or chancellor, who is in charge of archives and one who settles questions of discipline, disputes, and questions arising from *marriage regulations.

3. Protonatarios, or chief secretary of protonotary.

4. Kastrensios, one who is in charge of patriarchal insignia and who helps the patriarch vest.

5. Hypomnematographos, the secretary who writes up the synod's minutes.

6. Hieromnemon, who ensures that mistakes do not creep into the sacred and *liturgical books.

7. Protosynkellos, whose duty it is to witness all the Acts of the patriarch.

PAWELOS (Ethiopian)

See APOSTLE.

PEACE, KISS OF

Justin Martyr was the first commentator to note the kiss, which seems to have been part of the preliminary ceremonies. In his *First Apology* (ca. 150) he wrote, "Therefore we greet one another with a kiss" (65.2). This early position of the kiss was confirmed sixty years later by Hippolytus, and its position was then changed to take place just before the *Communion. The shift in position seems to reflect the African Church's tradition, where according to St. Augustine the kiss appeared just before the Communion. In Jerusalem in the middle of the 4th century the kiss of peace is followed by the offertory instead of preceding it, but among the *Copts and *Ethiopians its primitive position is still maintained.

The *Armenian tradition of giving the peace (srbouthean) is indicated by each member of the congregation bowing to his neighbor. For the *Byzantine practice, *see* ASPASMOS.

The Coptic peace (qublat-as-salam) is transmitted before the *Anaphora by the *priest placing the palm of his right hand against the person being saluted, then both bringing their fingertips to the mouth, although on occasion this last movement is omitted and the hand-to-hand gesture is sufficient. During the kiss of peace the *deacon proclaims, "Salute each other with a Holy Kiss."

The Ethiopians transmit the peace (*amcha) just before the Anaphora, and it is indicated by the deacon exclaiming, "Greet one another with a Holy greeting." Then the priests bow to one another, and the priest celebrant bows to the deacons, who bow to one another, and then a deacon bows to the congregation, who then bow to one another.

The *East Syrian/Nestorian tradition of the kiss of peace takes place with the sanctuary curtains drawn apart when the senior deacon, upon receiving the peace from the priest, kisses the dapa (altar board), the *chalice, *paten, and priest's hand saying, "Give peace to one another in the love of Christ." The peace is given to other deacons and to one of the congregation, usually a *reader, who in turn transmits the peace to the men, who then transmit it to the women. Its transmission is effected by the receiver of the peace taking the hands of the person from whom he is receiving it between his own and kissing them.

The Syro-Jacobites transmit the peace (sh'lomo) by the deacon taking the priest's hands between his own and then passing his own hands down his face, and it is thus transmitted to the other clergy and faithful. In the *Maronite rite, each takes the fingers of the cleric above him between his own fingers and then kisses his own fingers.

PEARL

A term occasionally used to describe a particle of consecrated *bread. In the *Syrian rite it is also known as the Margonitho. There is evidence from the 6th century that the word "pearl" was used to describe the particle, but this does not seem to be universal. The term recalls Matthew 7:6.

In the rubrical instruction in the *Coptic *Liturgy, just before the *Communion and as part of the rite of *elevation, *consignation, and *commixture, the *priest is instructed to lay "the pearls . . . on the *paten."

See MARGARITES.

PEDHITHO (Syrian)

See CUMMIN; VESTMENTS, TABLE OF; ZANDE; ZENDE.

PENANCE, SACRAMENT OF

Armenian Tradition

For *Armenian Catholics auricular confession is the norm, and it is administered in the Latin fashion. Among non-Catholic *Armenians, penance is administered either in the *sacristy or in the home of the *penitent, where the *priest, a married man, sits cross-legged on the floor while the penitent kneels with his head covered with a piece of the priest's *vestment. The priest recites

a long list of possible sins to the penitent. To each of these sins the penitent may reply either "I accuse myself" or not. After a penance has been imposed, the long Prayer of *Absolution is recited. Penance for children tends to be more general and collective, so that as the priest reads a long list of faults, each child will strike his chest unobtrusively if he should feel guilty of any particular fault. This *sacrament is expected to be received at least five times a year, and these occasions must include Epiphany and Easter.

Byzantine Tradition
(Metanoia [Greek]; Pokayanie [Slavonic])

This sacrament, also known as exomologesis, is usually received prior to receiving Holy *Communion. It is administered in some annex of the church at a folding stand on which has been placed a cross and *icon. The priest stands to one side of the stand, and the penitent approaches the priest and using a set formula usually accuses himself of particular sins.

The priest then imposes a penance (*epitimion) and places the *stole on the bowed head of the penitent and absolves, using a formula of absolution such as "May our Lord and God Jesus Christ . . . forgive you all your sins, my child, N., and I, an unworthy priest by the power which he has given me, forgive you and absolve you from your sins, in the name of the Father. . . ."

Coptic Tradition

This sacrament has always been observed except for one brief period in the middle of the 12th century when *Patriarch John is reputed to have abolished it, but it was later restored after Markus ibn Kunbari created a stir in 1174 when he declared that there could be no forgiveness of sin without confession.

Generally the *Copts try to confess before *marriage and, if possible, before death. One of the most usual forms is the confessing "to the thurible," as it is called, which is a kind of particular examination of one's conscience during the first censing at the *Liturgy, since this censing is followed by the Prayer of Absolution.

Ordinary auricular confessions do take place, a rather lengthy procedure in which the penitent stands before the priest with bowed head and both say the *Lord's Prayer; then after some prayers the priest gives the first absolution, and during the prayers the penitent makes three prostrations, one before the *altar, one to the confessor, whose feet he kisses, and one after the imposition of the penance when the priest gives the second absolution.

For the reconciliation of an apostate the priest blesses a vessel of water and pours *chrism into it; then *lessons from the Scriptures are read and the Prayer of Absolution is prayed over the penitent. The water is then blessed again, and the penitent is unclothed and sprinkled three times by the priest as he says, "I wash you in the name of the Father. . . ." The penitent resumes his clothes, more prayers are recited, and an absolution is given. *Dismissal follows, with the words "You are healed, go your way and sin no more."

Ethiopian Tradition

*Ethiopian Catholics are meticulous in their administration of this sacrament, as they are with the other sacraments, but non-Catholic *Ethiopians reserve the sacrament for the dying, and when a confession is made it is not very specific.

East Syrian Tradition

The *Chaldeans use the Syriac translation of the *Latin rite, whereas non-Catholic *Nestorians regard the rite of confession as being almost obsolete. Usually those who wished to communicate would gather in the porch of a church, and while kneeling they would have the Prayer of Absolution taken from the *Taksa d'husaya (Book of Pardon and Mercy) read over them.

The Nestorian rite of reconciliation was attributed to the *catholicos Ishu'yab III (7th century) for the reconciliation of apostates. Prior to its reception, such an apostate was expected to sit on ash-cloth and ashes for three days outside the door of the church with head and feet bared. After the Lord's Prayer and the recitation of Psalms 122 and 129 some hymns would be sung. The priest would then lay his hands on the penitent's head, and one of several varieties of the Prayer of Reconciliation would be said, with the ceremony concluding with the *sign of the cross and an anointing.

West Syrian Tradition

For Catholics in this tradition the Western form is observed, but making use of different formulas for different categories of sin. For non-Catholics the rite is usually performed at the church door and consists of a rather vague admission of faults, after which prayers are recited which, like the Catholic practice, are worded according to the category of sin. Then the confessor places his hand on the penitent's head, and the form of absolution employed varies according to whether the penitent is a cleric or not.

If the penitent is a cleric, the absolution is given in a deprecative form: "Sin is taken away from your soul and body in the name of the Father, Amen. May you be forgiven and share in the Holy *Mysteries in the name of the Holy Spirit, for everlasting life, Amen." But if the penitent is a layperson, the formula is given in an indicative form: "I forgive you . . . ." Among non-Catholics the reception of this sacrament is infrequent.

PENITENTS

Until the 4th century there was an idealized system of classifying those who sought reconciliation with the Church and who had been excluded from *Communion for varying periods so that they could progress and gradually become incorporated into full membership. The basis of the classification was according to the seriousness of the offense.

1. Weepers, or prosklaiontes, whose existence was attested by St. Gregory Thaumaturgus (233–270); they were not admitted to the church but had to stand outside the *doors in the *atrium and ask for people's prayers as they entered.

2. Hearers, or akrouomenoi, again attested by St. Gregory Thaumaturgus. They were expected to stand inside the door in the *narthex but below the

*catechumens; after the homily, they were dismissed.

3. Kneelers stood at the bottom of the *nave and were dismissed with specific prayers and blessings.

4. Consistents could stand with the faithful throughout the *Liturgy but could not receive Holy Communion; according to the *Apostolic Constitutions* (ca. 375) they were dismissed after the kiss of *peace.

PENQITHO (Syrian)

A liturgical book that contains the texts for *Vespers, *Nocturns, *Matins, and Terce for Sundays, the greater feasts, and the season of Lent.

See LITURGICAL BOOKS (West Syrian Tradition).

PENTEKOSTARION
(Byzantine/Greek)

A book similar to the *Triodion but containing the Proper of the season, that is, the variable prayers and *lessons for the services from Easter Sunday until the first Sunday after Pentecost (All Saints' Sunday). If allowance is made for borrowing and additions, it was largely the work of St. Theodore the Studite (d. 826) and St. Joseph of Thessalonica or their disciples.

See LITURGICAL BOOKS (Byzantine Tradition); TSVETNAYA TRIOD.

PERICOPE

A section of Holy Scripture read as a *lesson.

See LECTIONS.

PERIKEPHALAIA (Byzantine/Greek)
(also called Shlem)

See HABITS, COMPARATIVE TABLE OF; KOUKOULION.

PERIODEUTES
(Syrian and Maronite)

Literally, "visitor." These clerics are roughly equivalent to a Western vicar forane, but they have the privilege of carrying a *crozier and the authority to consecrate churches and administer *confirmation.

See BARDUTS.

PERISTERA (Byzantine)

A Eucharistic dove with outstretched wings, usually made of silver, and containing a wooden or silver casket. The opening of the peristera is in the dove's back. It is occasionally found hanging from the roof of the canopy (*kiborion) in place of the *artophorion.

PERISTERION (Byzantine/Greek)

This small kiborion, or ciborium, is located under the main *altar canopy, which is supported by four columns rising from the four corners of the altar. It serves as a shelter for the *peristera, or Eucharistic dove.

See KIBORION; PERISTERA.

PERITRACHELION
(Byzantine/Greek)
(also spelled Petrakhelion)

See EPITRACHELION; VESTMENTS, TABLE OF.

PESHITTO (Maronite)

The Bible, which for use by the *Maronites is written in Arabic. The Peshitto version of the Syrian Bible may have been as early as a 3rd- or 4th-century translation of the Hebrew Scriptures into the Edessene dialect.

PESNE (Byzantine/Slavonic)

See CANTICLE.

PETRAKHELION (Byzantine/Greek)

See EPITRACHELION.

PETSHAT (Byzantine/Slavonic)

See PROSPHORA; SEAL; SPHRAGIS.

PEVETZ (Byzantine/Slavonic)

See PSALTES; SINGER.

PHAILONES (Byzantine)

A chasuble.

See PHELONION.

PHAINA (East Syrian/Chaldean)
(also spelled *Paina)

A *vestment that is equivalent to the Western chasuble worn by *Nestorian and *Chaldean *priests. It resembles a hoodless cope and may be ornamented with many crosses. It is not fastened at the neck.

See MA'APRA; PAKILA.

PHAINO (West Syrian and Maronite)

See FAINO; RIDA.

PHAINOLION (Coptic)

See BURNUS; FELONION.

PHAKEGM (Armenian)

An obsolete 12th-century term referring to a *stole.

See PORURAR.

PHANAR

The world headquarters of the *ecumenical patriarch of Constantinople, located in the Greek quarter of Istanbul.

PHELGUTH-M'SHAMSHONO (Maronite)

Literally, "a half-deacon." The *minor order of *subdeacon, which may be given to a boy from his twelfth year.

PHELONION (Byzantine/Greek) (also spelled *Phenolion)

The *Byzantine chasuble, which is a very full bell-shaped *vestment, often severely cut away in front, as in the case of the *Russian clergy, whereas the *Greek phelonion tends to be fuller and deeper in front. From the 11th century, the *patriarch's phelonion has been covered with crosses (see POLY-STAVRION), and from the 14th century this decoration has been customary for all *bishops. Since 1453 and the fall of Constantinople, the phelonion has been replaced by the *sakkos for all Byzantine-rite bishops.

See FELON; VESTMENTS, TABLE OF.

PHELONO (Syrian)

In a 6th-century manuscript and in Renaudot's account there is evidence to suggest that the chasuble was once a full, flowing *vestment, but according to Assemani the vestment bore a greater resemblance to a cope, being open down the front.

See FAINO; PHAINO.

PHENOLION (Byzantine/Greek)

See PHELONION; VESTMENTS, TABLE OF.

PHILON (Armenian)

A black woolen cloak worn by an *Armenian *priest, but he may be permitted to wear a colored silk philon as a mark of distinction.

PHOKH (Armenian)

The verse of an antiphon.

See ANTIPHON.

PHOTISTERION (Byzantine/Greek)

Literally, "a place of enlightenment." An archaic word used to describe the rite of *baptism and the baptistery.

See BAPTISTERION.

PHOTOGOGIC(K)A (Byzantine/Greek)

The Lenten alternatives for the Hymn of Light (Exapostilarion; *Svyetilnie [Slavonic]).

PHRUMIUR (Maronite)

An introductory prayer that may be said before a *sedro.

See PROEM.

PILASA

See PINKA.

PILONION (Armenian)

A sleeveless black cloak (*mandyas) worn by clergy as part of their choir dress.

PINCO (West Syrian)

A linen purificator used to cleanse the *priest's fingers during the *Liturgy and as a substitute for a sponge (*espugo).

PINKA (East Syrian/Chaldean) (also called *Pilasa)

The Latin-shaped *paten used in this rite is unremarkable; the same term is sometimes used to describe both paten and *chalice.

PIRMO (Syro-Jacobite)

A Latin-shaped censer with short chains to which small bells are sometimes attached. It is swung in the *Byzantine fashion along its entire length. On occasion a chainless censer is used, being placed on the *altar or on graves during funerals.

See CENSER.

PISCINA

At the start of the *Byzantine *Liturgy this is the place where the *priest and *deacon wash their hands and where the final ablutions are made at the close of the Liturgy.

See THALASSIDION.

PISTOS (Byzantine/Greek)

See FAITHFUL.

PITHOM (Coptic)

See PITOTE; THOM.

PITOTE (Coptic)

See CURSI ALCAS; THRONOS NTE PIPOTERION; TOTE.

PIYALO (Syro-Jacobite)

See SINIYAH.

PLASHTSCHANITZA (Byzantine/Slavonic)

The area near the sanctuary where a small table used for requiem services and *memorials is kept, along with the requiem stand (*panikhidnik), which has places for tapers and a vessel to hold wheat grains.

PNEUMATIKOS (Byzantine/Greek)

Literally, "the ghostly father." The *priest who has permission to hear confessions; he must be at least forty years of age.

See DUHOVNEK; EPITIMION; EXAGOREUTES; PENANCE, SACRAMENT OF.

PODERES

See STIKHARION; STOICHARION; VESTMENTS, TABLE OF.

PODRIZNIK (Byzantine/Slavonic) (also spelled Podryasnik)

The inner *rason, a close-fitting cassock worn by *Russian Orthodox clergy.

See ANTERION; ESORASON; HABITS, COMPARATIVE TABLE OF.

POIMANTIKE RABDOS (Byzantine/Greek)

Literally, "pastoral staff."

See PATERISSA; POSOKH.

POKOYANIE (Byzantine/Slavonic)

See METANOIA; PENANCE, SACRAMENT OF.

POKROVY (Byzantine/Slavonic)

A general term to describe the three veils used to cover the sacred vessels. Two of these veils are used to cover the *paten and *chalice respectively, while the third veil, the *vosdukh or *aer, covers both paten and chalice.

See VEILS.

**POLAND,
ORTHODOX CHURCH OF**
(also called the Polish Autocephalous Orthodox Church)

The origin of the Orthodox Church of Poland, through Sts. Cyril and Methodius, dates from the 9th century in southern Poland; from 1772 to 1918 it was united with the *Russian Orthodox Church. Thereafter there was a period during which its *autocephality, although recognized by the *ecumenical patriarch, was not agreed to by the Russians, a matter that was not settled until 1948. At present the Church has five dioceses with a total of 1 million faithful and is governed by the *Metropolitan of Warsaw and All Poland, who administers the Church from Warsaw. While *Church Slavonic was previously used in the celebration of the *Liturgy, Polish is now more commonly used.

POLIELEY (Byzantine/Slavonic)

See POLYELAIOS.

POLUNOSHCHNITSA
(Byzantine/Slavonic)

See MESONU(Y)KTIKON; MIDNIGHT OFFICE.

POLYCHRONION (Byzantine)

The chant sung at the end of a pontifical *Liturgy in which the *bishop is wished a long life "for many years."

POLYELAION (Byzantine/Greek)

See POLYKANDELON.

POLYELAIOS (Byzantine/Greek)
(also spelled Polieley)

Literally, "much oil" or "much mercy." Part of the Office of *Matins for Sundays, some saints' days, and major feasts, when Psalms 134 and 135 are sung. Sometimes, just before Lent commences, Psalm 136 is added. The Psalms are not sung in their entirety but only selected verses, while "Alleluia" is inserted after each verse. During the singing of the polyelaios, *incense is offered and the shrine lamps are lit. The term "polyelaios" is probably derived from the concept of mercy as it appears in Psalm 135.

See ORTHROS.

POLYKANDELON
(Byzantine/Greek)
(also called Polyelaion)

A branched candlestick containing lamps of oil.

POLYKERION (Byzantine/Greek)

A many-branched candlestick.

POLYSTAVRION
(Byzantine/Greek)

Apart from its monastic use, the term refers to an early form of *phelonion worn by the *patriarch and later by some *metropolitans. This *vestment, which was decorated with many crosses, predates the introduction of the *sakkos as a vestment worn by hierarchs.

See ANALABOS; DEGREES OF MONASTICISM, HABITS OF; HABITS, COMPARATIVE TABLE OF.

POMA (Byzantine/Greek)

See POMATA.

POMATA (Byzantine/Greek)

The squares sewn on the mandyas, or *mantiya, where this garment is secured near the neck and feet. These pomata are said to represent the four Gospels and are traditionally embroidered with symbols of the Four Evangelists. In addition there are the "streams" of doctrine (Potamoi [Greek]; *Istotchniki [Slavonic]) represented by red and white bands sewn horizontally around the mandyas.

See MANDYAS; SKRIZHALI.

POPE

While this title usually refers to the head of the Roman Catholic Church, it is also employed by the *Coptic *patriarch of Alexandria.

See PAPAS.

POPRAZDNESTVO (Byzantine/Slavonic)

Literally, "after-feast." The period of time that follows the celebration of a feast; its length varies from a single day to a week.

POROORA (Armenian)

See PORURAR.

PORTER

See PREURATNEK; PYLOROS.

PORURAR (Armenian)
(also spelled *Poroora)

The stole, similar to the *Byzantine *epitrachelion and worn by *Armenian *priests. It differs from the Western stole in that the wearer's head is put through an opening in the upper part of the vestment, while the rest simply hangs down in front. The material from which this vestment is usually made is quite expensive, being either silk or brocade, often with jewels attached.

See VESTMENTS, TABLE OF.

PORUTCHI (Byzantine/Slavonic)

See CUFFS; EPIMANIKIA; VESTMENTS, TABLE OF.

POSLYSHNIK (Byzantine/Slavonic)

See DEGREES OF MONASTICISM, HABITS OF.

POSOKH (Byzantine/Slavonic)

The crozier, or pastoral staff, carried by *bishops and *archimandrites; it represents the spiritual authority over the monasteries and cities they rule and is a sign of their guardianship of Christ's flock. When an archimandrite has been newly installed, the bishop turns to him at the end of the *Liturgy and presents him with the posokh, saying, "Take this staff and establish and rule your flock, seeing that you must answer therefore to Our Lord God on the Judgment Day." The prayer and charge given by the consecrator to the newly consecrated bishop is similar but has more injunctions than that used for an archimandrite.

See PATERISSA; RABDOS.

POST (Byzantine/Slavonic)

See FASTS.

POSTNAYA TRIOD
(Byzantine/Slavonic)

A set of choir books, originally the work of the Studites but to which Philotheos, *patriarch of Constantinople (1354–1355 and 1361–1375), added the Office of St. Gregory Palamos because of the latter's opposition to Catholicism. The book is otherwise known as the Fasting Triodion because it contains the variable parts of the services during the Great Fast of Lent and because the *Canons have only three odes, or theme songs instead of the customary nine.

See LITURGICAL BOOKS (Byzantine Tradition); TRIODION.

POTAMOI (Byzantine/Greek)

See ISTOTCHNIKI; MANDYAS; MANTIYA; POMATA.

POTERION (Coptic)
(also called *Kas)

A *Coptic *chalice, which is usually a silver bowl with small and straight sides, long stem, and round knop, below which the base often slopes away rather abruptly. It has a circular foot on which it is unusual to find any inscription. There is evidence that glass or wood was once used for chalices, especially after the Muslim raids and following the troubles of 700 A.D. when there was considerable loss of gold and silver.

POTHURHAYE (Syro-Jacobite)

The *altar, which should stand clear of the east wall of the church to permit processions to pass around it. The altar should be made of either wood or stone and is often perfectly square. A canopy, or ciborium, is supported above the altar on four pillars. The *Syrians approach the altar by means of three steps, whereas the *Malabar Jacobites approach by means of one step only; in either case, these steps are kissed liturgically. It should be noted that it is customary to find a curtain hanging in front of the altar.

See MADB'HO; QUBB'THO; QUDSHO; THRONOS.

POTIR (Byzantine/Slavonic)
(also called *Poterion)

The *chalice, which is by custom taller and more ample than its Western counterpart, to which it bears a close resemblance.

POVECHERIE (Byzantine/Slavonic)

See APODEIPNON; COMPLINE.

POYAS (Byzantine/Slavonic)

The *girdle that is worn over the *stikharion. It is usually the same color as the *phelonion (chasuble) and may be lightly decorated; it is secured in the back by a small clasp and encloses the *epitrachelion. The girdle worn over the outdoor cassock is usually made of soft black material in the case of non-monastic clergy, but a leather girdle is usual for *monastic clergy.

See VESTMENTS, TABLE OF; ZONE; ZOSTER.

PRAXAPOSTOLOS
(Byzantine/Greek)

See APOSTOLOS.

PRAXIS (Coptic and Syrian)

See LECTIONS.

PRAZDITCHINAYA MINEYA
(Byzantine/Slavonic)

The service book that contains an abridged version of other books, for example, the Festal Menaion.

See ANTHOLOGION; LITURGICAL BOOKS (Byzantine Tradition).

PRECENTOR (Byzantine)
(also called *Protopsaltes; *Regentchora)

The first of the singers, who directs the choir.

PRE-CHALCEDONIAN

*Oriental Christian Churches.

PRECHASTCHENIE
(Byzantine/Slavonic)

See PRICHASTIYE.

PREDLOGENIE
(Byzantine/Slavonic)

See PROTHESIS.

PREDPRAZDNESTVO
(Byzantine/Slavonic)

The period that precedes a *great feast;

it could be only one day, or it might be as many as five days, as in the case of Christmas.

PREHOD (Byzantine/Slavonic)

A specific area bounded by limits. If the parish is administered by a monastery with the *monks taking it in turns to run the services and attend to the duties, the word "*ephemeria" is sometimes used.

See ENORIA; PARISH.

PRESANCTIFIED, LITURGY OF

See LITURGY OF THE PRESANCTIFIED.

P'RESTO
(also spelled P'risto)

See BREAD (Syro-Jacobite Tradition).

PRESTOL (Byzantine/Slavonic)

A term used to refer to the sanctuary in the sense of including within it both the *altar and the *throne.

See ALTAR; TRAPEZA.

PREVRATNEK
(also spelled Preuratnek)

See PYLOROS.

PRICHASTEN (Byzantine/Slavonic)
(also spelled Pritchasten)

The *Communion verse or hymn which is scriptural in content and which is sung after the *priest has raised the consecrated *bread at the *elevation and said, "Holy Things for the holy."

See KOINONIKON.

PRICHASTIYE (Byzantine/Slavonic)
(also called *Prechastchenie)

The order of receiving Holy Communion. The custom of receiving Communion after the clergy is an ancient tradition, according to the evidence of St. Silvia of Aquitaine in the *Pilgrimage of Etheria*, from the *Liturgy of the *Apostolic Constitutions*, books 2 and 8, and certainly from Justin Martyr's works.

The *priest breaks the consecrated *bread and puts the particles in the *chalice, covers it, and puts the *spoon on top. The *deacon opens the curtain and is handed the chalice by the priest, and together they go out through the *holy doors, sometimes called the *royal doors, of the *iconostasis to the *soleas. People approach with their arms folded crosswise on their chests. The priest takes the chalice from the deacon with his left hand and holds the spoon (*see* LABIS; LZHITZA) in his right hand. The deacon, having removed the *veil, places it on the *altar and brings the napkin with which to wipe the communicants' lips and stands to the left of the priest. Administering Communion, the priest says, "The servant of God, N., partakes of the Holy Precious Body and Blood of our Lord and God and Savior Jesus Christ unto remission of his sins and unto everlasting life." The napkin is held close by the chalice with one end held under the communicant's chin. When the mouth has been wiped, the communicant kisses the foot of the chalice and returns to a small table nearby in order to receive some blessed bread and a warm drink of wine and water. In the early days of the Church the bread and wine were received separately. This is mentioned by Tertullian and other early Church writers. Men were permitted to receive Communion in the bare right hand, while women were expected to veil their palm with a special covering.

From the writings of Tertullian, St. Cyprian of Carthage (ca. 200–258), and St. Basil the Great (ca. 330–379) it is apparent that the laity often took the Communion bread home with them. By the time of the Trullan Synod (692), the faithful were still receiving the elements separately, but not long after this the spoon was introduced so the Sacrament could be received under both kinds at the same time.

Communion to the infant has persisted in the East, but little infants are only communicated with the consecrated wine, since some infants may have difficulty or reluctance in swallowing the consecrated bread.

See COMMUNION (Byzantine Tradition).

PRIEST
See ORDERS, HOLY.

PRITVOR (Byzantine/Slavonic)

The inner portion, or vestibule, at the western end of a church, where in early times *catechumens and *penitents were expected to remain during part of the *Liturgy. It is here that the Office for the reception of converts is performed, as well as the *lity on major feast days.

See NARTHEX.

PRIZIVANIE (Byzantine/Slavonic)
See EPICLESIS; INVOCATION.

PRODIKI

See BRODIKI; CATHOLIC.

PROEGIASMENA (Byzantine/Greek)

A *Liturgy ascribed to St. Gregory Homiliastes (6th century), but its origins are unclear.

See PRESANCTIFIED, LITURGY OF.

PROEM (Syrian)

An introductory prayer, usually preceded by a diaconal exclamation but always introduced by a proclamation or a *shuraya. The proem forms part of the *hussoyo (literally, "propitiation"), which is made up of three parts—the proem, the occasional m'bass'yono bokhil, and the *sedro (long prayer), during the recital of which the church, clergy, and congregation are censed.

PROEMIA (Maronite)

A Greek term used by the *Maronites to describe the doxological introduction to the solemn prayers at the start of the *Liturgy of the Faithful; these solemn prayers are called *sedro.

PROEORTIA (Byzantine/Greek)

The period of one to five days that precedes a *feast of our Lord or of the Mother of God, during which time the hymns and *Gospels used anticipate the forthcoming feast.

PROEORTION (Byzantine/Greek)

A *troparion sung as part of the preparation services preceding a major feast.

PROKEIMENON (Byzantine/Greek)
(also spelled Prokimenon)

Literally, "what is set to be read." The verses taken from the psalms that are sung at *Vespers after the hymn "O Joyful Light," following the entrance of the *priest and *deacon into the sanctuary. The prokeimenon is also sung at *Orthros, or Matins, on Sundays and feasts, placed after the *Anabathmoi, which precedes the reading of the Gospel; in the *Liturgy they are sung preceding the Epistle.

PRONAOS (Byzantine/Greek)

An enclosed portico in which the *catechumens and the audientes (see PENITENTS) could gather and hear the hymns and psalms of the services.

See NARTHEX.

PROS HILARON (Byzantine/Greek)
(also spelled Phos Hilaron)

A hymn attributed to the martyr St. Athenogenes, probably of the 2nd century, who while being burned alive sang this hymn. It is sung at *Hesperinos, or Vespers.

PROSCHEMA (Byzantine)

See DEGREES OF MONASTICISM, HABITS OF.

PROSEUCHA (Byzantine/Greek)

A small chapel or oratory.

PROSFARIN (Coptic)
(also spelled Prospherine)

The large *veil, or corporal, used to cover the offerings at the start of the *Liturgy. This veiling occurs as part of the *enarxis, just before the *priest recites the Prayer of *Absolution to the Son, and it is removed just before the

*Anaphora. The veil is a white or colored silk or velvet 18′′ square with a cross embroidered in the middle, often with tiny bells attached to the center and corners. Some writers suggest that in desert churches it was used to wave over the *bread and wine during the Liturgy.

See IBRUSFARIN; LAFAFAH.

PROSFONESIS (Coptic)

The diaconal warning, which is made during the *Liturgy, for example, "All those who are sitting, stand up." This marks the start of the *Anaphora of St. Basil.

PROSFORA (Coptic)

The Eucharist.

See KORBAN.

PROSFORI (Byzantine)

See BREAD (Byzantine Tradition).

PROSKOMEDIA
(Byzantine/Slavonic)

See PROSKOMIDE.

PROSKOMIDE (Byzantine/Greek)
(also spelled *Proskomedia)

In the *Eastern Church this refers to the preparation of the offerings, which takes place before the *Liturgy proper commences. The ceremony of preparation takes place at a table known as the prothesis.

See ANAPHORA; PROSPHORA; PROTHESIS.

PROSKYNEMA (Byzantine/Greek)

A deep bow or reverence.

See PROSKYNETARION.

PROSKYNESIS (Byzantine/Greek)
(also called *Proskynema)

A deep bow or reverence that involves touching the ground with one hand.

See PROSKYNETARION.

PROSKYNETARION
(Byzantine/Greek)

A folding desk on which the *icon of the feast being celebrated (eikon tou proskynematos) is displayed. It stands outside the *iconostasis. When entering a church, one should approach the icon so displayed, and it is customary to bow deeply in reverence. Such a reverence is called a *proskynema, hence the name of this piece of church furniture.

P'ROSO (Syro-Jacobite)

See QUDSHO.

PROSPHORA (Byzantine/Greek)

Literally, "offering." In its original meaning, the offering referred to the food that was offered by the early Christians, part of which was selected for use in the Eucharist with the remainder being used for the *Agape, which followed. Nowadays, it is the *bread offered for use in the *Liturgy by members of the congregation. The bread is usually round, leavened, and somewhat flat and bears the inscription IC, XC, NI, KA (Jesus Christ conquers) and a cross. While it may recall the inscription of St. Constantine's banner, its origin is probably earlier.

In the Church of the *Old Believers, or the Edinovertsy, which reunited with the *Russian Orthodox Church in 1788, the design of an eight-pointed cross is permitted, while in some *monastic churches the *seal of the prosphora can portray a feast or even an *icon.

The prosphora is prepared by taking some fine best quality wheaten flour and mixing it with pure water and a little salt. The preparation is performed by a prosphornitsa, a devout person who repeats the *Jesus Prayer as the bread is being prepared.

The Russian Church makes use of five prosphora, the first and largest one being the "lamb" (see SEAL; SPHRAGIS; PETSHAT). The second prosphora honors the *Theotokos; the saints are honored from the third prosphora; the living from the fourth; and the departed remembered from the fifth prosphora. Particles may be removed from prosphora that are offered by members of the congregation in order to specifically commemorate living and dead relatives and friends.

See BREAD (Byzantine Tradition); KORBAN.

PROTAN KALYMMA
(Byzantine/Greek)

See DISKOKALYMMA; KALYMMATA; VEILS.

PROTHESIS

Armenian Tradition

During the prothesis (*matouthsaran) the great curtain is drawn across the sanctuary, and the unleavened *bread, having been handed to the *priest by the *deacon, is arranged on the *paten (*maghzmah); then wine is poured into the *chalice (*ski; *bashak) with a crosswise motion. Among the *Armenian Catholics a little water is then added. As Psalm 92 is recited, the offerings (*srboutheanch) are covered with a silk *veil (*kogh).

Byzantine Tradition

The term "prothesis" in this rite has one of three meanings:

1. It may refer to the rite of preparation before the *Liturgy is celebrated.

2. It may refer to the area, or chamber, just to the north of the sanctuary (the most usual meaning in ninth-century *Byzantine Liturgies).

3. It may refer to the table that stands to the north of the *altar, known as the paratrapezion (side-altar), while in the Slavonic tradition it is called the predlogenie or zhertvennik. The rite of preparation of the clergy is absent from early liturgical texts. It began to assume its present form, involving vesting and the washing of hands in the *diaconicum (south side of the altar), in the 13th century.

Coptic Tradition

The prothesis in this tradition commences with the fully vested priest going to the altar and, having placed three veils on the right side of the altar, opening the Missal, blessing himself, and then kissing the altar. After reciting the Prayer of Preparation of the Altar, he kisses it again, chooses the bread for the Liturgy, kisses the selected loaves, and after ensuring the soundness of the wine, he washes his hands on the right side of the altar. Having partially dried his hands, he rubs the bread; then, taking the bread in his hand in a silk veil, he walks around the altar preceded by a deacon carrying the wine with another deacon holding a lighted taper. This procession occurs on solemn occasions and is called the *Durat Alhamal (*Circuit of the Lamb). Returning to the front of the altar, the priest blesses both the bread and wine, the latter being put on the left of the altar, while the bread is placed on the paten, or *diskos; the wine is then poured into the chalice, or *poterion. Finally, both paten and chalice are covered with the veil and a third, larger veil is placed over both vessels. The priest then blesses the congregation with a hand cross.

Ethiopian Tradition

The prothesis commences with various prayers prior to the entry of the celebrant into the sanctuary, after which the sacred vessels and vestments are removed from the treasury and the altar and priest are vested. The priest then washes his hands but does not dry them, and he begins to recite the Prayer of Approach. Once the breads have been selected and blessed, they are rubbed with the priest's wet hand in order to test their soundness and to remove loose particles. A procession then forms in which the bread, chalice, and wine are carried around the altar by the clergy, who are preceded by a *subdeacon bearing a lighted taper. It has been known for the wine to be carried around the altar a second time as the deacon recites Psalm 22. Water is added to the wine and prayers are recited, followed by the Prayer over the Cross-Spoon. This is the *spoon from which the faithful receive Holy *Communion from the chalice. The bread and chalice are blessed again and

further prayers are recited, and the rite concludes with the priest facing east and reciting Psalm 116 alternately with the congregation.

East Syrian Tradition

The prothesis (*kubhtha), as observed by Catholic *Chaldeans, is quite a simple ceremony and starts with the lavabo (washing of the hands) by the celebrant. Prayers are recited during the vesting, after which the celebrant ascends the altar carrying the vessels. He places them on the altar with the paten lying to the right and the chalice to the left, and the *enarxis commences.

In the *Nestorian tradition, once the bread has been prepared the Prayer of the *Lachumura and further prayers and anthems are recited, after which the breads are taken out of the *oven by the priest, who puts them on the paten. He then takes a live coal from the oven and puts it in the *censer and throws a little incense haphazardly into the oven. Returning from the oven, he holds the paten in his right hand and the censer in his left and processes to the altar; he leaves the paten in the recess on the right side of the altar and hangs up the censer. Holding a cruet of wine in the right hand and the chalice in the left, the priest pours wine into the chalice in the form of a cross and similarly adds water and then more wine. The enarxis then commences.

West Syrian Tradition

For the alkhidmat alauwali (prothesis) the vessels are left uncovered on the altar with the veil on the left or north side hanging over the edge and the

Missal on the right or south side. The priest, dressed in outdoor clothes, comes to the foot of the altar, and with arms crossed on his chest he recites some prayers and Psalm 50, at the conclusion of which he ascends the altar, kisses it three times, and during the lighting of the altar candles, says more prayers. He then spreads the corporal and arranges the sacred vessels with the *sponge, spoon, and paten on the left and the chalice on the right. Syro-*Jacobite priests put on their *vestments at this point, but the practice observed by *Syrian Catholics varies, and they often vest after the prothesis. The bread is then arranged on the paten, crosswise if there are many breads, but if there are few they may lie one above the other. Wine and water are mixed; the Jacobites mix equal quantities in a vessel called the *deaconess, and this mixture is then poured into the chalice and the priest prays again. The prothesis ends with the covering of the paten and chalice.

See KUBHTHA; MATOUTH(SOUMN)SARAN; PROSKOMEDIA; PROSKOMIDE.

PROTIERE (Byzantine)

See ARCHIEREUS.

PROTODEACON (Byzantine)

The senior *deacon, whose role is roughly equivalent to that of archdeacon in the Western church. Unlike the practice in the West, the *Byzantine protodeacon is a deacon and never a *priest.

PROTOIEREUS (Byzantine/Greek)

The rank of archpriest is the highest grade that may be attained by married *priests.

See ARCHPRIEST.

PROTOPAPAS (Byzantine/Greek)

A *priest whose function is roughly equivalent to that of a dean in the Western Church.

PROTOPSALTES (Byzantine/Greek)

The term usually refers to a principal cantor.

See PRECENTOR; REGENTCHORA.

PROTOS (Byzantine/Greek)

The *Athonite *monk who has been chosen as the chairman of the committee that represents the twenty principal monasteries of the Athonite community.

See ATHOS, MOUNT.

PRUMION (Syro-Jacobite)

See PROEM; SEDRO.

PSAK (Armenian)

The term may have one of two meanings, (1) a marriage crown or garland that is put on the heads of both bride and bridegroom, or (2) the cross that is hung on a red and white thread and suspended around a newly baptized child's neck as part of the baptismal rite.

See BAPTISM; MARRIAGE.

PSALI (Coptic)

A liturgical Office in honor of the Mother of God.

PSALMODIA (Coptic)

See LITURGICAL BOOKS (Coptic Tradition).

PSALTERION (Byzantine/Greek)

One of the books required for the correct recitation of the Office in the *Byzantine rite. The psalms are divided into twenty kathismata, each *kathisma being divided into three *stasis. The divisions are called kathismata because of the early custom of singing the psalms while standing and then sitting during specific interruptions in the recital. These interruptions and the psalms between successive interruptions both came to be called "kathisma."

During the *Byzantine Office it is now customary to sit during a psalm's recitation but to stand at the doxology (*doxologia). When a kathisma is concluded, this interruption is filled with a *canon or *troparion. The Psalterion also includes the text of the nine biblical *canticles, or odes, that appear in *Orthros.

See LITURGICAL BOOKS (Byzantine Tradition).

PSALTES (Byzantine/Greek)
(also called Pevetz)

See SINGER.

PSALTU (Syrian)

See SINGER.

PSATHION (Byzantine/Greek)

Literally, "little mat."

See AETOS; ORLETZ.

P'SHTO (Syrian)

Literally, "extension." The outstretching of the arms, especially during the *great intercession during the *Anaphora; this occurs during the second part of each intercession, of which there are six. When this second part is said aloud (*t'litho: literally, "raising of voice"), the forearms are extended. At its conclusion the *priest lowers his arms to be near the consecrated *bread and wine.

PURIFICATOR

See ESPUGO; GOMURO; GUBKA; MOUSA; SPONGE.

PURSHONO (Syro-Jacobite)

Literally, "portion," "set apart."

See BREAD (Syro-Jacobite Tradition); BUCHRO.

PYLE (Byzantine/Greek)

See THYRA; VRATA.

PYLOROS (Byzantine/Greek)
(also called *Porter; Preuratnek [Slavonic])

The keeper of the *door of a church or monastery.

PYRGOS (Byzantine/Greek)

See KIBORION.

Q

QADISAT ALOHO (Syrian)

Literally, "You are holy, God." The opening words of the Trisagion, which is sung in eight *tones. Among the Syro-*Jacobites there are some variations. It is found in the *Liturgy of the *Catechumens just before the lessons are read, when the *priest ascends the *altar and blesses the *bread and wine three times and himself three times: "You are Holy, O God. Have mercy on us. You are Holy, O Strong One. Have mercy on us. You are Holy, O Immortal One. *Kyrie Eleison" (three times). The survival of the Kyrie may be a relic of an earlier litanic form. Catholic *Syrians present the Trisagion in this form, but there has been much controversy about its recitation and composition. It was probably used in the mid-4th century and is certainly found in the canons of the Council of Chalcedon (451).

See KADISHAT ALOHO; TRISAGION.

QANKE (East Syrian/Chaldean)

The sanctuary in a *Chaldean church; the same word may also refer to an *altar in terms of its being a place of sacrifice.

See MADB'HO.

QANONA (East Syrian)

An audible conclusion to an otherwise silent prayer, which roughly corresponds to a *Byzantine *ekphonesis, or audible conclusion. The qanona is sometimes accompanied by the clash of *cymbals.

QANUNO (Syrian)

See KANUNO.

QARUQTHO (Syro-Jacobite)

The black tarbush, worn on the head by secular *priests. It is customary for it to have seven white crosses sewn on it. This headwear is removed at the *Gospel and at the start of the *Anaphora and is resumed after the ablutions, which are taken at the close of the *Liturgy.

QARYANA (East Syrian/Nestorian) (also spelled *Qiryana)

A lectionary that contains the text of the liturgical Epistles and *Gospels.

See KERYANA; LITURGICAL BOOKS (East Syrian Tradition).

QASHISHO (Maronite)

A *priest, who must be older than thirty years of age in order to be ordained. Since the Council of Lebanon in 1736 he is obliged to recite the *Divine Office.

See KOHNO.

QATISMATA (Syro-Jacobite)

The chants sung during the *Fraction of the consecrated *bread in the *Liturgy.

QDHOSHO QUDHSHE (East Syrian/Nestorian and West Syrian)

See HOLY OF HOLIES.

QESTROMA (Syro-Jacobite)

See CATASTROMA.

QIRYANA (East Syrian/Chaldean)

A Book of Lessons; it can also refer to the Old Testament extracts which are read at the *Liturgy and which precede the reading from the *Apostle, or *Shuraya.

See LECTIONS; LITURGICAL BOOKS (East Syrian Tradition).

QOLE D'MATALTO (Syrian)

The *canticles that are sung during the *prothesis at the start of the *Liturgy.

QOLO (Syrian)

Literally, "voice" or "tune." Popular chants that are sung during the *Liturgy after a passage from the Holy Scriptures is recited. Alternatively, refers to a series of short anthems, each known as a "baito," which form a framework of extracts taken from the psalms with the "Glory be" being used to signal the extract's conclusion.

Q'ROITO (Syrian)

An invocation.

SEE DA'WAH.

Q(U)ADISH (Syrian)

The Sanctus, which in the West *Syrian rite is part of the *Anaphora and concludes the preface. The preface consists of two parts, the first part being said secretly (*Ghontho) while the *priest bows low and flutters his right hand over the *paten and his left hand over the *chalice. The second part is recited aloud with the priest stretching out his hands. At the conclusion of the Sanctus, with the words "Holy, Holy, Holy," *fans are shaken and bells are rung and the congregation responds, "Holy, Holy, Holy"; if a bishop is present he removes his *miter at this point in the *Liturgy.

QUBBA (Coptic)

See KUBBAH.

QUBB'THO (Syro-Jacobite)

The curtains that hang from the canopy over a Syro-*Jacobite *altar.

See QUDSHO.

QUBH'UNO (Syro-Jacobite)

See ESKHIM.

QUBLAT-AS-SALAM (Coptic)

See PEACE, KISS OF (Coptic Tradition).

QUDASHE (East Syrian/Chaldean)
(also spelled *Kuddasha)

The general name of the Anaphoras, or Hallowings, of the *Chaldean rite. Apart from the *Liturgy of the Apostles Addai and Mari, the Chaldeans call the Liturgy of Mar Theodore of Mopsuestia the "Second Hallowing," which is used from the start of Advent until the feast of Hosannas, or Palm Sunday; the other Liturgy, that of Mar Nestorius, or the "Third Hallowing," is used only five times a year: Epiphany; the Friday after Epiphany, called the Memorial of John the Baptist and commemorated on January 7 since the Synod of Rabban Hormizd (1853); the memorial of the Greek Doctors, observed on the Friday within the fifth week after Epiphany; the Wednesday of the Supplication of *Nineveh, observed in the third week of Lent; and Holy Thursday, or the Thursday of the Pasch.

See ANAPHORA.

QUDDAS (Syro-Jacobite)

See ANAPHORA.

QUDDOSHO (Maronite)
(also spelled Qudosho)

Literally, "Hallowing of the *Mysteries."

See ANAPHORA.

QUDHSHA (East Syrian/Nestorian)

See HOLY THING.

QUDSHO (Syro-Jacobite)

Literally, "holy place." The *Syrian sanctuary; this usually has three altars set in a row, with a canopy over the center altar supported by pillars set outside its perimeter and joined at the back and sides by trelliswork. On the gradines of the altar are usually two candles and a crucifix. A canopy curtain (*vilo; sometimes *qubb'tho) is drawn around the altar during certain parts of the *Liturgy and when it is not in use. The main altar is normally approached by means of three steps, with the *Malabar Jacobites using one step only. The top of the altar is made either of wood or stone and is covered by a cloth that conceals the *tablitho (altar stone). This embroidered cloth is folded four times and is in turn covered by colored cloths. The 18'' x 12'' altar stone lies lengthwise from east to west and, having been set into the altar, is consecrated by a *bishop using holy *chrism (*myron) on Holy Thursday or on any Thursday from Easter until the Ascension. The stone bears the name of the consecrating bishop and the date of consecration. For example, "The Holy Trinity has hallowed by the hands of N., Bishop, this Tablitho" and the words "Place NN., Year XY" are added.

A Syrian altar stands away from the end wall in order to permit processions to pass around it; the furnishings of the sanctuary are completed by the presence of two episcopal *thrones (*throniyon), which are both on the north side, one facing west and one facing south, for use during the Liturgy. The other side-altars are usually used as credence tables.

See ALTAR; BETH QUDSHO; Q'DHOSHO QUDSHE.

QUECONE (Armenian)

A musical instrument made from a staff topped by a cherub's figure and to which small bells are attached.

QUENAT (Ethiopian)

The *girdle which is given to an *Ethiopian novice by a superior and which signals the start of the religious life for this novice.

QUOROYO (Maronite)

The *minor order of *reader, or *lector, which may be given at the age of twelve. As part of the ordination ceremony the folded *orarion is laid across the candidate's extended hands.

QUQELION (Syrian)

A chant of psalms, the style of which traditionally dates from the 8th century; it is typified by being interrupted throughout by Alleluias.

QURARA (Coptic)

A cruet for holding wine during the *Liturgy. The *priest receives it from the *deacon and pours the wine into the *chalice from the right side, whereas water is poured in from the left.

QURBAN (Coptic)

Bread that is prepared by the bread-man (corbani), whose function has been taken over by a *deacon as part of the changes introduced by *Pope Shenouda III. Before the *Liturgy commences, the tray of breads covered with a cloth is brought in and placed on a table, shelf, or niche to the south of the *altar, and the wine cruet (*qurara) and a bottle of wine are placed by a deacon near this bread. The empty *paten is placed near the center of the altar, the *chalice in its box-like stand behind the paten, and the *Communion *spoon between the two vessels.

See BREAD (Coptic Tradition).

QURBORO (Maronite)
(also spelled Qurobo)

Literally, "offering."

See BURSHANAH; KURBAN.

QUROBHO (Syrian)

The *Liturgy.

See QUDSHO.

R

RABAN (East Syrian/Chaldean)

Literally, "our great one." An alternative title of a *Chaldean *monk.

See NAPQA.

RABDOS (Byzantine/Greek)

The term "chazranion" (Turkish) is sometimes mistakenly applied to a crozier, but a chazranion is more like an elaborate walking stick and is somewhat shorter than a crozier. The rabdos or, more correctly, poimantike rabdos, is different from a Western crozier: it is shorter and consists of a metal rod on top of which is a small orb that supports a small cross; on the side of this cross two arched serpents are positioned so that their heads are turned to face each other. The symbolism of the two serpents is obvious in that they represent the prudence necessary for those in pastoral authority. A small silk veil may cover the part of the crozier where it is held. As the rabdos is taken up Psalm 109:2 is recited: "The Lord will send out the scepter of your power out of Sion; Rule among your enemies."

See BAKTERIA; CROZIER; DIKANIKION OR DEKANIKION; DJEZL; PATERISSA.

RAB KAHNI (East Syrian/Chaldean)

A *bishop who is directly responsible to the *patriarch.

RAB-KUMRE (East Syrian/Nestorian)

An *archpriest, who ranks next after the *bishop in a diocese and who, at certain functions, may substitute for the bishop.

RADONITSA (Byzantine/Slavonic)

A ceremony that takes place on the Tuesday of the second week after Easter, when the faithful visit the graves of their families and scatter blessed Easter food (*paskha) on the graves.

RAF'AH (Syro-Jacobite)

See ZUYOHO.

RA'IS A-SHAMAMISH (Coptic)
(also spelled Ra'is a-shamamisah)

An archdeacon who has the right to wear a plain iron pectoral cross and may act as the *bishop's vicar-general. In the past the reception of this honor did not always involve a ceremony, but if a ceremony is performed, it is accompanied by a special prayer with an anointing and a laying on of hands as well as a ceremonial rearranging of the *orarion.

See ORDERS, HOLY (Coptic Tradition).

RAISED PLACE, THE
(East Syrian/Nestorian)
(also called Mactabhtha)

The footpace in front of the *altar.

RAKOHNO (Maronite)

Literally, "holy."

See EPISQUPO; KHASVO.

RAMBANS (Syro-Malankarese)

A solitary or eremitical religious.

RAMCHA (East Syrian)
(also spelled Ramsha)

Otherwise known as the Prayer of the Evening or Prayer of the Dusk; this Office of *Vespers is one of the only two compulsory Offices that must be recited by the clergy, the other being the Morning Office of *Sapra.

See EAST SYRIAN CHURCH, DIVINE OFFICE OF.

RASALAH (Melchite/Maronite)

See APOSTLE.

RASAM (Coptic)

The rite of *consignation, which consists of using an intincted *bread to touch the rest of the consecrated bread and then signing the *chalice with the intincted particle both inside the cup and on its outside. The particle is then dropped into the chalice and the chalice is covered.

RASKOLNIKI (Byzantine/Slavonic)

Literally, "schismatics." A comprehensive term describing that section of the *Russian Orthodox Church that refused to accept the many liturgical reforms introduced by *Patriarch Nikon; the schism (raskol) of 1666 followed.

See OLD BELIEVERS.

RASON (Byzantine)

A general term describing the wide-sleeved robe of the *Eastern clergy, but more specifically it refers either to the inner or outer rason.

1. The inner rason (*esorason; podryasnik [Slavonic]) resembles a Sarum-style cassock, the color being usually black, but dark blue and violet are commonly used. It is worn by all clergy, and in order to distinguish it from the outer rason it is often called the *anterion.

2. The outer rason (*exorason; paliya or ryasa [Slavonic]) is worn over the inner rason, has wider sleeves, and reaches to the ground. It is worn by all clergy and is usually black. If, in literature, a rason is referred to, it is usually this outer rason.

The rason worn by a *rasophore is less voluminous than that of the two higher types of *monks, the *stavrophore (krestonosets [Slavonic]) and *megaloschemos (skhimnik [Slavonic]).

See HABITS, COMPARATIVE TABLE OF.

RASOPHORE (Byzantine/Greek) (also called *Ryasonosets)

The lowest grade of *Eastern (*Byzantine) monasticism. An aspirant to the monastic life may be admitted to this grade after a few days or weeks and may elect to remain in this grade for the rest of his life, or after three years he can be admitted to the grade of *stavrophore.

See DEGREES OF MONASTICISM, HABITS OF; MONASTICISM (Byzantine Tradition).

RASPIATIE (Byzantine/Slavonic)

See ESTAVROMENOS.

RASTOYATEL (Byzantine/Slavonic)

See CENOBITIC SKETE.

RAZA (Syro-Malabarese)

A solemn celebration of the *Liturgy.

RAZA RABBA (East Syrian)

Literally, "Great Mystery." The *Liturgy.

RAZDROBLENIE (Byzantine/Slavonic)

See FRACTION (Byzantine Tradition).

READER

(also called Anagu'nstis [Ethiopian]; Quoroyo [Maronite]; Tchetz [Slavonic])

A minor cleric whose duty it is to read the *lessons and responsorial psalms. While the reader ranks below the *subdeacon, there is evidence from the *Byzantine *Liturgy before the 7th century that the readers read all the lessons, with the *Gospels read by the *deacon alone. However, at Alexandria, this privilege was restricted to the archdeacon.

In the Byzantine rite this *minor order may be conferred outside the Liturgy at the *throne set in the middle of the church, and it may take place before the Office that precedes the celebration of the Liturgy. The *bishop lays his hand upon the candidate's head, cuts a small piece of hair in the form of the cross, invests the candidate with a short chasuble, and following the ceremony, the ordinand may read a little portion from the Book of Epistles.

In the *Armenian rite this order is conferred, like all other orders, on a Sunday and with great solemnity. The ordinand is given a Book of Epistles together with an instruction by the bishop: "Take this book and be a preacher of God's Word, instructing yourself in it. If you fulfill your duties with a pure mind and heart, then you will have your reward among the saints. Amen."

In the *Syrian rite the order of reader (koruyo) is conferred at the *elevation during the Liturgy. The reader receives the Book of Prophecies and a *stole, which is worn around the waist like a girdle with the two ends crossed behind and brought to the front over the chest and tucked into the resulting belt-like arrangement.

See ANAGNOSTES; KORUYO.

REGENTCHORA
(Byzantine/Slavonic)

See PRECENTOR; PROTOPSALTES.

RELICS

See LEIPSANA; MOS(T)CHE.

RESERVED SACRAMENT

Armenian Tradition

Catholic churches of this rite always have a tabernacle placed on or near the *altar, before which a lamp burns. In non-Catholic churches there may be a tabernacle, or else the reserved Sacrament is retained in a niche in the north wall.

Byzantine Tradition

The Sacrament reserved for communicating the sick at home is prepared at the Holy Thursday *Liturgy in sufficient quantities for the whole year. At this time the consecrated *bread is broken into as many small particles as are thought necessary for the year and placed on a special plate, and then each particle receives a light drop of consecrated wine by means of the *Communion *spoon. The *priest then places a small piece of marble or even metal on the *antimension, and a specially constructed vessel is placed on this stand. Into this vessel, which has some small holes in it, a sieve-like cup containing burning coals is placed. The bottom of this cup reaches only halfway down the vessel. A deep plate with ring handles is placed on top of the vessel, and above this a *diskos is positioned. The holes in the base of this diskos are in the form of the cross, and it is on the diskos that the consecrated particles are placed and covered. From time to time the particles are stirred with the *lance until they are perfectly dry, then set aside in an *artophorion on the altar. This preparation can be undertaken at any time of the year as well as during Holy Week.

Melchite Tradition

The consecrated bread, which has been intincted with consecrated wine, is kept in a ciborium within a tabernacle. The Sacrament may be renewed in the following way: before cleansing the *paten, the priest takes the ciborium from the tabernacle, lays the consecrated bread on the paten, and purifies the ciborium with the *sponge. Taking the consecrated bread, he dips the end of it into the *chalice, and with this intincted bread he signs the bread that is to be reserved. He then places the intincting bread in the chalice, while the newly intincted bread is placed in the ciborium with the moistened side up. The ciborium is then returned to the tabernacle.

Coptic Tradition

*Coptic Catholics reserve the Sacrament in a tabernacle, while non-Catholic *Copts do not reserve the Sacrament at all. The common reason given for this nonreservation is that the consecrated bread undergoes quick deterioration in that part of the world. To reserve or not has been the subject of controversy for many years.

Ethiopian Tradition

As with the Copts, reservation was once practiced by the non-Catholics but is no longer. The *Ethiopian Catholics reserve in a tabernacle.

East Syrian Tradition

Catholic *Chaldeans reserve in a tabernacle, but the practice of reservation among the *Nestorians has fallen into abeyance, although they display considerable reverence for the *Malca.

West Syrian Tradition

In the 16th century there was an account by the *bishop of Sidon that the Sacrament used to be reserved in a wooden box, but no lights were burned before it. Nowadays the intincted consecrated bread is reserved in a chalice fitted with a cover or a Western-style pyx and placed in a cupboard (*paradiscus) in the center of the gradines of the altar. The container holding the consecrated bread stands on a corporal within the cupboard.

RHANTISMOS (Byzantine/Greek)

The ceremony of the sprinkling, for example at Epiphany as part of the great blessing of the waters, which takes place after the *Liturgy. During this ceremony the *priest, having blessed the water, plunges a cross into the water three times as a *troparion is sung, then a branch of basil is dipped into the water and the corners of the church are sprinkled with the blessed water. The rest of the congregation then approach, and after they have kissed the cross their heads are sprinkled with the water, which may also be drunk by the faithful.

RHANTISTRON (Byzantine/Greek)

An aspergil, which is used to sprinkle blessed or holy water.

See HAGIASTER; KROPELO; RHODISTAGMA.

RHODOSTAGMA (Byzantine/Greek)

Rosewater, with which people and things are sprinkled as part of the ceremonies of Holy Week. To perform this sprinkling use is made of a *kanion or *bikion, which is a flask fitted with a fine sieve at its narrow neck and which is also known as a *hagiaster or rhantistron.

RIDA (Maronite)

An ample chasuble, which is characteristic of the *Maronite usage.

See PHAINO; VESTMENTS, TABLE OF.

RIPIDIA (Byzantine/Greek)
(also called *Exapteryga; *Mirwahah; Ripidi)

Liturgical *fans, which are made of metal and designed to represent a cherub's head encircled by six wings. They are used to fan the *chalice during the *Anaphora, ostensibly to keep insects away. They may also be used to put out the lights after a service.

In the modern *Greek Church their use is now ceremonial rather than practical, being used just after the kiss of *peace and again just before the *diptychs when the *deacon fans the consecrated *bread and wine.

The fan is a distinctive insignia of a deacon. When it is presented in ordination at the close of the ceremony the *bishop exclaims, "Axios" (He is worthy), a tradition referred to by John Moschus in the 6th century. In the Greek tradition, when the holy *chrism is consecrated the box with the oil is carried in procession with seven deacons on either side, each holding a fan over the box.

Both the *Maronites and *Armenians use a brass or silver flabellum, a circular disc to which little bells are attached. In the Armenian rite this flabellum is waved at the *Trisagion to symbolize the wings of the seraphim.

The *Coptic ripidium (ripisterion; mirwahah) is mentioned in the Liturgy of St. Clement, translated from the *Apostolic Constitutions* (ca. 375). The gold or silver discs had a socket that secured them in a short wooden handle, and were engraved with figures of the seraphim. In the Coptic tradition these fans are used at the ordination of a *priest at the laying on of hands and are also used in the procession of the chrism, when as part of that oil's consecration twelve deacons, each bearing a fan, together with twelve *subdeacons carrying lamps and twelve priests bearing thuribles, accompany the bishop, who carries the vessel of oil, which is covered by a white cloth.

See CHEROUBIM; FLABELLA.

RIPIDION (Coptic)

See RIPIDIA.

RIPISTERION (Byzantine/Greek)

See RIPIDIA.

RISH-M'SHAMSHONO (Maronite)

A cleric, rather like an archdeacon, whose principal function is to supervise Church property.

RISH-QOLEH (Syrian)

The tune in which a hymn is to be sung. Each rish-qoleh has eight modes,

each with a title. The series of modes begins on the Sunday at the start of the Church Year, so that each week follows the mode of the preceding Sunday. Feasts usually have their own rish-qoleh.

RIZNITZA (Byzantine/Slavonic)

See SACRISTY.

ROMANIAN

See LITURGICAL LANGUAGES, TABLE OF.

ROMANIAN CATHOLIC CHURCH

The Romanian Catholic Church came into formal existence when the Orthodox Church of Transylvania united with Rome just after that principality came under Austrian rule in the 17th century, but in December 1948 the communist regime declared that the Church had voluntarily dissolved itself and had rejoined the *Romanian Orthodox Church.

At the time of this Church's suppression the Romanian Catholics had a *metropolitan See and four suffragan Sees, and all were forced into the Orthodox metropolitanate of Transylvania. Many clergy were imprisoned and all the *bishops died in prison, the last one being Mgr. Julia Hossu (d. 1970). Other bishops were consecrated by Mgr. O'Hara, an envoy from Rome, but they were all arrested and sent to monasteries after having promised that they would not perform any episcopal function. In 1975 an estimate of the number of faithful Catholics remaining suggested a population of around 900,000, with many *priests ministering clandestinely.

ROMANIAN ORTHODOX CHURCH

Eusebius of Caesarea recorded that St. Andrew and others brought Christianity to Romania. Certainly by the 3rd century Christianity was very strong in parts of the Lower Danube and the Black Sea region, today's Dobrogea (Dobruja).

Initially the *Liturgy was in Latin, but the Slavic Liturgy of Sts. Cyril and Methodius brought the Romanians into contact with Constantinople, and despite the Hungarian and Polish immigration of the 13th century and the arrival of the Dominican missionaries, their Liturgy remained stable and their *Orthodoxy unchanged. However, with the retreat of the Turks, religious pressures came to be felt, and the capture of Transylvania by Austria and the Hapsburgs in 1688 had the effect that many Orthodox became Catholics, especially under the influence of the Jesuits.

By 1733, there were 2,294 Catholic Romanian *priests in Transylvania as against 458 Orthodox priests, and by 1750 the faithful numbered 569,000 *Romanian Catholics as opposed to a mere 25,000 Orthodox.

In 1859 the states of Muntenia, or Wallachia, and Moldavia became united under Cuza. At the same time the two metropolitanates became united into one national Church, and the holder of the See of Bucharest took the title of primate of Romania. The Church's *autocephality was recognized by Constantinople in 1885, becoming a patriarchate in 1925.

Since then, Romanian Orthodoxy has flourished, and in 1969, 100,000 copies of the Bible were printed in Romanian. The Orthodox Church administers its own property, land, and printing presses and has responsibility for many religious journals. It provides education for the clergy in some minor seminaries, for example, the seminary at Cluj, which had 240 students, and two theological institutes, at Bucharest and Sibiu (1980).

Recently, there has been a growth of an evangelical movement within the Romanian Orthodox Church called the "Lord's Army," which was led by a later defrocked priest, Fr. Trifa. This movement, which is still in existence, has been suppressed by the state, and in the early 1950s many of its members were fined and jailed. In 1982 three of its leaders were imprisoned by the authorities; it is said to number some 300,000 members, both clerical and lay.

ROSARY

See CHOTKI.

ROYAL DOORS (Byzantine)
(also called *Beautiful Doors; *Holy Doors; Svyata Vrata; *Tsarskiya Vrata)

A term that normally describes the *doors set in the center of the iconostasis reserved for use by *bishops and officiating *priests. *Deacons rarely pass through the royal doors. Alternatively, the term may be applied to the door leading from the *narthex to the *nave of a church, with the term "holy doors" more correctly describing the central doors of the iconostasis, but the terms are often used incorrectly and interchangeably. It is a fairly open structure and is fitted with a curtain, which may be drawn at various points during the *Liturgy.

See BELOTHYRON; ICONOSTASIS; VELOTHYRON.

ROYAL HOURS (Byzantine)

The Royal *Hours are celebrated on Christmas Eve and the Eve of the Theophany. They are so called because in the past the *Byzantine emperors attended the celebration of the Hours at major festivals.

R'SHOM KOSO (Syrian)
(also called *Bryigyasmana)

The *Liturgy of the Presanctified, which used to be celebrated by the Catholic *Syrians on Good Friday morning and on the weekdays of Lent after Vespers. It is not observed by the *Syrian Jacobites.

RULE OF ST. ANTONY

A rule of life for hermits, unlike the *Rule of St. Basil, which is geared to those seeking a community life. The Rule of St. Antony, transmitted by oral tradition, was put together from St. Antony's writings (apothegms). A great deal is known of the life of St. Antony, "father of monks" (251–356), from the biography written by St. Athanasius, who knew him personally.

The eremitical life as seen by St. Antony differed somewhat from that of the usual hermit in that it envisioned hermits living together in an eremitical "community," which came to be known as a *lavra, as distinct from the mone, where *monks following the Rule of St. Basil lived. The lives of these semi-eremites was not the common life, for inside the lavra each monk was under the direction of a superior practiced in the degree of asceticism appropriate to his charge.

The Rule of St. Antony also forms the basis of a rule for Catholic Antonians, whose constitutions were approved by *Pope Clement XII in 1732; it is also used by *Coptic monks and by the *Orthodox community of Sinai.

RULE OF ST. BASIL

The monasteries of the East follow the Rule of St. Basil, reputed to date from 356 when St. Basil founded a monastery on the banks of the River Idris in Cappadocia.

The Rule is divided into two parts, the Greater and the Lesser Rules. The principal emphasis is on prayer, community life, and manual work, but despite its contemplative emphasis, it is flexible enough to permit almsgiving and guesthouse activities. The Rule is observed in some Western monasteries, and there are Basilian monks in Sicily, Calabria, and Rome who follow the *Byzantine rite but who conform to the *Latin rite in many things, especially in the addition of the *Filioque phrase to their *Creed.

RUSHMA (East Syrian/Nestorian)

The *seal on the Eucharistic bread.

See BREAD (East Syrian Tradition).

RUSHMO (Syrian)

The rite of the *consignation of the consecrated *bread follows the *Fraction (*Tukkoso dh'q'sayo), in which each portion of the broken bread is partially dipped into the *chalice and one portion of bread is then anointed with the other, while the small portion of bread intended for the *priest's

*Communion is placed into the chalice. Other breads are anointed with a piece of intincted bread and are set aside for the Communion of the people and other clergy.

See FRACTION.

RUSSIAN CHURCH IN EXILE

During the troubles that followed the Bolshevik revolution, the then Russian *patriarch, Tikhon, realized that in the event of his imprisonment he should authorize loyal Russian *bishops to set up a temporary and independent Church. As events turned out, with the collapse of the White armies, many found themselves in exile, and those bishops and clergy also in exile decided to execute the Tikhon ruling. A temporary ecclesiastical administration was designed in Yugoslavia, where a council was assembled at Karlovtzy at the behest of the Serbian patriarch. However, at the end of World War II the synod of bishops met and the Russian Church in Exile (or "Outside of Russia") became an established fact. Its synodal headquarters was established in New York.

RUSSIAN ORTHODOX CHURCH, PATRIARCHATE OF MOSCOW

Orthodoxy was first introduced into Russia officially when in 988 Vladimir of Russia, who reigned from 980-1015, was converted to Christianity upon his marriage to Anna, sister of the *Byzantine emperor. Until this time there had been some unofficial Christian proselytizing by way of Byzantium, Bulgaria, and Scandinavia. A patriarchate was established in January 1589 when *Patriarch Jeremias II of Constantinople officiated at the enthronement of the first Russian patriarch, after which the Church called itself the "Third Rome." This was alluded to in the famous letter written in 1510 by the *monk Philotheus of Pskov to Tsar Basil III: "All Christian empires are fallen and in their stead stands alone the empire of our rule in accordance with the Prophetical Books. Two Romes have fallen, but the third stands and the fourth there will not be."

For many years there was a close connection between Church and state, so that from 1613 to 1633 while *Metropolitan Filaret ruled the Church his son, Michael, ruled as the first Romanov Tsar. With the coming of Patriarch Nikon, one of the many aims was to introduce many needed liturgical reforms and to make the Church supreme over the state; this was emphasized when the patriarch claimed the right to intervene in civil matters. Following the Council of Moscow (1666-1667) when the liturgical reforms of Patriarch Nikon were approved, Nikon himself was deposed and Patriarch Adrian was appointed.

When Peter the Great came to power, he was influenced by an apostate, Prokopovitch, and the office of patriarch was abolished and a synod set up in 1721 composed of *bishops and an appointee of the Tsar, called an imperial procurator. It was this body that governed the Church. Catherine II completed much of the work of Peter the Great in restyling the Church, and much Church property was confiscated. When Tsar Nicholas II abdicated in March 1917, a Church council was summoned, and on November 5, 1917, the election of the patriarch Tikhon (Beliavin), the metropolitan of Moscow, took place. On November 7, 1917, the communist dictatorship commenced. Under communism, the Church suffered badly with the suppression of religion and the suspension of the patriarchate until the end of the war, during which time the Church gave considerable support and financial assistance. Stalin finally approved the appointment of Patriarch Sergius, who died after only three months in office and was succeeded by the metropolitan Alexis of Leningrad.

Following World War II, the number of churches that were open (in 1945) stood at 16,000 and rose (in 1956) to 20,000. There followed a series of mass closures, so that by 1967 the total had fallen to 11,500, and it continued to fall until in 1967 the estimated figure stood at 7,500 with between 25 million and 50 million faithful. (Timothy Ware, *The Orthodox Church*.)

RUTHENIAN RITE

A *Byzantine rite celebrated in the Old *Church Slavonic (*Staroslav) and used by Catholic *Slavonic people, called Ruthenians. While the Byzantine rite is used, there are some modifications, for example, the replacement of the *stikharion with an *amice and *alb, and the use of a *paten and *purificator instead of a *diskos and *sponge.

The *Filioque is retained in the text of the *Creed, and while the *zeon is added to the *chalice before *communion, there is no distribution of the *antidoron at the *Liturgy's end. However, during the *vigil service at *Great Vespers, where *bread, wine, and oil are blessed, the bread is distributed the following morning at the Liturgy.

The Roman sequence of liturgical colors is observed, but curiously the *Julian Calendar has been retained with many Western feasts being celebrated, for example, Corpus Christi and the feast of the Sacred Heart.

RUTHENIANS

Catholic Slavs, often called Little Russians to distinguish them from Great Russians, or Muscovites. These Little Russians, or Ukrainians, are found in southwest Russia, Poland, Czechoslovakia, Hungary, and Bohemia, with many groups in the New World.

RYASA (Byzantine/Slavonic)

See RASON.

RYASONOSETS
(Byzantine/Slavonic)

See DEGREES OF MONASTICISM, HABITS OF; HABITS, COMPARATIVE TABLE OF.

S

SA'AURE (East Syrian/Nestorian)

Literally, "visitors." Clergy who are not bishops in the sense of having been consecrated but who have jurisdiction over a group of country parishes.

See CHOREPISCOPUS.

SABANON (Byzantine)
(also called Sabbanon; *Sratchitza)

The term refers to the linen cloth worn by a *bishop as a protection for the *vestments against accidents, for example, during Holy Thursday ceremonies such as the washing of the feet, or when an *altar is being consecrated. The term also refers to the robe of the newly baptized.

See EMPHOTION; SINDON.

**SACRAMENTS,
COMPARATIVE TABLE OF**

See Table 5, page 332.

See under the English name for details:
PENANCE, ORDERS, etc.

SACRISTY

Armenian Tradition

The avandatoun (sarkavaganoths) is found on the north side of the *altar and may be entered by means of a *door. It is here that the table of the *prothesis (*entsaiaran; *matouthsaran) is located and where the *bread and wine are prepared for use in the *Liturgy.

See AVANDATOUN; BEITH ROZE; BETH SHAMASHA; DIAKONIKON; RIZNITZA.

Byzantine Tradition

See DIAKONIKON.

Coptic Tradition

The diakonikon appears to be used sometimes for the recitation of the prayers of the *enarxis according to the Greek Liturgy of St. Mark, whereas ordinarily the preparatory prayers are recited at the main altar.

East Syrian Tradition

The *Chaldean diakonikon and *Nestorian beth shamasha (literally, "house of the *deacon") are both found on the north side of the sanctuary. It is in the diakonikon, or *beth diyakun of the Chaldean rite, that the *priest washes his hands prior to vesting for the *Liturgy. Sometimes on the extreme left will be found the beth sahde (*beth kaddishe), which is where the *relics may be stored. Entry to this part of the sanctuary is by means of a door, called "the little door of the sanctuary."

West Syrian Tradition

See BEITH ROZE; DIYAQONIQON.

SAGHAVART (Armenian)

The cap, or crown, worn by *Armenian *priests during the celebration of the *Liturgy. The origins of this custom date to the 12th century. If a deacon is assisting a *bishop at the Liturgy, he may also wear a saghavart, but lower clergy substitute a silk bonnet with gold braid for this clerical miter. Bishops of this rite remove the miter during the Liturgy from the start of the *Cherubic Hymn until the end of the Liturgy. Armenian bishops wear a ring, a custom unique throughout the East. The ring of *Gregorian bishops is worn on the little finger of the right hand, since it is the privilege of the *catholicos to wear it on the ring finger.

See MITER; VESTMENTS, TABLE OF.

SAGHMOS JASCHOU (Armenian)

The Psalm of Dinner Time, which oc-curs just before the Old Testament *lesson in the Armenian *Liturgy; it may be omitted at ordinary celebrations. The Alelou Jaschou, or Alleluia of Dinner Time, is sung just before the *Gospel is read.

SAGHMOSERGOV (Armenian)

See APIR; SINGER.

SAHAL (Ethiopian)

The large *paten used by the non-Catholic *Ethiopians from which Holy *Communion may be distributed. The sahal is carried on a tray covered with a cloth and supported by two *deacons.

SAKKOS (Coptic and Byzantine)

A *vestment that replaces the chasuble and is worn by many *bishops of the *Eastern rite. Originally it was the tunic worn only by the emperor, but he granted the privilege of wearing it to the patriarchs, who in turn granted the privilege to the bishops following the fall of Constantinople to the Turks in 1453. It is said to represent the purple cloak that Christ wore during the Passion, while other sources suggest that it symbolizes the seamless robe of Christ. It is dalmatic in shape with short half-sleeves and is slit from top to bottom, the pieces being joined together either by ribbons or with tiny metal bells, as is the custom with the *Greeks.

SALAM (Maronite)
(also spelled *Sh'lomo)

The peace in this rite is exchanged among the clergy in the sanctuary by each cleric placing his joined hands between the hands of the cleric giving the peace. The receiver then withdraws his hands and places them over his heart. The *Maronite peace is given at the start of the *Canon, when the server kneels at the right of the *priest and extends his right hand. The priest kisses the *chalice *veil, touches the *altar, the chalice, and *bread and then exchanges the peace with the server. As the priest does this he says, "Peace be to you, the servant of the Holy Spirit," whereupon the server kisses the priest's hand and replies, "Come in peace, our father and holy priest."

See PEACE, KISS OF.

SALIB (Syro-Jacobite)

Literally, "cross." The arrangement of the broken consecrated particles of *bread in the form of a cross. This arrangement is conventionally employed from the feast of the Cross (September 14) until Christmas.

See FRACTION.

SAMDANION (Byzantine)

A corrupted word of Persian origin used to denote the candlesticks that are placed on the *altar during the *Liturgy.

SANCTUARY

A word that may be used variously: (1) in the sense of being a temple and so corresponding to the *Coptic *erphei, or *haikal, or (2) it may mean "*altar," and here the Syro-*Jacobite and *Nestorian word "*madhbh'ha" comes nearest to suggesting this sense.

See BETA MAKDAS; ERPHEI; KEDEST; MADB'HO; SRBARAN.

SANDARUS (Coptic)

A type of *Coptic *incense reputed to have a most penetrating odor; it is thought to have come from Java or Sumatra.

SANWARTHA (East Syrian)

An *amice-like vestment worn occasionally by *Chaldean and *Nestorian *bishops and *priests.

See VESTMENTS, TABLE OF.

SAPRA (East Syrian)

The Morning Office, which together with the *ramcha are the only compulsory Offices celebrated in this rite. It has many psalms, as the entire Psalter is read during one week together with many hymns attributed to St. Ephrem (ca. 306–373). At this Morning Office on Sundays and major feast days the "Glory Be to God on High" is sung.

SARKAVAGANOUTHS (Armenian)

See SANCTUARY.

SARKAVAK (Armenian)
(also spelled Sarkavag)

A *deacon, most of whom are in monasteries among the celibate clergy. During the *Liturgy his duties are concerned with censing and reading the liturgical *Gospel; his liturgical dress usually includes the *pakegh and *shapik.

See ORDERS, HOLY.

SATURDAY OF LIGHT (Coptic)

Holy Saturday, which is celebrated with special ceremonies and during which the entire Psalter is recited throughout the night. A procession is formed around the church while the choir sings the Song of the Three Children and the story of Nebuchadnezzar is read. The *Liturgy is celebrated as on Good Friday except that half the *lessons are read in a sad tone and half in a happy tone. After the Liturgy the Gospel of St. John is read in its entirety, and the silver Book of *Gospels is processed around the church accompanied by the singing of many hymns.

SCHEMA (Syro-Jacobite)

See DEGREES OF MONASTICISM, HABITS OF; ESKHIM; HABITS, COMPARATIVE TABLE OF.

SCHEMATOLOGION
(Byzantine/Greek)

A parchment manuscript containing the rite of profession; it was used on Mount *Athos as a substitute for a printed book.

SCHOORCHAR (Armenian)
(also spelled Schourdcharr; *Schurchar; *Shurtshar)

The chasuble, which resembles a Western hoodless cope but with a tall, stiff embroidered collar (*va(r)kas), which stands up around the neck; this vestment is worn by *bishops and *priests alike. It is suggested by some liturgists that it underwent the same sort of changes in style in the course of its history as the *Coptic chasuble (*phelonion) did. Neale seems to maintain that the chasuble was abandoned at the time of the *catholicos Isaac, when writing his condemnation of the errors of the Armenians in the 12th century, but Isaac was criticizing the clergy for

not using the chasuble rather than advocating its abandonment. The following prayer is said while putting on the vestment: "Lord of your mercy, clothe me with a bright garment and protect me against the wiles of the devil, that I may be considered worthy to glorify your glorious name. . . ."

See VESTMENTS, TABLE OF.

SCHOUSCHPHAH (Armenian)

See MARMNAKAL.

SCHURCHAR (Armenian)

See SCHOORCHAR.

SEAL

The term has several meanings, for example:

1. The Eucharistic *bread, called *tabh'o by the Syro-*Jacobites because the bread is sealed with crosses. It may also be called *p'resto (literally, "flat cake"). In the center of the *Byzantine *prosphora, or leavened Eucharistic bread, is a small central portion called the seal (*sphragis [Greek] or *petshat [Slavonic]). This has a cross stamped on it, in the four corners of which are the letters IC, XC, NI, KA, "Jesus Christ conquers." This seal is cut from the rest of the loaf with a *lance and placed on the *paten.

2. A final verse used, for example, in the Syro-Jacobite and *Nestorian rites, when the *khuthama concludes the latter part of the *prothesis ceremony, or "the Sacrifice of Melchizedek." Interestingly, if a *bishop is celebrating the Liturgy, this "Sacrifice of Melchizedek" is performed by the *deacon while the bishop remains on

the throne, and the second service of the *kurbono, or "Sacrifice of Aaron," follows immediately and is introduced by this seal.

3. A blessing, or khuthama, rather like an *apolysis, which occurs as the *dismissal rite at the close of the Nestorian *Liturgy. The blessing is pronounced by the *priest standing to the right of the *altar *doors. The text of the seal varies according to whether it is a special feast or not. The *eulogia follows.

SECOND ROME

A reference to Constantinople when, after the sack of Rome in 476, it became the capital of the Christian world. After Constantinople's fall to the Turks in 1453 Moscow claimed to be the Third Rome.

SECOND SERVICE OF THE KURBONO (Syro-Jacobite)
(also called Sacrifice of Aaron)

The second part of the *Liturgy, preceding the *lessons. Among *Syrian Catholics it includes the vesting ceremony, which follows the *prothesis, a *bishop being vested at the throne assisted by a *deacon. During this service the *priest returns to the *altar vested, kisses the step, ascends to the altar, uncovers the *bread and wine, and places the *paten and *chalice *veils to the south and north sides of the altar respectively. Crossing his hands, he picks up the paten in his right hand and the chalice in his left and recites the offertory prayer, at the end of which he places the chalice to the east and the paten to the west of the altar, covering both the paten and

chalice with the great veil. The remainder of the Liturgy continues and is known as the "Sacrifice of Jesus Christ."

See SEAL.

SEDALEN (Byzantine/Slavonic)

The short *troparion that is sung, while seated, at the end of each Psalter division during Matins or *Orthros.

See KATHISMA.

SEDRO (Syrian)

Literally, "order." A penitential prayer composed of verses set into a diffuse fixed framework, the recitation of which is preceded by a *proem. This prayer is recited by the *priest standing before the *altar while the *censer is being swung, for example, at the start of the *Liturgy of the *Catechumens. According to Moses bar Kepha (813–903) this combination of prayer and *incense during the sedro was quite unfamiliar. It was also commented upon by Denys bar Salibi (d. 1171).

The sedro is recited at the start of the Liturgy of the Faithful, when it is called the sedro of the Entrance (sedro d'ma'altho) and is preceded by the familiar *proem. This sedro of the Entrance suggests a *Byzantine-style *Entrance. According to bar Salibi, the *Jacobites had an Entrance of the offering, or gifts, which would appear to be pointless, since the *bread and wine were already on the altar. Some of the forms of this Entrance sedro, or supplication, are attributed to the *Monophysite *patriarch John (d. 650).

SELAN (Armenian)

See ALTAR.

SEMANTRON (Byzantine/Greek)
(also called *Bela; *Klepala)

Literally, "to give a signal." The wooden plank that is struck in order to call the people to worship. Some ten minutes later the final warning "bell" (sideroun) is struck to announce the imminent start of an Office or ceremony. The use of the semantron is attributed by Christian historians to an edict of Khalifat Omar about 637. Since the sideroun is an iron bar, it overcomes the early Muslim ban on the use of bells. The semantron may be struck in different ways so as to produce different notes. In monasteries with several semantra, the little one is used on ordinary days, while the large one is used on *great feasts.

SENAKSAR (Byzantine/Slavonic)

See SYNAXARION.

SENKESSAR (Ethiopian)

A Synaxary, or Book of the Saints. Many of the entries in this book are obscure because they have been adapted uncritically from the Arabic.

SENSATA (Ethiopian)

The feast of the Immaculate Conception, which is observed by *Ethiopian Catholics on December 8 (13 Tachsas) and by non-Catholics on July 31 (7 Nahase) or December 12 (16 Tachsas).

SENWARTA (East Syrian)

A white handkerchief, which may be worn as a *vestment over the head.

SERBIAN ORTHODOX CHURCH, HISTORY OF

The first Jewish convert Christians arrived in Dalmatia and Illyricum near the end of St. Paul's ministry, but organized Christianity came to Yugoslavia from Rome at the behest of the *Byzantine emperor Heraclius (610–641). The Roman missionaries were not successful, since Latin, an unfamiliar language to the Serbs, was used liturgically. It was for this reason, with the death of Heraclius and the weakening of Byzantium, that paganism grew stronger among the Serbs.

It was through the efforts of Emperor Basil I the Macedonian (867–886) that the influence of Byzantium grew, especially since he had helped Grand Duke Mutimie of Serbia win a victory over African Saracens in Dalmatia. The Serbs requested the emperor to send Christian preachers, who turned out to be Greeks, and the Serbian parishes began to depend on Constantinople and not on Rome to the extent that it was in Constantinople that their *bishops were consecrated, and the *patriarch was commemorated in the *Liturgy.

Between the 9th and 12th centuries, the Serbs were under Latin influence and then under the Greek patriarchate and even, at one time, under the Bulgarian hierarchy. This confusing state of affairs continued until the coming to power of Prince Stephen Nemanya of Rashka (1114–1200), who became the unifier of the Serbian lands. Although he had been baptized in his early years by a Roman *priest, he received holy *baptism from the *Orthodox bishop Leontije of Rashka in 1143 and was the father of St. Sava, whose name is associated with the foundation of an independent Serbian Church.

It was St. Sava who in 1219 went to Asia Minor to request the Greek emperor and the patriarch of Constantinople, who were then in Nicea, to grant *autocephaly to the Serbian Church and to appoint a Serbian archbishop to Serbia, which was granted provided that St. Sava would head the Serbian Church. From that time on the Serbian Church, which had previously been headed by Greek bishops, was autocephalous, and Serbia was divided into twelve dioceses but maintained its ties with the *ecumenical patriarch.

In 1346, the Serbian archiepiscopate was upgraded to a patriarchate at Pec during the reign of Stephen Douchan, but when the Serbs were defeated at the battle of Kossovo (1389), the Turks favored Ohrid as the patriarchate instead of Pec, which was suppressed but was reestablished in the 16th century. Pec continued as patriarchate until 1766, when the ecumenical patriarch persuaded the Sultan to revoke its establishment by an edict, most probably because of the growing Greek influence at the Sultan's court.

In 1832 the Serbian Orthodox Church was granted authority to elect *metropolitans and bishops and in general was able to exercise a fair degree of internal *autonomy, but metropolitans still had to go to Constantinople to be consecrated. With the decline of Turkish power before World War I, the Serbian Orthodox Church was split into three autocephalous Churches—Serbia, Montenegro and Dalmatia, and Austria-Hungary—all officially under the ecumenical patriarch.

One of the effects of the war was political unity, and the Serbian Orthodox Church attempted to mirror this unity with the establishment of the Belgrade patriarchate in 1922, which was recognized by the ecumenical patriarch. In the interwar period the Serbian Orthodox Church was targeted by ideologies both at home and abroad, which, in order to implement their anti-Serbian and anti-Yugoslav strivings, aimed to split the Serbian people as a single and distinct unity in the Balkans. This culminated in the physical and cultural genocide of the Serbian people during World War II, accompanied by the martyrdom of many bishops, priests, and laity.

After World War II many of the Church's privileges were removed by the communists after the 1945 proclamation, which severed any connection between Church and state. In 1975 in Yugoslavia the Serbian Orthodox Church had 81 monasteries, 72 convents, 3,368 churches, 4 major seminaries, a monastic school, a theological faculty in Belgrade with 120 students, and 172 students in St. Sava's Seminary.

SERVICE BOOKS

See LITURGICAL BOOKS.

SESLE (Syro-Jacobite)

The *cymbals, which together with the *noqusho are sounded to warn of the approach of the more solemn moments of the *Liturgy, such as the Sanctus, institution, *Epiclesis, *elevation, and the blessing before the people's *Communion.

SETHRO (Syro-Jacobite)

These obsolete curtains may occasionally be found hanging in each of the *doors in the screen of a Syrian-rite Church.

SHABBUQTO (West Syrian)

A crozier. *Jacobite prelates use a staff, the head of which bears two entwined serpents with a small orb between them with a cross at the top. *Syrian Catholics generally use a Latin-style crozier, although they have been known to use the Jacobite style of crozier. When the crozier is being held by a *bishop during a pontifical *Liturgy, it is not to touch the floor and must be held a few inches above the ground.

See HUTRO; MURONITHO; PASTORAL STAFF; VESTMENTS, TABLE OF.

SHABHO'A (East Syrian/Chaldean)
(also spelled Shabu'a; Shawu'i)

Literally, "set of seven." The name given to each of the seven-week periods into which the Church Year is divided. Some of these periods are not actually seven weeks in length, since the occurrence of Easter may shorten or lengthen these periods of special commemoration.

SHABTO DAMYOKHTO (Maronite)
(also called Shabto d'k'hewose)

Literally, "week of rest." Easter week.

SHAHARA (East Syrian/Nestorian)
(also called *Awakener)

One of the *Nestorian *minor *orders, the others being that of *reader and *subdeacon. This *order is one exercised by a reader or by an old *priest whose function it is to preside at the Night Office or at funerals.

SHAMAMOUT (Armenian)
(also spelled *Jhamamout)

An introit that marks the start of the *enarxis; it is the *Monogenes of the *Byzantine rite and is employed on Sundays, but the text varies according to the day and season of the year. According to De Meester, the Sunday Monogenes found its way into the Byzantine *Liturgy in the 7th and 8th centuries. Some authorities ascribe it to the emperor Justinian (reigned 527–565), while others think it was composed by Severus of Antioch (d. ca. 536).

SHAMASHA (East Syrian/Nestorian)
(also called *Dyakna)

A *deacon.

See ORDERS, HOLY (East Syrian Tradition).

SHAMASHUTHA
(East Syrian/Nestorian)

Literally, "herald." The Book of the Diakonika, as used by *Nestorian *deacons (*shamasha), so called because it is the deacon who addresses the congregation. The term was used by Narsai (399–502), who was called "the leper" by the *Monophysites.

SHAMLAH (Coptic)
(also spelled Chamlah)

A word often used to describe what is more properly the tailasan, but shamlah is not synonymous with the ballin.

The shamlah is a long white band of linen or silk up to six meters in length embroidered with gold crosses at the ends and worn by both *priests and *archpriests (*kummus), a term much disliked by *Copts. It is worn twisted around the head like a turban with one end hanging down the back, while the other end passes under the chin and is secured on top of the head.

The ballin worn by the *patriarch and *bishops resembles the shamlah but is made of colored silk and is embroidered with texts and crosses. The strip of material is doubled, then placed on the head in such a way that both sides are of equal length. These ends are brought to the front and crossed on the chest, then passed under the opposite arms, across the back, over the opposite shoulder, and straight down in front to be confined beneath the *girdle. The patriarch wears the ballin on Good Friday but never during the *Liturgy, whereas if a bishop is celebrating the Liturgy without a *miter, he must wear the ballin.

See BALLIN; TAILASAN.

SHAPIK (Armenian)

A long *alb-like vestment that is fuller than the Western equivalent; while it is usually made of silk it is sometimes made of linen or velvet and may be of any color.

See VESTMENTS, TABLE OF.

SHARAKAN (Armenian)
(also spelled Sharagan)

A book of hymns, or *canticles, not found in the Book of Hours (*Jamarkik).

SHAUTHOPHUTHO (Syrian)
(also called *Tanawal)

Holy Communion.

See COMMUNION.

SHAWU'I (East Syrian/Chaldean)

See Shabho'a.

SHEHIMO (West Syrian)
(also spelled Shimo)

The West Syrian Daily Office, which exists in three *Jacobite editions, those of 1890, 1913, and 1936 as well as in many Catholic editions. The obligation to recite the Office may be fulfilled by substituting the recitation of the *Trisagion and the *Lord's Prayer for each *Hour of the Office. A more elaborate Office, the *Fenqith, exists but is rarely used.

SHENTO (Coptic)

See STOICHARION.

SHER'ATA GECAWE (Ethiopian)

A lectionary; among non-Catholic *Ethiopians it is used to provide the texts of the psalms and *Gospels for *Vespers and also the four lessons and psalms used in the *Liturgy.

See LITURGICAL BOOKS (Ethiopian Tradition).

SHER'ATA KEDDASE (Ethiopian)
(also called *Mashafa Keddase)

This is often called the Book of the Oblation, since it is the Missal used by *Ethiopian Catholics. It contains the Ordinary text of the *Liturgy as well as the principal *Anaphoras used in this rite.

See LITURGICAL BOOKS (Ethiopian Tradition).

SHESTOPSALMIE
(Byzantine/Slavonic)

See EXAPSALMOS.

SHIRAZ WINE (Armenian)

The wine normally used in the *Armenian *Liturgy.

SHKINTA (East Syrian/Nestorian)

A table found below the steps leading to the sanctuary, on which may be placed a wooden cross with floriated ends and a Bible. Before dawn on a day when the *Liturgy is to be celebrated, candles are lit on either side of the shkinta to provide light for the readings from the Scriptures that precede the making of the sacramental bread (*see* BREAD [East Syrian Tradition]). A person coming into the church goes to the shkinta, lifts up the cross and brings it to the lips, saying, ''We worship the Lord, your undivided Godhead and Manhood.'' When receiving *Communion, the communicants kiss the shkinta and leave an alms offering.

SHLEM (Byzantine/Slavonic)

See KOUKOULION; PERIKEPHALAIA.

SH'LIHO
(Syro-Jacobite and Nestorian)

See LECTIONS.

SHLIKA (East Syrian)

The text of the Epistles found in the *East Syrian Lectionary (*Qaryana). The *Apostle, as it is sometimes called, is read from the right side of the *altar and is preceded by the announcement ''Amen. Be silent. Paul the Apostle's Epistle to N., my brethren; bless Lord.''

See LITURGICAL BOOKS (East Syrian Tradition).

SHLIKHA (East Syrian)
(also spelled Sh'liho)

See SHLIKA.

SH'LOMO (Syrian)
(also spelled *Salam; Shlama)

The peace, or kiss of peace; if it is to be received by a cleric below the order of *deacon, the *priest kisses the *altar and then the cleric does so, then kisses the hand of the priest, and then the other side of the altar. If the cleric is a deacon or priest, he censes the altar, receives the greeting, and kisses the hand of the celebrant. A deacon, however, takes a priest's hand between his own and then passes his own hands down his face. The principal layman comes to the door of the sanctuary and places his joined hands between the deacon's hands, brings them to his mouth and forehead, and then conveys the peace to others in the same manner.

See PEACE, KISS OF.

SH'MASH (Syrian)

Literally, ''minister.'' The term ''minister'' may refer either to the vessel used for the cleansing of the vessels after the *Communion or to the washing of the vessels and hands at the close of the *Liturgy.

SHOMU'O (Syrian)

See CATECHUMEN.

SHORDION (Coptic)

A *Coptic *stole; the way it is worn is determined by the wearer's status. If, for example, he is a *subdeacon, the stole is worn by being passed across the chest, under the arms, crossed on the back, and drawn over the shoulders, and the free ends are then tucked into the band (*zinnar) in front. If the cleric is a *deacon, it is worn under his right arm with the free ends hanging over the left shoulder. A *priest wears the stole in a *Byzantine manner, but it is allowed to hang outside the zinnar.

See BATRASHIL; ORARION; VESTMENTS, TABLE OF.

SHOSHEPA (East Syrian/Chaldean) (also spelled Shushepa; Shushipa)

The large, stiff *veil used to cover the consecrated *bread and wine in the *Liturgy. At the time of consecration this large veil is folded in four in such a manner that its embroidered cross is prominently on display. The veil is then placed around the consecrated bread and wine on three sides. It is only after the *Fraction, *elevation, and intinction that the shoshepa is removed and returned to the north side of the *altar.

SHOURE (Coptic)

An *Oriental-type *censer, usually heavily ornamented with tiny bells and used extensively throughout the *Coptic *Liturgy.

See CENSER.

SHUBBOHO (West Syrian)

The short anthem that precedes the *priest's *Communion.

SHUNOYO (West Syrian)

The feast of the Dormition of the Virgin Mary (Assumption) is celebrated August 15. On this day in Aleppo, *Syrians go to the cemeteries, where they eat blessed grapes; what remains uneaten is distributed to the poor. For this reason a medieval Syrian calendar of the 13th century refers to the feast as "The Decease of the Mother of God over the Grapes."

SHURAYA (East Syrian/Nestorian) (also spelled Shuroyo)

Literally, "beginning." The *antiphon that precedes the Prayer Before the Apostle. The term may sometimes refer to the lesson from the *Apostle. When the *deacon says, "Stand for prayer," the *priest recites the first verse of the shuraya, to which the choir responds with the second verse. In form it is quite similar to the *Byzantine *prokeimenon.

See LECTIONS; SH'LIHO.

SHURTSHAR (Armenian)

See SCHOORCHAR; VESTMENTS, TABLE OF.

SHUSHEPO (West Syrian) (also spelled *Shoshepa)

Literally, "clouds." This word has several meanings:

1. The small hand cross with a veil that is held by *bishops in their right hand when giving a blessing. When not in use the cross is carried in the left-hand pocket.

2. The *veils, of which there are three, used to cover the sacred vessels during the *Liturgy. Those that cover the *paten and *chalice are known as the huppoyo and are about eight inches square, flexible, colored, and sometimes designed with a flap on each of the four sides, while the large veil (keltho) is used to cover both paten and chalice.

See ANNAPHURO; HUPP(A)OYO; VEILS.

SHVOT (Coptic)

The episcopal pastoral staff at the apex of which are two entwined serpents on either side of a small round sphere with a cross at the top. Near the top of the staff a small green silk veil is usually attached.

See CROZIER; DIKANIKION.

SIGN OF THE CROSS

See CROSS, SIGN OF.

SINAI, CHURCH OF

A small independent *Orthodox Church ruled by the archbishop of Mount Sinai, who is in charge of the Monastery of St. Catherine, whose *monks are Antonian rather than Basilian. Though this Church's independence was confirmed in 1782, the *patriarch of Jerusalem consecrates the archbishop following his election by an assembly of the senior monks of the monastery. This assembly acts as the *synaxis, or advisory council, to the archbishop.

SINAKSAR (Coptic)

See SYNAXAR.

SINDON (Byzantine/Greek)

A linen cloth used by *bishops. The term has sometimes been applied generally to all liturgical *veils and cloths.

See SABANON.

SINGER

A *minor order, that of *taperer-reader (*singer), which in the *Byzantine tradition is one of the two minor orders, the other being that of *subdeacon. Both of these orders may be received outside the *Liturgy. The order of psaltes (singer) is conferred before the Office that precedes the Liturgy and involves a *tonsure; the order of subdeacon is conferred after that Office.

In the *Syrian rite the order of psaltu (mzamrono) is conferred at the *elevation during the Liturgy, when the singer receives a Book of Psalms. He is expected to make the responses when the rubrics indicate that the congregation should respond. Readers (singers) of the Syrian rite wear a *stole (*uroro) around the waist with the two free ends crossed and brought over the chest, then tucked into the part that forms the belt.

See APIR; MAZAMER; MZAMRONO; PEVETZ; PSALTES; PSALTU; SAGHMOSERGOV.

SINIYAH (Syro-Jacobite)
(also called *Pinco; *Piyalo)

The linen *purificator, which can be substituted for the *sponge and which is used to gather up the particles of consecrated *bread during the *Liturgy.

SINODOS (Ethiopian)

An Ethiopic translation of the Sahidic Heptateuch.

SIS (Armenian)

See CILICIA.

SITARAH

See KATAPETASMA.

SKETE (Byzantine/Greek)
(also spelled Sket [Slavonic])

A minor monastery usually associated with Mount *Athos, but the term can be applied to similar settlements dependent on a monastery. There are two kinds of sketes, *cenobitic and *idiorrhythmic.

See CENOBITIC SKETE; IDIORRHYTHMIC SKETE.

SKEUPHYLAION (Byzantine/Greek)

The area to the right of the *altar where the sacred vessels and *vestments are stored and whose security is the responsibility of the *deacon.

See DIAKONIKON.

SKHIMNIK

See DEGREES OF MONASTICISM, HABITS OF; MEGALOSCHEMOS; MONASTICISM (Byzantine Tradition).

SKI (Armenian)

A *chalice, usually of Western design and dimensions.

See BASHAK.

SKOUPHOS (Byzantine/Greek)

A small cap worn by *monks under their veils; it may also be worn by a minor cleric. The term is derived from the Arabic for "basket" and resembles a brimless hat. Among the *Russian clergy it is worn by *priests and *archpriests who have received the skouphos as a token for service. In the profession ceremonies the skouphos and veil are collectively called the *perikephalaia (Greek) or *shlem (Slavonic).

See KAMILAFKA.

SKRIZHALI (Byzantine/Slavonic)

Literally, "The tables of the law." The squares of velvet that are sewn on a bishop's mantle at the neck and where it is secured at the feet. They symbolize the Old and New Testaments or the Four Evangelists.

See MANDYAS; POMATA.

SLAVA (Byzantine/Slavonic)

See DOXASTIKON.

SLAVONIC

See LITURGICAL LANGUAGES, TABLE OF.

SLAVOSLOVIE
(Byzantine/Slavonic)

See DOXOLOGIA.

SLEEPLESS LAMP (Byzantine)

The lamp that burns perpetually in the apse behind the *altar. It is so called because it is never extinguished.

SLOVAK RITE

The name of the rite observed by *Byzantine Catholics in Czechoslovakia. The population of this rite numbered 176,000 members in 1970.

SLUTHA DLILYA
(East Syrian/Nestorian)

Literally, "prayer at night." The Night Office, which, if sung, may be joined with Shara (*Lauds) and *Slutha Dsafra (Prime).

SLUTHA DSAFRA
(East Syrian/Nestorian)

The Office corresponding to the Western Office of Prime, which, if joined with *Lauds, constitutes the Morning Prayer.

See SLUTHA DLILYA.

SLUZHEBNIK (Byzantine/Slavonic)

The service book that contains the fixed parts of the *Liturgy of St. John Chrysostom, the *Liturgy of St. Basil, and the *Liturgy of the Presanctified. There may additionally be an abridged version of the *Euchologion containing some fairly common ceremonies such as *baptism, *chrismation, *matrimony, *unction of the sick, and *penance. For this reason the Sluzhebnik is sometimes called the Little Euchologion in contrast with the Great Euchologion.

See AGIASMATARION; HIERATIKON; IERATIKON; LITTLE EUCHOLOGION; LITURGICAL BOOKS (Byzantine Tradition); LITURGIKON.

SMALL COMPLINE (Byzantine)

The closing Office of the day. Following the blessing by the *priest the prayer "O Heavenly King, the Comforter" is read; the *Trisagion and *Lord's Prayer follow together with Psalms 50, 69, and 142, the small doxology, the Nicene *Creed, *Canon of the *Theotokos, the Trisagion, and Lord's Prayer. The Office concludes with a *kontakion or *troparion, the prayer of the Hour, the priest's *dismissal, and final *litany.

See GREAT COMPLINE.

SMALL EUCHOLOGION
(Byzantine)
(also called Mikron Euchologion)

See AGIASMATARION; BOOK OF NEEDS; IERATIKON; LITURGICAL BOOKS; LITURGIKON; SLUZHEBNIK.

SMALL LITANY

See LITY; MALAYA EKTENIYA; ORTHROS.

SMALL VESPERS (Byzantine)

Small Vespers commences with the *priest's blessing, "Blessed is our God, always now and ever and to the ages of ages," and the *Trisagion, *Kyrie (three times), *Lord's Prayer, Psalm 103, and *Litany of Peace follow. The congregation prays, "Lord I have cried to You, hear me . . .," which prayer is made up of a series of verses from Psalms 140 and 141. Verses for the day are read, followed by the Evening Hymn, or Vesper Song to the Son of God, the Litany of Supplication, and Nunc Dimittis. The Office concludes with the Trisagion, Lord's Prayer, the *apolytikon, threefold litany, and *dismissal.

See GREAT VESPERS; HESPERINOS.

SMIESHEVANIE
(Byzantine/Slavonic)

See COMMIXTURE; ENOSIS.

SOBOR (Byzantine/Slavonic)

See SYNAXIS.

SOBORNIE (Byzantine/Slavonic)

See CONCELEBRATION; SYLLEITOURGON.

SOBORNOST (Byzantine/Slavonic)

A term denoting the unity of many within the organic fellowship of the Church. Inside this unity each retains individual and full freedom while sharing in the corporate life of the whole.

SOLEAS (Byzantine/Greek)
(also spelled Solea [Slavonic])

The platform located outside the *iconostasis. It is on the same level as the sanctuary and may be approached by a step or two. In times past the soleas was reserved for the *subdeacons and *readers, but it is now used by the choir, and it is to the soleas that the faithful come to receive Holy *Communion. If there is no *ambo, the *Gospel may be sung here.

See KLIROS.

SOROS (Byzantine/Greek)

A chapel used to house the *relics of saints.

SPHRAGIS (Byzantine/Greek)

See PETSHAT; PROSPHORA; SEAL.

SPONGE (Byzantine)
(also called G'Muro; Spongos)

A small triangular *sponge sewn into a red silk cover, the sides of which measure about one or two inches. It is used to gather up the pieces of *bread at the *prothesis and at the *Communion of the faithful, and it may sometimes be used to purify the fingers of the celebrants. When not in use it is kept with the *antimension.

See ESPUGO; GOUBA; GUBKA; MOUSA.

SPONSOR

The person who, at baptism, presents the candidate at the font and who makes the baptismal promises on behalf of an infant. It is the sponsor's privilege subsequently to crown this godchild as part of the godchild's *marriage ceremonies. Likewise, during the profession of a *monk, the sponsor (*staretz) is responsible for the postulant's direction and will present him when he is to be clothed.

See ANADOCHOI; BAPTISM; GERONTAS; KRESTNAYA ATIETS.

SPOON (also called Ljitza)

The use of the spoon in distributing Holy *Communion seems to be Syrian in origin and is reputed to date from the time of St. John Chrysostom (ca. 347–407). In the *Syrian rite, the *tarwodho is laid across the top of the *chalice after the consecrated *bread and wine have been covered, just before the Communion.

See IZHITZA; KALB'THO; KOKLIARION; LABIS; MYSTER; MYSTHERI; TARWODHO.

SPOUDIKON (Coptic)
(also spelled Isbodikon)

See ASBADIKON.

SQEM (Armenian)

The *monastic *habit.

SRBARAN (Armenian)

In an *Armenian church this is the raised sanctuary; the *altar within it is usually approached by seven steps.

SRBASATHSOUTHIUN (Armenian)

The hagiology, or account of the festival being commemorated on that particular day.

SRBITSCH (Armenian)
(also called *Thasch-kinak)

A fine linen *purificator.

SRBOUTHEANCH (Armenian)

A collective term referring to the *bread and wine, or oblation, which is presented at the offertory as part of the *Liturgy.

STARETZ (Byzantine/Slavonic)

Usually a *Russian *monk, but occasionally it may be a layman or laywoman. The staretz is often a religious leader who is sought by many to act as a spiritual adviser, but his sole authority lies in his personal spirituality.

See GERONTAS; SPONSOR.

STAROSLAV

An alternative name for *Church Slavonic.

See LITURGICAL LANGUAGES, TABLE OF.

STASIDIA (Byzantine)

See THRONOS.

STASIS (Byzantine/Greek)

See KATHISMA.

STAVROPEGION (Byzantine/Greek)

A *monastic term referring to a monastery that is independent of a *bishop or *metropolitan but directly dependent on the *patriarch.

STAVROPHORE (Byzantine/Greek)

Literally, "crossbearer." For this grade of *monasticism the candidate is re*tonsured and takes the four oral vows of poverty, chastity, obedience, and stability. The lowest age limit for men is twenty-five, for women it is forty years. The term also applies to one who has the right to wear the pectoral cross.

See DEGREES OF MONASTICISM, HABITS OF; KRESTONOSETS; MIKROSCHEMOS; SKHIMNIK.

STAVROS (Byzantine/Greek)

The *sign of the cross, which is made by a *bishop or *priest with the right hand in blessing, the fingers being so arranged that they form the shape of the letters IC, XC (Jesus Christ); or the word may refer to the making of the sign of the cross, which is done by joining the thumb and the first two fingers to represent the three-in-one. The sign is made from right to left and not from left to right as in the West and other *Eastern rites.

See CROSS, SIGN OF.

STAVROSIMON (Byzantine/Greek)

A *troparion that has the Crucifixion as its theme.

STAVROTHEOTOKION
(Byzantine/Greek)
(also called *Krestobogoroditchen
[Slavonic])

A *troparion that is recited to honor
both the cross and the Mother of God
on those days in which a commemoration of our Lord's passion is made,
for example, on Wednesdays and Fridays. This may substitute for the more
usual *Theotokion or *Bogoroditchen,
"Hymn to the Birth-Giver of God."

STEPENNYI ANTIFONI
(Byzantine/Slavonic)

See ANABATHMOI; DEGREE OF THE
ANTIPHON.

STEPHANOMA (Byzantine/Greek)

Literally, "the crowning."

See BRAK; GAMOS; MARRIAGE (Byzantine
Tradition).

STEPHANOS (Byzantine/Greek)

See CROWN; MITER; VIENETZ.

STICHARION (Byzantine)

See STIKHARION.

STICHERA (Byzantine)

See STICHERON.

STICHERON (Byzantine/Greek)
(also called Stikhiri [Slavonic])

A hymn sung at *Matins and *Vespers
that is usually attached to a verse of
a psalm or some other scriptural passage. The text varies according to the
*tone appointed.

STICHOLOGIA (Coptic)

See ALLELUIA.

STICHOS (Byzantine/Greek)
(also spelled Stikhos [Slavonic])

A short verse, usually taken from the
Psalms or elsewhere in Scripture, that
may be used to introduce the *sticheron in the Office.

STIKHAR (Slavonic)
(also called Stichar)

An *alb-like vestment worn by *readers, *subdeacons, and *deacons.

See VESTMENTS, TABLE OF; STIKHARION.

STIKHARION (Byzantine/Greek)
(also called *Sticharion; *Stikhar)

An *alb-like vestment, originally a
secular garment. An early reference
dates from the 4th century when St.
John Chrysostom mentioned a liturgical stikharion, which he called a
khitoniskos.

Originally made from linen, it was
later superseded by more expensive
materials such as silk or velvet. While
it is worn by all *Byzantine clergy,
there are some differences in style and
design according to the clerical status
of the wearer. The *bishop's garment
may be embroidered at the bottom,
and from the shoulders to the hem of
the garment there are red and white
bands called *potamoi. The stikharion
of a *deacon is very full and more ornate than that of a *priest and has
shorter sleeves than that of a bishop or
priest but is not confined by a *girdle.
The stikharion is most commonly
white or dark red and is split from top

to bottom at the sides with the two parts joined by little ribbons.

See PODERES; STOICHARION; VESTMENTS, TABLE OF.

STIKHERES (Byzantine/Greek)

See APOSTICHA.

STOICHARION (Coptic)

A long robe that extends to the ankles is called the tuniyah, according to the *patriarch Gabriel II ibn Tarik (1131–1146), and is mentioned by Renaudot. It is worn by all clergy including *subdeacons and is described as being "tight-fitting and of white color." Butler described it as a dalmatic, but in the West this implies a tunic with long sleeves, whereas the tuniyah (stoicharion) more closely resembles the earlier *colobion, which had short and close fitting sleeves. Although this *vestment was abolished in Egypt by *Pope Sylvester (314–335), its use has persisted until now. A canon of Basil declared that the vestment must always be white, although colored stoicharions are found in murals.

The stoicharion of a *priest and *deacon differ in that the priest's vestment has a figure of the *Theotokos on the chest and an angel embroidered on each sleeve, whereas the deacon's vestment has small colored crosses embroidered over its surface. Stripes on the sleeve are also a common form of decoration.

See COLOBION; MAPPA; MARPPA; POTERION; SHENTO; STYCHARI; TUNIYAH.

STOLE

See EPITRACHELION; ORARION.

STRATCHITZA (Byzantine/Slavonic)

Either the first *altar covering, said to represent the shroud of Christ, or the linen cloth a *bishop wears over his *vestments to protect them, especially during the feet washing ceremony on Holy Thursday.

See ALTAR CLOTHS; KATASARKION; SABANON.

STYCHARI (Coptic)

See STOICHARION.

SUBDEACON

A *minor order in the *Eastern Church; according to the Council of Laodicea (363) *subdeacons, along with *readers, *singers, exorcists, and *doorkeepers, were forbidden to wear *stoles or even to enter the sanctuary. A subdeacon was forbidden to handle the sacred vessels and was expected to keep watch on the *doors; since the role of the doorkeeper was largely concerned with the women's doors, the subdeacon had the care of the men's doors in those churches where the separation of the sexes was rigidly enforced by the nature of the building's architecture.

See ABUDIYAKUN; EEPODIACON; HIUPATHI'AQNA; HYPODIAKONOS; KISARKAVAG; NEFKA DIYAKON; ORDERS, HOLY; YPODIAKON.

SUBOHO (Syrian)

A type of hymn sung during the *Liturgy.

SUDR (Coptic)

See ORARION.

SUDRA (East Syrian/Nestorian)
(also called *Kotina)

A cotton *alb-like vestment decorated with three black or red crosses on the shoulder, which may be worn by a *reader.

SUGUBAYA EKTENIYA
(Byzantine/Slavonic)

The augmented *litany.

See LITIYA.

SULH (Coptic)

A variable hymn sung during the *peace.

See ASPASMOS.

SULOQO (Syrian)

Ascension Thursday.

SULTANA (Syro-Jacobite)

See ABA.

SUNDAY OF ABSTINENCE FROM FLESH (Byzantine/Greek)

The equivalent of Sexagesima Sunday; it is so named because it is the last day on which meat is allowed before Lent commences. On the previous Saturday a requiem *Liturgy is celebrated for all departed *Orthodox; this Saturday is known as Ancestors' Saturday.

SUNHADUS (East Syrian)

The Breviary, which traditionally provides the seven *Hours of Prayer. The four that are of general obligation are as follows:

1. *Ramsha, or Dramshna ("at evening"), which is like the *Byzantine *Hesperinos and is sung at sunset after which

2. *Compline, or Suba'a, like the *Apodeipnon, is sung. This Office is only sung in *Nestorian churches during Lent and at the feast of the *Ninevites and is frequently joined with the Office of *Vespers to form a *vigil service.

3. The Night Office, or *Slutha Dlilya (literally, "prayer at night"), corresponding to the *Mesonu(y)kti-kon and followed by

4. a Vigil, or *Shahra (*Lauds), like the Byzantine *Orthros, after which the first Day Prayer (*Slutha Dsafra) follows, which corresponds to the first Hour of the Byzantine rite. Generally speaking, the last two Offices, Shahra and Slutha Dsafra, are joined as a Morning Office. The *Chaldean Breviary for use by Catholic clergy was reedited from the earlier Roman edition at Leipzig in 1886 by the Chaldean Lazarist Paul Bedjan.

SUPARA (East Syrian)
(also spelled *Suphora)

A *monastic *tonsure.

SUPHORA (Syro-Jacobite)

See SUPARA.

SURB (Armenian)
(also called Surb Seghan)

See ALTAR.

SURB KHATHS (Armenian)
(also called *Neshkhar)

See BREAD (Armenian Tradition).

SUTAFE (Ethiopian)

Holy Communion is received by the clergy and congregation in a fixed order starting with the *bishops and *priests, after which newly baptized infants, *deacons, the rest of the male congregation, and finally the women receive Communion. When a communicant receives, the hand is placed over the mouth until the Sacrament is consumed. After receiving the consecrated *bread, the communicant says, "Amen," and after the *chalice, responds, "Amen. Amen."

Among *Ethiopian Catholics there had been some controversy as to whether Communion could be received under both species. In general it was the custom to give Communion under one species at the "ordinary" celebrations, but on more solemn occasions it could be received under both species.

The non-Catholic *Ethiopians receive Communion infrequently, and the consecrated bread is distributed from a large *paten placed on a cloth-covered tray which is supported by two deacons.

See COMMUNION.

SVASHSHTENIK
(Byzantine/Slavonic)

A *priest.

See BATOUSHKA; IEREUS; ORDERS, HOLY (Byzantine Tradition); PAPAS.

SVATEA (Byzantine/Slavonic)
See HAGIA.

SVYATHAYA (Byzantine/Slavonic)
See ALTAR.

SVYETILNIE (Byzantine/Slavonic)
(also spelled Svyetilny)

The Hymns of Light.

See EXAPOSTILARION.

SYEN (Byzantine/Slavonic)

A canopy suspended over the *altar and said to represent the heavens.

SYLLEITOURGON
(Byzantine/Greek)

See CONCELEBRATION.

SYMBOLON (Byzantine/Greek)
(also called Symvol Veri [Slavonic])

See CREED.

SYNAPTE (Byzantine)

Literally, "joined." A prayer designed like a *litany and used in the *Liturgy and other church services. It consists of a series of short petitions that, because they are recited by the *deacon, are called the diaconals, or ta diakonika. To these petitions the congregation responds, "*Kyrie eleison," after which the *priest recites a closing prayer.

See EKTENE.

SYNAXAR (Coptic)
(also spelled *Sinaksar)

A martyrology written in Arabic that contains the shortened summary or commentary on the lives of the saints. The author is thought by some to be Peter al-Gamil, *bishop of Malig (12th or 13th century), but is now thought to be Michail, bishop of Athrib and Malig (15th century). The Copts read the Synaxar (*Synaxarion) before the

*Trisagion in the *Liturgy, and sometimes *lessons from the Synaxar are substituted for the *Praxis.

See LITURGICAL BOOKS (Coptic Tradition); SYNAXARION.

SYNAXARION (Byzantine/Greek)
(also called *Menologion [Greek]; *Senaksar [Slavonic])

A word having several meanings; it may be either a short account of the life of a saint or a brief homily on the significance of the feast being celebrated. It is read at *Orthros after the sixth ode of a saint's *Canon. Alternatively, it is the book that contains these passages arranged according to the calendar, in which case it is known as the Greater Synaxarion. The word may yet again refer to that book that lists the feasts to be observed every day, with reference to the appropriate biblical *lessons. One of the most famous is the *Menology* of St. Basil (10th century).

SYNAXIS (Byzantine/Greek)

Literally, "an assembly." (1) A feast for which the faithful gather to honor the saints associated with the *Mystery celebrated the previous day. For example, the synaxis of Sts. Simeon and Anna (February 3) is celebrated because the previous day's feast was the Purification. (2) Sometimes the term is used with reference to the *Liturgy and refers to a collection of short prayers. (3) Occasionally it may have a *monastic meaning and refers to a gathering or synod of elder *monks in a monastery.

See SOBOR.

SYNCELLUS (Byzantine/Greek)
(also spelled Synkellos)

Literally, "a person who shares a cell." In the *Byzantine Church this term is applied to a cleric whose role is that of domestic chaplain or *bishop's secretary. The title may also be given to any *Melchite or *Syrian titular bishop.

SYNTAGMA

A collection of laws and commentaries written by Matthew Blasteres, a 14th-century *monk of St. Basil.

See NOMOCANON.

SYNTHRONON (Byzantine)

The area to the rear of the *altar where the ruling *bishop's *throne is located on a raised dais with the stalls of the *priests radiating out on either side.

See THRONOS.

SYRIAC

An Aramaic dialect with Western pronunciation and characters used in the *Syrian *Liturgy.

See LITURGICAL LANGUAGES, TABLE OF.

SYRIAN JACOBITE CHURCH
(also called Syro-Jacobite Church)

The common name applied to *Monophysite Syrian Christians together with a semi-independent branch in *Malabar. The Church, which affirms only the first three *ecumenical councils and is in communion with the *Copts, is governed by a *patriarch of *Antioch assisted by *metropolitans and *bishops. Use is made of the West Syrian rite, with much of the language being Arabic.

SYRIAN ORTHODOX CHURCH, HISTORY OF

The origins of this Church are a little obscure and many accounts are clearly apocryphal, but following the Council of Chalcedon (451), which condemned the Syrian Church for its *Monophysitism, the *patriarch of *Antioch vacillated between the *Orthodox and the *Monophysites. It does seem possible that the Monophysite struggle provided the opportunity for the discontent that had been raging between Antioch and Constantinople to be resolved. In any case, Monophysitism took root in Syria, and Antioch's vacillation between heresy and orthodoxy continued until 518, largely dependent on whether the current emperor favored the heresy or not. For example, the emperor Justin (518–527) warred against Monophysitism; his nephew Justinian (527–565) imprisoned all who openly believed and taught this heresy.

The empress Theodora, who secretly favored the heresy, sought the help of the imprisoned Monophysite patriarch Theodosius of Alexandria to secure the episcopal consecration of two *monks, Theodore and Jacob Baradai, in order to set up a new hierarchy (543). Disguised as a beggar to avoid arrest, Mar Jacob Baradai preached and traveled extensively, founding independent Monophysite Churches; it is in recognition of Mar Jacob's work that the Syrian Monophysites call themselves *Jacobites. Continued persecution by the emperor was fairly fruitless, since the heresy was bound up with the nationalist aspirations of Syria, so when the Muslim Arabs entered Syria in 633,

the imperial troops could not expect total support from the populace. It transpired that the Syrian Christians separated into two principal divisions, the Orthodox Catholics, or *Melchites, and the Monophysites, or Jacobites.

During the patriarchate of Gregory in the early 7th century the caliphs of Babylon began to spread their influence throughout Syria and Antioch. Arabic was imposed upon the people, and the Greek language was forbidden even in the celebration of the *Liturgy. The Jacobites were quite successful in their missionary activities in Persia, and, as expected, they encountered considerable opposition from the *Nestorians, but it was not long before the Jacobites established a primate in Persia (7th century). There were attempts in the 10th, 12th, and 13th centuries to bring the Jacobites into union with either orthodoxy or Rome, but, as at the Council of Florence in 1439, these attempts failed.

In the centuries that followed, attempts by Rome to establish a patriarchate were met with a campaign of violent reprisals. Eventually in 1830 a Catholic patriarch returned to Aleppo on the understanding that the Catholics would be recognized as a distinct body from the Jacobites, and many converted to Rome. Following renewed persecutions from the Muslims and the more militant Jacobites, the patriarch was forced to move from Aleppo to Mardin. The start of World War I gave many lay Jacobites a greater role in the administration of the Church, but following attacks by the Turks many fled into exile. The events that finally resulted in the murder of Mar Flavian and some of his clergy in

1915 persuaded the Catholic patriarch Ephrem II Rahmani to leave Mardin and to take up residence in Beirut.

As recently as July 1984 the Roman Catholic and Syrian Orthodox Churches signed a joint statement affirming a common faith in the nature of Christ and a reciprocal arrangement for the pastoral care of each other's faithful. According to this agreement both Churches accept the Nicene *Creed, which affirms that Christ was "one in being with the Father" and was "born of the Virgin Mary and became man."

SYRIAN RITE, EAST

See CHALDEAN EAST SYRIAN CHURCH.

SYRIAN RITE, WEST

For details of the administration of the *sacraments in this rite see under the headings for individual sacraments: PENANCE, etc.

The *Syrian rite is used by *Syrian *Catholics, *Malabar Syrians, and *Jacobites of Syria. The *Liturgy, commonly called that of St. James, dates from the 4th century, and while the language is largely *Syriac, some parts are in Arabic. The *proskomide is performed before the celebrant vests, while the Epistle is sung by a *deacon and the *Gospel by a *priest. The preparation for the distribution of Holy *Communion is most complicated and is always under both kinds.

See ANAPHORA; BREAD (Syro-Jacobite Tradition); SYRO-JACOBITE CALENDAR; SYRO-JACOBITE DIVINE OFFICE; SYRO-JACOBITE PATRIARCH.

SYRIANS, CATHOLIC

These are usually converts from the *Jacobites and are governed by a Catholic *patriarch of Antioch from Beirut. The clergy are usually celibate but dispensations are normal.

See ANTIOCH, PATRIARCH OF; CATHOLIC.

SYRO-ANTIOCHENE RITE

See SYRIAN RITE, WEST.

SYRO-CHALDEAN RITE
(also called Chaldean Rite)

See EAST SYRIAN.

SYRO-JACOBITE CALENDAR

The Church Year begins on October 1 and follows the *Julian reckoning, whereas the Catholic West Syrians use the *Gregorian Calendar, which they adopted before the 1853 synod.

SYRO-JACOBITE DIVINE OFFICE

The Syro-Jacobite Divine Office, researched thoroughly by Baumstark in 1910, is very ancient. The *Hours are *Vespers (*Ramcha), *Nocturns (Lelya), followed by the Morning Office (Safra), which resembles the Western Office of *Lauds (*Tesebhotho). The Day Hours correspond to Terce, Sext, and None followed by *Compline or Suttara (literally, prayer of protection). Each Hour of the Office begins with a triple *Trisagion and *Lord's Prayer, followed by the rest of the Office. It is based on the Psalter, which is sung in the *Antiochene order and contains *lessons, either scriptural or hagiographical, together with various hymns and prayers.

SYRO-JACOBITE PATRIARCH

The present (1986) *patriarch lives in Damascus and is advised by a council that includes two *metropolitans who do not have dioceses. The council is responsible for all appointments, ordinations, and consecrations. When a Jacobite patriarch is elected, the name Ignatius is always added to his own in memory of the *bishop of Antioch who was martyred in Rome in 107. The Syrians believe that St. Ignatius taught the *Orthodox Christians to bless themselves with the three touching fingers of the right hand in honor of the indivisible Trinity.

SYRO-MALABAR RITE

The chasuble used in this rite resembles a Western cope with an embroidered Greek cross on the back, but the *stole is wider than a Western stole and is worn crossed in front. The cincture is usually of a matching color, and *cuffs enclose the sleeves of the *alb. *Altar vessels are of Western shape and design.

The Divine Office is composed of three Hours: (1) *Ramcha, or Ramsha (*Vespers); (2) *Lilia, or Lilya (the Night Office); and (3) *Sapra (the Day Office). These were rearranged so that the Psalter is read entirely in one two-week period. The Roman calendar is used, with a few Eastern commemorations that include a holy day of obligation for the feast of St. Thomas and for that of Sts. Peter and Paul. The Lenten *fast commences on the Monday preceding Ash Wednesday.

SYRO-MALABARESE

Either the *Orthodox St. Thomas Christians of India, who remained in communion with the *Jacobite Church and independent of Rome (1,581,000 in 1980), or the Catholic St. Thomas Christians, whose submission to Rome dates from 1599 and who use the *East Syrian rite in Malayalam (2,811,000 in 1980).

SYRO-MALANKARESE

The Catholic St. Thomas Christians, who submitted to Rome in 1930 and who use the West Syrian liturgical rite; in 1980 they numbered 280,900.

T

TA'AMANI (Ethiopian)

See FAITHFUL.

TABAK (Coptic)

Circular mats five or six inches in diameter made of silk and backed with coarser material. Each mat has an embroidered cross on it with small crosses set into the branches of the main cross. While various colors may be used, the most common are red, pink, and green. During the *Anaphora of St. Basil, just before the Consecration, the red tabak is removed from the *chalice and held in the right hand, while the green tabak is held in the left.

See MATS; THOM.

TABELLA
(West Syrian, Catholic and Jacobite; Coptic, Ethiopian and Nestorian)

An *altar board.

See ANTIMENSION.

TABH'O (Syro-Jacobite)

See BREAD, (Syro-Jacobite Tradition); BUCHRO.

TABIEH (Maronite)

A soft, round, quilted, dark blue turban, part of the outdoor dress of *Maronite clergy. A *bishop wears it over the *masnaphtho.

TABLITH
(Maronite and Syro-Jacobite)
(also spelled *Tablitho)

An *altar stone measuring about 18" x 12" which strictly speaking should be made of wood. According to one source, the use of wood was permitted after the persecution by Sapor II in the early 4th century. This altar "stone" is anointed with *chrism on Holy Thursday or on any Thursday during the period from Easter to Ascension Thursday. It is inscribed with the words "The Holy Spirit has hallowed this Tablith by the hands of Mar N. [name of the consecrating *bishop]," and across it is inscribed the year of consecration.

See ANTIMENSION.

TABLITHO
(Syro-Jacobite and Ethiopian)

See ANTIMENSION; TABLITH; TABOT.

TABOOT (Ethiopian)
(also spelled Tabut)

See TABOT.

TABOT (Ethiopian)

Literally, "ark." Usually an *altar stone, but the term is sometimes applied to the altar. The tabot, or tabut, may be made of a stone such as agate or a hard piece of cedar. *Non-catholic *Ethiopians inscribe the names of our Lord, the Blessed Mother of God, and the consecrating *bishop on the stone (tablitho), and this is then placed in a box called the tabot. It is referred to by the *Monophysite Ethiopians as the model of the ark of the covenant, and much of the attention and reverence it receives might be considered nearly idolatrous.

See ANTIMENSION; PARADISCUS.

TAILASAN (Coptic)
(also spelled Tailsana; Tilsin)

Renaudot (1640–1720) mistook this garment for a *Coptic *chasuble, whereas the 17th-century Vansleb correctly described the tailasan as an amice-like garment, in that is was a long band of white linen worn by *priests and *deacons and twisted around the head, doubtless over a small cap. The garment is retained until the start of the preface in the *Liturgy, where there is a clear rubric instructing the clergy to remove it.

See BALLIN; EPHOUT; KIDARIS; SHAMLAH.

TAJ (Coptic and West Syrian)
(also spelled Tag)

See KLAM; METRA.

TAKHSHEPHTHO (Syro-Jacobite)

The petition in a *litany.

TAKSAD'HUSAYE
(East Syrian/Nestorian)

Literally, "rite of mercy." The book that contains the prayers and rites of *penance and absolution.

See LITURGICAL BOOKS.

TAKSAD'MADA
(East Syrian/Nestorian)

The Book of *Baptism; this book is usually bound with the Taksa, or principal liturgical book containing the texts of the *Anaphoras.

See LITURGICAL BOOKS (East Syrian Tradition).

TAKSAD'SYAMIDA
(East Syrian/Nestorian)

The book used in the ordination ceremonies; it is usually bound with the Taksa of the *Liturgies and the *Taksad'mada, or Book of *Baptism.

See LITURGICAL BOOKS (East Syrian Tradition).

TALLIA (Syro-Jacobite)

Literally, "youth." The arrangement of the broken and consecrated particles after the *Fraction, which resembles the outline of a person and is customarily performed from Christmas until Easter in Iraq.

See FRACTION.

TANARETZ (Armenian)

An *Armenian married parish *priest, who receives his support by means of voluntary gifts from the parish. Parish priests are elected by the parish, either by a direct vote or by a deed of presentation. Once the candidate has been selected, a religious council is summoned and presided over by the *bishop so that an estimate can be reached concerning the fitness and suitability of the candidate before ordination can proceed.

TANAWAL (Coptic)
(also spelled Tanowwal)

See COMMUNION; SHAUTHOPHUTHO; TSCHI.

TANURTA (East Syrian/Nestorian)

The *oven set aside for the baking of the bread, or *Bukhra, that is to be used for the *Liturgy.

See BREAD (East Syrian Tradition).

TAPERER-READER (Byzantine)

See READER.

TARBUSH (Coptic)

A red cap or fez.

TARHIM (Coptic)

See DIPTICHON.

TARWODHO (Syro-Jacobite)
(also called *Kalb'tho)

The Communion spoon, which is used to give Holy Communion to those in holy *orders; occasionally, it may be used to administer Holy Communion to the faithful, who receive the consecrated particles directly into the mouth from the *chalice.

See COMMUNION; SPOON.

TCHASOSLOV (Byzantine/Slavonic)

The Book of *Hours, containing the Hours and Typical Psalms, together with those portions of *Vespers, *Compline, *Matins, and *Midnight Office (*Mesonyktikon), and Hymns that may be used on various occasions. This book is used by *singers and *readers.

See HOROLOGION; LITURGICAL BOOKS (Slavonic Tradition).

TCHETZ (Byzantine/Slavonic)

A reader, one of the two *minor orders.

See ANAGNOSTES; READER.

TCHINOVNIK (Byzantine/Slavonic)
(also spelled *Chinovnik)

The pontifical service book, which contains the fixed portions of the *Liturgies as celebrated by a *bishop. The book also contains the details for all episcopal ceremonies such as ordinations, various kinds of ecclesiastical promotion, as well as the blessing of the *antimins, or *antimension.

See LITURGICAL BOOKS (Slavonic Tradition).

TCHLAS (Byzantine/Slavonic)

See ECHOS.

TERBROUTIUN (Armenian)

A book of *canticles and Office hymns.

See LITURGICAL BOOKS (Armenian Tradition).

TESEBHOTHO (Syrian)
(also spelled Teshebhotho)

A hymn of praise honoring Christ the King, which is sung on major feasts before the *Gospel at the *Liturgy and *Vespers and which is based on Exodus 15:2. The term also refers to the Office of *Lauds in the West Syrian *Divine Office.

TESHBOTA (East Syrian)

A post-*Communion hymn of thanksgiving.

TESHMESHTO (Syrian)

Among the *Syrians this service of psalms is recited before the entry into the sanctuary. The *Syro-Jacobites recite it while squatting on their haunches. The term may also refer to a prayer for the dead, which is said by the *priest as he unvests after the *Liturgy has been concluded.

TESHTENIE (Byzantine/Slavonic)

See LECTIONS.

TESSARAKOSTAI
(Byzantine/Greek)

See FASTS.

TESTON (Byzantine/Greek)

The vessel containing the water used for the washing of the *altar on Holy Thursday.

TETRAEVANGELION
(Byzantine/Greek)

The *Gospel book.

See EVANGELION.

TETRAVELA (Byzantine/Greek)

The curtains that hung between the four columns of the *Kiborion, once commonly found above a *Byzantine *altar.

See KIBORION.

THALASSA (Byzantine/Greek)

Most probably corresponds to the *altar cavity in *Coptic churches, down which the rinsings from the ablutions and the ashes of holy things could respectfully be poured and so disposed of by means of a special drain. The thalassa was sometimes used to house *relics.

See KHONEUTERION; THALASSIDION.

THALASSIDION (Byzantine/Greek)

See PISCINA.

THANKSGIVING, THE GREAT
(Byzantine)

The great thanksgiving marks the opening of the *Anaphora and is made up of three portions, the preface, Sanctus, and post-Sanctus.

THASCH-KINAK (Armenian)

See SRBITSCH.

THEOPHANY (Byzantine/Greek)
(also called *Bogoyavlenie [Slavonic])

Literally, "manifestation of God." The equivalent of the Western feast of

Epiphany and designed to celebrate Christ's baptism (January 6). A strict *fast is observed on the eve of the feast, the *Royal Hours are read, and the *Liturgy of St. Basil is celebrated. There is also a first blessing of the waters that are intended for the use of *catechumens who are going to be baptized. On the feast itself there is a second blessing of waters with which the people are sprinkled.

THEOTOKARION (Byzantine/Greek) (also called Bogorodichen [Slavonic])

A liturgical book containing the *Canons of the *Theotokos. These are divided into eight series, corresponding to the eight modes to which they are sung. Each series comprises seven Canons, one for each day of the week.

See LITURGICAL BOOKS (Byzantine Tradition).

THEOTOKIA (Coptic)

An Office in honor of the Mother of God, which is usually sung during December; it is divided into four principal parts: (1) psali, an invitation to everybody to sing the praises of the Virgin Mary; (2) Theotokia proper, a long hymn composed in the Virgin Mary's honor and set out in the style of chapters; (3) lobsh, an explanation or commentary on what has been sung; and (4) tarh, a supplementary or further explanation and commentary.

THEOTOKION

A *troparion in honor of our Lady, for example, the Theotokion sung on Wednesdays and Fridays commemorating her sorrows at the foot of the cross is called the *Stavrotheotokion.

THEOTOKOS (Byzantine)

Literally, "Mother of God." A title of the Blessed Virgin Mary; this term was adopted by the Councils of Ephesus and Chalcedon (431 and 451 respectively) as an assertion of the doctrine of the divinity of our Lord's person. Although two natures are united in one Christ, yet there are not two persons, but one; so when God became incarnate he did not cease to be that divine person but took on a human nature. Although the nature he took from the substance of his mother was human, the person who was born was divine. This was the truth declared when the term "Theotokos" was adopted for describing the Blessed Virgin Mary.

THERMARION (Byzantine/Greek)

The vessel used to introduce the zeon, or warm water, into the *chalice during the *Liturgy. This vessel may also be used in the washing of the *altar prior to the dedication ceremony.

See ORKIOLION; ZEON.

THIYAB ALTAKDIS (Maronite)

A general term used to describe the older and more traditional style of *vestment used in this rite. There has of late been a tendency to Westernize the vestments of this rite, and this has been countered by a strong reaction in favor of retaining *Eastern vestments.

THOM (Coptic)

Literally, "a plate." A small mat which is used to cover the top of the *chalice and on which the *paten is laid. The whole is placed in the *tote.

See MATS; PITHOM; TABAK.

THOUTH (Coptic)

The first month of the Coptic calendar, which corresponds to the period from August 29 to September 27.

THREE HOLY HIERARCHS, THE

Sts. Basil the Great, Gregory the Theologian, and John Chrysostom. Their feast is celebrated in the *Byzantine rite on January 30.

THRONE

See THRONOS.

THRONIYON (West Syrian)

An episcopal *throne in the sanctuary with its back to the screen on the north side. At a solemn Office among the *Syrians, the throne is on the north side of the sanctuary but turned so it faces west. During a solemn *Liturgy, however, it is on the north side but faces south. The number of steps leading to it indicates the status of the throne's occupant, five steps for a *patriarch, three for *metropolitans and diocesan *bishops, and one for coadjutor bishops. If a bishop is visiting and is outside his diocese, a provisional throne is placed on the south side of the altar.

THRONOS
(Byzantine, Coptic, and Syro-Jacobite)

Literally, "table of life." The principal *altar, which is at the east end of the church. For the Coptic Tradition *see* TOTE OR PITOTE. In the *Byzantine rite it may mean either (1) the *antimension, which may be called a thronos because it has direct contact with the consecrated *bread and wine, or (2) it

may refer to the high-backed chair located at the back of the apse to the rear of the altar. The *bishop sits here during pontifical ceremonies, while on either side of him are arranged the seats (stasidia), the whole arrangement being called the *synthronon.

The term should not be confused with the archieraticos thronos (*despotikon), which is a second, more ornate seat on the south side of the *nave under a canopy and approached by several steps. It was called the despotikon because of its Constantinopolitan usage when a throne behind the altar was reserved for the emperor, but later the name came to be used for the *patriarch's throne.

See POTHURHAYE.

THRONOS NTE PIPOTERION
(Coptic)

See CURSI ALCAS; PITOTE; TOTE.

THYMATERION (Byzantine/Greek)
(also called Thymiaterion; Thymatos)

An Eastern-style *censer which has shorter chains than its Western counterpart. In the east it is swung at its full length, and the right hand alone controls the entire movement of the censer. Small bells are often attached to the censer.

See CENSER.

THYMIAMA (Byzantine/Greek)

*Incense.

THYRA (Byzantine/Greek)
(also called Pyle; Vrata)

The general term referring to the *doors; it is quite unspecific, and in a

*Byzantine-rite church the usual doors are the great west door, the *royal doors, the *holy doors of the *iconostasis, the south or deacon's door, and the north or server's door.

THYROROS (Byzantine/Greek)

See DOORKEEPER.

THYSIASTERION
(Byzantine/Greek)

A reference to the altar that connotes the sense of sanctuary.

See ALTAR; TRAPEZA.

TIARA (Melchite)

See KLAM; METRA; TSCHREPI.

TIMKAT (Ethiopian)

The festival of Epiphany, during which there is a blessing of the waters. During its celebration, the clergy form two parallel lines facing each other with a *koboro (drum) at each end; then, while holding their *mekamia (crutches) in their right hands, they dance toward and then away from each other as the drums are beaten. This dance is performed to the accompaniment of chanting. The same ritual is observed at Easter and on the feast of the Holy Cross.

TISTOLE NIERATIKON (Coptic)

A general term used to describe all the Eucharistic *vestments used in this rite.

T'LITHO (Syrian)
(also spelled T'Loitho)

Literally, "elevation." A reference to the posture, which should be erect when certain prayers are recited in a loud voice, as distinct from *g'hontho, which is a rubric calling for a low voice and inclined head.

See GREAT INTERCESSION.

TOGHO (Syrian)

A *miter, which among the *Syrian Catholics is of Latin design and is worn over the *schema. The use of a miter has been noted among some *Jacobites, notably the *Malabarese.

TONES (Byzantine)

There are eight tones arranged in two major groups of four each, but the style in which these tones are sung varies within the *Orthodox community. Each week has a set tone, and the cycle commences with Tone 1; on each Saturday evening the tone is changed for the following week. The text of these tones may be found in the *Octoechos.

See GLASY.

TONSURE
(also called Tonzura [Slavonic])

The tonsure symbolizes the dedication of a candidate to God's service and is signaled by a cutting of hair from the forehead, crown, and each side of the head in the form of a cross. It is given at *baptism by a *priest. The tonsure given to *singers and *readers is a clerical tonsure and is called the koura klerike (Greek) or hieratike (Slavonic). The *monastic tonsure (monachike kourac or apokarsis), is given by the superior of a community when the *habit is given and may be repeated when the religious is admitted to any degree of monasticism.

See KOURA.

TOTE (Coptic)
(also called *Pitote)

The box or "ark" in which the *chalice stands during part of the *Liturgy and which is arranged so that the top of the chalice lies flush with the top of the box.

See CURSI ALCAS.

TOUPTIKON (Coptic)
(also called *Tarhim)

See DIPTICHON.

TOUT (Coptic)

This marks the start of the Church Year in the month of Tout, which is approximately September 10.

See COPTIC CALENDAR.

TRAPEZA (Byzantine and Coptic)
(also called *Ma'idah)

An altar. A more ancient term, thysiasterion (Heb 13:10), is occasionally encountered, with other terms (trapeza kyriou and hagia or hiera trapez) more commonly employed.

In the *Byzantine rite in early times, the table of the altar in Constantinian basilicas was supported either by a single block or by four slabs. The table of the altar is called the *calamos or sometimes the *bomos when it is supported on a cylindrical or square central column. Pope St. Sylvester (314–335) insisted that all altars be made of stone, but whether this ruling referred to the entire altar or just the mensa of the altar is unclear. When the altar is consecrated it is secured to its support by a cement known as *keromastikos.

In the *Coptic tradition the Arabic term "ma'idah" is most frequently used and emphasizes the sacrificial aspect of the altar's function. In Coptic-rite churches the altar is detached from the east end-wall and is usually on the same level as the floor of the *haikal (sanctuary) without any approaching steps. While it is usually a four-sided mass of bricks or stones, wooden examples are known, which are sometimes hollow but may be solid and covered with plaster. Set into the mensa of the altar is an oblong rectangular well 1′′ deep into which the altar board (*lax) is set. There are no incised crosses set into the altar itself except those cut into the altar board. As part of the consecration, three crosses of *chrism are used to anoint the altar, about which Renaudot makes specific mention. On the east side of the altar and level with the ground is a small opening that leads into a larger cavity in which it was customary to bury the bodies of saints and martyrs, but today such *relics are more properly housed in reliquaries.

Coptic churches have three altars, the side altars being used only occasionally, for example at Christmas, Easter, Palm Sunday, and the Exaltation of the Holy Cross (March 6 [10 Barmahat] and September 13 [16 Tout]). In this way several celebrations may occur on one day without violating the canons that prohibit a second *Liturgy on the same altar on the same day, a tradition that applies not only to the altar but to the *vestments and vessels as well. Over Coptic altars and side altars there may be a decorated wooden canopy (*baldachino) resting on four columns, the decorations usually being paintings of our Lord in the center of the dome of the canopy, surrounded by angels.

See ALTAR.

TREASURY (East Syrian/Nestorian)
(also called *Beth Kudsha)

Literally, "house of the Holy Thing." A recess in the north wall of the sanctuary into which vessels are placed until the offertory in the *Liturgy. The same term may occasionally mean simply a table set against the north wall in the sanctuary.

See BETH GAZZA.

TREBNIK (Byzantine/Slavonic)

See LITURGICAL BOOKS (Byzantine Tradition).

TREBOUTION (Armenian)

Literally, "Book of the Choir Boys." A book containing the text of those portions of the *Liturgy that are specifically sung by the choir.

See LITURGICAL BOOKS (Armenian Tradition).

TRENTSVA (Byzantine/Slavonic)

See SACRAMENTS, COMPARATIVE TABLE OF.

TRIADIKON (Byzantine/Greek)

A *troparion honoring the Holy Trinity.

See TROICHEN.

TRIKERION (Byzantine/Greek)
(also called Trikeri [Slavonic])

A triple-branched candlestick with tapers, so arranged so that the wicks of each, though distinct, blend into one flame. It is used to sign the *Gospel book and by a *bishop when giving blessings, in which case it is held in the bishop's right hand while the *dikerion is held in the left.

See DIKERION.

TRIODION (Byzantine/Greek)
(also called Postnaya Triod [Slavonic])

One of a set of choir books originally produced by the Studites, but Philotheos, *patriarch of Constantinople (1354–1355 and 1361–1375), insisted on the inclusion of an Office for St. Gregory Palamas, archbishop of Thessalonica and a vigorous opponent of Catholicism, whose commemoration is kept by the *Orthodox on the second Sunday of Lent. The book contains the variable parts of the services from the tenth Sunday before Easter (the Sunday of the Publican and Pharisee) until Holy Saturday, after which the *Pentekostarion follows. The name derives from there being three odes in the *Canon instead of the customary nine.

TRISAGION
(also called *Trisyatoe)

The hymn "Agios O Theos," which according to tradition was revealed to a boy, a *priest, and even the *patriarch at Constantinople during the mid-5th century and is reputed to be the hymn that the angels sing in heaven. What is certain is that it was about this time that the hymn made its appearance in the liturgical text. It was Nestorius who between 430 and 450 insisted that it be included in the *Liturgy of Constantinople, and it was one of the recorded exclamations of the Fathers at the Council of Chalcedon in 451. Certainly it had been included in the Liturgy at *Antioch before 471 because of the trouble that followed when Peter the Fuller (patriarch of Antioch, 470–488 A.D.) included the clause ". . . immortal, who was crucified for us, have mercy." This addition had the effect of asserting the *Monophysite doctrine of the single divine nature of Christ, and so this Trisagion was used by Coptic and Syrian *Monophysites, but the clause was condemned by the second Council of Trullo (692) by Canon 81.

In the *Byzantine rite the following text is sung after the *Entrance of the Gospels, otherwise known as the Little Entrance: "O Holy God, Holy Mighty, Holy Immortal One, have mercy upon us" (three times). At other times of the Church Year such as Christmas, Theophany, Eve of Palm Sunday, Holy Saturday, Easter, and Pentecost another prayer is substituted.

During the *Coptic Liturgy the Trisagion is recited by priest and people immediately before the Gospel is announced. The *Coptic Catholics omit various insertions that are part of the non-Catholic Trisagion such as the doxology and the repetitive "Have mercy on us." At its conclusion, the congregation is blessed with a hand cross held by the priest, and the prayer of the Gospel is started.

The *Ethiopians follow the Coptic custom, while the *Ethiopian Catholics have an interpolation-free Trisagion, which is simply the triple repetition of "Holy God, Holy Mighty, Holy Living Immortal, have mercy on us."

In the *Armenian tradition, the Trisagion marks the start of the Liturgy of the *Catechumens, which is accompanied by the Little Entrance in the form of a procession around the *altar. A clause was inserted, "who was crucified for us," which suggested that the Trisagion was addressed to the Son and not to the Holy Trinity. This insertion was defended by the patriarch Naslian, but the *Armenian Catholics were forbidden its insertion by Propaganda in 1677 and 1833. The Armenians agreed to this in the patriarchal Synod of Constantinople in 1890 and later in the National Council at Rome in 1911.

In the *East Syrian tradition a commentary by the catholicos Jesu Yab in 596 referred to the Trisagion, and in the 9th century Abraham Bar Lipheh spoke of the Trisagion as "the Mystery of the preaching of the angels." The Chaldean text reads, "Holy God, Holy and Strong, Holy and Immortal. Have mercy on us. Glory be to the Father . . . . Holy God, Holy and Strong, Holy and Immortal. Have mercy on us. From everlasting to everlasting. Amen."

During a West Syrian Catholic Liturgy, after the Gospel book has been placed on a lectern in the sanctuary at the start of the Liturgy of the Catechumens, the priest ascends the altar steps and, blessing himself three times, recites the Trisagion, the text of which follows: "You are Holy, O God. Have mercy on us. You are Holy, O Strong one. Have mercy on us. You are Holy, O Immortal One. Kyrie eleison, Kyrie eleison, Kyrie eleison.'' The *lessons are then read.

See ERECHSRBEANN; QADISAT ALOHO.

TRISKELION (Byzantine)
(also called *Diskelion)

A portable lectern from which the *Gospel may be read. It is so called because it is made up of three shafts, whereas the lectern, which is made of two shafts to form a large X-shaped structure, is called the diskelion.

TRISYATOE (Byzantine/Slavonic)

See TRISAGION.

TRITEKTI (Byzantine/Slavonic)

This specifically describes the reception of the *catechumens.

See CATECHUMENS.

TROICHEN (Byzantine/Slavonic)

A stanza or verse honoring the Trinity; usually the penultimate *troparion takes up this theme whereas the last verse honors the *Theotokos.

See TRIADIKON.

TROPARIA EOTHINA
(Byzantine/Greek)

See OCTOECHOS.

TROPARION (Byzantine)

A stanza of religious poetry, for example, the *apolytikion, known as the troparion of the day. Originally it was a short prayer but later became modified as poems, a number of which became known as the heirmoi, which were models for others. Some developed individual rhythms and melodies and became known as the idiomela or automela (*see* IDIOMELON). Each strophe of the hymn is really a troparion, several of which make up an ode, while the nine odes, which allude to the scriptural *canticles, make up a *Canon, so the term could really be applied to the stanzas of the Canon.

There are different classes of troparia, for example a *kontakion refers to the feast of the day, an *oikos serves to expand this, while a *Theotokion is in honor of the Mother of God.

TRULLION (Byzantine)

See KIBORION.

TRUMUS (Syro-Jacobite and East Syrian/Nestorian)
(also called Trunus)

An altar. *Nestorian altars have a ciborium over them that usually extends beyond the perimeters of the altar. The use of a ciborium (*kiborion) was quite common in Constantinople in the 6th century.

See ALTAR; MADB'HO.

TSARSKIYA VRATA
(Byzantine/Slavonic)

The royal doors, which form the central opening in the *iconostasis, are also called the svyatya vrata (*holy doors) because it is through these doors that the holy gifts are brought during the *Liturgy. Women and unordained men are forbidden to pass through these doors.

See ROYAL DOORS.

TSATSKOTHS SKIH (Armenian)

The second *veil, which in addition to the *kogh is used to cover the *chalice during the *Liturgy.

TSCHI (Coptic)
(also called *Tanawal)

The rite of the reception of Holy Communion. When a *priest communicates, he kisses the *bread before receiving it and blesses himself with the *chalice before receiving some of its contents. A *Coptic *deacon may receive Communion while standing, whereas the laity traditionally kneel in order to receive. Among non-Catholics it is the custom for men to receive the chalice and for women to receive an intincted particle of bread. If there is danger of death, Communion is received under the species of bread that has been intincted; this bread has two crosses on it. During the distribution of Holy Communion the deacon stands behind the *altar facing west while each communicant has a mat or veil held under his mouth, which is wiped with the cloth after Communion. Each communicant is expected to drink a little water after receiving Holy Communion.

See COMMUNION.

TSCHREPI (Coptic)

See KLAM; METRA.

TSELOVANIE (Byzantine/Coptic)

See ASPASMOS.

TSVETNAYA TRIOD
(Byzantine/Slavonic)

See PENTEKOSTARION.

TSVIETOSLOV (Byzantine/Slavonic)

See ANTHOLOGION.

TUKAS RAZI (East Syrian)

In the *East Syrian rite, this marks the point in the *Liturgy when the remains of the Blessed Sacrament are consumed; in the *Nestorian rite it is at this point that the celebrants and ministers receive Holy *Communion.

TUKKOSO DH'Q'SAY W'RUSHMO
(West Syrian)

Literally, "order of breaking and signing." A ceremony during which the *deacon says the *Catholic (*Kathuliki).

See FRACTION.

TUNIYAH (Coptic)

See STOICHARION.

TURBAN (Syrian)

The headgear of *Jacobite Syrian *bishops, who wear the *schema beneath an episcopal turban.

TURGAMA (East Syrian)

Literally, "interpretation." A book of hymns attributed to Ebed Jesu to Barsauma (d. 489), which are largely interpretative and are sung responsorially as an explanation prior to the New Testament *lessons on Sundays and feast days, hence the literal translation of the term.

See LITURGICAL BOOKS (East Syrian Tradition).

TURIKES (Byzantine)

Cheese Week, which starts seven weeks before Easter and follows the Meat

Fast week. During Cheese week, no cheese, eggs, butter, or milk may be consumed. Because the Cheese-Fast Sunday *Gospel read at the *Liturgy (Matt 6:14-21) emphasizes the importance of forgiveness, this Sunday is often called Forgiveness Sunday.

TWELVE GREAT FEASTS, THE

In the *Byzantine rite these are divided into two major groups, those of our Lord and those of the Theotokos (Mother of God).

The Feasts of Our Lord

The Feast of Feasts—Easter.
1. The Nativity of Our Lord.
2. Epiphany.
3. The Purification of the Virgin.
4. Palm Sunday.
5. The Ascension.
6. Pentecost.
7. The Transfiguration.
8. The Exaltation of the Cross.

The Feasts of the Theotokos

9. The Nativity of the Theotokos.
10. The Presentation.
11. The Annunciation.
12. The Dormition of the Theotokos.

See GREAT FEASTS.

T'WILAITA (East Syrian/Nestorian)

See ANTIMENSION.

TYPIKA (Byzantine/Greek)
(also called *Izobrazitelnaya [Slavonic])

A service of prayer and praise celebrated on days when there is no celebration of the *Liturgy and inter-posed between Sext and None (Western style). The service is composed of hymns, prayers, and various liturgical readings such as Psalms 103 and 145, the *Beatitudes (Makarismoi), *troparia and verses, the Nicene *Creed, prayers, and the *Lord's Prayer. The service concludes with the *kontakion, a prayer, Psalm 33 (sometimes), and a *dismissal.

TYPIKON (Byzantine/Greek)
(also called *Ustav)

Literally, "a decree." A liturgical manual that daily sets out how the services for the Proper of the saints and season as well as the *fast days are to be observed. It details as well the rules concerning the concurrence of feasts. In an appendix one may find further information concerning the performance of such ceremonies as an akathistos, ordinations, and funeral rites.

According to tradition St. Sabbas of Jerusalem (439–532) drew it up, and it was subsequently revised by St. Sophronius, *patriarch of Jerusalem (560–638), who added material from the usage of St. Catherine of Sinai.

The Typikon of St. Theodore the Studite (759–826) was used by St. Athanasius the *Athonite (ca. 920–1003) as a directive for Mount *Athos, from where its influence spread to Russia and Europe. However, in the 19th century a new edition appeared edited by *Protopsaltis George Violakis (d. 1911), which was issued with the blessing of the *ecumenical patriarch. This new edition introduced many changes, especially in the order of *Orthros or Matins on Sundays. For example, the concluding stanzas of the *canticles or odes of a *Canon were to be sung at the end of the eighth canticle, and the *Gospel to be read at Matins was positioned between the eighth and ninth canticles. The *Russian Church, however, continued to make use of the Typikon of St. Sabbas. The old Typikon, that of St. Theodore, is still observed by some *Greek monasteries, especially those on Mount Athos and at St. John of Patmos.

See LITURGICAL BOOKS (Byzantine Tradition).

TZVYETNAYA TRIOD
(Byzantine/Slavonic)

The book, often called the Flowery *Triodion, that contains the order of service during Easter until Pentecost and includes the service for Whitmonday.

See PENTEKOSTARION.

U

UKRAINIAN CATHOLIC CHURCH

The Catholic Ukrainian community dates to the 1595 union of Brest-Litovsk, when six *Orthodox dioceses in Poland and Lithuania accepted the authority of the *pope. By 1939 in what was then Polish Galicia, there were 3.5 million Ukrainian Catholics under an archbishop and two other *bishops. In 1945, most of the Church's hierarchy and their congregations were forcibly amalgamated with the *Russian Orthodox Church, thus revoking the union of 1595.

UKRAINIAN ORTHODOX CHURCH

The Ukrainian Orthodox Church was founded in the ancient Ukrainian state of Kiev by Prince Vladimir (Volodymyr) in 988, with its own *metropolitan coming under the oversight of Constantinople. In 1686 the *patriarch of Constantinople transferred his jurisdiction of the Ukraine from Kiev to Moscow without the knowledge of the metropolitan of Kiev, and thus the Ukrainian Church found itself integrated into the *Russian Church and its independence at an end. With the fall of the Tsarist empire (1917–1920) the Ukrainians seized the opportunity to try to revive Church independence even though political independence could not be achieved, and in October 1921 the first all Ukrainian synod in Kiev announced the establishment of the Ukrainian *Autocephalous Orthodox Church. After World War II when all of the Ukraine came under Soviet control, large numbers of Ukrainians fled to the West.

Non-Catholic Ukrainians are now united by the annual synod that meets under the title "The Ukrainian Orthodox Church in the Free World," and they have been seeking recognition for the Church's *autonomy from the patriarch of Constantinople.

UNAYA (East Syrian)

A congregational response or refrain to verses of a psalm read by a *reader during the *Liturgy.

UNCTION OF THE SICK

Following the injunction in James 5:14-15 that the sick should be anointed and prayed over to restore health and forgive sins, this *sacrament is observed in the *Eastern Church but with considerable variation in its practice.

Armenian Tradition

As observed by non-Catholic *Armenians in the past, the sacrament resembles a *Coptic service in its use of a seven-branched lamp, but unlike the Coptic usage, it can be conducted at the sick person's bedside. It is administered with a view to restoring a person to good health and is not restricted to the dying. *Armenian Catholics use a Roman form of administration.

Byzantine Tradition
(also called *Euchelaion [Greek]; *Eleosvastchenie [Slavonic])

The sacrament may be administered when a person is simply ill and not in danger of death and is therefore repeatable. Ideally seven *priests should perform this rite, but in practice one will suffice. The oil that is used has wine mixed with it in commemoration of the Parable of the Good Samaritan; the blessing of this oil by a priest involves lengthy prayers in which the *Theotokos and Sts. Cosmas and Damian are invoked. A table with seven lighted candles and a small dish of wheat to symbolize new life are prepared, and the room is incensed. If one priest performs the anointings, the forehead, lips, cheeks, both sides of the hands, nostrils, and breast are all anointed by means of a fine brush. Each anointing is preceded by an Epistle, *Gospel, *litany, and a long prayer, and during the anointing the priest says, "Heal your servant, N., from the ills of body and soul." The person who receives this sacrament, often called "prayer oil," may receive Holy *Communion either before or after the unction. The ceremony concludes with the Gospel book being laid on the sufferer's head with the printed words facing down; this symbolizes that the same physical and spiritual healings recounted in the Gospels may be accomplished in the sufferer.

Coptic Tradition

The sacrament, often called "The Office of the lamp," is rather lengthy, and as among the Armenians, its reception does not imply that the person is dying. Either a seven-branched lamp or seven lamps are lit, and the lamps are lit by each of the seven priests usually attending, accompanied by an appropriate *lesson, psalm, Gospel, and prayer. If the person to be anointed is in the church, he comes to the *door of the *haikal (sanctuary) and faces east, then the senior priest present holds the silver Gospel book and cross high over the person and then lays his hands on the person's head. After further blessings, Gospel readings selected by chance are read followed by further prayers. The seven-branched lamp is then carried around the church in procession and the sick person returns to the door of the hai-kal, where he is anointed with oil on the throat, wrists, and forehead. Because the sacrament may not be administered outside the church, if the person is too ill, a substitute for the sick person comes to the church and acts as a proxy and the rite is more intercessory in character.

Catholic *Chaldeans use the Roman Ritual translated into *Syriac, but the blessing of the oil is a local and ancient variant. The anointings are performed on the mouth, hands, and feet.

Among the *Nestorians this sacrament has fallen into disuse, in fact the sick were more commonly administered with *henana, a dust gathered from the graves of martyrs and mixed with oil and water to form small tablets, which were then blessed. This was never regarded as a sacrament.

West Syrian Tradition

For Catholic West Syrians this sacrament is administered according to the Roman usage translated into *Syriac, but among non-Catholic *Syrians it is usually administered by one priest only, who blesses the oil as it is required. In times past, even the dead were anointed.

UNIATES

*Eastern-rite Catholics are often incorrectly described as Uniates, a rather contemptuous term employed by the opponents of the union of Brest, which refers to the union of the *Ruthenians or *Ukrainians with the Holy See, effected on December 23, 1595. A bitter opposition followed this union. The term is not usually found in an ecclesiastical Act or official publication. The preferable term is "Eastern-rite Catholic."

UNITHA (East Syrian/Nestorian)

See ANTIPHON.

UNITHA D'IWANGALIYUN (East Syrian)

The anthem of the *Gospel, the text of which is read at the *Liturgy on solemn occasions and refers to the dominant theme of the *Gospel.

UNITHA D'QANKI (East Syrian)
(also spelled *Onitha dh'qanke)

An anthem that may be sung responsorially when the *reader recites the verses from a psalm.

URARA (East Syrian/Chaldean)

A *subdeacon's *stole, which is worn so that one end hangs down in front and the other end hangs in back on the left side under the *girdle.

See VESTMENTS, TABLE OF.

URORO (Syrian)

A general term used to describe the *stole worn by all the clergy, whose ecclesiastical rank is indicated by the manner in which the stole is worn.

When a *Syrian *priest is to be ordained, he comes vested as a *deacon with the stole hanging loose back and front over the left shoulder, and during the ordination ceremony the *bishop takes the end of the stole at the back and brings it around the right shoulder where it remains uncrossed.

An *archdeacon wears the stole fastened on the right but worn over the left shoulder, while a *subdeacon has a stole on the left shoulder with the part hanging behind brought around under the right arm and thrown back over the left shoulder.

A *reader wears the stole like a cincture, around the waist with the two ends crossed behind and brought over the chest, then tucked into the belt thus formed.

As a pontifical *vestment, the uroro (*omophorion; uroro rabbo) is like a priestly stole except that it is wide and double, hanging down in front and behind and with large crosses on it. It is worn over the *phaino, and the *masnaphtho, when thrown back from the head, falls over it.

See BITRASHIL; HAMNIKHO; URARA.

URORO RABBO

See URORO.

USPLENIE (Byzantine/Slavonic)

See KOIMESIS.

USTAV (Byzantine/Slavonic)

See TYPIKON.

UTRENYA (Byzantine/Slavonic)

See ORTHROS.

V

VARAPOCHUMN (Armenian)

The feast of the Assumption, known also as the Dormition or the Falling Asleep of the Mother of God. It is observed in this rite on the Sunday nearest August 15.

VA(R)KAS (Armenian)

An *amice-like vestment which has a stiffened collar resembling a medieval apparel and which may be put on after the tunic (*shapik). *Deacons and clergy in *minor orders now wear a short cape embroidered with crosses.

See VESTMENTS, TABLE OF.

VARTABED (Armenian)
(also spelled Vartaped; Vartapet)

An *Armenian order of clergy thought to have been institutcd in the 5th century; in general these clergy are thought of as being *hieromonks of distinction or doctors in the Church. Their ranks denote the authority they have to preach, and this is indicated by their *crozier, which has two or four intertwined serpents with heads apart but facing each other. Vartabeds are celibate *priests from whose ranks *bishops are chosen, but since they are celibate, they are not permitted to hear confessions. Many have been noted for their teaching expertise in seminaries and universities. The minor and supreme doctors are grades of vartabeds, and these are divided into subgrades: the minor grade (*maznavor) is divided into four subgrades, while the major grade is divided into ten subgrades. Progression through these grades is signaled by a gradual elaboration of the ceremonies that form part of the ceremonial institution into a grade. Vartabeds have the privilege of preaching sermons while standing on the platform of the *altar, whereas the privilege of sitting belongs to a bishop.

If a vartabed is of a lower order, the crozier (*gavazan) has only a single serpent's head and a little cross at the top, but if he belongs to a higher order, a globe on the staff with a cross at the top is taken to represent authority to preach throughout the world. Occasionally a veil is attached to the staff, but since the 14th century this has not always been the case. Additionally vartabeds had the right to a *throne, but this privilege was abolished in the closing years of the 19th century.

Like all Armenian clergy, vartabeds have the right to wear the *philon (cloak), which for lower-grade vartabeds is often embroidered with flowers, while that worn by a superior vartabed is often made of violet silk. An ornamented doctoral cross may be worn. The *miter worn by a vartabed is like that worn by a priest, but if his mandate is of the grade of an *aradchenord (or aratshnord) and authorizes the administration of a diocese, he wears the episcopal miter within that diocese. The episcopal miter is Western in shape; the adoption of such miters seems to date from the 12th century.

VARTAVAR (Armenian)

Literally, "festival of roses." The feast commemorating the Transfiguration and the festivities associated with this are said to take their origin from St. Gregory the Illuminator.

VECHERNYA (Byzantine/Slavonic)

See GREAT VESPERS; HESPERINOS.

VEGHAR (Armenian)

The veil worn by celibate *priests over the *Pakegh.

VEILS

A general term used to describe the coverings of the offerings in the *Liturgy.

Paten Veils

In the *Byzantine rite, the *paten veil may be called the *kalymmata or kalymma, but more specifically it is called the proton kalymma or *diskokallyma. It is supported above the *discos by the *asterisk.

The *Copts use an 18″ square veil of white or colored silk, the *lafafah, to cover the *bread and wine at the start of the Liturgy. The huphayo d'pinco is the paten veil used by the *Syro-Jacobites. This veil is placed on the right or south side of the altar as part of the offertory ceremonies.

In the *Ethiopian rite, the *cedan'-awed is specifically referred to in the rubrics when it is removed from the paten just before the celebrant washes his hands and the *peace is given.

Chalice Veils

In the Byzantine rite it is known as the *deuteron kalymma. Sometimes this veil is substituted for by special metal domes that are used to cover both paten and *chalice. In the Coptic rite the *pitote is used as a stand in which the chalice remains during the Consecration.

Syro-Jacobites use the huphayo d'coso, which is removed at the offertory and placed on the left or north side of the altar during the offertory ceremonies. In the *East Syrian/Chaldean rite use is made of the *kaprana (*mcaprana) as the chalice veil. This is a white veil of stiffened material embroidered with a cross and folded in three.

Paten and Chalice Veils

In the Byzantine rite, the *aer or bolshoi vozdouch (Slavonic) is used. When this large veil is removed, it is gently shaken as part of the ceremonies surrounding the recitation of the *Creed during the Liturgy.

The Syro-Jacobites use the *annaphuro, which at the start of the Liturgy of the *Catechumens covers both chalice and paten. The aimo or cloud (mentioned in the rubrics to be observed during the preparation of the altar) is an alternative to this annaphuro.

The *prosfarin (Coptic) and *macdan (Ethiopian) are the veils used to cover both the chalice and paten in the Coptic and Ethiopian rites, just before the Prayer of *Absolution to the Son in the *enarxis.

The East Syrians/Nestorians use one veil (*shoshepa) to cover both chalice and paten; this is possible since the paten fits into the well at the top of the chalice. This veil is removed at the start of the *Anaphora when it is folded around both the paten and chalice. The Nestorians use a humeral veil (*m'kablana), which is received by the *deacon prior to reading the *Apostle, when he receives the paten from which *Communion is to be distributed.

VELICHANIE (Byzantine/Slavonic)

A hymn known as the Exaltation.

See MEGALYNARION.

VELIKAYA EKTENIYA
(Byzantine/Slavonic)
(also called *Great Litany)

A litany normally recited by the *deacon or sometimes by the celebrant, who stands in front of the *holy doors of the *iconostasis during Matins or *Orthros after the reading of the customary psalms.

VELOTHYRON (Byzantine/Greek)
(also called *Vemothyron)

The veil which may be hung behind the *holy doors of the *iconostasis and which conceals the upper part of these central *doors. It is drawn aside at various moments during the *Liturgy.

See BELOTHYRON.

VEMOTHYRON (Byzantine/Greek)

See VELOTHYRON.

VERARKOU (Armenian)
(also spelled Verarku)

Part of the outdoor dress of the clergy; it is a generously sleeved mantle worn loosely over the blue cassock of married *priests (*derders).

VEROYUSCHIE
(Byzantine/Slavonic)

See FAITHFUL.

VERVITZA (Byzantine/Slavonic)

Literally, "string."

See CHOTKI; KOMBOSCHOINION; L(I)ESTOVKA; ROSARY.

VESPERS

See GREAT VESPERS; HESPERINOS; SMALL VESPERS.

VESTMENTS, TABLE OF

See Table 6, pages 333 and 334.

VIENETZ (Byzantine/Slavonic)

See CROWN.

VIGIL

Among the *Russian Orthodox the vigils (vzenoshchnoe edenie) are maintained in both parishes and monasteries, but in *Greek churches they are generally observed only in monasteries. If there is a vigil, *Small Vespers are read early in the afternoon, then the vigil proper commences with *Great Vespers or *Great Compline with the *lity, followed by *Matins and the first *Hours.

VILO (Syro-Jacobite)

See QUDSHO.

VKHOD (Byzantine/Slavonic)

See EISODOS.

VKHODNOE (Byzantine/Jacobite)

See EISODIKON.

VLADYKA (Byzantine/Slavonic)

A *Slavonic form of address to a *bishop.

VOSDUKH (Byzantine/Slavonic)

The *aer, or third veil, which is used to cover both *chalice and *paten during the *Liturgy.

VOSNESENIA (Byzantine/Slavonic)

The commemoration of the Ascension.

See ANALEPSIS.

VOZDNOSHT SHENIE
(also called Voznoshenie)

See HYPSOSIS; WERATHSOUOMN; ZUYOHO.

VRATA (Byzantine/Slavonic)

See THYRA.

VZENOSHCHNOE EDENIE
(Byzantine/Slavonic)

See VIGIL.

W

WANGEL (Ethiopian)

The liturgical *gospel, which is read by a *priest facing east assisted by taper-holding deacons standing on either side. At the Gospel's conclusion a verse is read, the text of which is distinctive for each evangelist.

WARAGUIR (Armenian)

The two curtains that are stretched on wires in front of the *altar in such a way that one curtain hangs in front of the other. They are used to conceal the altar, *priest, and *deacon at various moments in the *Liturgy; for example, the second curtain is drawn to conceal the priest from the deacon during the priest's *Communion, and it is drawn after the Liturgy.

WARDA (East Syrian/Chaldean)

A collection of hymns that are sung after the *Gospel or during the distribution of Holy *Communion.

See LITURGICAL BOOKS (East Syrian Tradition).

WEGHERET (Ethiopian)

A linen collar worn over the shoulders of superiors of *monastic communities.

See HEBANIE; KESELA.

WEM (Armenian)

See ANTIMENSION.

WERABEREOUTHIUN (Armenian) (also called Weraperum)

The Great Entrance proceeds around the altar by way of the rear of the altar.

See ENTRANCE; GREAT ENTRANCE.

WERATHSOUOMN (Armenian)

A brief reference to the elevation made in the Liturgy when the priest says aloud, "To the Holiness of the Holies."

See ELEVATION.

WEST SYRIANS

Alternatively known as Syrian Ortho-dox, often, more simply known as Jacobites.

See SYRIAN ORTHODOX CHURCH, HISTORY OF.

WILA (East Syrian/Chaldean)

The veil that hangs before the sanctu-ary door leading west out of the sanc-tuary. There is reference to a wila in a letter to Theophilus, patriarch of Alexandria, in 411.

WIPE THE FACE (Coptic)
(also called Massah Wajh)

Part of the *dismissal rite in the *Coptic *Liturgy when the *priest scat-ters holy water on the *altar and over the people, after which it is customary to distribute the *eulogia, or *baracah. The phrase refers to the occasional practice of the priest passing his still-wet hands over his face and over those of the faithful present.

X

XEROPHAGIA (Byzantine/Greek) Literally, "dry nourishment." A strict *fast lasting from Monday to Thursday in Holy Week in which one may eat only bread, salt, onions, garlic and some herbs. Water is permitted.

Y

YAYSMAVURK (Armenian)
(also spelled *Haysmavurk)

Literally, "this very day." The Synaxary, or *Menologion, containing abridged versions of the saints' lives and some small homilies suitable for various Sunday feasts. These extracts are read to the congregation before *Vespers.

YEFE TSAMIE QOB (Ethiopian)

The tall white hat that is presented to the solemnly professed *monk.

YERETZ (Armenian)

See KAHANA.

YPODIAKON (Coptic)

Literally, "a little deacon." A *subdeacon.

See ABUDIYAKUN.

YUGOSLAV RITE

A *Byzantine rite for Catholics in Yugoslavia. In 1970 they numbered around 58,000.

YUQNO (Syro-Jacobite)

An *icon, for example, of the Virgin Mary.

Z

ZAHAWARIAT (Ethiopian)

The *Anaphora of the Apostles, which is commonly used by the *Ethiopians. While it may be based on the *Apostolic Tradition* of Hippolytus (3rd century), the version in use was probably translated from an early Arabic one in the 13th century. It was Dix's opinion that the Anaphora of the Apostles is largely identical with the *Coptic *Liturgy of St. Cyril.

ZAMESHTIR (Ethiopian)

See ANAPHORA; ENFORA; KEDDASE.

ZAND (Syrian and Maronite)

See ZUNNAR.

ZANDE (East Syrian/Chaldean) (also spelled Zenda; *Zende)

The *cuffs worn by a *priest; they are no longer used in the *Nestorian rite.

See CUMMIN; PEDHITHO; VESTMENTS, TABLE OF.

ZATIK (Armenian)

The feast of Easter.

See ARMENIAN CHURCH CALENDAR.

ZAVIESA (Byzantine/Slavonic)

See BELOTHYRON.

ZENAR (Ethiopian)

The *girdle, which is overhung by the *stole so that it encloses only the *alb, or kamis.

See KAMIS.

ZENA-ZIL (Ethiopian)

A rattle-like musical instrument sometimes used to accompany the singing in this rite.

ZENDE (Syro-Jacobite) (also spelled Zendo)

The *cuffs used to hold back and confine the sleeves of the *cuthino, or *alb. Sometimes these cuffs are long and narrow, extending to the elbows, and may be made of the same material as the other *vestments. They should not be considered to be simply like Western maniples.

See CUMMIN; PEDHITHO; ZANDE.

ZEON (Byzantine)

The practice of adding warm water to the *chalice containing the consecrated wine just before Holy *Communion. The word sometimes refers to the vessel that contains the hot water.

See ORKIOLION; THERMARION.

ZEWD (Ethiopian)

The crown used by clergy in the order of *deacon and above as part of their liturgical *vestments. Catholic *bishops use a Western-style *miter.

See VESTMENTS, TABLE OF.

ZEZLE (Syro-Jacobite)

*Cymbals which, together with the *noqusho (a type of gong), are sounded at the Sanctus, institution, *Epiclesis, *elevation, and blessing before Holy *Communion. Among the *Malabarese they may be sounded also at the *Trisagion.

ZHERETVENNIK
(also called *Predlogenie)

The table of oblation, otherwise known as the credence table, or *prothesis.

ZIJAH (Coptic)
(also called Aklil-Al)

Literally, "the crowning."

See MARRIAGE.

ZINNAR (Coptic)

A *girdle; according to Renaudot, it was Al-Hakim (996–1021) who imposed the wearing of the girdle on Christians in order to distinguish them from the Muslims, but Butler claims that it was imposed some 150 years earlier by Caliph Mutawakkil. The girdle, highly decorated with a strong, ornamented clasp, was thought to have been worn only as part of the ceremonial dress suitable for great occasions. Its first clear mention as an ecclesiastical *vestment was in the 8th century by St. Germanus of Constantinople. Unlike the Catholic clergy, non-Catholic *Copts do not wear the girdle consistently. It is made of silk or velvet and may be of any color.

See MINTAKAH; ZOUNARION; ZUNARION.

ZINZGHA (Armenian)

A Turkish musical instrument consisting of two bronze plates, which are struck against each other like *cymbals to announce certain moments in the *Liturgy.

ZONARION (Byzantine)

A cincture.

See BAPTISM (Byzantine Tradition); ZONE; ZOSTER.

ZONE (Byzantine)
(also called *Zoster)

This word commonly has two meanings:

1. It may refer to a narrow band of material usually the same color as the chasuble (*phelonion [Greek]; *felon [Slavonic]). It may have either one or

three crosses on it and is secured at the back by hooks or cords, unlike the practice of the *Melchites, who secure it in front with an elaborate fastening device. The zone is meant to signify spiritual strength and innocence, as the text of the prayer that is recited while the zone is being put on suggests: "Blessed is God, who girds me with strength and has made my path blameless and has given me feet like those of a hart and has set me on high."

2. It may be used to describe the black cotton band worn by secular clergy as part of their outdoor dress; *monastic clergy use a leather belt.

See VESTMENTS, TABLE OF.

ZOSTER (Byzantine)

See ZONE.

ZOUNARION (Coptic)

See ZINNAR.

ZQIFUTHO (Syro-Jacobite)

Literally, "cross." The arrangement of particles of the broken consecrated *bread to resemble the Crucifixion and commonly performed by traditionalists from Christmas to Easter.

ZUMARA (East Syrian/Nestorian)

Literally, "song." Part of the preparatory rite preceding the reading of the *Gospel and consisting of a few psalm verses; it was not included in the *Chaldean Catholic Missal, which was published at Mosul in 1901.

See ALLELUIA.

ZUNARA (East Syrian/Chaldean)

A *girdle worn by a *Chaldean cleric.

See VESTMENTS, TABLE OF.

ZUNARION (Coptic)

See ZINNAR; ZOUNARION.

ZUNNAR (Syrian and Maronite)

Among the *Maronites it refers to the girdle used to enclose and confine the *alb, over which the cleric may put on the *masnaphtho.

See ZANDE; ZUNNORO.

ZUNNARA (East Syrian/Nestorian) (also called Hasa)

This resembles a *Coptic *girdle and is secured by clasps.

ZUNNORO (Syrian)

A cincture, which is not worn by inferior clerics; it is used to enclose the *alb. A *priest's zunnoro is usually embroidered and is secured by a clasp.

ZUYOHO (Syro-Jacobite)

The *elevation of the *paten and *chalice during the *Liturgy, but it should be noted that the vessels are elevated separately. The *priest first takes the paten in both hands and raises it, moving it crosswise from east to west and then from north to south saying: "The Holies to the holy and pure are given," to which the congregation responds: "One Holy Father, One Holy Son, and One Living and Holy Spirit." The priest then replaces the paten on the *altar after he has touched his eyes with it and kissed it. The same procedure is adopted for the chalice, after which the priest takes the paten in his right hand and the chalice in his left, and holding the right hand over the left so as to form a cross, he says: "The One Holy Father is with us, who formed the world by his grace," and the people respond, "Amen."

"The One holy Son . . . ." "Amen." "The One Living and Holy Spirit . . . ." "Amen."

ZVYEZDITZA (Byzantine/Slavonic)

See ASTERISK.

A Quick Reference Guide

Familiar English language terms are listed in the left hand column against which are listed approximate equivalent entries for the different Eastern Rites; therefore, the appropriate entry may be found effortlessly within the Dictionary proper.

ABBESS	Hegoumenissa (Greek)
ABBOT	Archimandrite; Hegoumenos; Kathegoumenos (Greek) Hegumen (Slavonic) Mamher (Ethiopian)
ALB	Shapik (Armenian) Kamision; Stikharion (Greek) Stikhar (Slavonic) Stoicharion; Shento; Mappa; Marppa (Coptic) Tuniyah (Coptic/Arabic) Cuthino; Kuthino (Syrian) Citunah (Syrian & Maronite) Kotina; Sudra (East Syrian)
ALTAR	Khoran; Selan; Surb; (Armenian) Aghia Trapeza; Thronos; Thysiasterion; Trapeza (Greek) Prestol; Svyathaya (Slavonic) Ma'idah; Manershooushi; Trapeza; Thronos (Coptic) Meshwa'e (Ethiopian) Pathora; Pothur Haye; Qudsho; Trumus; Thronos (Syro-Jacobite) Trumus (East Syrian/Nestorian)
ALTAR, CANOPY OF	Kiborion; Pyrgos (Greek) Syen (Slavonic) Baldachino (Coptic)

ALTAR CLOTHS   Antimension; Eileton; Endyte; Katasarkion (Greek)
   or LINENS   Inditia; Stratchitza (Slavonic)

ALTAR STONE   Marmnakal; Schouoschphah; Wem (Armenian)
  or CORPORAL   Antimension; Kathierosis; Thronos (Greek)
                   Antimins (Slavonic)
                   Lax; Nakis; Tabella (Coptic)
                   Andimisi; Lauh (Arabic)
                   Tabella (Ethiopian)
                   Tabella; T'wilaita (East Syrian)
                   Kethons; Mandil; Tablith(o) (Syro-Jacobite & Maronite)

AMICE   Va(r)kas (Armenian)
                   Ballin; Ephout; Kidaris; Palin; Shamlah; Tailasan
                      (Coptic & Coptic/Arabic)
                   Ghelab; Hebanie; Kesela; Wegheret (Ethiopian)
                   Birun; Sanwartha (East Syrian)
                   Masnaphtho (West Syrian & Maronite)

ANAPHORA   *See* ANAPHORA.
                   Kuddas (Arabic)
                   Agiasmos; Anafora (Coptic)
                   Enfora; Keddase; Zameshtir (Ethiopian)
                   Kuddasha; Qudashe (East Syrian/Nestorian)
                   Quddosho (Maronite)
                   Kurobho; Qurobho (West Syrian)

ANOINTING OF SICK   *See* UNCTION OF THE SICK.
                   Euchelion (Greek)
                   Eleosvastchenie (Slavonic)
                   Henana (East Syrian/Nestorian)

ANTIDORON   *See* Bread, Blessed in this reference guide.

APOSTLE   *See* LECTIONS.

APSE   *See* APSIS.

APSE, SOUTHERN   Beth Diyaqon; Beth Roze; Diyaqoniqon (Syro-Jacobite)

ARCHANGEL   Archistrategos (Greek)

ARCHDEACON   Ra'is a shamamishah (Coptic)
                   Nebrid (Ethiopian)
                   Rish-M'shamshono (Maronite)
                   Arkidyakna (East Syrian)

ARCHPRIEST   *See* ARCHPRIEST.
                   Avagueretz; Kahanayapet (Armenian)
                   Protoiereus (Greek)
                   Rab-Kumre (East Syrian/Nestorian)

ASTERISK	*See* ASTERISK. Asteriskos (Greek) Zvyezditza (Slavonic) Dome; Kubbah (Coptic/Arabic)
BAPTISM	*See* BAPTISM. Baptisma (Greek) Krestshenia (Slavonic)
BAPTISTERY	Baptisterion; Kolymbethra; Photisterion (Greek) Beth'mada; Bit Qanki (East Syrian/Nestorian) M'amuditho (West Syrian)
BEATITUDES	Makarismoi (Greek)
BELFRY	Campanarion; Kodonostasion (Greek)
BELIEVER	*See* FAITHFUL. Hhavatathseal (Armenian) Pistos (Greek) Veroyuschie (Slavonic) Ethnahti (Coptic) Ta'amani (Ethiopian) M'haimno (Syrian)
BELL	Kodon (Greek)
BISHOP	*See* ORDERS, HOLY. Episcopos (Armenian) Archiereus; Episkopos (Greek) Protiere (Slavonic) Abbas; Anba (Coptic) Episqupo; Khasvo; Rakohno (Maronite) Efiskufa; Rab-Kahni (East Syrian/Chaldean)
BISHOP'S SECRETARY	Syncellus (Greek)
BISHOP'S THRONE	Synthronon; Thronos (Greek)
BREAD	*See* BREAD. Neshkar; Surb Khaths (Armenian) Prosphora (Byzantine) Korban; Prosfora; Qurban (Coptic/Arabic) H'bst; Korban (Ethiopian) Burshanah; Purshono; Qurboro (Maronite & Syrian) Buchro; Katzto; Paristo; Tabh'o (Syro-Jacobite) Bukhra; Kaprana; Malca; Melkaita (East Syrian/Nestorian)
BREAD, BLESSED	Antidoron; Eulogia (Byzantine) Baracah; Khubz Moubarak (Coptic/Arabic) M'caprana (East Syrian/Nestorian) Burc'tho (Syro-Jacobite)

BREAD, CONSECRATED *See* COAL; HOLY OF HOLIES.
Masn (Armenian)
Margarites; Pearl (Byzantine)
Asbadikon; Kedsat; Spoudikon (Coptic & Ethiopian)
G'murtho; Lahma Dkudasha; Qudhsha
(East Syrian/Nestorian)

CANDLESTICK

Single Kerostates; Lampas; Manoualion (Greek)

Branched with candles Dibampoulos; Kerion; Keropegia; Polykerion (Byzantine)

Branched with oil lamps Polyelaion; Polykandelon (Byzantine)

Liturgical, 2 tapered Dikerion (Greek)
Dikiri (Slavonic)

Liturgical, 3 tapered Trikerion (Byzantine)

Collective for above Dikeretrikeria (Byzantine)

CASSOCK Verarkou (Armenian)
Anterion; Rason (Greek)
Podriznik; Ryasa (Slavonic)
Aba; Sultana (Syro-Jacobite)

CATECHUMEN *See* BAPTISM.
Erekhah (Armenian)
Oglashenniy; Tritekti (Slavonic)
Katechoumenos (Coptic)
Ne'us Crestiyan (Ethiopian)
Shomu'o (Syrian)

CENSER Bourwarr (Armenian)
Thymaterion (Greek)
Kadilnitza (Slavonic)
Shoure (Coptic)
Ma'etant (Ethiopian)
Pirmo (Syrian)

CHALICE Bashak; Ski (Armenian)
Potir (Byzantine)
Poterion; Stoicharion (Coptic)
Cenae; Cewa'e (Ethiopian)
Coso; Kas (Syrian)

CHALICE STAND Cursi Alcas; Pitote; Thronos nte Pipoterion; Tote
(Coptic/Arabic)

CHASUBLE *See* VESTMENTS, TABLE OF.
Schoorchar (Armenian)
Phailones; Phelonion (Greek)
Felon (Slavonic)

Amforion; Burnus; Falunyun; Felonion; Kouklion;
    Phainolion; Phelonion (Coptic)
Cappa; Kaba (Ethiopian)
Ma'pra; Paina; Pakila (East Syrian)
Faino; Phaino; Phelono; Rida (Syro-Jacobite)

CHOREPISCOPUS — *See* CHOREPISCOPUS.
Kurepisqupo (Maronite)
Sa'aure (East Syrian/Nestorian)

CHRISM — *See* CHRISM.
Meron (Armenian)
Myron (Coptic)

CINCTURE — *See* GIRDLE.

CLERIC — Dpir (Armenian)
Kahenat (Ethiopian)

COMMIXTURE — Kharrnoumn (Armenian)
Enosis (Greek)
Ispolnenie; Smieshevanie (Slavonic)

COMMUNION — *See* COMMUNION.
Khaghordouthiun (Armenian)
Koinonia (Greek)
Obshcheniye; Prichastiye (Slavonic)
Tanawal; Tschi (Coptic/Arabic)
Sutafe (Ethiopian)
Shauthophutho (Syro-Jacobite)

COMMUNION SPOON — Labis (Greek)
Izhitza (Slavonic)
Kokliarion (Coptic)
Myster; Mystheri (Ethiopian)
Kalb'tho; Tarwodho (Syro-Jacobite)

COMPLINE — *See* COMPLINE.
Apodeipnon (Greek)
Povecherie (Slavonic)

CONCELEBRATION — *See* CONCELEBRATION.
Sylleitourgon (Greek)
Sobornie (Slavonic)

CONFESSOR — *See* PENANCE.
Epitimion; Exagoreutes; Pneumatikos (Greek)
Duhovnek (Slavonic)

CONFIRMATION — *See* CHRISMATION.
Meropomazanie (Slavonic)
Myron (Coptic)

CONSIGNATION	*See* CONSIGNATION. Rasam (Coptic) Ataba (Ethiopian) Rushmo (Syro-Jacobite & Nestorian)
CREDENCE TABLE	Entsaiaran; Matouthsaran (Armenian) Predlogenie; Zheretvennik (Slavonic) Kenfo (Syro-Jacobite)
CREED	*See* CREED. Khavatamch (Armenian) Symbolon (Greek) Haiyimonutho (Syrian)
CROSS, SIGN OF	Stavros (Greek)
CROWN	*See* MITER. Stephanos (Greek) Vienetz (Slavonic)
CROZIER	Dekanikion; Paterissa; Rabdos (Greek) Djezl; Posokh (Slavonic) Akaz; Bakteria; Dikanikion; Shvot (Coptic) Hutro; Muronitho; Shabbuqto (Syro-Jacobite)
CRUCIFIX	Estavromenos (Greek) Raspiatie (Slavonic)
CUFFS	*See* VESTMENTS, TABLE OF. Bazpan (Armenian) Epimanikia; Hypomanika (Greek) Porutchi (Slavonic) Kamision (Coptic) Cumm; Cumman; Kaman (Coptic/Arabic) Acmam; Edjge (Ethiopian) Cummin (Maronite) Pedhitho; Zande; Zende (East Syrian)
CURTAIN	*See* VEILS. Belothyron; Velothyron; Vemothyron (Greek) Zaviesa (Slavonic)
DEACON	*See* ORDERS, HOLY. Sarkavak (Armenian) Devterevon; Diakonos (Greek) Diakon (Slavonic) Diacon (Coptic) M'Sham-Shono (Maronite) Shamasha (East Syrian)
DEACON, SENIOR	Protodeacon (Byzantine)

DEACONESS	*See* DEACONESS. M'Sham-Shonoitho (Maronite & Syro-Jacobite)
DIPTYCHS	*See* DIPTYCH. Diptich (Slavonic) Diptichon; Tarhim; Touptikon (Coptic & Arabic) Diupatcin (East Syrian) Diphtucho; Kanuno; Qanuno (Syro-Jacobite)
DISMISSAL	Apolysis (Greek) Otpust (Slavonic) Wipe the Face (Coptic) Massah Wajh (Coptic & Arabic)
DOORKEEPER	*See* ORDERS, HOLY. Drpnapan (Armenian) Pyloros (Greek) Dvernik; Prevratnek (Slavonic)
DOORS	*See* HOLY DOORS; ROYAL DOORS. Basilikos; Pyle; Thyra (Greek) Vrata (Slavonic)
EAGLE	Aetos; Psathion (Greek) Orletz (Slavonic)
ELEVATION	Werathsouomn (Armenian) Hypsosis (Greek) Vozdnosht Shenie (Slavonic) Raf'ah; Zuyoho (Syro-Jacobite)
ENTRANCE	*See* ENTRANCE. Werabereouthiun (Armenian) Eisodos (Greek) Bohod; Vkhod (Slavonic)
EPICLESIS	*See* EPICLESIS; INVOCATION. Kathschoumn (Armenian) Epiclesis (Greek) Prizivanie (Slavonic) Da'wah; Kerytho; K'royotho (Syrian)
EPIGONATION	*See* EPIGONATION. Hypogonation (Greek) Nabedrennik; Palitza (Slavonic)
EPISCOPACY	*See* ORDERS, HOLY (Bishop).
EPISTLE	*See* LECTIONS. Arrachealch (Armenian) Apostolos (Greek)

Apostol (Slavonic)
Apostolos; Catholicon (Coptic)
Bulus (Coptic/Arabic)
Pawelos (Ethiopian)

EUCHARIST
See ANAPHORA.
Anaphora; Koinonia (Greek)
Anafora (Slavonic)
Agiasmos; Anafora; Korban; Prosfora (Coptic)
Enfora; Keddase; Zameshtir (Ethiopian)
Kuddasha (East Syrian/Nestorian)
Annaphura; Kurbono; Kurobho (Syro-Jacobite)

EUCHARISTIC VESSELS
See ASTERISK; CHALICE; LANCE; PATEN; SPOON.

FANS *or* FLABELLA
Chschoths; Keshotz; Kshotz (Armenian)
Exapteryga; Ripidia; Ripidion; Ripisterion (Greek)
Cheroubim; Mirwahah; Ripidion; Ripisterion
  (Coptic/Arabic)
Marwah'tho (Syro-Jacobite)

FRACTION
See FRACTION.
Bekanel (Armenian)
Melismos (Greek)
Razdroblenie (Slavonic)
Fosh (Coptic)
Kism (Coptic/Arabic)
Kasyo; Tukkoso dh-q'sayo (West Syrian)

GIRDLE
See VESTMENTS, TABLE OF.
Goti; Kodi (Armenian)
Zonarion; Zone; Zoster (Greek)
Poyas (Slavonic)
Mintakah; Zinnar; Zounarion; Zunarion
  (Coptic/Arabic)
Kamis; Zenar (Ethiopian)
Zunara; Zunnara (East Syrian)
Zand; Zunnar; Zunnoro (West Syrian & Maronite)

GOSPEL
See GOSPEL; LECTIONS.
Avat(h)ran (Armenian)
Evangelion; Tetraevangelion (Greek)
Evangelie (Slavonic)
Anjil; Evangelion (Coptic/Arabic)
Wangel (Ethiopian)
Ewangeliyun; Iwangallyuna (East Syrian)

ICON
See ICON.
'Nkar (Armenian)
Ikon (Slavonic)
Yuquo (Syro-Jacobite)

ICON STAND	Proskynetarion (Greek)
INCENSE	Thymiama (Greek) Ladan (Slavonic) Maia; Sandarus (Coptic)
INTERCESSION	Brodiki; Catholic; Kathuliki (Syrian)
LECTERN	Analogion; Diskelion; Triskelion (Greek) Golgotha (West Syrian)
LESSONS	*See* LECTIONS. Arrachealch; Avat(h)ran; Margarech (Armenian) Lexis; Praxis (Coptic) Menbab (Ethiopian) Keryana (Syrian)
MARRIAGE	*See* MARRIAGE. Gamos (Greek) Brak (Slavonic)
MATS	Pithom; Tabak; Thom (Coptic)
MITER	*See* MITER; VESTMENTS, TABLE OF. Saghavart (Armenian) Mitra (Greek) Metra; Vienetz (Slavonic) Klam; Metra; Taj; Tschrepi (Coptic & Arabic) Zewd (Ethiopian) Taj; Togho (Syrian) Tiara (Melchite)
MONASTERY	*See* MONASTICISM; CENOBITIC; IDIORRHYTHMIC. Lavra; Skete; Stavropegion (Greek) Rastoyatel (Slavonic)
MONASTIC CEREMONY	Apokoukoulismos (Greek)
MONASTIC HABIT	*See* HABITS, COMPARATIVE TABLES OF. Pakegh; Sqem; Veghar (Armenian) Analabos; Koukoulion; Mandyas; Megaloschemos; Polystavrion; Skouphos (Greek) Kamilafka; Mantiya; Paraman; Skhimnik (Slavonic) Askema; Wegheret (Ethiopian) Eskhim; Jubba; Qubh'uno; Schema (Syro-Jacobite)
MONASTICISM	*See* DEGREES OF MONASTICISM, HABITS OF.
MONK	Abegha (Armenian) Calogers; Kalogeros; Mikroschemos; Rasophore; Stavrophore (Greek) Krestonosets; Poslyshnik; Ryasonosets (Slavonic) Napqa; Raban (East Syrian/Chaldean)

MONK-DEACON	Hierodeacon (Byzantine)
MONK-PRIEST	Hieromonk (Byzantine) Raba(o)n (East Syrian/Chaldean)
MONK, SUPERIOR	Archimandrite (Byzantine)
OVEN	*See* BREAD. Bethlehem (Ethiopian) Tanurta (East Syrian/Nestorian)
PALLIUM	Emiphoron (Armenian) Homophorion; Omophorion (Greek) Omofor (Slavonic) Omoforion (Coptic) Martuta (East Syrian) Hemnicho; Homophorion; Uroro; Uroro Rabbo (Syro-Jacobite)
PARISH	Enoria (Greek) Prehod (Slavonic)
PATEN	*See* PATEN. Maghzmah (Armenian) Discos; Diskarion (Byzantine) Diskos (Coptic) Ained; Awed; Cachel; Sahal (Ethiopian) Pilasa; Pinka (East Syrian/Nestorian)
PATRIARCH	*See* PATRIARCH. Amba (Coptic) Abuna (Ethiopian)
PEACE, KISS OF	*See* PEACE. Hampuir Srboutian (Armenian) Aspasmos (Greek) Tselovanie (Slavonic) Sulh (Coptic) Amcha (Ethiopian) Salam (Maronite) Sh'lomo (Syro-Jacobite)
PENANCE	*See* PENANCE. Epitimion; Exomologesis; Metanoia (Greek) Pokoyanie (Slavonic)
PRECENTOR	Protopsaltes (Greek) Regentchora (Slavonic)
PRELATES, ARMENIAN	*See* CHOREPISCOPUS; VARTABED.
PRIEST	*See* ORDERS, HOLY. Eretz; Tanaretz (Armenian)

Iereus; Pap(p)as (Greek)
Batoushka; Svashshtenik (Slavonic)
Kassis; Kess (Coptic)
Kohno; Qashisho (Maronite)
Kahna; Kasha; Kashisha (East Syrian)
Kachicho (West Syrian)

PRIEST, SENIOR   Protopap(p)as (Greek)

PRIESTS, CELIBATE   Abegha (Armenian)

PRIESTS, MARRIED   Derders (Armenian)

PROTHESIS   Entsaiaran; Matouth(soumn)saran (Armenian)
                          Proskomide (Byzantine & Coptic)
                          Proskomedia (Slavonic)
                          Kubhtha (East Syrian/Nestorian)

PURIFICATOR   *See* PURIFICATOR; SPONGE.
                          Srbitsch; Thasch-Kinak (Armenian)
                          Pinco; Piyalol; Siniyah (Syro-Jacobite)

READER   *See* ORDERS, HOLY.
                          Anagnostes (Greek)
                          Tchetz (Slavonic)
                          Anagnostes; Karianjili (Coptic & Arabic)
                          Amura; Karuya (East Syrian/Nestorian)
                          Quoroyo (Maronite)

RELICS   Leipsana (Greek)
                          Mostche (Slavonic)

RELIQUARY   Beth Kaddishe; Beth Sadhe (East Syrian)

RING, WEDDING   *See* MARRIAGE.
                          Daktylios (Greek)

ROSARY   Kombologion (Greek)
                          Chotki; Komboschoinion; Liestovka; Vervitza (Slavonic)

ROYAL DOORS   *See* BEAUTIFUL DOORS; HOLY DOORS; ICONOSTASIS.
                          Belothyron (Greek)
                          Zaviesa (Slavonic)

SACRAMENTS   For Greek and Slavonic equivalents, *see* SACRAMENTS.

SACRISTY   Avandatoun; Sarkavaganouths (Armenian)
                          Diakonikon (Greek & Coptic)
                          Diakonnik; Riznitza (Slavonic)
                          Beith Roze; Beth Diyakun; Beth Shamasha (East Syrian)

SANCTUARY   Srbaran (Armenian)
                          Hierateion (Greek)
                          Erphei; Haikal (Coptic)

Beta Makdas; Kedest; Kedsat; Macdan Kedus; Magdas;
 Makedes (Ethiopian)
Kedush (East Syrian)
Madb'ho (Syro-Jacobite & Nestorian)

SERVICE BOOKS   *See* LITURGICAL BOOKS.

SINGER   Apir; Saghmosergov (Armenian)
Psaltes; Pevetz (Byzantine)
Defteras; Mazamer (Ethiopian)
Mzamrono; Psaltu (Syrian)
Mazmorono (Maronite)

SPONGE   *See* PURIFICATOR; SPONGE.
Mousa (Greek)
Gouba; Gubka (Slavonic)
Espugo; Gomuro (Syrian)

SPOON   Labis (Greek)
Izhitza; Lzhitza (Slavonic)

SPONSOR(S),   Anadochoi (Greek)
 BAPTISMAL

SPONSOR(S), MONASTIC   Gerontas (Greek)
Krestnaya Atiets; Staretz (Slavonic)

STOLE   *See* VESTMENTS, TABLE OF.
Ourar; Phakegm; Porurar (Armenian)
Epitrachelion; Orarion; Peritrachelion (Greek)
Epitrakhil; Orar (Slavonic)
Shordion (Coptic)
Mothat (Ethiopian)
Urara; Uroro (East Syrian/Chaldean)
Bitrashil; Hamnikho (Syrian)

SUBDEACON   *See* ORDERS, HOLY.
Kisarkavag (Armenian)
Hypodiakonos (Greek)
Eepodiacon; Ypodiakon (Slavonic)
Abudiyakun; Ypodiakon (Coptic & Arabic)
Nefka Diyakon (Ethiopian)
Hiupath'aqua (Ethiopian)
Houpodiacono (West Syrian)
Phelguth-M'shamshono (Maronite)

TABERNACLE   *See* RESERVED SACRAMENT.
Artophorion; Hierophylakion; Peristera (Greek)
Kovtcheg (Slavonic)
Beth Qurbana (East Syrian)
Beit Qurban; Paradiscus (Syro-Jacobite)

THRONE, BISHOP'S	Archieraticos Thronos; Cathedra; Thronos (Byzantine & Coptic) Throniyon (Syro-Jacobite)
TONSURE	*See* TONSURE. Koura; Monachike Koura (Greek) Apokarsis (Byzantine) Supara (East Syrian) Suphora (Syro-Jacobite)
TRISAGION	*See* TRISAGION. Erechsrbeann; Ergsrbeann (Armenian) Agios O Theos (Greek) Trisyatoe (Slavonic) Ajus (Coptic) Kadishat Aloho (Maronite)
UNCTION	*See* CHRISMATION; UNCTION OF THE SICK. Euchelion (Greek) Eleosvastchenie (Slavonic) Henana (East Syrian/Nestorian)
VARTABED	*See* VARTABED. Aradchenord; Dzairakouyn; Maznavor (Armenian)
VEILS, CHALICE	Tsatskoths Skih (Armenian) Deuteron Kalymma (Greek) Pitote (Coptic) Hupp(a)oyo (Syrian) Gita Alcas (Maronite)
VEILS, PATEN	Diskokallyma; Kalymmata; Proton Kalymma (Greek) Cedana'awed (Ethiopian) Gita Absainiyah (Maronite)
VEILS, PATEN & CHALICE	Kogh (Armenian) Aer; Nephele (Greek) Pokrovy (Slavonic) Ibrusfarin; Lafafah; Prosfarin (Coptic/Arabic) Macdan; Shoshepa (Ethiopian) Shushepo (East Syrian/Nestorian) P'roso (Syro-Jacobite) Gita; Nafur (Maronite)
VEILS, SANCTUARY	Waraguir (Armenian) Belothyron; Tetravela; Velothyron; Vemothyron (Greek) Zaviesa (Slavonic) Hijab; Katapetasma; Sitarah (Coptic) Wila (East Syrian) Qubb'tho (Syro-Jacobite)
VESSELS FOR OILS	Alabastron (Greek) Alavastr (Slavonic)

Tables

	Lowest Degree	*Middle Degree*	*Highest Degree*
Slavonic Monk	Ryasonosets	Krestonosets	Skhimnik
Greek Monk	Rasophore	Stavrophore/ Microschemos	Megaloschemos
Name of Habit	Fore-Habit	Little Habit/ Little Schema	Great Habit/ Angelic Habit
Parts of Habit	Inner Rason	Inner Rason (Paramandyas & Cross)	Inner Rason (Paramandyas & Cross)
	Girdle	Girdle	Girdle
	Outer Rason	Outer Rason	Outer Rason
	Skouphos	Skouphos & Veil	Cowl *or* Skouphos & Veil *or* Koukoulion
			Analovos
		Mandyas	Mandyas
	Sandals	Sandals	Sandals

Table 2   Comparative Table of Hours (Divine Office)

West	Greek	Slavonic
Matins	Mesonyktion	Polunoshtchnitza
Lauds	Orthros	Khvalitnyi
Prime (7 A.M.)	Hora Prote	Tchas Pierve
Terce (9 A.M.)	Hora Trite	Tchas Trietie
Sext (12 noon)	Hora Hekte	Tchas Schiestie
None (3 P.M.)	Hora Enate	Tchas Devyatie
Vespers	Hesperinos	Vetchernya
Compline	Apodeipnon	Nediela

Table 3   Summary of Byzantine Liturgical Books

	Slavonic	Greek
1.	Bolshoi Ieresky Molitvoslov	Euchologion, Great
2.	Trebnik	Euchologion, Small
3.	Sluzhebnik	Hieratikon
4.	Tchinovnik	Archieratikon
5.	Tchasoslov	Horologion
6.	Oktoikh	Oktoechos/Parakletike
7.	Postnaya Triod	Triodion
8.	Tzvyetnaya Triod	Pentekostsarion
9.	Mineya	Menaia
10.	Irmologion	Heirmologion
11.	Evangelie	Evangelion
12.	Apostol	Apostolos
13.	Psaltir	Psalterion
14.	Ustav	Typikon
15.	Prazditchnaya Mineya	Anthologion

TABLE 4   331

Table 4   **Table of Liturgical Languages**

Rite	Language
Alexandrian	
Coptic	Coptic and Arabic
Ethiopian	Ge'ez
Antiochene (West Syrian)	
Malankara	Malayalam
Maronite	Syrian and Arabic
Syrian Orthodox	Syrian and Arabic
Armenian	
Catholic	Armenian
Gregorian (non-Catholic)	Armenian
Byzantine	
Albanian	Albanian and Old Greek
Bulgarian	Church Slavonic
Byelorussian (White Russian)	Church Slavonic
Georgian	Georgian
Greek	Old Greek
Hungarian	Church Slavonic
Italo-Albanian	Old Greek and Albanian
Melchite	Old Greek and Arabic
Romanian	Romanian and Church Slavonic
Russian	Church Slavonic
Ruthenian	Church Slavonic
Slovak	Church Slavonic
Ukrainian	Church Slavonic
Yugoslav	Church Slavonic
Chaldean (East Syrian)	
Chaldean	Syrian and Arabic
Syro-Malankarese	Malayalam
Nestorian	Syrian and Arabic

Table 5   **Comparative Table of Sacraments**

English	Greek	Slavonic
Baptism	Baptisma	Krestshenie
Confirmation	Chrism	Meropumazania
Eucharist	Eucharistia	Prechastchenie
	Koinonia	
Penance	Metanoia	Pokayanie
Orders	Hierosyne	Svyastchenstvo
Marriage	Gamos	Brak
Unction	Euchelaion	Eleosvastchenie

TABLE 6   333

Table 6   **Table of Vestments**

English	Byzantine	Arabic	Slavonic
Alb	Sticharion	Tuniyah	Stikar
		Istikharah	Stichar
Cuffs	Epimanikia	Cumm	Narukavni
		Kaman	Kavnitza
Stole	Epitrachelion	Bitrashil	Epitrachil
			Epitrachie
Stole (deacon)	Orarion		Orar
Girdle	Zone	Zunnar	Poyas
Chasuble (priest)	Phelonion	Iflunyah	Felon
	Phenolion		Phelon
Chasuble (bishop)	Sakkos	Burnus	Sakkos
Pallium	Omophorion		Omofor
Crozier	Rabdos		Djezl
Miter	Mitra	Tag	Mitra
Cross (pectoral)	Stavros		Krest

English	Chaldean	Nestorian
Alb	Kuthino/Kotina	Sudra/Cudhra
	Cuthina	
Cuffs	Zenda/Zende	Kepi
Stole	Urara	Urara
Girdle	Zunara	Zun(n)ara
Chasuble	Phaina	Ma'apra/Paina
Amice (bishop)		Biruna
Amice (priest)		Senwarta

(continued on page 334)

Table 6 (continued)   **Table of Vestments**

English	Syro-Jacobite	Catholic Syrians	Maronites
Alb	Cuthino	Kamis	Citunah
Cuffs	Zendo	Zunnar	Cumm
	Pedhitho		
Stole	Uroro/Urara	Bitrashil	Bitrashil
Girdle	Zunnoro	Zunnoro	
		Zunnar	Zunnar
Chasuble	Phaino		
	Faino	Badlah	Rida
Pallium	Hemnicho/Uroro	Bitrashil	
Miter	Togho	Taj	
Amice	Masnaphtho		Masnaphtho

English	Armenian	Coptic	Ethiopian
Alb	Schapik	Stoicharion	Kamis
	Shapik		
Cuffs	Bazpan	Kamasion	Acmam
			Edjge
Stole (deacon)	Ourar		
	Urar	Orarion	Mothat
Girdle	Goti	Zinnar	
		Zounarion	Zenar
Chasuble	Shourdcharr	Felonion	
	Shurtshar	Kouklion	
		Amforion	Kaba Lanka
Pallium	Emiphoron	Omoforion	
		Pallin/Ballin	
Miter	Saghavart	Mitra/Klam	Zewd
Amice	Varkas	Tailasan